Alfred Kazin has risen to eminence as one o
widely read critics in America. The breadth of his interests is forcefully
revealed in this major volume, now published in the first new, revised
edition since 1962. When it appeared critics stressed its authoritativeness
on so wide a range of subjects, making up a critical history of writing and
thought from the Romantics to the present:

"Whether he is outlining the background of modern literature, examining Freud and his consequences in life and art, or solving the puzzles of
contemporary mores and values, Kazin comes to terms with the relationship of society and the artist."   — *New York Herald Tribune*

"A diversity of interests rare in this age of literary specialists."
                      — Albert J. Guerard, *New York Times Book Review*

Contemporaries opens with a broad discussion of the forces which have
shaped our literature and leads into analyses of many individual writers:
Melville, Emerson, Thoreau, Stephen Crane, Dreiser, D.H. Lawrence,
Gertrude Stein, Faulkner, Ezra Pound, Graham Greene, Mann, Camus,
Sholom Aleichem, I. B. Singer, Elie Wiesel.

An important section deals with the writers who came into prominence
after World War II: James Agee, Pasternak, Malamud, Bellow, Robert
Lowell, Salinger, Mailer, James Baldwin.

There are five essays on Freud and the effects of psychology; essays on
politics and society; and on the critic's role.

In this new edition Mr. Kazin has concentrated on the present, pruning
the 1962 edition of matters of topical interest two decades ago, and adding
extensive new essays of interest today: "The Self as History" (the writing of
autobiography from Henry Adams and Whitman to Hemingway, Conrad
Aiken and Malcolm X); "New York from Melville to Mailer"; "Edward
Hopper" (painter of the city); "The Happy Hour" (on teaching poetry,
chiefly the current influence of T.S. Eliot's *The Waste Land*); "Uprooted
Writers" (the effects on the lives and work of writers in exile: Mann,
Nabokov, Hannah Arendt, etc.); "To Be a Critic" (the function and responsibilities of the critic in our culture); "Rome: A Meditation on John
Keats" — the one essay rooted entirely in the past, a masterly and moving
piece.

Books by Alfred Kazin

ON NATIVE GROUNDS: AN INTERPRETATION
    OF MODERN AMERICAN PROSE LITERATURE

A WALKER IN THE CITY

THE INMOST LEAF

CONTEMPORARIES

STARTING OUT IN THE THIRTIES

BRIGHT BOOK OF LIFE: AMERICAN NOVELISTS
    AND STORYTELLERS FROM HEMINGWAY TO MAILER

NEW YORK JEW

Editor:

THE PORTABLE WILLIAM BLAKE

F. SCOTT FITZGERALD: THE MAN AND HIS WORK

THE STATURE OF THEODORE DREISER
    (WITH CHARLES SHAPIRO)

MELVILLE'S *Moby Dick* (RIVERSIDE EDITION)

RALPH WALDO EMERSON: A MODERN ANTHOLOGY
    (WITH DANIEL AARON)

THE OPEN FORM: ESSAYS FOR OUR TIME

THE SELECTED STORIES OF NATHANIEL HAWTHORNE

HENRY JAMES, *The Ambassadors*

Contemporaries

Alfred Kazin

 Horizon Press, New York

Contemporaries

From the 19th Century to the Present

New and Revised Edition

LIBRARY OF CONGRESS CATALOG CARD NO. 81-82850

ISBN 0-8180-1132-7

Acknowledgment: The author wishes to thank the following for permission
to reprint copyrighted material:

Dell Publishing Co., Inc., for Alfred Kazin's Introduction for their Laurel
Dreiser series, © copyright, 1959, by Alfred Kazin; Doubleday and Com-
pany, Inc., for "The Background of Modern Literature" by Alfred Kazin,
from AN OUTLINE OF MAN'S KNOWLEDGE OF THE MODERN
WORLD, edited by Lyman Bryson. Copyright © 1960 by Catherine Mc-
Grattan Bryson, Executrix of the estate of Lyman Bryson, reprinted by
permission of Doubleday and Company, Inc., and published by McGraw-
Hill Book Company; Houghton Mifflin Company, for the Introduction to
MOBY-DICK by Herman Melville; Random House, Inc., for Mr. Kazin's
essay reprinted from SELECTED STORIES OF SHOLOM ALEICHEM,
by permission of Random House, Inc., © 1956 by Alfred Kazin; Wayne State
University Press, for "William Faulkner: The Stillness of LIGHT IN AU-
GUST," copyright 1958 Wayne State University Press; *Psychoanalysis and
Psychoanalytic Review* for Mr. Kazin's "Psychoanalysis and Literary Cul-
ture," Volume 45, Numbers 1 and 2, Spring-Summer 1958, © copyright
1958; seven lines from "Howl" by Allen Ginsberg, © 1956 & 1959 by
Allen Ginsberg, by permission of City Lights Books; 250 words from
NIGHT by Elie Wiesel, © Les Editions de Minuit, 1958, English translation © MacGibbon and Kee, 1960, reprinted by permission of Hill and
Wang, Inc.; six lines from "The Second Coming" by W. B. Yeats, reprinted
with permission of The Macmillan Company, Mrs. W. B. Yeats and Macmillan & Co. Ltd. from THE COLLECTED POEMS OF W. B. YEATS,
© 1924 by The Macmillan Company, © 1952 by Bertha Georgie Yeats;
240 words from "In Haste" from THE OLD COUNTRY by Sholom
Aleichem © 1946 by Crown Publishers, Inc., used by permission of the
publisher.

For Edmund and Elena Wilson
in loving memory

Acknowledgments

MOST OF THESE essays appeared first in the following publications, and are republished here with their permission: the *Reporter*, the *Atlantic Monthly, Harper's*, the *American Scholar, The New Republic, The New York Times Book Review, The New York Times Magazine, Esquire, Partisan Review, Commentary*, the *Griffin, The New Yorker, Psychoanalysis and The Psychoanalytic Review, The New Leader*. "The Background of Modern Literature" appeared first in *An Outline of Modern Knowledge*, edited by Lyman Bryson, and is republished here by permission of Doubleday and Company; "Ishmael and Ahab" is the introduction to the Riverside Press edition of *Moby-Dick*, and is republished here by permission of Houghton Mifflin Company; "Dreiser: The Esthetic of Realism" is the general introduction to the novels of Theodore Dreiser published by Dell Publishing Company, and appears here by their permission; "The Stillness of *Light In August*" was written for *Twelve Original Essays on Great American Novels*, edited by Charles Shapiro, and is republished here by permission of Wayne State University Press; "Sholom Aleichem: The Old Country" was written as an introduction to the Modern Library edition of *Selected Stories of Sholom Aleichem*, and is republished here by permission of Random House; "Rome: A Meditation on John Keats" was first published in the *American Scholar*; "The Happy Hour" was first published in *Esquire*; "Isaac Bashevis Singer: God May Be A Novelist" was first published in *The New York Times Book Review*; "Edward Hopper" was first published in *The New York Times Magazine*; "Uprooted Writers" was originally read at the Smithsonian Institution, Washington, February 9, 1980, at the Colloquium,

"The Muses Flee Hitler," in honor of Albert Einstein during the centennial of his birth. "The Self as History" was originally a lecture delivered at the University of California, Santa Barbara, and was first published in *Telling Lives*, New Republic Books. "New York From Melville to Mailer" was first read at the conference on Literature and the Urban Experience, Rutgers University, Newark, 1980.

The author also wishes to thank the following for permission to use excerpts: Basic Books, for *The Letters of Sigmund Freud*; Farrar, Straus and Cudahy, for *Life Studies* by Robert Lowell, and for *Gimpel the Fool* by Isaac Bashevis Singer; David McKay Company, Inc., for *Warrior's Rest* by Christiane Rochefort; Random House, Inc., for *Light in August* by William Faulkner, *The Legacy of the Civil War* by Robert Penn Warren, and *Breakfast at Tiffany's* by Truman Capote; The Viking Press, for *Henderson the Rain King* by Saul Bellow, and for an excerpt from *Herzog* by Saul Bellow as it appeared in *Esquire*; and Little, Brown and Company, for "Because I Could Not Stop for Death" from *The Complete Poems of Emily Dickinson*, edited by Thomas H. Johnson.

I am particularly grateful to Mr. Robert B. Silvers for his editorial advice and for his invaluable help in arranging the order of these essays.

Contents

I
To Be a Critic

FORTY AND MORE YEARS AGO, when I began practicing this peculiar trade of criticism, I had the good fortune to fall in love with a then unfashionable subject, American literature. I say "fall in love with," not "specialize in," for it never occurred to me to devote myself exclusively to this literature. There was not enough of it, yet what there was would still have been too much for me even if I had had the patience to give up everything else for it.

I certainly did not want to do that. I was under no illusion that American literature was more significant than English or French or Russian literature, or that it could be understood in itself apart from English its mother tongue, English its mother literature, its connections with German literature at the beginning of the nineteenth century and with French and Russian literature at the end of it. To devote oneself exclusively to American literature would have seemed to me a confession of mediocrity. And in any event literature, or at least some of the literature of Western man, was practically all the culture I had. It composed for me, in T.S. Eliot's phrase, a simultaneous order. It included such writers as America never had: all the great dramatists; great novelists of manners who were also among the most profound critics of human nature, like Tolstoy; great poets of the sensuous life — Villon, Shakespeare himself, Goethe, Baudelaire; great philosophic and critical spirits who were knife blades opening up the imagination — Montaigne, Rousseau, Voltaire, Diderot, Nietzsche.

So it was not in fond illusion that American writing was food enough for the mind that I settled down to practice some criticism of it. I fell in love with it because in a sense this literature was mine — I felt part of it and at home with it. I reacted with intellectual affection to the tone of certain American writers — I was charmed and stimulated and satisfied by certain American books because I felt that I really understood them. I felt, as the French have learned to say about certain moral problems, *authentic* in my critical reactions to certain American writers. I seemed to know what they were talking about; I thought I recognized what they were aiming at; I liked the voices in which they spoke. I was at home with certain texts; I responded with intellectual kinship and pleasure. I knew the modulations of their language; I could see their landscapes. And very important indeed, I shared much of their belief in the ideal freedom and power of the self, in the political and social visions of radical democracy. I felt I had started from the same human base and was accompanying some writers to the same imaginative goal.

Behind all these friendly and interested reactions was the fact that my judgment was real to me, too real to distrust. I felt free to like what I liked, not to like what I didn't, and to support my critical reactions by formulating esthetic reasons. It was easier forty and more years ago to feel this pleasant confidence in one's critical judgment, for American literature was still in the making, and the best writers and critics rather condescended to it. If you settled down to it with any passion, you realized that you were eccentric and were making claims for writers that no distinguished mind would look at for a moment. In those days the total approval now extended to Henry James (even as a political mind) was by no means shared by everyone. Criticism was still a matter of individual knowledge and taste, not a way of introducing students to literature; people still thought they could learn more about life from a good story than from the most brilliant exegesis of the story. So I was left, in delicious isolation, to read books that no one else had looked at in years, to have reactions that were wild but which I didn't know enough to tame — to be, without shame, what in those days was considered the absolute second choice and consolation prize: a critic.

"Criticism" is just a word, but critics are very real if their opinions are real to themselves. A critic lives in a buzz of culture and in a vast exchange of opinions like everyone else. Being a critic, dedicated to opinion, he often sets too much store by other people's opinions. If you tell him that *King Lear* is an unbelievable play, full of rant and uncontrolled opinions, he will not ignore you, as a poet would, but will in his own mind figure out what it is in *King Lear* that would allow a presumably good head to think such a thing. A critic deals in considerations about art, not in life as drama, not in the psychic situation that an imaginative writer sees everywhere he goes. A critic is more naturally considerate of opinions than a novelist; his world is made up of opinions. For him literature is not himself seeking to put the widest amount of experience into dramatic consciousness; it is literature, many literatures, many writers, books, forms, styles, traditions — all of which add to the burden on him of other people's opinions; he takes off from them. No critic is ever one by himself; criticism takes place in society, it is a dialogue with the past and one's contemporaries. The circle of examples and tradition and opinions draws tighter and tighter around the critic trying to add something useful and honest to the many libraries that have put him into being.

Nevertheless, a critic is someone whose reactions to a work of art are so real as to be binding on himself and meaningful to others; he will use, not imitate, the learning and insight of other people. The critic is someone whose reactions are so authentic to himself as to become, above all else, *interesting* for others because illuminative of their own unconscious experience in the presence of art. By reactions I mean the ability to take pleasure in what is good, to recognize in the concrete instance the classical truth of those esthetic laws that are so few and incontrovertible, yet meaningful only in the practice of art and in profound critical response to art.

What is "personal" is what is most deeply experienced by the whole person of the critic. Taste cannot be, and should not be, made so "objective" that opinions become simply right or wrong. The value of a particular work in criticism never depends on the critic's *position* alone. In our day critical fashion tyrannizes over many innocent minds. But it does not follow that a book attacking Henry James derives any necessary merit from opposition to the vast herd of sophisticates who hold that James is the last word in the English novel, which in their experience he may well be. A good critic can uphold any reasonable opinion, if only he will *hold* it and engage himself with the work of art that inspired him to it. Jean-Paul Sartre may not convince us in his essays on Dos Passos and Faulkner that Dos Passos is so bold in technique as to be the greatest twentieth-century novelist, that Faulkner is so traditionalist in his thinking as to kill the future for his characters. But Sartre engages *U.S.A.* and *The Sound and the Fury* with an understanding and conviction that make his own critical thinking in these essays an experience to us — Dos Passos and Faulkner have already been great experiences to Sartre.

What counts is that the critic should be really involved with a work; that he should follow the track of his curiosity into it just as long and as passionately as may be necessary. This follows from what I call being-at-home-with-a-text, from feeling in one's bones that one knows what the work is about, that one knows the tone of voice in which the writer speaks, that one is present, oneself all present, at every stage. Criticism exists, after all, because the critic has an intense and meaningful experience of a work. And if he doesn't, why pretend that he does? Why bother, if what one is doing is not intensely real to oneself?

This is the first condition, not of "criticism" but of being a critic. When I read Shakespeare, I am dazzled by the speed and force of his mind. But I

also know when I read him that there is something fundamental about
Shakespeare that I do not truly understand. I do not mean that Shakespeare's characters use expressions that have to be explained. Historical
matter can be learned. But even if I were immensely learned, I would not
feel that I understand Shakespeare for myself — which is all the fun and all
the use of being a critic. Many people have written importantly *around*
Shakespeare without convincing me that they understand him for themselves. Most readers are in fact uneasy with Shakespeare, which is why the
silly snobbish question of who wrote his plays rages in every generation.
Shakespeare is the unknown whom even the greatest critics, like Johnson
and Goethe, have redrawn in the character most suitable to themselves.
Perhaps only John Keats, because he was a virtuoso of language like
Shakespeare, saw him "whole." In the famous letter of October 27, 1818,
he wrote in clairvoyant excitement that "the poetical Character... is not
itself — it has no self — it is everything and nothing. ... It has as much
delight in conceiving an Iago as an Imogen.... A Poet is the most unpoeti-
cal of anything in existence; because he has no Identity — he is continually
infor[ming] and filling some other Body...."

These orphic revelations make a dependable guide to the subtle and
mischievous imagination that bars our full understanding. Keats, at least,
mastered Shakespeare's protean mind; because in his own way he duplicates Shakespeare's sense for language, he is confident that his own reaction of wild delight is also a path to new knowledge. Keats does not preach
Shakespeare the romantic, Shakespeare the monarchist, Shakespeare the
cynic, as so many other critics have done. It is not Shakespeare's *opinions*
that impress Keats; it is his pure poetic intelligence that in turn becomes
each character it can create and takes its force from each dramatic event.
Shakespeare discovered Keats to himself. The Shakespeare text, which is a
chore to students and an intellectual maze to scholars, was to Keats a
release, of the kind that Herman Melville was later to find in Nathaniel
Hawthorne: "For genius, all over the world, stands hand in hand with
genius, and one shock of recognition runs the whole circle round."

Keats *knew* Shakespeare as only one great poet knows another, can
imitate him without really knowing the other's language. To know, not just
to know about, is the highest aim of criticism, and depends on sensibility
intellectually cultivated, on the most urgent instinct for esthetic achievements and distinctions. Of course, one great writer talking about another
can be subjective and may well seem tendentious to a later generation. But

the condition of being-at-home-with-a-text that I am setting forth here as crucial to criticism, the reality compelling response, is important because it risks being fallible. To be a critic, nothing else is so important as the ability to stand one's ground alone. This gets more important as criticism gets more standardized and institutionalized, as the critic gets more absorbed in literary theory rather than in the imaginations who are his *raison d'être*. The more abstractions we deal with, the more we look for proof; since this is not possible in literature, we look for confirmation from other persons. This now usually means the captive audience of half-literate students.

Criticism is a branch of literature, not of science. Like any form of literary expression, criticism can satisfy nothing but our sense of imaginative truth: its judgments operate only within our inner sense, and depend on our taste and culture. Critical statements are not binding on everyone, as are proofs of scientific truth. Keats on Shakespeare, Melville on Hawthorne, are operating within a realm that most people have never heard of, and which does not touch on their lives in the slightest. Literature operates significantly only on exceptional individuals fortunate enough to afford the luxury of pleasing their imaginations. "I went far enough to please my imagination," said Thoreau. Criticism operates on even a smaller number. If Keats's reaction to Shakespeare seems more "personal" than a scientist's findings can ever be, that is because literature exists only in the realm of minds, and takes its sanction from laws of art that are understood only in relation to the human mind.

Keats is one of the few writers on Shakespeare who help me to read *him* and not just to read about him. Shakespeare is entirely real to Keats, and so Keats makes Shakespeare less unreal to me. That is what I look for in a critic — his use to me; I can use critics whose general point of view is outrageous to me, but who in specific matters have this capacity for making a writer real and a text real. A useful critic is someone who has already begun to use a text in a significant personal way, who is not in doubt about his fundamental reaction, who is not arbitrary but is convinced, in his reading of Shakespeare (or Dos Passos), that he knows what there is to know. Of course, this is not enough for the ages; only the greatest critics survive, for as Johnson said, they raise opinion to knowledge. These are the lawgivers of art, and there are very few of them — far fewer, it turns out, than there are original minds in science. But opinion in criticism, if held at a level deep enough to become interesting, can vivify our sense of what writing is all about and may even excite us to write in new ways. If I ever make an anthology of criticism, it will be called *The Useful Critic,* and will feature only writings that have helped me.

It would come from all sources, and would be an odd mixture indeed. The conversation of Johnson, Goethe, Auden. An early criticism of Vladimir Nabokov by Isaac Babel. The art criticism of Baudelaire, the music criticism of Nietzsche. A few lines from Whitman, interviewed by Horace Traubel, on Emerson's essential genius as a "critic or diagnoser." Marx on Balzac, showing how important it is for "revolutionaries" to respect genius on any side. Emerson on "The Poet," because this rhapsody is the most eloquent and uncompromising revelation of the artist as hero who stands behind his prophetic writings. William James delighting in Emerson, William James curtly correcting Henry Adams's attempts to apply "science" to history. Melville's magnificent praise of his as yet unmet friend in "Hawthorne and His Mosses," because it shows in every free and flowing line of praise how Hawthorne's insistence on becoming a storyteller in Calvinist New England could help another genius to recognize himself. Henry James's preface to *The Portrait of a Lady,* not because it reveals the "laws" of any art but James's own, but because James's art is founded on the celebration of civilized beauty with which this preface begins.

Among twentieth-century critics in English, my anthology would include (poets make my favorite critics; they have the most intense personal consciousness of art) Eliot on Pascal, D.H. Lawrence on Hardy, Randall Jarrell on Frost, Conrad Aiken on Faulkner, Wallace Stevens for his general reflections on intellectual nobility, Robert Penn Warren on Conrad. It would include V.S. Pritchett, because he is a genius at truly *literary* journalism, and for any of dozens of appreciations of the English and European novel, but especially for his essays on the comic novel; Edmund Wilson, for many illuminations of different literatures, but especially for the observations on American style in *Patriotic Gore.*

This list could go on, just as personally, to include A.C. Bradley, whom in my unfashionable way I still deeply admire on Shakespeare; Erich Auerbach, the great German refugee scholar, whose *Mimesis,* on the representation of reality in Western literature, is the most useful contemporary work in criticism that I own. I can never turn to Auerbach on Homer or Montaigne or even Shakespeare without being enlightened in the deepest and most active way. My anthology would include Lessing on the contrast of actor and audience; Whitehead on Shelley; Erich Heller, for his moving intellectual sympathies with Nietszche, Rilke, Thomas Mann; Joseph Frank for his work on Dostoevsky.

My list would *not* include academics whose sense of their own authority has never instructed or even provoked me. What I ask of a critic is that he usefully show the impact on his own consciousness of anothers artistic power. If the critic cannot reveal to others the power of art in his own life, he cannot say anything useful or even humane in its interest. He will scrawl, however learnedly, arbitrary comments on the text.

Literary thought starts in the most intimate, the closest possible touch with subject-matter, not critical method. To be absorbed, to be involved at every point with the implications of a subject is to see the text in context, and this alone turns the mind back ever more freshly to the rest. Literary thought means to me reaction to a unique act. The *force* of the act breaks up something already existent and "makes new." A book is not just the precious lifeblood of a master spirit; it has consequences in many minds as well as origins in many minds. It *connects* in all sorts of unspoken ways; then it becomes the act of a particular culture; and as an image of a particular time turns the past into the present. From text to text the aroused reader, the true critic, lives in *all* these time-worlds, space-worlds, dream-worlds.

≤ 2 ≥

To be a critic, to exercise thought on the literature of a developing culture, means that one wants to influence and not just to show that the flowers entombed in a certain well-wrought urn had never been moved into the light. The critic should be an agent of change, moving from concrete — even physical — reactions into unexpected realizations of all that may be embedded in a writer's unique force. No critic, alive to his subject matter rather than to a critical formula, comes to close grips with a text without changing a reader's mind. The experience of literature can be, it used to be, a particularly concentrated and driving force for transforming a person's life. There can be a reorientation to the physical, mental, and political universe in the writer's mind. One shares a new universe, if ever so briefly. Even when our minds drift on to other mental universes, we ourselves have been altered in unsuspected ways.

But of course this may be absurd just now. We live in a period when literature provides information, has no influence moral or political compared with the visual power of television, films, advertising, the screaming headline. So it is also an age — if only in the universities — of endless theorizing about what literature cryptically is. The emphasis is on the "reader" (meaning the critic not the common reader). The critic becomes the central figure in every "creative" transaction. Language as such contains the intrinsic authority once ascribed to individual talent; "text replaces voice." But not without the fond belief, typical of critical intelligence rather than of creative power, that what a "strong" poet is really thinking about when he writes a poem is supplanting his predecessors.

≤ 3 ≥

The connection between illiteracy (or even anti-literature) in the mass and critical theory in the universities, between the atrocity of best-sellerdom and what Coleridge called the multiplication of secondary distinctions is ignored. These are political phenomenona, but criticism today battens on the increasing evidence of political chaos. Consider the futility of any teacher in the 1980s invoking what Eliot in a famous passage called "the historical sense." This "we may call nearly indispensable to anyone who would continue to be a poet beyond his twenty-fifth year; and the historical sense involves a perception, not only of the pastness of the past, but of its presence; the historical sense compels a man to write not merely with his own generation in his bones, but with a feeling that the whole of the literature of Europe from Homer and within the whole of the literature of his own country has a simultaneous existence and composes a simultaneous order."

I grew up with the historical sense; it was a sign that history had a discernible pattern and might even have a manifest end. Whether the writer was a Christian like Eliot, a transcendental novelist like Proust, a mythologist like Joyce, or a radical critic in the Hazlitt tradition like Orwell, the historical sense seemed as natural as a sense of time. The last great writer among us to believe this was Jean-Paul Sartre, for whom philosophy came down to a contest between being and nothingness, between man as the creator and embodiment of value and a universe that does not exist without man. Sartre the philosopher, critic, novelist, dramatist, polemicist, veering over the postwar years toward a more and more revolutionary contempt for existing institutions, expressed more than anyone else, in a generation of radical writers often demoralized by Communism, the God That Failed, the will to remain faithful to the perennial dream of revolution in France. There the radical intellectuals write the best books, but the bourgeoisie and the bureaucracy never relinquish the actual power. Revolution traditionally remains the intellectuals' imaginary paradise.

The more the actual oppressiveness of Communism finally came through to this class (Solzhenitsyn's *The Gulag Archipelago* turned around many left intellectuals), the more Sartre, despite his anguish over the suppression of the Hungarian Revolution, *tried* to remain faithful to his fundamental idea. All value is embodied in revolutionary change, transferring vital being to new elements in society. The author of such works essential to our time as *L'Être et le néant*, of *La Nausée*, of *Huis Clos*, *Les Séquestrés d'Altona*, had already shown himself an innovative critic in his *Baudelaire*, in three volumes of essays with the perfect Sartrean title of *Situations*. His uniquely objective memoir of childhood, *Les Mots*, his research into Flaubert, *L'Idiot de la famille*, showed again that the most trenchant studies of the nature of literature, of the reason for its power, are made by philosophers.

Sartre's blend of existentialist psychoanalysis, his unrelenting scorn for French bourgeois life (that cradle of their best authors) could not conceal his own increasingly exasperated culture revolution. He did his best to get arrested, rejected his Nobel Prize. But the French do not arrest their most famous authors even when they make a point of hawking some inflammatory leftist paper. De Gaulle, then president, noted that the French had arrested François Villon and it hadn't helped.

But after Sartre, socialism as the secular religion of the intellectuals lost its punch. The continuing practice in every café and classroom of *le discours* (whether or not the subject requires so much impersonation of intelligence) has often survived belief, conviction. Sainte-Beuve said that in France one remains Catholic after one has ceased to be Christian. With the dissipation of classic leftism there became prominent in the newly technological and modernized France a more ironic and neutral intellectual — the essayist Roland Barthès, the philosopher Jacques Derrida, the psychoanalyst Jacques Lacan. They stimulated that ever-present audience in France for an intellectual formula that upsets convention, for the necessarily literary that has shock value promising a new way of seeing things.

France in this period significantly became a center of advanced technique, of discoveries in molecular biology; linguistics had been a tradition since Ferdinand de Saussure. The New Wave in fiction produced nothing lasting, but it had a significantly close association with film. The prominent new literary theorists, whether structuralists like Lévi-Strauss or post-structuralists like Derrida, were experts in literary form, writers bound to the scientific idea that language has an innate structure and authority all its own that has more effect on the individual writer than the writer has on it.

The universal structures of language, the fact that comparative study always shows more resemblances between languages than contrasts, was as a scientific observation held to be superior to the romantic cult of individual genius and the supposedly discredited phenomena of inspiration.

The appeal of literary theory was that it was a wholly new, more "scientific" form that also became literature. It upheld the impersonal authority of what the French like to call *literarité*, the literariness in discourse itself. The poet's touch was not always necessary to turn words into literature, but the critic was necessary to explain that language itself was more interesting than the poet who used it.

The critic in the university had with the New Criticism become an authority rather than a mere interpreter. Contemporary literature had somehow come to take all preceding literature under its wing, but it was always the next line in a contemporary poem that had to be explained by some Great Big Explicator to students who had no Latin, no French, no German, had never read the Bible, knew Oedipus as a character in Freud. Mencken said that nobody ever went broke underestimating the American audience. Modernism became the favorite dish in the English Department just when the best minds tended to go elsewhere and what was required of an English major was not that he know how little the great English novels resembles Henry James's but that he make obedient sounds of comprehension and addiction about works so packed with learning as *The Waste Land* and Pound's *Cantos*.

Nevertheless, the New Criticism soon took a back seat to advanced literary theory. This was easy, because the habit of reading, reading for yourself, reading indifferent to fashion and ideology, reading because it is at least one way of puzzling out your life and the world's, was becoming more and more difficult to practice. There emanates from the many new authorities over our lives a real censorship; there is also — "also"? — a staggering indifference to reading insofar as reading itself still represents some personal determination to change habits of seeing and thinking. No bibliomaniac today can honestly affirm that reading maketh the whole man — that literature represents *any* force of change equal to technology, political violence, insurrection, war — to films, television, the endless reversals of images, to proclamation and visual threat. Change is so incessant that the individual secretly torn apart by its flux is no longer under the old Sartrean illusion of the self moving beyond itself while retaining its metaphysical unity — but of losing identity. That identity once seemed the very ground of life. We see now that it rested on the twin pillars of religion and capitalism, which have survived as institutions, not objects of respect. Change is beyond our present categories, even when they are about nothing else.

≤ 4 ≥

I grew up as what my old teacher and friend Mark Van Doren called a "private reader." Nothing in the world was so delightful, my own pleasure principle, as taking more and more books every day out of the Public Library — an institution then open every other day. I spent the better part of every day reading; I lived to read. There were never enough books for this — never words enough to describe the transformations taking place in me as I read. The private experience of books, as Saul Bellow once put it in a beautiful essay, was some unknown person's "sealed treasure." There was that in me, reading myself into the writing of my first book year after year at the golden tables in Room 315 above Forty-Second Street, that was an experience of human advancement and liberation too subtle to be shared. Only writing about it, an act of criticism, confronting a text, could express some of the pent-up thinking involved in absorbing, moving with all those black marks on paper.

And what did one read for? Why so *much?* Because it was understood, as Isaac Babel put it in the title of a story, that "you must know everything." If reading was not indiscriminate and omnivorous, endlessly exploratory, seeking knowledge at every turn and from the most neglected of books as well as the most famous, what was it?

It was their orthodoxy — by which I understood their limitation largely to poetry and only to a certain kind of lyric poetry — that made me shy away from the New Criticism. I felt that everyone had a right to read in his/her own way and to admire just what had given one the greatest pleasure. It was absurd to think that what Henry James called "form" was more essential than what James's own adored Balzac knew as the human comedy. It was absurd of James, who knew nothing about it, to call the great Russian novelists "loose and baggy monsters." It was absurd of F. R. Leavis to leave Dickens out of the "great tradition" of the English novel — absurd of R. P. Blackmur, the most brilliant and elusive of the New Critics, to put down Frost as easily as he put down Cummings — absurd, when Eliot became in effect literary dictator, to read Donne and Marvell as if Keats and Whitman had never existed.

What I most objected to in the New Criticism was that the act of criticism became a star performance, annihilating earlier performers — not so much advancing knowledge as impressing students. Students took the severity of their master's voice as another excuse for not reading beyond the assignment. And what was assigned was not just Brooks and Warren, but a certain mildewed way of looking at the world that I found ludicrously uninformed, as when Cleanth Brooks informed an audience that Emerson was responsible for Hitler. When I began to teach regularly in the fifties, I was staggered by the medievalism of my students: they knew just a few chosen texts, and all the rest was commentary by brilliant critics whose *names* you had only to mention for everyone to recognize that you had consulted Authority.

The real success of the New Criticism was not in the realm of ideas or taste, but in teaching our blissfully uneducated students and children "how to read." I had not realized that a movement against illiteracy could be considered a movement in criticism. Then taste shifted from the untimely classicism of the New Criticism. The counterculture adored the Freudian critique of repression, pan-sexual poets like Whitman. The well-wrought urn was bombed by cultural terrorists (one even became president of the Modern Language Association) who could have shouted with Goering, "When I hear the word culture I reach for my revolver." The private reader in old-fashioned solitude confronting a text had to yield to the public clamor, to the thundering simultaneity of film, television, advertising, political atrocity. Nihilism, posing as revolution, exulted in the post-humanist observation of Jean-Luc Godard — "We are interested only in process. Form and content are process." On the murder of the Israeli athletes at the Munich Olympics, Godard pronounced: "The Palestinians were right with their basics, but not their external conditions. They didn't realize the world was just watching a looking-machine — the television — and the killings didn't have the effect they wanted." A will-o'-the-wisp was strenuously pursued at our best universities by the exasperated children of the bourgeoisie. Not the text counted but, in good anarchist style, The Act.

The Act was many things now in the revolutionary consciousness of the alienated young. It was Action painting, where as one especially observant critic noticed, the idea was "to fuck up the painting." It was populism of the most frenzied antinomian sort: all cultures are equal, especially if some of them have no culture. It was what a marginal group proudly asserted as Camp, and what Susan Sontag in *Against Interpretation* held up as the necessary erotics of art. A certain diffuse and even vicarious eroticism indulged in the fable of the everlasting Id — to which Ego, that Victorian patriarchal self so marked among chauvinistic males, had to yield. Outmoded Freud had hoped for the reverse.

Meanwhile, any real advance intellectually was taking place not in imaginative literature, but in structuralism and in its growing perception of the real unity of cultures based on universal identity. There was developing in France and there would soon emerge in the United States more evidence that what really fascinated literary theory was the innate creativity of language itself.

The romantic transcendentalist Emerson had guessed that language is "fossil poetry," that words alone, contracting their expressive history, exert the appeal that gets the poet to listen and obey. Emerson was an orphic mind and soul, and foretells the curious religiousity behind our present view of language. Hegel thought that the World-Spirit moved to some inherent destiny through gifted individuals. Just now literary theorists (a different breed from students of linguistics) celebrate language as itself more the real author of some text than the individual author.

My prime requirement for a critic has always been sureness of touch, the firmest possible contact with the subject in hand (which can be not just a particular text but one moving *through* the text into a whole series of contexual relationships). This requires the necessary separation between the private reader and his book. The current breakdown of traditional political relationships, as well as the way in which films and television (Godard's "looking-machine") absorb us into the process itself, show that a clearly defined subject matter becomes more and more remote and even unnecessary to literary theory.*

Harold Bloom is a prodigy of learning, memory, exegesis. We owe him a great deal for bringing the English romantics — especially Blake and

---

*Just how unaware of one's purported subject matter an intelligent critic can now be is seen in an essay on "political novels" in the New York Times Book Review of August 10, 1980, by Robert Alter. Alter compares novels so removed in space and time as Stendhal's Charterhouse of Parma, Robert Penn Warren's All the King's Men, Robert Coover's The Public Burning, E. L. Doctorow's The Book of Daniel, Thomas Pynchon's Gravity's Rainbow. There is no intimation in Alter's analysis that these novelists are writing about political issues so different as Italy after Napoleon, Louisiana under Huey Long, the Rosenberg case in the 1950s, and possible universal destruction by nuclear war.

I, too, dislike Coover's book for its false frenzy, as I object to Doctorow, a more equable novelist, for being able to write a novel around the Rosenbergs without intimating their

Shelley — back into critical favor after the Eliot dictatorship fell. Bloom's early books are wonderfully stimulating — not least because his sense of Jewish tradition has benefited from Gershom Scholem's recreation of Jewish mystical tradition. There is a frustration of religion in Bloom that excitedly finds expression in English romanticism; as Whitehead said, romanticism is spilled religion. But under the spell of Freud's "family romance," Bloom has cultivated ideas of the necessary rivalry between poets, the necessary "misreading" of long established texts, that totally mistake the critic's power and responsibility. Bloom, essentially orphic in his pronouncements, is attempting to make of the universal spirit-in-time-and-space-as-the-genius-of-poetry (this was German orphic romanticism) something that will enable *him* to slip into it as a kind of poet.

I have observed Bloom lecture; I have been in the audience of eager but baffled note-takers as he examines a poem like Wallace Stevens's "Sea Surface Full of Clouds" and piles so many allusions to other writers onto it that the audience is not so much enlightened as intimidated. It may be essential to Harold Bloom that his audience not know quite what he is talking about. In his contribution to *Deconstruction and Criticism*,* "The Breaking of Form," he comes out with this:

> Angus Fletcher, in his studies of Spenser, Milton, Coleridge, and Crane, has been developing a liminal poetics or new rhetoric of thresholds, and I follow Fletcher both in my notion of the topoi or "crossings" as images of voice, and in my account of the final revisionary apophrades or reversed belatedness, which is akin to the classical trope of *metalepsis* or transumption and to the Freudian "negating" (Verneinung) with its dialectical interplay of the defenses, projection and introjection. I will re-expound and freshly develop these Fletcherian ideas in the reading of Ashbery that follows.

---

complicity in their own fate. Pynchon, a more intelligent and resourceful novelist than most, is writing about the bomb hanging over our minds — the bomb ticking away in our minds. Mr. Alter writes about novels he thinks equally "political" without making it clear that Parma in the early nineteenth century, Louisiana under Huey Long in the 1930s, cannot be related to the novel that now comes out of the threat of universal destruction.

In a recent interview Truman Capote explained that "Subject matter is not important." "It's just style," Capote says hitting the fan on his palm for emphasis, "It's all style."

Compare Edmund Wilson to Vladimir Nabokov, 1942: ". . . everything around me seems of an emptiness that opens right out on the interstellar spaces. I think that airplanes in changing our point of view on the permanence and authority of human habitations, are also damaging our intellectual and imaginative constructions."

*New York: The Seabury Press.

This staggering pronouncement reminds me of Ross Chambers in *Critical Inquiry* (Winter issue, 1979):

> The structuralist revolution, or more precisely the trend towards linguistic analysis of texts manifesting the so-called poetic function of language, has immeasurably increased our understanding of the types of relationships, paradigmatic and syntagmatic, which constitute the "literarité" of texts. But it has necessarily left out of account those relationships which, because they are hierarchical, do not so easily admit of contrastive analysis in terms of binary equivalences; these are the "interpreting relationships" which exist between a specific segment of discourse within a text and the text as a whole.
>
> If such is the duplicity of commentary, then interpretation only compounds the problem by further contextualizing the intratextual contextualization! Literature, in some ways, is like a gift which comes with its price tag attached in the form of commentary — and to which, through interpretation, we endlessly strive to restore the value it has, for that very reason, lost.

Everyone who "teaches" literature now knows that there are fewer and fewer private readers among students, still fewer each year who would understand the old culture dream of wanting to "know everything." There seem to be practically none who will say to the critical "performance" of Harold Bloom that it is now all personal myth-making, barbarously and self-hallucinatingly arcane and, to impress innocent students, a form of aggrandizement.

On the other hand, is there another way just now, in and out of the universities, to make students respect "literature"? Of keeping the subject serious under the onslaught of all in this disruptive period that keeps a private reader from his old dream that by thinking in new ways he will yet help others to rethink the world? That rethinking, new ways of seeing past our outworn connection with the world, must be the silent force behind our reading?

For many people just now, the private reader asserting his own thinking as a sufficient act may not seem enough. There are just too many forces against him. There always are. Those forces were never stronger than when Nadezhda Mandelstam memorized her husband's work in order to keep it alive. When Solzhenitsyn was arrested for writing a private letter and in the Gulag had to write whole plays and essays in his mind, apportioning the words there by the bricks he once had to lay in the prison camp. When Andrey Sinyavsky, arrested for writing his defiance of "Socialist Realism," had to explain to a Soviet judge in defense of his fellow-prisoner Yuri

Daniel that a character's speeches are not to be identified with the personal views of the author.

Sinyavsky is out of Russia now, like Joseph Brodsky, Vasily Aksyonov, Anatoly Gladilin, Viktor Nekrasov. Aksyonov in New York: "Sometimes I think it is not a tragedy, that it is our duty as writers now in the West to try to restore the links between Russian culture and Western culture, to prove we haven't become people without any spiritual life."

The forces in Latin America were never more depressing, endlessly cruel and fanatical when such writers as García Márquez, Jose Donoso, Vargas Llosa, Carlos Fuentes, Márcio Souza, Julio Cortázar — émigrés all — dazzled the outside world with the centuries of solitude their Latin America represents. Exiles. I think of Naipaul, for me the greatest contemporary novelist in English, as I think of Conrad; of Nabokov; of Nelly Sachs driven to the edge of madness by the Holocaust but at the edge of sanity writing her best poems in Sweden; of Samual Beckett deciding to write in French; of Elias Canetti sticking to German (wherever he lives). When is the true writer and the creative deed *not* wrung out of oppression and the most freezing solitude? Freud escaped to England, described himself as "an island of pain in a sea of indifference." Just now the primary task of the critic may be not only to expound the deed but to demonstrate its continuity, resisting every imaginable threat and emptiness.

But to do this requires a sense of the radical insufficiency of language itself. Language is not a god. Flaubert, describing Rodolphe tiring of Emma Bovary's passionate protestations: "Because lips libertine and venal had murmured such words to him, he believed but little in the candor of hers; he thought that exaggerated speeches hiding mediocre affections must be discounted; — as if the fullness of the soul did not sometimes overflow into the emptiest metaphors, since no one can ever give the exact measure of his needs, nor of his conceptions, nor of his sorrows; for human speech is like a cracked kettle, on which we hammer out tunes to make bears dance when we long to touch the stars to tears."

[1981]

II
The Background of
Modern Literature

EVER SINCE the end of the eighteenth century, when great poets like Goethe and Blake denounced experimental science as partial and inconclusive, the distinctively modern writers have been those who have claimed that literature gives us a more direct and more comprehensive access to reality than science can. It is not knowledge as such, or even the power over nature that can be won through knowledge, that the modern writers have questioned; it is knowledge gained by scientific method. Wordsworth says disapprovingly that we murder to dissect, and Whitman condescendingly turns his back on the "learn'd astronomer" to look up "in perfect silence at the stars." Poe cried out in his sonnet "To Science" that science had robbed the world of its magic, and later in the nineteenth century the great French visionary poet Arthur Rimbaud, himself in the tradition set up in France by disciples of Poe, protested that "our pale reason hides the infinite from us." As early as the seventeenth century, the particular concern of the *modern* writer is typified by that genius in both mathematics and literature, Blaise Pascal, who wrote that the heart has its reasons — which reason cannot know. Yet the spell of even scientific knowledge is so great that Goethe made investigations in botany and optics, realistic novelists from Balzac to Zola have conceived of fiction as a branch of biology, and in the twentieth century an extraordinary poet and would-be mathematician, Paul Valéry, wrote certain poems as if he were preparing theorems.

Valéry's master, the Symbolist poet Stéphane Mallarmé, had already shown (on a hint from the stories of Poe) that the effects of one sense can be described as if gained through another. A sound can be expressed as a vision and each vowel in a word can suggest a different color. Through this doctrine of "synaesthesiae" Mallarmé had proclaimed that unity of the poetic imagination that had been broken ever since science had taught men to separate reason from intuition. One reason why Poe was such a profound influence on these French poets, starting from Baudelaire, is that he conceived of himself as a seer, a poet who was a genius at ratiocination. Those demigods of popular literature — the amateur detectives who are never at a loss for a solution — actually have their beginning in the fantasies and ambitions of Edgar Allan Poe, who may be said to have invented the detective story, and whose hero, C. Auguste Dupin, is the very type of the modern literary intellectual — an aristocrat temporarily down on his luck who lives alone, works by night, and, entirely by superior guesswork, has a knowledge of crime and the human heart that confounds the stupid representatives of the official police, with their reliance on common sense and laboratory methods.

This contempt for the official police on the part of poets who prize their independence is really a dramatization of the everlasting contempt that the Romantic writers — the first self-consciously modern group — felt for the conventional picture of the world and the conventional morality that narrowed the possibilities of man. Whether it is Goethe's Faust or Shelley's Prometheus or Melville's Captain Ahab, the characteristic heroes of the Romantics are those who know that reality is more mysterious and intangible than the ruling gods will admit — and who try to meet this reality on every side of their personal experience. The great insight of the Romantics — and of those who have become the fundamental type of modern writer in our day, Joyce and Proust and Yeats — is that the world which science seeks so laboriously to understand must be grasped through man, not despite him. A contemporary social scientist has contemptuously defined personality as "the index of inefficiency." But Yeats wrote in "The Tower" (1928) that "Death and life were not/Till man made up the whole." Where the scientists studied "the facts," unrelated and external to man, the modern writer, as early as the eighteenth century, took his stand on human consciousness as the key to reality.

It is this claim that explains the extraordinary inner consistency of modern literature from the fall of the Bastille to the fall of mechanistic conceptions in twentieth-century science, as it is this claim that explains the actual influence of literature on science. Although science and technology seem pre-eminent in our present culture, the really suggestive thing about the very greatest twentieth-century writers, like Proust, Joyce, Lawrence, Yeats, Mann, is that they have never felt outdone or outclassed by scientific investigation. Although literary people often complain that they feel isolated and anomalous in a world where scientists exert so much influence and get so much prestige, the greatest writers of our time have celebrated in literature man's increasing contact with the profundities of his own experience. In a book of startling encouragement to writers, *Science and the Modern World* (1925), Alfred North Whitehead, speaking from his immense prestige as a mathematician and philosopher, substantiated the criticism first made by the Romantic poets of mechanistic conceptions of the external world. In his tribute to Wordsworth, Whitehead noted that the philosophy which had reached its ultimate expression in the eighteenth-century dream of ordering human nature and society in a fixed mode, through reason, had a fatal weakness: "It involves a fundamental duality, with material on the one hand, and on the other hand mind. In between there lie the concepts of life, organism, function, instantaneous reality, interaction, order of nature, which collectively form the Achilles' heel of the whole system." And Whitehead added: "We are witnessing a conscious reaction against the whole tone of the eighteenth century. That century approached nature with the abstract analysis of science, whereas Wordsworth opposed to the scientific abstractions his full concrete experience. Wordsworth in his whole being expressed a conscious reaction against the mentality of the eighteenth century. What moved him was a moral repulsion. He felt something had been left out, and that what had been left out comprised everything that was most important."

In one form or another, much that had been left out by nineteenth-century science was brought back by modern literature. For the missing "life," "organism," "function," "instantaneous reality," "interaction," one could now fill in William James's radical empiricism, Henri Bergson's *élan vital*, Sigmund Freud's theory of the unconscious. Such men are not merely philosophers and psychologists but superb writers, whose greatest contributions to knowledge, as in *The Principles of Psychology* (1890), *Matter and Memory* (1896), *The Interpretation of Dreams* (1900), have not only exerted enormous influence on the modern movement in twentieth-century literature, but have themselves become classic parts of this literature.

In writers like James, Bergson, and Freud, modern literature and modern science have gone hand in hand, and despite the efforts of second-rate poets to cut themselves off from difficult subject matter and of second-rate psychologists to dismiss the insights gained by modern writers, literature and science have shown themselves in the best hands to be profoundly respectful of each other. Freud, who was a very beautiful writer—he was awarded the greatest German literary honor, the Goethe prize, even if he was steadily refused a Nobel Prize in science — typified the intelligence of an original scientist when he wrote, in a famous essay on Dostoevsky: "Unfortunately, before the problem of the creative artist, analysis must lay down its arms." The influence of Freud on modern literature and art, so overwhelming that no one can trace it completely, can be attributed to the belief that Freud had confirmed the creative role of the imagination, that necessary and valuable projection of human symbols upon the world, which Wordsworth, as early as 1798, had summed up as "the mighty world of eye, and ear — both what they half-create, and what perceive."

It is this identification of personal consciousness with the hidden areas of reality that explains why the language in modern poetry, which to so many readers seems unintelligible and even willfully so, is so often regarded by the poet as "ultimate" and irreducible in its truth. The poet regards his words not as signs or referents, but as direct images of the world. "Poetry is not written with ideas," said Mallarmé the Symbolist, "it is written with words." This could have been said by the Romantics as well, and one can find in so Romantic a poet as Whitman the same reliance on words whose import is mysterious and unknown to himself that one can find in the Symbolist poets. Where Symbolism broke with Romanticism was on the question of form, not belief. Romantics like Whitman assumed that the revelations they made in their poems were in line not only with their own unconsciousness but with the moral order of the world, and that the "rapt" inspiration of the poet was in perfect correspondence with God, society, science, and truth. The Symbolists — their idol, Poe, significantly insisted that a successful poem must be short and strict in form — did not think of themselves as nature's priests but as nature's alchemists: they were fabricators rather than "revealers." For them poetry was not in line with society but in opposition to it. A poem had to be not "open" but "closed": for the hermetic images on which the poem was founded were absolute in themselves, and the experience to be gained from the complex interweaving of human sensations together would finally be unstatable. By opposing sensation to conscious understanding, the poem to prose, the poet to society, the Symbolists diverted poetic imagination from the transcendental to the subjective. The implied despair of the outside world, of commonplace human experience, even of sexual love, became elements of which the poem was hardened in form, and what had been sponsored by Wordsworth, Hugo, and Whitman as revelation was now adored as magic. The typical Symbolist poets — Mallarmé in France, Stefan George in Germany — had cults around them which regarded them as "magicians," celebrating the mystery of the word. The religion of the individual genius which the Romantics had formed was based on the image of the poet as an oracle and great national leader: Emerson in America, Carlyle in Britain, Goethe in Germany, Dostoevsky in Russia. The poet was akin to God because he was the voice of God. The Romantics had emphasized "creativity" because they had wished to establish the value of originality, and this, founded on the image of Shakespeare, had meant an analogy between genius and nature. Even the most famous Romantic definition of Shakespeare's creative power — Keats's conception of "negative capability," that the poet in himself is nothing but becomes in turn all the personages he creates — implies that genius is as mysteriously recreative of itself as nature is. But the cult of the *poet* among the Symbolists is significantly opposed to that of the *bard* among the Romantics; with the Symbolists the poet not only becomes the highest human being, but is privileged by understanding which he cannot share with anyone else and which, since it cannot even be *stated* in the poem itself (it is merely suggested), cannot be grasped at all outside the immediate experience of the poem.

Much of what is said in explanation of modern poetry is based on the doctrine of the Symbolists and is misleading when it is used to substantiate the particular achievement of *all* poetry. Because of the overwhelming success of modern poetry in the style of Eliot and Pound, their followers often speak of poetry as if it had always been a rite, as it was to the Symbolists. When Allen Tate declares that poetry gives us a higher form of knowledge than science does, a knowledge that is "complete" in itself, he is speaking of poetry as in itself a religious experience — which is what it was to the Symbolists, but is not to Eliot himself, as it was not to Dr. Johnson or to Shakespeare. Everyone knows Archibald MacLeish's famous lines: 'A poem should not mean / But be." But since the victory of the specifically modern poetry that grew out of Symbolism, not everyone remembers that many a great poem before the nineteenth century — and in it — could both mean *and* be.

The particular emphasis which the Symbolists put on the being of a poem rather than its meaning grew out of their revolt against the narrow-minded science of the mid-nineteenth century. The quality of this period comes back to us when Matthew Arnold reports in his essay on *Literature and Science* that a young man in an English training college for teachers, having to paraphrase the passage in *Macbeth* beginning "Can'st thou not minister to a mind diseased?" turned this line into: "Can you not wait upon the lunatic?" Arnold commented in his official report as an inspector of schools that it would be a curious state of things if every pupil in English national schools knew in exact figures the diameter of the moon but thought that these two lines came to the same thing. In the heyday of nineteenth-century science, the poets reacted so strongly against the cocksure materialism of the scientists that they made a cult of experiences that could be only suggested, not represented or defined. Arnold collected the most affecting single lines of poetry and read them as if he were a priest reading his breviary. The Symbolists relied for their art entirely on the thaumaturgic power of words, which can affect us in the same way that we are affected by actual physical representations in the fine arts and by sounds in music.

« 2 »

If we look now at the way Symbolism triumphed—in the invigorating atmosphere of artistic "modernism" that just before World War I began to sweep everything before it—we can see that, as in all periods, the poetry which it ridicules and destroys, the poetry that has been too long in favor, confesses its weakness by proclaiming its "moral" intentions. A characteristic sign of creative weakness is talk about doing good. Such talk was particularly rife at the end of the nineteenth century, when the more "genteel" poets, in the now diffused poetic tradition of the Romantics — "Tennyson-and-water" — could not respond directly enough to the challenge offered by science and escaped into a religion of beauty. It was the period when the poets of the future, like Eliot and Pound, were as students significantly turning away from nineteenth-century English poetry to the hard, biting, eccentric poetry of Jules Laforgue and Tristan Corbière. Elsewhere, even the greatest poet of the future, William Butler Yeats, was still writing wistfully pastoral poems like "Innisfree," based upon his reading of Thoreau's *Walden*; it often seemed in those days that poetry had no future but would yield to fiction based on the documentary methods of those naturalistic novelists who were followers of Ernst Haeckel and Herbert Spencer.

Characteristically, it was in the poetry of the Symbolists and in the philosophy of James and Bergson that the challenge to mechanism was first made, thus living up to the boast of so many writers that literature is a swifter, more prophetic apprehension of reality. This is what Ezra Pound meant when he said that writers are the "antennae" of the race, but have to work against the "bullet-headed" many. In the late 1890s and early 1900s, however, the "antennae" were often invisible, a minuscule advance guard of literature. In literary circles in America, there was a sickly belief that poetry meant either roundelays or the hearty "athletic" verse that came in with Kipling and the celebration of imperialism. Though a remarkable group of young poets — Trumbull Stickney, William Vaughn Moody, George Cabot Lodge — had sprung up at Harvard in the 1890s, and had significantly been concerned in their verse dramas with the martyrdom of Prometheus, they soon gave up or died off; visibly killed, says their contemporary George Santayana, by the lack of air to breathe. At the time when Edwin Arlington Robinson was working in the New York subways and Stephen Crane's vinegary little poems were regarded as jokes, when Whitman was still indecent and the poetry of Emily Dickinson was "corrected" by her first editors, one saw the great tradition of the English Romantics reduced to an academic cult of beauty. The philosophical purposiveness which had sought God in nature was replaced by a worship of nature itself. The Georgians, as the more introverted cultists of nature were to be called in England — the genteel tradition, as it was later to be called in America when it was directly under attack — these represented that dependence on literature as consolation rather than as exploration of reality which was soon to mark off traditional poetry from that of the modern group. In the verse that was so soon to seem old-fashioned, the poet saw himself as a victim rather than as an observer, and it is this self-pity that peculiarly character- izes the literary tradition that succumbed to the devastating insights of twentieth-century poetry.

By contrast, the poetry of Eliot and Pound, which grew out of Symbolism, went back to Baudelaire's conception of the poet as a "dandy," an ironic observer of big-city life. Poetry in the hands of the Symbolists had become a little too arcane, too prone to cherish itself as a mystery. Eliot and Pound gave their poems a quality more immediately dry and biting, an ironic tang. Instead of the seclusion that had figured so largely in the Symbolists, the center of interest now became the self-mockery in "The Love Song of J. Alfred Pru- frock" (1917), the ". . . muttering retreats / Of restless nights in one-night cheap hotels / And sawdust restaurants with oyster-shells." In Eliot's poem there were "Streets that follow like a tedious argu- ment / Of insidious intent," and one felt in his early poems not only contempt for the genteel tradition of the Boston Brahmins, but the insidious emptiness of modern life, the loneliness and dinginess of big cities — which Eliot was able to realize with the sardonic dramatic emphasis that explains his power to reach so many people. But this was dramatic monologue in poetry as incongruous and flip as the distortions in the new paintings of Picasso and Braque. Eliot went beyond the trancelike effect of Symbolist poetry, so often weak in poetic power, to catch the unaccountability of modern experience. And to the prevailing sense of meaninglessness, which he suggested with such poignant irony in the actual texture of poems like "Pru- frock," he added a startling genius for lines that made sense only because they laughed at sense, for epithets that clowningly reduced pompous or much-used words to their sickening banality. One of the French poets whom Eliot learned his manner from, Tristan Cor- bière, once appeared in Rome with a miter on his head, circles painted around his eyes, leading a pig decorated with ribbons. Eliot's early poetry had this deliberate provocation, this dramatic wit. In terms that by now have become the clichés of modern criticism, but that once were needed to describe the actualities of Eliot's verse, he emphasized paradox and ambiguity and tension. And though he himself gravely attributed his literary debts to the Jacobean dramatists, the seventeenth-century metaphysicals, and marginal figures in French poetry like Laforgue and Corbière, it was the immediate dramatic verve of this poetry, besides its content of fashionable hopelessness, that made it so tonic and effective.

« 3 »

Ezra Pound, who was actually the instigator of many of Eliot's experiments, was the leading spirit behind a movement that was influential in fiction as well as in poetry, and it was Pound who first campaigned for Henry James when he seemed to be undervalued at his death in 1916, as it was Pound who insisted, against the documentary methods of the realists, on the importance of style in the novel and the legacy of Flaubert. And significantly, it was through Pound's influence that original writers of fiction like James Joyce began to appear in American *avant-garde* reviews.

Pound's influence on fiction, though he does not write it himself, indicates the direction in which literary expression was moving. Some of the greatest twentieth-century novelists — Joyce, Hemingway, Lawrence, Faulkner — began as poets; of others — James, Conrad, Woolf, Proust — one feels that if they did not themselves write poetry, they certainly brought a poetic sense to the novel. Even the novelists of the nineteenth century who have been notable influences on the twentieth, like Melville, have been distinguished more for their poetic power, the freedom and originality of their language, their power to suggest the mythical and the supernatural in ordinary events, than for the kind of lifelike realization of commonplace events and ordinary people for which the great novelists of the nineteenth century were famous. The most influential figures in twentieth-century fiction are distinguished precisely by their feeling for language. Although even their admirers apologize for the stylistic crudities of Balzac or Dreiser, one thinks of certain passages in Proust, Joyce, or Lawrence as splendors of language in themselves. In some of the later novels of Virginia Woolf, like *The Waves*, and in Joyce's last book, *Finnegans Wake*, the language is central, not what is described; "ordinary" life, life as it is, rude and accidental, becomes a function of language. The contents of such books are the actual contents of the human mind — dreams, longings, memories, thoughts. The emphasis in modern fiction on "the stream of consciousness," on "interior monologue," on "point of view," on the organizing of events around a "foreground observer," as in the novels of Henry James — all illustrate how much in a modern novel is presented to us by a mind initially conscious of itself. The narrator, and central figure, in Proust's great novel, *Remembrance of Things Past*, lies in bed, gathering his dreams and memories around him, for Proust believed that "when a man is asleep, he has in a circle around him the chain of the hours, the sequences of the years, the order of the heavenly host." The whole of James Joyce's *Ulysses* takes place on a single day, the outward events reverberating in the interior thoughts of the characters. If Proust's novel begins in the sleeper's mind, *Ulysses* ends in the "night-thoughts" of a heartily sensuous woman falling asleep. And the world of man's unconscious that Proust and Joyce used as a bridge to the world of society becomes itself the ideal in the novels of D. H. Lawrence, for what Lawrence celebrates in the name of sex is actually that ideally unrestricted consciousness which makes us feel our primitive connection with the world.

The "poetic" reconquest of the novel has led to grand, even profound achievements. Certain complex works of twentieth-century fiction — *Ulysses, Remembrance of Things Past*, Franz Kafka's *The Castle*, seem to us as intellectually revealing as discoveries by Einstein and Rutherford and Planck. But the limitations of this emphasis on personal consciousness is that the "I" who is behind each of these books, who seeks to unite the free world of his consciousness to the ordinary world, is restricted to what can be grasped by *his* consciousness. In this theory of relativity, nothing can be reported which is not imagined by an observer, that is not initiated or expressed in a human mind: which means a glorification of contemplation and a minimizing of the actual world process. The self-conscious vision of the world which the Romantics inaugurated is symbolized by the fact that none of the great Romantic poets (or their descendants in the nineteenth century) was able to achieve a great drama. And grand in conception as Joyce's last work is, it represents art which is relatively stationary and inert, a picture rather than a story, lacking in the full sense of human conflict that we get from the great realistic novels of the nineteenth century. Such twentieth-century novels are usually defended on the basis of their intellectual wit rather than their literary power. The novels of Joyce and Virginia Woolf, so plainly triumphs of prophetic intelligence as well as of the ability to represent life powerfully, deepened the division of the reading public between highbrow and lowbrow. Where Dickens, Balzac, Dostoevsky wrote for the largest possible public, and figured before this public as national leaders as well as popular storytellers (a relation typified by Dickens's public justification, in the magazine which he himself edited, of his separation from his wife), the form in which even the great twentieth-century novelists have first appeared has proverbially been the little magazine, the coterie, the advance-guard fighting to establish the new literature. The great seminal figures in the modern movement — Gertrude Stein, Joyce, Eliot, Pound — remind one in their early days of old-fashioned conspirators and revolutionaries. And like modern revolutionaries, they were leaders and instigators, not brothers of those they led.

« 4 »

Yet if these writers have been right to distrust popularity, popularity has gone after them. The recent interest in literary criticism can be traced in large part to the position which certain critics in this country and in England — the New Critics — have taken up as explicators and interpreters of the difficult modern writers. There is no better instance of what the advance guard has been in modern literature than the success of the New Critics, who have been nearest to modern poetry, and who, without any effort at deliberate popularization, have been notable mediators between a remarkably complex group of writers and a public which — even in the universities — seems to know nothing of literature but what the critics can tell it.

The *effect* of the New Criticism, which one can now see institutionalized in American colleges, where "modern literature" has become the canon, tends to fit too well with the pragmatic temper of Americans. Undergraduates can get the same pleasure from taking apart a poem by Eliot or a passage from Joyce that they get from working on a car. Yet the intention of the New Criticism, particularly as one traces it in the critical essays of T. S. Eliot — the most influential critic in English of this century and the spiritual father of this movement in criticism — was just the opposite. For what Eliot emphasized, against the impressionistic critics before him who liked to dwell on their personal enjoyment of certain works, was the need to explain and to understand a poem in its own terms. For Eliot, criticism became an analysis of the poem in itself, the poem in the context of its immediate words; it meant conveying the necessity of those difficulties that were the greatest stumbling block to the reader. Like all true critics, Eliot's prime intention was to inspire enjoyment through greater understanding, and like all the great creator-critics in whose line he naturally follows — Ben Jonson, Dr. Johnson, Coleridge, Matthew Arnold — he was understandably a partisan of one literature and deeply opposed to another. But superb and extraordinarily effective as Eliot's early critical essays are — they created a new standard of taste — it was impossible even for Eliot, who as a critic functions on the highest level, brilliant shop-talk, not to give the impression that the great works of literature, which exist as created organic forms, become entirely accessible through the analysis of language. The result, as one can see in so many examples of the remarkable body of contemporary criticism, which is probably unrivaled for the passion and brilliance of its marginal comments on certain texts, is that the original emphasis on the purpose of the difficulty has been replaced by a passion for interpretation itself. When the sharp methods of the New Criticism are picked up by people who, unlike Eliot, know only the literature over which Eliot presides, they often miss the point of criticism and use it to establish their own ingenuity rather than to contribute to the understanding of literature.

The difference between Eliot and some of his routine followers is best established by the difference between his neo-Catholicism and their conventional liberalism. Eliot insisted on the necessary difficulty and complexity of modern literature because he thought that modern life, through debasement of culture and feebleness in belief, had so destroyed right standards that only work that symbolically conveyed the necessary complexity and forgotten profundity of human experience — like Dante's The Divine Comedy — could encompass and describe the anarchical flood of modern life. In 1923, writing in tribute to Joyce's *Ulysses,* he said:

In using the myth, in manipulating a continuous parallel between contemporaneity and antiquity, Mr. Joyce is pursuing a method which others must use after him. . . . It is simply a way of controlling, of ordering, of giving a shape and significance to the immense panorama of futility and anarchy which is contemporary history. . . . Instead of narrative method, we may now use the mythical method. It is, I seriously believe, a step toward making the modern world possible for art. . . .

This pronouncement, at once so lofty and despairing, is a key document of the belief that only through difficulty and complexity can one represent — and by implication, reverse — the drift of modern life and the tragedy of disbelief. In Eliot's eyes, a work of literature has to be highly formal, concentrated, hard — in the same way that the Church, by hierarchy, dogma, and ceremony, saves man from the welter of mere subjective emotion. The conservative American critic Paul Elmer More could not understand why, despite this belief, Eliot's own poetry seemed to be, in the defiant fashion of the 1920s, so "chaotic" and disorderly. Poetry, replied Eliot, shows the world as it is: criticism, as it should be. And the world "as it is" — reflected not only in the actual content of Eliot's most famous poem, *The Waste Land* (1922), but in the deceptive chaos on the surface of the poem — represents in Eliot's mind (and in the minds of so many of his admirers) a contrast between the age of faith and the age of chaos in which we live. For Eliot "the immense panorama of futility and anarchy which is the modern world" is always to be compared with some other period — when art was not a religion but served religion. In the formal structure and ritualistic symbolism of *The Divine Comedy,* Eliot finds his favorite symbol of the order and complexity that he opposes to the present.

In one form or another, this despair of the present age is one of the staple themes of modern literature and art. This characteristic historical nostalgia is represented in the very plan of Flaubert's *Three Stories* (1877), which portrays man's degeneration in time from the world of paganism to the present age. And while the Homeric parallels in *Ulysses* do not signify devaluation of the present in favor of antiquity, there is in Joyce's great work, as in all the key works of twentieth-century literature, a profoundly felt complaint that human experience today is meaningless, that man has been deprived of fundamental values, that he has lost that sense of the miraculousness of his existence with which, historically, religion has always provided him.

In his horror of "the waste land" and "the hollow men" who live in it, Eliot comes to the very heart of modern literature as a criticism of life, and explains the power of this literature over the minds of people who have come to it reluctantly. For nothing is more central to contemporary experience, more obvious, than the increasing loss of religious faith — of belief in the providential, the sacred, the mysterious. In Eliot's *The Waste Land* quotations from classical and religious literature are put side by side with instances of modern chaos, so as to direct the reader's mind back toward the authority that he has lost, toward institutions. But however one may agree with Eliot as to the decline of religion in our period, Eliot's conception of tradition as synonymous with religion has had a sentimentalizing effect on the critical movement associated with his name. Before World War I, Eliot, along with Pound, helped to inaugurate experimental, reckless, sardonic modern poetry; after the war, he encouraged an unhistorical piety about the past, a haughty squeamishness about the present. In the writings of Eliot's more sedulous followers, there is a constant reiteration of modern "anarchy" and "heresy" that makes such defenders of modern poetry deny the actual strength and courage of literature and that portrays modern writers as if they were simply surrogates for the past. Eliot's notion of history as closed, his conception of order as necessarily aristocratic and hierarchical, minimizes the actual achievement of the modern movement. The revolutionary faith in personal consciousness from which the modern writer started is not merely an esthetic tool but a philosophical and religious achievement. Joyce significantly called himself, in Blake's phrase, "a priest of the eternal imagination." Proust, like Wordsworth and Blake before him, described the world of imagination as the only eternity to which man has access. D. H. Lawrence celebrated in sexual love man's ability to transcend his ordinary experience. Eliot's addiction to words like "heresy" and "orthodoxy," his churlish criticism of so bold and revolutionary a writer as Lawrence, contradict the complex personal experience that is expressed in his own poetry. When Eliot praises Joyce, who was even less of a believer than Lawrence was, one feels that he is mixing admiration of Joyce's genius with an American's envy of a traditional education. There is a cultural snobbery rather than a religious passion about Eliot's neo-Catholicism that reminds one of Henry James's complaint that America had no established church, no Oxford and Cambridge, no aristocracy. Expatriation can take place in time as well as in space, and Eliot seems to have accomplished both.

Yet there is a special irony in Eliot's nostalgia, for no student of twentieth-century literature can overlook the enormous role played in it by Americans like Eliot, Pound, Gertrude Stein, Ernest Hemingway. American writers are forced to deal with the chaotic modern world on its own terms, for they lack any tradition of ideas before the modern epoch began with the French and American Revolutions, and they are so different in origin that they naturally think in planetary terms — in terms of man as he is and can be, not as he might possibly have been in the twelfth century. This situation has been a constant stimulus to modern literature. For the American writer, like Ezra Pound of Idaho, tends naturally to feel that all traditions potentially belong to him, that all cultures fertilize each other into one. And just as the mélange of languages and traditions in Eliot's *The Waste Land* and Pound's *Cantos* are both as typically American in their feeling for the world scene as *Leaves of Grass* and *Moby-Dick*, so the very eagerness to build a "modern" tradition, so much associated with Ezra Pound, starts from Pound's concern with French and Provençal poetry in *The Spirit of Romance* (1910), and is seen in a whole series of works characteristically entitled *Instigations* (1920), *How to Read* (1931), *Make It New* (1934). Eliot's assumption that tradition is always behind us, something lost, contrasts strangely with the American passion for creating tradition, with Eliot's own creation of modern poetry as a tradition. Eliot said of Pound in 1946: "Pound did not create the poets: but he created a situation in which, for the first time, there was a 'modern movement in poetry' in which English and American poets collaborated, knew each other's works, and influenced each other." And in the same way, the American need to create, out of modern literature, the only real body of literature it has explains why Americans have been at the center of the modern movement, from the time that Gertrude Stein settled in Paris and gathered around her not merely Hemingway and Sherwood Anderson but Picasso and Braque. American expatriates like the painter Whistler, Stephen Crane, Henry James, Ezra Pound, show that the American, even when he goes abroad to learn, remains to instigate; that he marries his American importunity to the European tradition of art in such a way as to make a new kind of art.

This "new" literature in America is virtually a story in itself, for it is not merely the most remarkable body of writing that we have produced, but peculiarly an adaptation of the characteristically modern sensibility to the problems of modern man. But it is not actually a story in itself, and many Americans overlook the exciting historical dimension in the work of men like James, Eliot, Hemingway, Faulkner, because they overlook the extent to which the American concern with individual consciousness, with the lack of tradition, with the challenge from modern science, has seemed to European writers an unconscious prophecy of their own struggles. It is only when we see American literature against the background of European thought that we can understand why D. H. Lawrence thought the modern epoch began with Whitman; why Italian novelists like Cesare Pavese and Elio Vittorini translated and interpreted American literature as part of their struggle against Fascist dictatorship; why Hemingway became the sacred god of the new Italian concern with artistic "truth"; why Sartre was so carried away by the experimentalism of *U.S.A.* that he proclaimed John Dos Passos the greatest twentieth-century writer.

One of the essential elements in modern art has been its *élan*, the energy of challenge and not of "despair," as moralistic critics call it. The kind of creative wit and irreverent skill which one associates with the continuing energy of old men like Picasso and Stravinsky was long ago marked in the violence of H. L. Mencken, in the satire of Sinclair Lewis, in the dazzling originality of Faulkner, in the crushing experimentalism of Dos Passos. Such energy was one of the most interesting aspects of the modern movement. There is almost a special sanctity to rhythm in modern music. One of the reasons why there was such an immediate rupture between the old and the new can be seen in the virtual physical terror, the inability to respond without disturbance, to the charged-up beat of Stravinsky's *Rites of Spring*, to the confusing typography of Cummings's poems, to the almost physical assault on the eye made by Cubism, to the actual screams and bellowing of locomotives in the music of Arthur Honegger, of machines in that of Edgard Varèse. In a highly charged industrial civilization, with its emphasis on quick effects, on the rapid turnover of impressions, a civilization where life seems to proceed with intensified color, violence, quickness, as it so often does under the influence of the American atmosphere and American high spirits, art becomes synonymous with energy, with change, even with disturbance. And it is this that from the outset put Americans directly at the center of the "modern movement," and that, in unison with the increasing mechanization of American life, reversed the traditional thinness, academicism, and moralism of American art. Eliot said that "myth," or the sense of tradition, had made the modern world possible for art. It would probably be more true to say that only he who can assimilate the modern world — not perhaps on its own terms, but at least with an effort to discover what its terms actually are — can make art in the modern world. It is this *élan* of writers in the 1920s, which corresponds to the high spirits of so many Americans at the time, that helps to explain the extraordinary technical achievement behind Scott Fitzgerald's *The Great Gatsby* (1925) and Faulkner's *The Sound and the Fury* (1929), the rise of important new magazines like the *American Mercury*, *Time*, and the *New Yorker*, the social criticism behind Sinclair Lewis's *Babbitt* and Mencken's *Prejudices*.

The 1920s were everywhere the apogee of modern art. It was the last free period in Russia; the great period of experimental drama and painting in Germany; the time of the last authentic geniuses writing in English — Yeats, Lawrence, Joyce. But nowhere was this experimentalism so much at home with the times as in America, where for the first time we were getting a national literature, a literature that had been in the making from the 1880s on. For the first time there was modern drama in America as well as modern poetry, and even magazines now of mass circulation, like *Time*, characteristically took off from literary and "advanced" experiments in style, while the *New Yorker* became a byword for its satire and for a precision in style characteristic of the time when American writers prided themselves on being artists. The 1920s marked a true renaissance, with recognized cultural centers. Eliot, recalling his editorship of the *Criterion* in London, says that it belonged to a time when it represented literary authority, along with the *Nouvelle revue française* and the *Deutsche Rundschau*. It was a time when films were consciously an art, under Griffith, Pabst, Pudovkin, Eisenstein, Clair, Vidor; when there were great expressive artists of the silent screen — Chaplin, Garbo; a time when, starting from the prewar tradition of Picasso's sets for the Russian ballet under Diaghilev, Cubists and Expressionists still did the sets for Soviet productions of the classics. It was a time when the famous advance guard of modernism became more and more a cultural influence over the other public whom Mencken called the "booboisie," and when it seemed that the "intelligentsia" (a term borrowed from the traditions of the Russian Revolution) had become the advance guard of humanity itself.

« 5 »

The mid-1920s were the moment when typically modern writers and artists came into their kingdom. Then it seemed that the enormous preparations for freedom, challenge, spontaneity, individuality, which had been the essence of modernism ever since the eighteenth-century philosophers and poets had destroyed so much more than the old regime, were at last in the ascendancy. This was the moment not merely of success but of realization, when the moderns felt that at last it was possible to say fully what it meant to be modern, as they confronted the century on its own terms. This was the moment when certain names became great names: Hemingway, Joyce, Eliot, Picasso, Braque, Stravinsky, Bartok, Faulkner, Bertolt Brecht, Malraux, Yeats, Valéry, Gide, Céline, Colette; the moment when the last of Proust's thirteen volumes was finally published, completing the immense structure like a cathedral built over centuries. Now all the exciting "tendencies" and "trends" and "crusades" and "insurgencies" arose out of the manifestoes of Cubism, Dadaism, Vorticism, Futurism, and it was possible to see modern man at the apex of his freedom, confident of his integrity, sure that he had learned from the lessons of World War I — like

Picasso, a man beset by his own creativity, confronting into old age the infinitely expanding universe of skill and knowledge.

It is important to emphasize this pride because despite the "despair" in *The Waste Land* and the shivery warnings of dissolution sent down from Thomas Mann's *The Magic Mountain* (1924), it is a fact that the 1920s were a time of expansion in art as well as in society, and when the sense of freedom, the possibility of recklessness, the joy in open criticism, were matched by respect for the individual and by that general advance in the standard of living which in all periods is a necessity of artistic vitality. The very emphasis which was put on "style" — seen in the new magazines, in the acceptance of modern furniture and functional architecture, in the sense of economic power, in the growing feeling for luxury which was behind the esthetic posturing of writers ashamed of the realism that had preceded them — indicated how much artistic self-confidence depends on a general advance in society.

An essential reason for this modern *élan*, as one can see from the perpetual high spirits of Bernard Shaw, was the sense that the Victorian nineteenth century was falling to the standards of the new writers. Creative vitality in a group rests on attack — the Encyclopedists of the eighteenth century gave each other strength in attacking the superstitions of the old regime; the Romantics spoke together against the rationalism of the eighteenth century. Now writers like Shaw, Mencken, Gide, Colette, minor writers like Lytton Strachey in *Eminent Victorians*, proved the enormous effect of the long-standing battle against "moralism." One can even date the success of the new writers in America from the time when "Babbitt" became a term of opprobium. The nineteenth century fell over and over to the diatribes of Mencken and the laughter of Shaw; the genteel tradition was trampled underfoot, the old gods were done away with. The symbolic novel of the period, at least in America, was against the small town — *Main Street; Winesburg, Ohio; Moon-Calf* — and embraced the excitement of the big city — *Manhattan Transfer, The Great Gatsby*. The symbolic heroine was the "emancipated" woman; the symbolic crusade was against snoopers and vice-leaguers and book-censors. The common characteristic of the remarkable group of novelists who became famous in the 1920s — Dreiser, Anderson, Lewis, Hemingway, Willa Cather, Fitzgerald —

is that they were all from the Midwest, provincials seeking in the city a philosophy from which to attack the old values. The symbolic issue of the period was freedom.

But what we can see about the 1920s now is that the cause they fought for had long since triumphed and was on its way out. The effectiveness of a literary movement seems to be greatest when its *raison d'être* is past. The sense of triumph emerges only at the point when the movement is really over. It can be shown, in fact, that the real ascendancy of modern art lies in the exciting years before World War I. Jacques Barzun, in *The Energies of Art*, claims that by the end of the war, a quality of bitterness and self-pity, or hardness and insensitivity, had come into modern art — qualities which were not only falsely identified with modernism, but which actually diverted it from its original goals. Compare prewar and postwar works by the same man (Mencken, Gide); contrast those peculiarly pure writers who flourished before the war (Charles Péguy in France, Randolph Bourne in America) with the Dadaists and tough guys who came after it; think of the generation of poets who died in the war — from the group of "Whitmanesque" poets in Germany to British poets like Wilfred Owen and Isaac Rosenberg — and it becomes clear that the 1920s produced a particular hardness that is unmistakable in the fashionable poses of Hemingway's art, in the drift of Eliot's poetry away from satire and toward frenzied salvation-seeking, in the coarsening of Pound's verse and the paranoiac brutality of his political views. The decade was not an inauguration but a culmination. Writers and artists attacked the Victorian tradition as if it were still alive, but the crisis of modern art, perhaps even its eclipse, came at Verdun and Ypres, at Chemin des Dames and the Somme. In those terrible slaughters, the last idealism and political hopefulness of Europe disappeared, and from then on society was seen, even in periods of seeming health, to be impersonating health like a madman who has quieted down, but who may break out again at any time. In a famous short story, Hemingway insisted that all is *nada*, nothing. As early as 1921, in "The Second Coming," Yeats saw that

> Things fall apart; the centre cannot hold;
> Mere anarchy is loosed upon the world,

The blood-dimmed tide is loosed, and everywhere
The ceremony of innocence is drowned;
The best lack all conviction, while the worst
Are full of passionate intensity.

When Robert Graves offered the work of a young poet to Yeats for *The Oxford Book of Modern Verse,* Yeats declined it, saying: "Too simple, too sincere." The tone of hardness literally contracts; it does not expand or free, as one can see from the total career of Hemingway. Hardness has the unmistakable limitation of making the writer self-conscious, of confining him to the pose he first adopted. From now on, Eliot must always sound like a disapproving deacon; Hemingway may never desert the famous Hemingway style. It was once said of Victor Hugo — who was the most famous, probably the best, certainly the most uneven, French poet of his time — that he was a madman who thought he was Victor Hugo. This concern with one's own legend has become the staple of modern art, and museums are now erected to perpetuate it.

The "crisis" of modern art, perhaps even the "end" of modern art, came when it was made clear in the 1930s that the twentieth century had finally arrived in force — not just for writers and artists, but for everyone. In contrast to the eminent Victorians, the booboisie, the stuffed shirts, the genteel tradition — easy marks for a writer to attack, especially when the butt of the joke applauds — there now came the economic desperation of the 1930s, the hardening of Communism into Stalinism, of Nazism into the unspeakable slaughter of civilian populations on the basis of race. In 1914, when war was declared, the English Foreign Secretary Earl Grey, watching at nightfall the lamps being lighted on the Thames Embankment, remarked that "the lamps are going out all over Europe, and we shall not see them lit again in our lifetime." But only in 1929, 1933, 1939, did all men begin to see how dark it really was. Now was the time when so many writers of the 1920s died — either by their own hand, like Hart Crane, or, as with D. H. Lawrence, of long-standing illness brought to a crisis by the incongruity of his values in the period. Now Joyce, almost entirely blind, became the frenzied monologist and punner of *Finnegans Wake* where once he had spoken for all artists as young men. Now one felt the bitterness of the writers who had found themselves, in the 1920s, after so many early struggles for recognition, only to find themselves outside again — Willa Cather, Sinclair Lewis, Sherwood Anderson. The characteristic new writers of the 1930s are Auden, roaming over the gray debris of depression England, and Jean-Paul Sartre, whose *Nausea* (1938), one of the greatest books of our time, proclaims the broken connection between man and the world. In America the 1930s were a period of political literature, of "proletarian" literature, a literary period that was painful not only because so many bad books were written, but because so many writers were honestly misguided and did not realize that in giving themselves to a programmatic literature they were signing their death warrants as writers. Those who did not learn this in the Thirties or Forties learned it in the Fifties; but they all learned it, sooner or later.

The 1930s marked the end of the modern movement. One can tell this very easily: the essential ideals of freedom, spontaneity, individuality, were openly rejected by writers themselves. Whatever "modernism" may mean, it does not mean a fear of freedom. Yet as soon as this political episode ended among writers, at the end of World War II, one saw how completely the modern movement had become an institution. Now the Nobel prizes began to roll in — Lewis, O'Neill, Gide, Eliot, Faulkner, Hemingway. Now modern literature became the staple of literature in the universities, and the heresies of the first period became the academic clichés of the last. Modern literature and art now became not merely the subject of routine scholarship, the staple of mass taste, but had become its own tradition. The young writer no longer knows whether he is part of a continuing movement of modern literature or whether he is not justified, in view of the mummified modernity that surrounds him on every hand, in treating it as his enemy. The modern — modern literature, modern furniture, modern houses, modern taste, modern advertising — has become the enemy of the contemporary. Worse, modern as a routine description has become a mark of participation rather than of creation, and the vapidity of the term is shown in the thoughtlessness with which people assume that modern art can be accepted apart from its connection with modern politics, modern science, and modern people. In a notable description of some unusually humanistic war memorials in Europe, Lewis Mumford recently denounced the widespread belief that art is produced merely as a response to psychological stimuli, and noted that certain examples of modern art look as if our world had been recorded "in a decapitated brain, severed from heart and guts, from feeling and meaning."

Modern art as a fashion, a profession, a business has become so much its own justification for being that now that its histories are being written — and for the first time, they can be — one is not surprised to find art itself being interpreted wholly as a religion. The idea of literature itself as a sacrament is laughable — or pitiful; for it implies a subjective manipulation of materials which is akin to magic. But it is truer to say, as André Malraux does, that "One lives *in* art as if in a religion." Modern literature may have become an institution, a church, but for many people it is now simply a passion, and as modern life gets increasingly more organized and impersonal, literature may take its place simply as an odd human skill, as it appeared to Flaubert. What man, creative man, seeks above all else is a sense of his continuing creativeness, of possibility for the work of his hands in the universe. Like Ford Madox Ford, many a writer can now humbly describe himself as "an old man mad about writing." Literature as an activity can become a life in itself. In the course of things this cannot last forever, for literature can never be too "pure" an art, and whenever it seeks to become self-contained it loses much of its point. But at the moment we can see that "modern literature" has exhausted much of the strength that came from the attack on old institutions.

[1958]

III
Relevance of the American Past

Ishmael and Ahab

MOBY-DICK is not only a very big book; it is also a peculiarly full and rich one, and from the very opening it conveys a sense of abundance, of high creative power, that exhilarates and enlarges the imagination. This quality is felt immediately in the style, which is remarkably easy, natural and "American," yet always literary, and which swells in power until it takes on some of the roaring and uncontainable rhythms with which Melville audibly describes the sea. The best description of this style is Melville's own, when he speaks of the "bold and nervous lofty language" that Nantucket whaling captains learn straight from nature. We feel this abundance in heroic types like the Nantucketers themselves, many of whom are significantly named after Old Testament prophets and kings, for these, too, are mighty men, and the mightiest of them all, Captain Ahab, will challenge the very order of the creation itself. This is the very heart of the book — so much so that we come to feel that there is some shattering magnitude of theme before Melville as he writes, that as a writer he had been called to a heroic new destiny.

It is this constant sense of power that constitutes the book's appeal to us, that explains its hold on our attention. *Moby-Dick* is one of those books that try to bring in as much of life as a writer can get both hands on. Melville even tries to create an image of life itself as a ceaseless creation. The book is written with a personal force of style, a passionate learning, a steady insight into our forgotten connections with the primitive. It sweeps everything before it; it gives us the happiness that only great vigor inspires.

If we start by opening ourselves to this abundance and force, by welcoming not merely the story itself, but the manner in which it speaks to us, we shall recognize in this restlessness, this richness, this persistent atmosphere of magnitude, the essential image on which the book is founded. For *Moby-Dick* is not so much a book *about* Captain Ahab's quest for the whale as it is an experience *of* that quest. This is only to say, what we say of any true poem, that we cannot reduce its essential substance to a subject, that we should not intellectualize and summarize it, but that we should recognize that its very strength and beauty lie in the way it is conceived and written, in the qualities that flow from its being a unique entity.

In these terms, *Moby-Dick* seems to be far more of a poem than it is a novel, and, since it is a narrative, to be an epic — a long poem on a heroic theme, rather than the kind of realistic fiction that we know today. Of course Melville did not deliberately set out to write a formal epic; but half-consciously, he drew upon many of the traditional characteristics of the epic in order to realize the utterly original kind of novel *he* needed to write in his time—the spaciousness of theme and subject, the martial atmosphere, the association of these homely and savage materials with universal myths, the symbolic wanderings of the hero, the indispensable strength of such a hero in Captain Ahab. Yet beyond all this, what distinguishes *Moby-Dick* from modern prose fiction, what ties it up with the older, more formal kind of narrative that was once written in verse, is the fact that Melville is not interested in the meanness, the literal truthfulness, the representative slice of life, that we think of as the essence of modern realism. His book has the true poetic emphasis in that the whole story is constantly being meditated and unraveled through a single mind.

"Call me Ishmael," the book begins. This Ishmael is not only a character in the book; he is also the single voice, or rather the single mind, from whose endlessly turning spool of thought the whole story is unwound. It is Ishmael's contemplativeness, his *dreaming*, that articulates the wonder of the seas and the fabulousness of the whale and the terrors of the deep. All that can be meditated and summed up and hinted at, as the reflective essence of the story itself, is given us by Ishmael, who possesses nothing but man's specifically human gift, which is language. It is Ishmael who tries to sum up the whole creation in a single book and yet keeps at the center of it one American whaling voyage. It is Ishmael's gift for speculation that explains the terror we come to feel before the whiteness of the whale; Ishmael's mind that ranges with mad exuberance through a description of all the seas; Ishmael who piles up image after image of "the mightiest animated mass that has survived the flood." It is Ishmael who, in the wonderful chapter on the masthead, embodies for us man as a thinker, whose reveries transcend space and time as he stands watch high above the seas. And of course it is

Ishmael, both actually and as the symbol of man, who is the one survivor of the voyage. Yet utterly alone as he is at the end of the book, floating on the Pacific Ocean, he manages, buoyed up on a coffin that magically serves as his life-buoy, to give us the impression that life itself can be honestly confronted only in the loneliness of each human heart. Always it is this emphasis on Ishmael's personal vision, on the richness and ambiguity of all events as the skeptical, fervent, experience-scarred mind of Ishmael feels and thinks them, that gives us, from the beginning, the new kind of book that *Moby-Dick* is. It is a book which is neither a saga, though it deals in large natural forces, nor a *classical* epic, for we feel too strongly the individual who wrote it. It is a book that is at once primitive, fatalistic, and merciless, like the very oldest books, and yet peculiarly personal, like so many twentieth-century novels, in its significant emphasis on the subjective individual consciousness. The book grows out of a single word, "I," and expands until the soul's voyage of this "I" comes to include a great many things that are unseen and unsuspected by most of us. And this material is always tied to Ishmael, who is not merely a witness to the story — someone who happens to be on board the *Pequod* — but the living and germinating mind who grasps the world in the tentacles of his thought.

The power behind this "I" is poetical in the sense that everything comes to us through a constant intervention of language instead of being presented flatly. Melville does not wish, as so many contemporary writers do, to reproduce ordinary life and conventional speech. He seeks the marvelous and the fabulous aspects that life wears in secret. He exuberantly sees the world through language — things exist as his words for them — and much of the exceptional beauty of the book lies in the unusual incidence of passages that, in the most surprising contexts, are so piercing in their poetic intensity. But the most remarkable feat of language in the book is Melville's ability to make us see that man is not a blank slate passively open to events, but a mind that constantly seeks meaning in everything it encounters. In Melville the Protestant habit of moralizing and the transcendental passion for symbolizing all things as examples of "higher laws" combined to make a mind that instinctively brought an inner significance to each episode.

Everything in *Moby-Dick* is saturated in a mental atmosphere. Nothing happens for its own sake in this book, and in the midst of the chase, Ishmael can be seen meditating it, pulling things apart, drawing out its significant point.

But Ishmael is not just an intellectual observer; he is also very much in the story. He suffers; he is there. As his name indicates, he is an estranged and solitary man; his only friend is Queequeg, a despised heathen from the South Seas. Queequeg, a fellow "isolato" in the smug world of white middle-class Christians, is the only man who offers Ishmael friendship; thanks to Queequeg, "no longer my splintered heart and maddened hand were turned against the wolfish world. This soothing savage had redeemed it." Why does Ishmael feel so alone? There are background reasons, Melville's own: his father went bankrupt and then died in debt when Melville was still a boy. Melville-Ishmael went to sea — "And at first," he tells us, "this sort of thing is unpleasant enough. It touches one's sense of honor, particularly if you come of an old established family in the land." But there is a deeper, a more universal reason for Ishmael's apartness, and it is one that will strangely make him kin to his daemonic captain, Ahab. For the burden of his thought, the essential cause of his estrangement, is that he cannot come to any conclusion about anything. He feels at home with ships and sailors because for him, too, one journey ends only to begin another; "and a second ended, only begins a third and so on, for ever and for aye. Such is the endlessness, yea, the intolerableness of all earthly effort."

Ishmael is not merely an orphan; he is an exile, searching alone in the wilderness, with a black man for his only friend. He suffers from doubt and uncertainty far more than he does from homelessness. Indeed, this agony of disbelief *is* his homelessness. For him nothing is ever finally settled and decided; he is man, or as we like to think, modern man, cut off from the certainty that was once his inner world. Ishmael no longer has any sure formal belief. All is in doubt, all is in eternal flux, like the sea. And so condemned, like "all his race from Adam down," to wander the seas of thought, far from Paradise, he now searches endlessly to put the whole broken story together, to find a meaning, to ascertain — where but in the ceaselessness of human thought? — "the hidden cause we seek."

Ishmael does not perform any great actions, as Ahab does; he is the most insignificant member of the fo'c'sle and will get the smallest share of the take. But his inner world of thought is almost unbearably symbolic, for he must think, and think, and think, in order to prove to himself that there is a necessary connection between man and the world. He pictures his dilemma in everything he does on board the ship, but never so clearly as when he is shown looking at the sea, searching a meaning to existence from the inscrutable waters.

What Melville did through Ishmael, then, was to put man's distinctly modern feeling of "exile," of abandonment, directly at the center of his stage. For Ishmael there are no satisfactory conclusions to anything; no final philosophy is ever possible. All that man owns in this world, Ishmael would say, is his insatiable mind. This is why the book opens on a picture of the dreaming contemplativeness of mind itself: men tearing themselves loose from their jobs to stand "like silent sentinels all around the town . . . thousands of mortal men fixed in ocean reveries." Narcissus was bemused by that image which "we ourselves see in all rivers and oceans," and this, says Ishmael when he is most desperate, is all that man ever finds when he searches the waters — a reflection of himself. All is inconclusive, restless, and endless flow. And Melville's own style rises to its highest level not in the neo-Shakespearean speeches of Ahab, which are sometimes bombastic, but in those amazing prose flights on the whiteness of the whale and on the Pacific where Ishmael reproduces, in the rhythms of the prose itself, man's brooding interrogation of nature.

« 2 »

But Ishmael is a witness not only to his own thoughts, but also to the actions of Captain Ahab. The book is not only a great skin of language stretched to fit the world of man's philosophic wandering; it is also a world of moral tyranny and violent action, in which the principal actor is Ahab. With the entry of Ahab a harsh new rhythm enters the book, and from now on two rhythms — one reflective, the other forceful — alternate to show us the world in which man's thinking and man's doing each follows its own law. Ishmael's thought consciously extends itself to get behind the world of appearances; he wants to see and to understand everything. Ahab's drive is to *prove*, not to discover; the world that tortures Ishmael by its horrid vacancy has tempted Ahab into thinking that he can make it over. He seeks to dominate nature, to impose and to inflict his will on the outside world — whether it be the crew that must jump to his orders or the great white whale that is essentially indifferent to him. As Ishmael is all rumination, so Ahab is all will. Both are thinkers, the difference being that Ishmael thinks as a bystander, has identified his own state with man's utter unimportance in nature. Ahab, by contrast, actively seeks the whale in order to assert man's supremacy over what swims before him as "the monomaniac incarnation" of a superior power:

If man will strike, strike through the mask! How can the prisoner reach outside except by thrusting through the wall? To me, the white whale is that wall, shoved near to me. Sometimes I think there's naught beyond. But 'tis enough. He tasks me; he heaps me; I see in him outrageous strength, with an inscrutable malice sinewing it. That inscrutable thing is chiefly what I hate; and be the white whale agent, or be the white whale principal, I will wreak that hate upon him. Talk not to me of blasphemy, man; I'd strike the sun if it insulted me. For could the sun do that, then could I do the other; since there is ever a sort of fair play herein, jealousy presiding over all creations. But not my master, man, is even that fair play. Who's over me? Truth hath no confines.

This is Ahab's quest — and Ahab's magnificence. For in this speech Ahab expresses, more forcibly than Ishmael ever could, something of the impenitent anger against the universe that all of us can feel. Ahab may be a mad sea captain, a tyrant of the quarter-deck who disturbs the crew's sleep as he stomps along on his ivory leg. But this Ahab does indeed speak for all men, who, as Ishmael confesses in the frightening meditation on the whiteness of the whale, suspect that "though in many of its aspects this visible world seems formed in love, the invisible spheres were formed in fright." So man, watching the sea heaving around him, sees it as a mad steed that has lost its rider, and looking at his own image in the water, is tortured by the thought that man himself may be an accident, of no more importance in this vast oceanic emptiness than one of Ahab's rare tears dropped into the Pacific.

To the degree that we feel this futility in the face of a blind impersonal nature that "heeds us not," and storm madly, like Ahab, against the dread that there's "naught beyond" — to this extent all men may recognize Ahab's bitterness, his unrelentingness, his inability to rest in that uncertainty which, Freud has told us, modern man must learn to endure. Ahab figures in a symbolic fable; he is acting out thoughts which we all share. But Ahab, even more, is a hero; we cannot insist enough on that. Melville believed in the heroic and he specifically wanted to cast his hero on American lines — someone noble by nature, not by birth, who would have "not the dignity of kings and robes, but that abounding dignity which has no robed investiture." Ahab sinned against man and God, and, like his namesake in the Old Testament, becomes a "wicked king." But Ahab is not just a fanatic who leads the whole crew to their destruction; he is a hero of thought who is trying, by terrible force, to reassert man's place in nature. And it is the struggle that Ahab incarnates that makes him so magnificent a *voice*, thundering in Shakespearean rhetoric, storming at the gates of the inhuman, silent world. Ahab is trying to give man, in one awful, final assertion that his will *does* mean something, a feeling of relatedness with his world.

Ahab's effort, then, is to reclaim something that man knows he has lost. Significantly, Ahab proves by the bitter struggle he has to wage that man is fighting in an unequal contest; by the end of the book Ahab abandons all his human ties and becomes a complete fanatic. But Melville has no doubt — nor should we! — that Ahab's quest is *humanly* understandable. And the quest itself supplies the book with its technical *raison d'être*. For it leads us through all the seas and around the whole world; it brings us past ships of every nation. Always it is Ahab's drive that makes up the *passion* of *Moby-Dick*, a passion that is revealed in the descriptive chapters on the whale, whale-fighting, whale-burning, on the whole gory and fascinating industrial process aboard ship that reduces the once proud whale to oil-brimming barrels in the hold. And this passion may be defined as a passion of longing, of hope, of striving: a passion that starts from the deepest loneliness that man can know. It is the great cry of man who feels himself exiled from his "birthright, the merry May-day gods of old," who looks for a new god "to enthrone . . . again in the now egotistical sky; in the now un-haunted hill." The cry is Ahab's — "Who's to doom, when the judge himself is dragged to the bar?"

Behind Ahab's cry is the fear that man's covenant with God has been broken, that there is no purpose to our existence. The *Pequod* is condemned by Ahab to sail up and down the world in search of — a symbol. But this search, mad as it seems to Starbuck the first mate, who is a Christian, nevertheless represents Ahab's real humanity. For the ancient covenant is never quite broken so long as man still thirsts for it. And because Ahab, as Melville intended him to, represents the aristocracy of intellect in our democracy, because he seeks to transcend the limitations that good conventional men like Starbuck, philistine materialists like Stubb, and unthinking fools like Flask want to impose on everybody else, Ahab speaks for the humanity that belongs to man's imaginative vision of himself.

Yet with all this, we must not forget that Ahab's quest takes place, unceasingly, in a very practical world of whaling, as part of the barbaric and yet highly necessary struggle by man to support himself physically in nature. It is this that gives the book its primitive vitality, its burning authenticity. For *Moby-Dick*, it must be emphasized, is not simply a symbolic fable; nor, as we have already seen, can it possibly be construed as simply a "sea story." It is the story of agonizing thought in the midst of brutal action, of thought that questions every action, that annuls it from within, as it were — but that cannot, in this harsh world, relieve man of the fighting, skinning, burning, the backbreaking row to the whale, the flying harpoons, the rope that can take you off "voicelessly as Turkish mutes bowstring their victims." *Moby-Dick* is a representation of the passionate mind speaking, for its metaphysical concerns, out of the very midst of life. So, after the first lowering, Queequeg is shown sitting all night in a submerged boat, holding up a lantern like an "imbecile candle in the heart of that almighty forlornness . . . the sign and symbol of a man without hope, hopelessly holding up hope in the midst of despair." Melville insists that our thinking is *not* swallowed up by practical concerns, that man constantly searches for a reality equal to his inner life of thought — and it is his ability to show this in the midst of a brutal, dirty whaling voyage that makes *Moby-Dick* such an astonishing book. Just as Ahab is a hero, so *Moby-Dick* itself is a heroic book. What concerns Melville is not merely the heroism that gets expressed in physical action, but the heroism of thought itself as it rises above its seeming insignificance and proclaims, in the very teeth of a seemingly hostile and malevolent creation, that man's voice *is* heard for something against the watery waste and the deep, that man's thought has an echo in the universe.

« 3 »

This is the quest. But what makes *Moby-Dick* so fascinating, and in a sense even uncanny, is that the issue is always in doubt, and remains so to the end. Melville was right when he wrote to Hawthorne: "I have written a wicked book, and feel as spotless as the lamb." And people who want to construe *Moby-Dick* into a condemnation of mad, bad Ahab will always miss what Melville meant when he wrote of his book: "It is not a piece of fine feminine Spitalfields silk — but it is of the horrible texture of a fabric that should be woven of ships' cables & hawsers. A Polar wind blows through it, & birds of prey hover over it." For in the struggle between man's effort to find meaning in nature and the indifference of nature itself, which simply eludes him (nature here signifies the whole external show and force of animate life in a world suddenly emptied of God, one where an "intangible malignity" has reigned from the beginning), Melville often portrays the struggle from the side of nature itself. He sees the whale's view of things far more than he does Ahab's: and Moby-Dick's milk-white body, the tailfeathers of the seabirds streaming from his back like pennons, are described with a rapture that is like the adoration of a god. Even in the most terrible scenes of the shark massacre, where the sharks bend around like bows to bite at their own entrails, or in the ceaseless motion of "my dear Pacific," the "Potters' fields of all four continents," one feels that Melville is transported by the naked reality of things, by the great unending flow of the creation itself, where the great shroud of the sea rolls over the doomed ship "as it rolled five thousand years ago." Indeed, one feels in the end that it is only the necessity to keep one person alive as a witness to the story that saves Ishmael from the general ruin and wreck. In Melville's final vision of the whole, it is not fair but it is entirely *just* that the whale should destroy the ship, that man should be caught up on the beast. It is just in a cosmic sense, not in the sense that the prophet (Father Mapple) predicts the punishment of man's disobedience in the telling of Jonah's story from the beginning, where the point made is the classic reprimand of God to man when He speaks out of the whirlwind. What Melville does is to speak for the whirlwind, for the watery waste, for the sharks.

It is this that gives *Moby-Dick* its awful and crushing power. It is a unique gift. Goethe said that he wanted, as a writer, to know what it is like to be a woman. But Melville sometimes makes you feel that he knows, as a writer, what it is like to be the eyes of the rock, the magnitude of the whale, the scalding sea, the dreams that lie buried in the Pacific. It is all, of course, seen through human eyes — yet there is in Melville a cold, final, ferocious hopelessness, a kind of ecstatic masochism, that delights in punishing man, in heaping coals on his head, in drowning him. You see it in the scene of the whale running through the herd with a cutting spade in his body, cutting down his own; in the sharks eating at their own entrails and voiding from them in the same convulsion; in the terrible picture of Pip the cabin boy jumping out of the boat in fright and left on the Pacific to go crazy; in Tashtego falling into the "honey head" of the whale; in the ropes that suddenly whir up from the spindles and carry you off; in the final awesome picture of the whale butting its head against the *Pequod*. In all these scenes there is an ecstasy in horror, the horror of nature in itself, nature "pure," without God or man: the void. It is symbolized by the whiteness of the whale, the whiteness that is not so much a color as the absence of color. "Is it that by its indefiniteness it shadows forth the heartless voids and immensities of the universe, and thus stabs us from behind with the thought of annihilation, when beholding the white depths of the milky way?" And it is this picture of existence, as one where man has only a peephole on the mystery itself, that constitutes the most remarkable achievement of Melville's genius. For as in the meditation on the whiteness of the whale, this becomes an uncanny attempt to come to grips with nature as it might be conceived with man entirely left out; or, what amounts to the same thing, with man losing his humanity and being exclusively responsible to primitive and racial memories, to the trackless fathomless nothing that has been from the beginning, to the very essence of a beginning that, in contradiction to all man's scriptures, had no divine history, no definite locus, but just *was* — with man slipped into the picture much later.

This view of reality, this ability to side with nature rather than with man, means an ability to love what has no animation, what is inhumanly still, what is not in search, as man himself is — a hero running against time and fighting against "reality." Here Melville puts, as it were, his ear to reality itself: to the rock rather than to the hero trying to get his sword out of the rock. He does it by constantly, and bitterly, and savagely, in fact, comparing man with the great thing he is trying to understand. Ahab may be a hero by trying to force himself on what is too much for him, but Melville has no doubt that man is puny and presumptuous and easily overwhelmed — in short, drowned — in the great storm of reality he tries to encompass.

This sense of scale lies behind the chapters on the natural history of the whale, and behind the constant impressing on our minds of the contrast between man and the whale — man getting into a small boat, man being overwhelmed by his own weapons. The greatest single metaphor in the book is that of bigness, and even when Melville laughs at himself for trying to hook this Leviathan with a pen — "Bring me a condor's quill! Bring me Vesuvius' crater for an inkstand!" — we know not merely that he feels exhilaration at attempting this mighty subject, but that he is also abashed, he feels grave; mighty waters are rolling around him. This compelling sense of magnitude, however, gets him to organize the book brilliantly, in a great flood of chapters — some of them very small, one or two only a paragraph long, in the descriptive method which is the great homage that he pays to his subject, and which so provides him with an inexhaustible delight in devoting himself to every conceivable detail about the whale. And, to go back to a theme mentioned earlier, it is this sense of a limitless subject that gives the style its peculiarly loping quality, as if it were constantly looking for connectives, since on the subject of the whale no single word or statement is enough. But these details tend, too, to heap up in such a staggering array as to combine into the awesomeness of a power against which Ahab's challenge is utterly vain, and against which his struggle to show his superiority over the ordinary processes of nature becomes blasphemous. The only thing left to man, Melville seems to tell us, is to take the span of this magnitude—to feel and to record the power of this mighty torrent, this burning fire.

And it is this, this poetic power, rather than any specifically human one, this power of transcription rather than of any alteration of life that will admit human beings into its tremendous scale, that makes up the greatness of the book — by giving us the measure of Melville's own relation to the nature that his hero so futilely attempts to master or defy. For though Melville often takes a grim and almost cruel pleasure in showing man tumbling over before the magnitude of the universe, and though much of the book is concerned, as in the sections on fighting and "cooking" the whale, with man's effort to get a grip on external nature, first through physical assault and then by scientific and industrial cunning, man finds his final relatedness to nature neither as a hero (Ahab) nor by heeding Father Mapple's old prophetic warning of man's proper subservience to God. Though all his attempted gains from nature fail him, and all goes down with the *Pequod* — all man's hopes of profit, of adjustment to orthodoxy (Starbuck), even of the wisdom that is in madness (Pip) — man, though forever alien to the world, an Ishmael, is somehow in tune with it, with its torrential rhythms, by dint of his art, by the directness with which his words grasp the world, by the splendor of his perceptions, by the lantern which he holds up "like a candle in the midst of the almighty forlornness." Man is not merely a waif in the world; he is an ear listening to the sea that almost drowns him; an imagination, a mind, that hears the sea in the shell, and darts behind all appearance to the beginning of things, and runs riot with the frightful force of the sea itself. There, in man's incredible and unresting mind, is the fantastic gift with which we enter into what is not our own, what is even against us — and for this, so amazingly, we can speak.

[1956]

Dry Light and Hard Expressions

"I LIKE," said Emerson, "dry light, and hard clouds, hard expressions, and hard manners." The writers who become our saints and sages, the wise men of our tribe, they who help us to live—there is only one way by which we can know them: their genius for compression. They are the ones who are always stripping life down to fundamentals and essentials, to aphorisms and parables and riddles, and if we ask what is holy about men whose life sayings often shock and hurt as much as they illuminate, the answer is that the final compression they get into their speech is a compression they have attained in their lives. The absolute in their writing is an absolute they have learned to live, and the sometimes overemphatic sharpness, the well-known intolerance by holy men, the cutting blow, the very quickness with which they sum up life and eternity in a sentence, is only the expression in words of the attempt to meet existence with the greatest possible directness.

This is what Thoreau meant when he said that he wanted to "drive life into a corner," when he appealed to his distracted countrymen: "Let us settle ourselves, and work and wedge our feet downward through the mud and slush of opinion, and prejudice, and tradition, and delusion, and appearance . . . till we come to a hard bottom and rocks in place, which we can call *reality*, and say, This is, and no mistake." The imagery — one might better say the music — with which he brings to an ecstatic end this second chapter of *Walden* is a whirl of variations on the single theme of the ultimate, the *"point d'appui* below freshet and frost and fire" — bedrock, facing a fact until it divides you through the heart and marrow like a sword, the sky whose bottom is pebbly with stars, the deep deep earth through which the intellect works like a cleaver. Thoreau, because he yearned to possess the infinite spaces suggested to him by his imagination, wanted to base this infiniteness on some image that would be immediately graspable, that would *look* so sharp and definite and accessible, in his telling of it, that he could lead you up to it, make you feel it, give it to you. Blake spoke of "the world in a grain of sand"; Thoreau's desire was to make you feel this in the ultimate sensation that man could possibly express of his connection with nature. If he could have rolled himself up in the world, have tasted it in every cell of his being, this and this alone would have made him feel that he was communicating his supreme privilege of ecstasy. And it is the attempt to mark this sensation of maximum contact that he tried to get into his prose — "wildness," the taste of a muskrat eaten raw, walking blind through dark woods at night, a swim in the infinite silence of Walden Pond. Fundamentally, Thoreau's best writing is an attempt to get up to the point where he can reduce human experience to communion with nature and this communion to images of total physical ecstasy.

But this same need of compression, of the absolute expression, of the ultimate in speech that will condense and contract your whole experience, can find easier forms. In Emerson, whom we tend these days to underestimate because of the priggishness that so often wars with his genius, the poet's need of condensation takes the form of epigram. There are epigrams in Thoreau, too, perhaps even more of them; but they are the steps up to his temple, the rehearsals of his style; they do not express the reaches of his ultimate feelings. In Emerson, on the other hand, epigrams, *aperçus*, bare notations which seem to cross his journal in a single motion from his eye to his hand, serve for that sidelong glance into things which expresses him far more characteristically than the ecstasies described in his first book, *Nature*. For Emerson's conception of himself was not as a solitary in nature but as an oracle, a clairvoyant, a seer; and his truest moments come when he speaks in slightly veiled disclosures from on high, when he exemplifies the quality that Thoreau missed in Carlyle — he retires "behind the truth he utters."

Emerson's compressiveness takes the form of intellectual wit, of the sentence that gives you not a description of external nature to be embraced, but a definition of things in which you can rest. He exemplifies the traditional role of the founder of new religions by providing his audience, his possible disciples, with a set of maxims which give spiritual tangibility to the otherwise nameless and indistinct blur of the outside world. Such maxims are definite names for spiritual things and so convince us of their reality; they lay down a pattern of stepping-stones across what would otherwise be the terror of an utterly alien world. Without man, there is utter silence; a true sentence cuts into this silence and gives man a habitation in the universe. "The maker of a sentence, like the other artist," Emerson wrote in 1834, "launches out into the infinite and builds a road into Chaos and Old Night, and is followed by those who hear him with something of wild, creative delight." Emerson's sentences are compressed because they are pronouncements; they show the way; they teach. He thought so habitually in "sayings" that he himself found "each sentence an infinitely repellent particle."

Emerson's professional task was to build up his scattered sentences into essays, but he naturally began with just those pronouncements that someone else would have thought it necessary to prove. He once noted of a new lecture "that it was a very good house, only the architect had unfortunately omitted the stairs." And the genius of Emerson is that he did not try to change himself, that his professional need to write essays and to deliver lectures did not pressure him out of his natural tendency to the orphic, the fragmentary, the epigram. By the 1870s, when his powers had begun to fail him, he allowed his daughter Ellen and James Elliot Cabot to put together new essays by "excerpting and compounding" from old manuscripts exactly as he had done for himself. He was not merely dependent upon such help but, in a very significant sense, indifferent to the final result.

« 2 »

Emerson's genius is in the sudden flash rather than in the suavely connected paragraph and page. He is a writer who is so natural a stylist that even in his masterpiece, the *Journals*, certain sentences come from the habit of writing well rather than from having anything to say. His good things, however, are always neat. "Love is the bright foreigner, the foreign self." "Dante's imagination is the nearest to hands and feet that we have seen." He will refer to Alcott as a "tedious archangel" and remark of the British that they remind him of old Josiah Quincy, "always blundering into some good thing." "Every new writer is only a new crater of an old volcano." "Life is in short cycles or periods; rapid rallies, as by a good night's sleep."

In that superb book, *English Traits*, he noted that "Loyalty is in the English a sub-religion. They wear the laws as ornaments," and went on to say that "The religion of England is part of good-breeding. When you see on the continent the well-dressed Englishman come into his ambassador's chapel and put his face for silent prayer into his smooth-brushed hat, you cannot help feeling how much national pride prays with him. . . . So far is he from attaching any meaning to the words, that he believes himself to have done almost the generous thing, and that it is very condescending in him to pray to God." He could be wonderfully sharp. "Their religion is a quotation; their church is a doll; and any examination is interdicted with screams of terror. In good company you expect them to laugh at the fanaticism of the vulgar; but they do not; they are the vulgar." "If Socrates were here, we could go and talk with him; but Longfellow, we cannot go and talk with; there is a palace, and servants, and a row of bottles of different coloured wines, and wine glasses, and fine coats."

The best examples of Emerson's compressiveness, his gnomic gift, lie in those sentences with which he surprised himself. Emerson's genius is so contentedly solitary (where Thoreau's is lonely) that one feels that for him the high point of his writing was the discovery of some aspect of nature (often human nature) which was an uncovered secret. Like his famous Aunt Mary, whom he called a sibyl, a Cassandra with a terrible gift of penetration, he had the clairvoyant's gift for letting life come to him. "A man finds out that there is somewhat in him that knows more than he does. Then he comes presently to the curious question, Who's who? Which of these two is really me? The one that knows more, or the one that knows less? The little fellow or the big fellow?" One feels about Emerson not merely that there was a private self concealed behind the public self, but that this private self was continually making discoveries that Emerson knew instantly how to seize.

In reading Thoreau's *Journals*, one senses always the heroism of a will tensing itself almost to the breaking point, a quest for details in nature that would distract Thoreau from his inwardness — details which he could assemble and fuse for that final encounter with nature in which he anticipated the consummation of his existence. "I come to my solitary woodland walk as the homesick go home." All of Thoreau is in that sentence. It is this everlasting preparedness, militancy, expectancy before nature, this perpetual gathering of arrowheads and meteorological data and Oriental scriptures, that makes Thoreau's lifework, the *Journals*, all one tension and that invests his frustration in the end with the truest quality of human tragedy — which does not make the effort to "drive life into a corner" any less heartbreaking. Sentence after sentence, gathered like the stones in David's sling, whitened and sharpened and polished — to be flung against a power too great to be conquered and too indefinite to be embraced! Emerson does not go forth to battle, he waits; and the communion with nature that he describes is not one which he has gone out to find but one that has revealed itself to him.

It is this that in a way makes Emerson a truer *observer* than Thoreau, though Emerson did not consciously look so much or so far — or so hard. Thoreau looked for the immanent connection; he saw in nature details that had been flung off from some larger whole that he still hoped to find; his most characteristic symbols are poignant, like the Indian arrowheads he was always finding under his feet in Concord, fragments of the vanished Indian past which he tried to reassemble in his notes. Thoreau is a true mystic: for him there is always a lost Eden, a divine background in nature. To this he can relate what he picks up on his walks, but of this he has lost something incommunicable, "a hound, a bay horse, and a turtle-dove." His description of the simplest objects in nature can be unbearably moving: one feels so keenly his own trembling at the veil that keeps the world from us. Who, after all, can possess the world, put all nature into our hand? Thoreau's imagery has all the characteristically painful longing, the *Schmerz*, of the romantic mystic. But Emerson lights upon truths that delight in themselves, that reveal a hidden law. There is the well-known passage in his *Journals*, repeating his experience at the Jardin des Plantes in Paris:

The universe is a more amazing puzzle than ever, as you glance along this bewildering series of animated forms — the hazy butterflies, the carved shells, the birds, beasts, fishes, insects, snakes, and the upheaving principle of life everywhere so incipient, in the very rock aping organized forms. Not a form so grotesque, so savage, nor so beautiful but is an expression of some property inherent in man the observer — an occult relation between the very scorpions and man. I feel the centipede in me — cayman, carp, eagle, and fox. I am moved by strange sympathies; I say continually, "I will be a naturalist."

Emerson looks upon the universe as a witness, not as a lover. He waits for things to display themselves before him so that he can "yield to the law of their being." Without being in the least a scientist, he is often impressively disinterested and curious about phenomena. He complained that "Now many are thought not only unexplained but inexplicable; as language, sleep, madness, dreams, beasts, sex." Emerson is at his best not when he is announcing the Oversoul to the people or flattering his audience, but when he is idiosyncratic, spare and strange; in those moods of almost sleepy reflection and passive wonder one feels that he is entirely open to his unconscious, that he can get it to speak through him in the same way, to use his own image, as the tree puts itself forth through its leaves and branches. "The secret of the world is the tie between person and event. . . . The soul contains the event that shall befall it, for the event is only the actualization of its thoughts and what we pray to ourselves for is always granted." It is in this understanding that, as Thoreau says, the poet retires "behind the truth he utters," and then we feel that Emerson's writing arm somehow moves exactly to the pressure of the vision in his brain. Like Blake "taking down" the *Songs of Innocence*, he has only to dip his pen and write.

It is then that Emerson attains a greatness beyond that of the moral philosopher and national prophet. He can openly rejoice in the fact that he really has no disciples, and he shows himself not merely shrewd but uncomfortably penetrating. At his best, in his most private mood, his only aim is quiet understanding, to find the law which is spanned by the mind of that representative man whom he called "the poet." It is in these little bits of Emerson's *Journals* — scattered portraits, wayward reflections, fragments that are witty not only in the exactness of their expression but in the effect they have on the reader, for they disconcert and undercut — that we see the particular essence of a genius which, beginning as "self-trust," has made itself a kind of open channel by which truth can reach men, has converted itself wholly into an instrument of meditation and of style.

[1957]

Thoreau's Lost Journal

THE GREAT WORK OF Henry Thoreau's life — and of his art — is the *Journals,* published in fourteen volumes. There is no other work in American literature, perhaps no other writer's journal, which is quite like it. Although it is entirely a personal document in appearance, it is a formal literary work, often rewritten from rough field notes. It is not a "savings bank" for publishable essays, as Emerson called his own journal; even less is it an intimate confession, on the style of Baudelaire's famous challenge to writers to lay their "hearts bare." It is a highly stylized and endlessly deliberated work on the stark Romantic-Transcendentalist subject of man's solitary communion with the divinity of the world.

It can be compared, in style and intention, to other works of the same school — Whitman's "Song of Myself," Wordsworth's Immortality Ode, Emerson's early essays, the "mystical" sections of *Moby-Dick* which show us the world as seen directly by Ishmael the poet. But of course Thoreau's *Journals* contrast oddly with such works. For this greatest act of his life Thoreau perfected a particularly disciplined kind of prose and yet celebrates in his self-portrait the most mulishly solitary character in modern literature. The *Journals* are a wholly deliberate, plastic and imaginative work that became not a reading of life but Thoreau's only life. Without his ceasing to be an artist (except at the very end, when he faltered into

Consciousness in Concord: The Text of Thoreau's Hitherto "Lost Journal" (1840-1841). Notes and a commentary by Perry Miller. Boston: Houghton Mifflin Company.

imitating the scientist he had never wanted to be), his *Journals* became not only his art, but his mode of existence. He did not merely live for his book, as other great writers have; he lived nowhere else. The box he built of yellow pine to hold the thirty-eight manuscript notebooks was also to serve as his coffin.

It is Thoreau's psychological complexity that has so long kept people from recognizing the artistic grandeur of his *Journals*. Yet there is always the equal temptation: to forget just how peculiar Thoreau's literary lifework is and to read him as a pure visionary. Perry Miller has taken advantage of an unusual editorial opportunity to review the problem of the *Journals* in a more systematic and passionate way than, to my knowledge, has ever been done before. The occasion is the first publication of the so-called "Lost Journal" — which is simply the third notebook in a group of six composed during the earliest period of the *Journals*, but of which only five appeared in Volume One of the published journal itself. This "lost" notebook, which covers the period from July 30, 1840, to January 22, 1841, appears to have been mislaid by Harrison Blake, to whom Thoreau's sister Sophia had bequeathed the entire work in the famous pine box. It was Blake who first printed sections of the *Journals* under seasonal titles — a very misleading introduction to the inner mind of Henry Thoreau. The box passed through various hands and eventually went to the Morgan library, which in 1956 acquired the "Lost Journal" and for the first time in many years was able to fit the whole journal snugly into place.

The "Lost Journal" is a characteristic document of Thoreau's early journalizing, before he went to Walden and began to make deliberate literary use of his personal experience. It belongs to the period before Thoreau realized all that he could make of the journal as a form. As Mr. Miller says, it is really an anthology of his previous thoughts, and goes back to the period when Thoreau used the journal as a commonplace book rather than as the labor toward the full revelation of his consciousness that it eventually became. The greatest moments of the *Journals* — they record some unforgettable flights of the solitary mind — are not here. But Mr. Miller has seized the occasion for a thorough analysis of Thoreau's peculiar literary situation. If the book is more Miller than Thoreau, it is because there is something endlessly frustrating as well as fascinating in Thoreau's double use of the *Journals*: first as art, then as life.

The situation may be summed up this way. Thoreau, a Transcendentalist artist with unlimited faith in the symbolic resources and objective reach of his personal consciousness, conceived of his journal as a "song of myself" which, theoretically, could have had as much objective artistic validity in its daily "nature notes" as other works that have come out of the romantic cult of the imagination. It is not absurd to say that Thoreau's *Journals* have the same broad intention — to show the meeting of the inner and external worlds — that Proust shows in erecting his great symphonic novel on the foundation of introspective analysis. Thoreau's favorite myth — the imagination (or "soul") in the material world is like Apollo condemned to work as a shepherd for King Admetus — was especially dear to Proust, who in the form of a quotation from Emerson used it as the epigraph to his first book, *Pleasures and Days*.

Mr. Miller stresses the resemblance between Thoreau as the hero of his own book to Joyce's Stephen Dedalus. But whether one thinks in terms of Proust or Joyce, it is clear that like all the great twentieth-century writers whose concern with the stream-of-consciousness really starts from the romantic discovery of man's unconscious as a power of divination, Thoreau's whole literary faith is based on the mystic bonds between the private imagination and reality. Our generation is beginning to understand that Thoreau is not a "naturalist," and that the subject of his work is not the external scene, "nature," but the greater world of being with which the imagination claims affinities.

What makes Thoreau so different from the great modern Symbolist novelists is that he really had no subject but himself, and so had to strain for an "objectivity" that he could only simulate, not feel. Living in Concord with no real respect for anyone but himself, being a person with a shattering gift for holding his experience down to his image of what it should be, he let nothing grow wildly under his hand, allowed nothing to surprise him. He was always in control — in the *Journals* — and the life he held in such harsh control finally evaporated in his hands. He did not let the world flower under his benevolent gaze, as Whitman did — and Proust;

he kept it as *his*, all the time, until there was nothing to possess but the *Journals* which the world rather tends to see as the dead records of his vanished love.

If the essence of the romantic artist's faith in "consciousness" is that he thinks it puts him in touch with the Absolute, the tragedy of Henry Thoreau, as Mr. Miller succinctly names it, is that he tried to be the Absolute himself. The world which Proust was able to *discover* through his personal consciousness, Thoreau lost by trying to assimilate it entirely into his own. At the end of the *Journals*, as Thoreau himself seems to have acknowledged with dismay, he was forced to impersonate the deliberate and "scientific" observer of nature, to limit himself to the artificial "facts" and external shell of things he had always been able — in his rapturous and marvelous flights — to bypass before.

[1958]

Called Back

EMILY DICKINSON died in Amherst on May 15, 1886. A few days before, she had written her Norcross cousins, "Called back," and this phrase is on her stone in the Dickinson family plot.

Called back. Whatever the faith that this old-fashioned phrase may seem to express, it is more typical of Emily Dickinson's verbal economy than of her religion. No one who reads far into the 1775 poems that Thomas H. Johnson has edited with such scrupulousness and literary intelligence in *The Complete Poems of Emily Dickinson* (substantially the same text as the definitive three-volume edition Mr. Johnson prepared for the Harvard University Press in 1955, but without the variants for each poem) can miss the fact that Emily Dickinson was not sure of what being "called back" could mean. In poem after poem she expressed, in her odd blend of heartbreaking precision and girlish winsomeness, the basic experience, in the face

The Complete Poems of Emily Dickinson. Edited by Thomas H. Johnson. Boston: Little, Brown and Company.

of death, of our fear, our awe, our longing — and above all, of our human vulnerability, of the limit that is our portion. It is this sense of our actuality, this vision without certainty, this dwelling only on our possibility, that makes her poems so awesome and so witty, for she likes to catch things exactly, and implicitly expresses her delight in hitting the target.

> I cannot dance upon my Toes —
> No Man instructed me —
> But oftentimes, among my mind,
> A glee possesseth me. . . .

Until recently, however, it was exactly this quality of precision, bringing home the felt sensation, that in many instances her editors missed or blurred or omitted. The reason for this is a tragic-comic tale of genius in a provincial setting.

During her lifetime, Emily Dickinson had only seven poems published — all of them appeared anonymously and, as Mr. Johnson has said, almost surreptitiously. Each of them had in some way been changed and damaged by Victorian editors who distrusted her originality. Her only contact with the "literary world" had been the Boston critic Thomas Wentworth Higginson, to whom she had written in 1862 for guidance, and who advised her with a kindly obtuseness that did not make the seclusive Emily less lonely. After her death, in helping to edit the first volume of her poems (1890), he changed many lines in order to make them immediately acceptable. One mass of Emily Dickinson's poems, almost nine hundred of them, had been discovered by her sister Lavinia only after her death, and most of them, as Mr. Johnson explains in his introduction to the Harvard Press edition of the poems, were in different stages of composition and sewn together in little packets. No one in her immediate circle had guessed at Emily's productivity, and the discovery of a major poet by no means rejoiced everyone she had loved. When her sister Lavinia went for help to their brother Austin's wife Sue, who had been Emily's special friend, Sue sulkily sat on the poems until Lavinia went to the wife of an Amherst College astronomer, Mrs. Mildred Todd, who with Higginson's help put out a first selection of the poems in 1890.

Slowly, as Emily Dickinson's unexpectedly large reputation came

home to Amherst, a contest over manuscripts began. The parties
were Sue's daughter, Martha Dickinson Bianchi, who with Alfred
Leete Hampson issued several editions of her aunt's poetry, and
Mrs. Todd and *her* daughter, Millicent Todd Bingham. Eventually,
Mrs. Bianchi's share was bought up and donated to Harvard, while
the Todd-Bingham interests, so to speak, were transferred to Amherst College. Surely there is a new version of Henry James's *The
Aspern Papers* in this tale. Even now, although Mr. Johnson was
able to gather all the poems together for this great edition, rival
claims persist. Yet aside from this purely human story, the real
significance of the contest over the manuscripts lies in the amateurish
and willful editing of the text. There is a well-known and very
beautiful poem, number 712 in the present edition, that runs:

> Because I could not stop for Death —
> He kindly stopped for me —
> The Carriage held but just Ourselves —
> And Immortality.
>
> We slowly drove — He knew no haste
> And I had put away
> My labor and my leisure too,
> For His Civility —
>
> We passed the School, where Children strove
> At Recess — in the Ring —
> We passed the Fields of Gazing Grain —
> We passed the Setting Sun —
>
> Or rather — He passed Us —
> The Dews drew quivering and chill —
> For only Gossamer, my Gown —
> My Tippet — only Tulle —
>
> We paused before a House that seemed
> A Swelling of the Ground —
> The Roof was scarcely visible —
> The Cornice — in the Ground —
>
> Since then — 'tis Centuries — and yet
> Feels shorter than the Day

> I first surmised the Horses' Heads
> Were toward Eternity —

This poem was written about 1862. (Mr. Johnson has been the first to date many of the poems, and one of the significant features of his chronological arrangement is that it emphasizes how many of Emily Dickinson's poems, and especially her best, were written in the early 1860s, after the clergyman she had fallen in love with, Charles Wadsworth, had moved to San Francisco.) The poem was included in the first published selection of her poems under a title that the poet never gave to it, "The Chariot," and a fourth stanza was omitted! Where the poet had written, in the third stanza,

> We passed the School, where Children strove
> At Recess — in the Ring —

Higginson and Mrs. Todd replaced *strove* with *played*; for *At Recess — in the Ring —* they substituted *their lessons scarcely done.* In the penultimate stanza,

> The Roof was scarcely visible —
> The Cornice — in the Ground —

in the Ground became *but a mound*, and where in the last stanza Emily Dickinson had written

> Since then — 'tis Centuries — and yet

they replaced *and yet* with *but each.*

Look up the same poem in the so-called "Centenary Edition" that Martha Dickinson Bianchi and Alfred Leete Hampson put out in 1935. The fourth stanza is still missing; there are the same alterations in lines 9, 20, and 21, and, where the poet had written *where Children strove/At Recess—in the Ring*, the children now played *at wrestling in a ring.* And Mrs. Bianchi and Mr. Hampson nicely smoothed out the punctuation, replacing the poet's sometimes girlish but always meaningful dashes with proper commas and semicolons and periods.

I like Emily Dickinson's dashes. I am glad that Mr. Johnson has put them back. If that is the way she wrote, that is the way she wrote. The dashes have a light fierceness; they set the rhythm of her thinking. And in this great poem of Death's taking a lady out for a drive, the dashes help to create that "shudder of awe" that Goethe thought was man's only proper response to life and death. It is her ability to make us shudder that is Emily Dickinson's greatest achievement. No wonder that where some nineteenth-century American writers seem great, she is merely deep. "Deep" is not "great," for she does not have Whitman's scope, his ability to make us think of his poetry as the instrument of the world-process. On the other hand, greatness of a certain kind — greatness of subject, of vision, of voice — which we associate with Emerson and Whitman and Melville, has been so much more frequent than deepness that we rarely notice such a distinction. We do not even know that it can exist. The chief quality of our greatest writers is that each of them brings a wholly new world into being: each is the prophet of a new consciousness, virtually the teacher of a new religion. Their virtues are always rebelliousness, independence, self-sufficiency.

But the originality of a new religious teaching, though it can be electrifying in its power to change our minds, to make us see the world with new eyes, is not the only literary virtue. As literature, Whitman and Emerson and Thoreau do not have the texture constantly to engage and to surprise us, to uncover distinctions and to reveal new subtleties. Emily Dickinson does. She does not create a new world, as Whitman does; she gives us the range of this one.

Perhaps the quality that so fascinates me in her work is only the inherent quality of poetry itself, which with every word, stroke on stroke, establishes the poet's inner consciousness as our true world. It may be that in this country we have had all too little poetry (as opposed to declamation in the last century and fine word-painting in this), and so are constantly surprised by the precision of feeling, the depth of sound, that are found in so great a beginning as

> Because I could not stop for Death —
> He kindly stopped for me —
> The Carriage held but just Ourselves —
> And Immortality.

But surely the great quality of this poem, on the surface so painfully witty, so ironically demure, is that it remains enigmatic. The poem describes Death calling for a lady, and the journey they take, although described with touching brief glimpses of the world fast vanishing from her consciousness, remains mysterious and incommunicable. The horses' heads were toward Eternity; there is no going back. We can no longer see behind us, yet what Eternity itself is we cannot say.

To write of death with this wonder, this openness, this overwhelming communication of its *strangeness* — this is to show respect for the lords of life and death. This respect is what true poetry lives with, not with the armed fist of the perpetual rebel. But to know the limits is to engage subtlety and irony and humor; it is to write with a constant wariness of the gods. Emerson thought he had licked the problem of the gods by replacing worship with personal imagination. Thoreau, whose whole work is a mystic's quest for certainty, drove his entreaty into those overcharged single sentences that represent his artistic achievement. Whitman hoped that on occasion he might be mistaken for a god. Melville, who loved the myth of Prometheus, insisted on his antagonism to the gods. But all these are attitudes, whistlings in the dark, sharply in contrast with Emily Dickinson's provisional, ironic, catch-as-catch-can struggle with her own fears. She gave as her primary reason for writing poetry — "I had a terror — since September — I could tell to none — and so I sing, as the Boy does by the Burying Ground — because I am afraid." Perhaps she was thinking of the love she had never had, the pain of separation that can be like death, that is a death. So many of her poems are about death that the word, in her poems, finally becomes the symbol and the effect of all separation. In the great poem that I have been discussing, death is a journey out of the known world; it is a gradual separation from the light. Yet the tone of the poem on the surface is playful, even coy. The emotional charge of the poem, the mysterious sense of submission that it leaves us with, lies in the contrast between the whimsicality of language and the mystery of the destination even after the journey is over. There is even a particular achievement in identifying a Victorian lady's submission and weakness with the human condition!

> We slowly drove — He knew no haste
> And I had put away
> My labor and my leisure too,
> For His Civility —

With the next stanza (the third), the sense of the passage, of the slow separation from life that absorbed her in so many poems, is borne home to us in significant images of human struggle:

> We passed the School, where Children strove
> At Recess — in the Ring —

and of the ebbing world:

> We passed the Fields of Gazing Grain —
> We passed the Setting Sun —

The sense of increasing cold, the gradual passage toward death, the lady's finding herself inadequately dressed and armed against the hill of death — this reaches its unforgettable apogee in the revelation:

> Since then — 'tis Centuries — and yet
> Feels shorter than the Day
> I first surmised the Horses' Heads
> Were toward Eternity —

This last image catches first the drawn-out sense of intimation, and then the shock of irrevocability that is our strongest sense of death. When one thinks of how many human beings have tried to get around this fact, and how few have succeeded in expressing it, we have a sudden sense of the most that human beings can know and feel. We are "with it," as they say, all the way. We have a sense of the human soul stretched to the farthest, of valor encompassing the most that it can know.

[1960]

Good Old Howells

IN HIS own lifetime (1837-1920), William Dean Howells was a great success. He belongs to the generation of Midwestern country boys who became industrial pioneers and millionaires, and in his own way he resembled the businessmen of the new generation and spoke for them. He was a self-taught Ohio boy who made his way up as a printer and reporter. A campaign biography of Lincoln made him American consul in Venice during the Civil War, and after the war he so quickly endeared himself to the Boston Brahmins that he became editor of the *Atlantic Monthly* and their petted symbol of the "good" Midwesterner, the faithful disciple of the genteel tradition.

Howells soon became restive in this role, and, in turning to the novel, he caught the historical moment when the Midwesterners of his own generation and background came into conflict with the pretentious culture of the Eastern seaboard. He became the most influential voice for "realism," and when he moved to New York in the 1880s, it was widely believed that he had taken the literary center of the country with him. He wrote with the undeviating industry of a librarian cataloguing books; he earned prodigious sums by his writing. He was the intimate friend of both Mark Twain and Henry James. He lived to be the first president of the American Academy of Arts and Letters — and a symbol to the 1920s of everything that a modern writer should *not* be.

This recoil was unfair, and for at least twenty years, starting in the 1930s, when politically minded critics began to defend Howells because of his brief flirtation with socialism in the 1880s and the Christian Socialist values in his novels of the period, there have been isolated attempts to revive interest in Howells. They have not succeeded. So far as I can see, Howells's novels mean even less to the general reader today than they did in the 1920s, when novel-

The Realist at War: The Mature Years of William Dean Howells, by Edwin H. Cady. Syracuse: Syracuse University Press.

ists like Sinclair Lewis took Howells seriously enough to attack him. Howells has come back only as a subject of academic research.

This biography (now concluded with the present volume) by Edwin H. Cady, though intelligent and interesting, is a perfect proof of how little Howells figures in literary thinking today. If it were a wholly biographical and evocative work, frankly nostalgic in the style of Van Wyck Brooks, one could at least enjoy such a book as a period piece. But this is a two-volume biography of a nineteenth-century literary eminence that symbolically carries no illustrations. Since Howells spent most of his eighty-three years writing books and editing magazines, his biography is essentially the history of his publications, and in this second volume Mr. Cady really does little more than go through Howells's literary opinions, year by year.

It is true that after 1885, when Howells more or less deserted Boston and in the "Editor's Study" column of *Harper's Monthly* became the American defender of "realism" on the French-Russian model, he broke, for the first time in years, with the established taste. And soon after, when the Haymarket Anarchists were hanged, Howells's defense of them brought the enmity of the respectable. But the "realism war," though a fascinating chapter in the emergence of writers like Stephen Crane and Frank Norris, whom Howells supported, cannot be studied, as Mr. Cady largely does, as a significant story in itself. By this time it is of no particular interest to know what Thomas Bailey Aldrich, H. C. Vedder and William Roscoe Thayer thought of Howells. What we would like to know is what it was about Howells (though he was generalissimo of the realists) that made it impossible for him to support Dreiser's *Sister Carrie* — a fact that Mr. Cady does not mention.

In attacking "romanticism," in speaking up for "realism," Howells was not only defending middle-class American experience against the old snobbish attachment to English literature, he was speaking, as he did all his life, for the emergent class of self-made businessmen who identified "romance" with the aristocratic culture in which they had no share. Now the problem of the American novelist, as Henry James pointed out with annoyance when Howells tried to enlist him in the "realism war," is just that "realism," though a vital social question at the end of the nineteenth century, did not answer to all his needs as an artist. Mr. Cady touches on this point when he notes that James fought alongside of Howells "up to the point where the integrity of his balanced insights seemed threatened."

It is just this "balanced insight" that one needs today in order to understand the limitations of Howells's own fiction. It has often been "romance" (not the Graustarkian kind that Howells hated, but the fantastic imagination that got into *Moby-Dick*, *Huckleberry Finn* and *The Wings of the Dove*) that has made the significant contribution to American fiction.

If one is not going to write a wholly old-fashioned and purely historical life of Howells, one should discuss his work with critical freedom. Mr. Cady writes with intelligence but not with critical freedom, as one can tell from his emotional complaint that there was "a monstrous legend of Howells current in 'modernist' circles of the Twenties and Thirties." He writes out of loyalty to Howells, but does not attempt to understand why, when so many critics have been writing about Howells with sympathy, it has still proved impossible to make out a real case for even Howells's "major" novels.

Every possible argument has been made out for Howells in our day. He had been admired for his political courage, his personal nobility, his devotion as a family man, his encouragement of younger writers. Hardly anyone has explained why his novels are so peculiarly thin and unsatisfying. The excited Freudian critics of the Twenties naturally thought that Howells was afraid of sex. No one seems personally to have been more afraid of sex than Henry James, who therefore was able to suggest its power far more convincingly than does Henry Miller.

Perhaps one explanation of Howells's almost self-induced smoothness is that he was such a steady producer, with such an immediate audience, that he could never break with anything for very long or allow himself to be disturbed. In his excellent recent book on the American novel, *The American Novel and Its Tradition*, Richard Chase goes to the heart of the matter when he complains that "the trouble with Howells . . . is that he never tried hard enough. There is a real laziness, as well as a prudishness, about his mind, and in his novels he was always making great refusals." It is this very self-saving quality, indeed, that helps to explain Howells's fantastic productivity — one might almost call it the ooze of his hundred books. It was so necessary for him to write easily, plentifully and publicly that he was rarely stopped by what he wrote.

The pity of Howells's smoothness is that he *was* so attractive and above all so intelligent a writer. Like his friend Mark Twain, he is a natural stylist — with a fresh, cool, easy style that makes him irritating precisely when he uses his virtuosity to gloss over difficult matters. There are few literary memoirs in the English language that are so beautiful as *My Mark Twain,* and there are many powerful scenes in his novels that make one angry at the fatal ease with which Howells drops them. Howells had got into the habit of success: success expressed not only as money, but as the instant understanding and approbation of his audience, his kind. He very rarely disappointed this audience, and when contact with it was lost, he quickly recovered it. The "realism war" did not last very long, for realism, like science and big business, was in the air. He was a good man and a great success.

[1958]

Stephen Crane's Scarlet Woman

ONE DAY in November, 1896, the twenty-five-year-old author of *The Red Badge of Courage* arrived in Jacksonville, Florida, and while waiting for a blockade-running ship to take him across to Cuba, then seething with revolt against the Spaniards, became extremely friendly with the proprietress of a high-class "sporting house." The Hotel de Dream (this sounds like the setting of a play by Tennessee Williams) was not exactly a brothel, and Cora Taylor, who was to live with Crane in England for the last three years of his life as Mrs. Stephen Crane, was certainly not anything like the nature of her business. She had been born in Boston of an extremely

Cora Crane, by Lillian Gilkes. Bloomington, Indiana: Indiana University Press.

good family, and technically at least she was still the wife of a well-known British colonial official whose father was a field marshal and had formerly been commander-in-chief in India. Cora was a cultivated, gifted, and well-bred woman who was soon to move in the company of Henry James, Joseph Conrad, H. G. Wells, and now lesser-known figures like Harold Frederic and Robert Barr. Crane had been her greatest literary admiration before she met him, and afterward they went together as correspondents to the Greek-Turkish War.

Stephen Crane, six years younger than Cora and infinitely more complicated in every respect, was to become the great passion of her life. And whether or not it was her dark past that appealed to the need of something "sinful" in his love affairs, there is no doubt that she was his only wife. Since the whole story of "Mrs. Stephen Crane" has been unwritten until now, Lillian Gilkes's full and sometimes breathlessly detailed biography, which draws on the collection of Crane papers recently acquired by Columbia, will be fascinating to anyone interested in the peculiar genius behind *The Red Badge of Courage* and "The Open Boat." This is the kind of exhaustive biography that really helps us to see people of another epoch — how they lived and what they thought about.

Yet the deeper interest of the book lies in the theme of illegitimate passion, of sexual daring — the revolutionary theme of so many novels of the end of the century. Publicly, at least, the Victorian repressions were all in force, and the underlying theme of writers like Crane, Norris, and Dreiser was the power of sex. This was exactly the period in which Freud was beginning to work up his first and perhaps most important book, *The Interpretation of Dreams*. The timid and thus infinitely suggestive treatment of sex that Henry James would soon get into novels like *The Ambassadors* and *The Golden Bowl* now marks the same revolt as Dreiser's *Sister Carrie* and Crane's obsessive concern with prostitutes in his early stories. Yet in a society still externally dominated by anxious middle-class prudery, the concern with sex was more challenging than social radicalism. The Socialists, already outside respectable society, had nothing to lose by threatening to overturn it; but there were writers of reputation who by dealing frankly with sex challenged the class that had established and now supported them.

This was true of Crane, who could not live with Cora in America; even in England, to which they went, George Gissing "reaped the social punishments meted out to those entering into a union outside wedlock"; H. G. Wells and Ford Madox Ford had their troubles. The American novelist and *Times* correspondent Harold Frederic, unable to get a divorce from his wife, lived openly with another woman and their children, and, after Frederic's death, many leading English writers put up a special fight to get his common-law wife recognized as his lawful heir. This was the golden age of "the line," the cocotte, the "fast" woman, the private room at fashionable restaurants — all of which, now translated from Colette's *Gigi* into words by Lerner and music by Loewe, seems as quaint to us as George Washington at his cherry tree. But many an innocent was helpfully made wicked by the self-righteous respectability of the times. When Cora first came to New York to live with an aunt, "nice" girls did not stay unchaperoned in New York, and the better-class boardinghouses "let in" no one without an introduction. Miss Gilkes has discovered that "In New York, in the 1880s, a woman could be arrested for appearing in public 'red in the face.'"

Judge now the effect that a woman of real individuality and unquestioned experience would have on Stephen Crane's timid relatives in Port Jervis, New York. As it happened, Crane and Cora could live in England — Crane always brought out the most amazing devotion and admiration in writers like James, Conrad, Wells, and Kipling; even the timid William Dean Howells always championed him. The really "advanced" and gifted people were all enthusiastic about Crane. It is significant that Cora herself appealed to many of these people as well. It is impossible to say how many of them knew about the Hotel de Dream, but it was also typical of the great company in which Crane moved that they admired her for herself as well as for her boundless devotion to Crane.

The exception was Henry James. Whether it was rumors of Cora's "dark past" or his usual snobbery, it is a fact that James seems to have been as covertly hostile to Cora as he was solicitously admiring of Crane himself. An American friend of Crane's reported that he "had to hear a great deal from some English friends about Mr. Henry James and his intense sufferings when he had to 'endure'

Mrs. Crane. Maybe! I do know that he came bowling over from Rye one day with a carriageload of people, all stuffed shirts, and announced that he had brought them to lunch. Mrs. Crane was mad as a hornet, but did not show it. She vanished into the kitchen and concocted a lot of extra lunch in a chafing dish." My own suspicion is that James, whose imagination was so much stronger than his experience — it had to be — could not stand so vital a woman. The more intensely repressed he felt, the more silky in his pomposity he became. Harold Frederic said flatly that James was an "effeminate old donkey who lives with a herd of other donkeys around him and insists on being treated as if he were the Pope." One of the incidental pleasures of reading so fully detailed an account of literary life sixty years ago is that we can see James's affectations minus the rosy hue that has been conferred on all of James's doings by our revival of his work. Even the actual rewards of reading James have been misrepresented as more significant than they really are. James never engages life at any really critical level; fundamentally, he is more concerned with the rich textures of life than with the shoals and abysses of human conflict. Despite his extraordinary gifts as a verbal artist, there is an essential heaviness of spirit to him, an inordinate pessimism, that speaks of complete sexual repression. The vitality that comes with personal hope was missing from James's later work, and the reason, I believe, was his inability to champion the instincts even as a symbol of social revolt against the middle classes who had made a cult of virtuousness.

Actually, many of the really good novelists of the period were concerned with the "primitive" instincts and the "lower" classes who were identified with these instincts. Crane was driven to seek out life on the lower East Side and on the Bowery. (He called the Bowery his old "university," and someone at Constance Garnett's thought he was referring to a school of fine arts.) His importance lies not only in those few works of his which completely come off, like "The Open Boat," but in his constantly seeking the primitive facts, the forbidden places, the dangerous people. Crane always got on badly with popular idols of the time like Richard Harding Davis, "the dandified idol of college youth," as Miss Gilkes calls him, "who deemed the author of *Maggie* and the Bowery tales a gifted but unwashed lunatic, a boor with suicidal proclivities and unfortunate leanings toward low associations." And as Crane himself said to an old friend, "Of course I am admittedly a savage. I have been known as docile from time to time but only under great social pressure."

Crane, worn out with trying to support by hackwork the immense establishment he and Cora kept up in England, died at twenty-eight of tuberculosis. Cora tried to finish some of his works herself, but unable to market them successfully or to get any money from Crane's relatives, went back to Jacksonville. Yes, and opened another house, the Court. In 1905 she married a man younger than herself, who eventually murdered another man in a jealous rage over her. She helped get him off, but he divorced her. She died in 1910, aged forty-five. A car had got stuck in the mud, and when she saw it, she rushed up to help pull it out. She died that day.

[1960]

A Leftover Transcendentalist: John Jay Chapman

THIS BOOK came out just as the Little Rock crisis began, and one morning, when the *New York Herald Tribune* reproduced on its editorial page the words that John Jay Chapman once spoke in Coatesville, Pennsylvania, after a lynching, there was a flare-up of the old pride and faith in many a soured American heart. For John Jay Chapman (1862–1933) was the last Emersonian, a man who tried to live by conscience as if it were an absolute, and, a year after a mob had burned a Negro to death under particularly horrifying circumstances, Chapman had gone down to Coatesville entirely on his own, and had held an individual prayer meeting there, exactly as Thoreau had once taken the Concord Town Hall in order to honor the memory of John Brown.

Chapman's great quality was always a gift for stirring up again

Selected Writings of John Jay Chapman, edited and with an introduction by Jacques Barzun. New York: Farrar, Straus and Cudahy.

the embers of our old faith. In a culture like ours, which possesses so few traditions in common that it must emphasize certain spiritual episodes in its past, a figure like Chapman, who on every side of him, up to his very name, incarnates continuity, serves with peculiar emotional force to remind us of the heroic period in our history, to revitalize the symbolic theme of our experience. And Chapman himself, like so many American literary critics, was himself so nostalgic, so imprisoned in memory by the epoch to which he thought he belonged, that he did his best work in magnificent essays on Garrison and Emerson — both included in this long-needed selection from Chapman's work.

Each of these essays — the first appeared as a book in 1913 — has a peculiar emotional vibrancy which reveals Chapman's passion and relief at being able to live again in his rightful period. In each, Chapman assumes the greatness of his subject as a matter of course, and though Garrison and Emerson are very different, Chapman manages to make the reader feel that they are part of the same movement of greatness in the American mind.

In reading these essays, one has the sense of being recharged and uplifted — not by mere partisanship of old causes, such as professional liberals give us when they invoke the past as a slogan, but through imaginative reinvolvement. Chapman prefaces the second edition of his book on Garrison by telling us of a historian who, while the Civil War was in progress, actually felt no interest in it, but who in 1895 became so absorbed and excited in writing a biography of Lincoln that "he lived it over again and could not sleep at night." Chapman had that gift of imaginative participation to an astonishing degree. But what is most astonishing about it — and peculiarly the mark of a critic rather than of a historian — is that he was excited by old ideas, fought them over again, saw them at work in his own life, wrote about them with a vehemence that makes the reader of these two extraordinary essays believe that Chapman wrote about Garrison and Emerson because he felt that he was engaged in exactly the same struggle.

But he was not. And it is this lack of actual historical sense, despite his strong identification of himself with the past, that makes Chapman so passionate and yet so baffling a figure. Chapman is "religious," a visionary, in the sense that he sees his own ideals as permanent and classic features of thought, cannot admit that the ideal may be present under another name, sees Emerson and Garrison struggling for the light against the commercial interests that, of course, particularly oppressed Chapman's own generation in the years between the Civil War and the First World War. Although Chapman's material is history, always history, he has actually little historical detachment, and this is why he excitedly relived Garrison's life instead of writing *about* him. Equally, the essay on Emerson, though magnificent in its moral exaltation, is really a portrait of the superior individual in the Industrial Age threatened by the mob; it does not come to grips with the first — and decisive — phase of Emerson's thought, his attempt to convert the religion of his fathers into a personal ritual. "If a soul be taken and crushed by democracy till it utter a cry, that cry will be Emerson." That cry was uttered by John Jay Chapman, not by Ralph Waldo Emerson. Emerson never cried out at all — at least not in public (and not very much, we may be sure, in private). Chapman *always* cried out. His tragedy, as everyone who has studied his career knows, is the tragedy of a man born out of his time (or who thought that he was, which can be the same thing), a man dominated by historical wistfulness and forced to posturings in his immediate circle, a man who kept fighting for causes that had long since been won because he was not able to define to himself the causes — partly personal, mostly circumstantial — that oppressed him in his own lifetime.

« 2 »

The proof of this is Chapman's telltale reliance on "passion" for its own sake, on "religion" as a self-conscious gesture, on vehement outbursts against "America" and the "modern" rather than against the comfortable clubmen among whom he lived and whom he always enjoyed, in his own complacent way, far more than he could admit. The causes that Chapman gave himself to in his own time were always incidental or incoherent. Exactly like Theodore Roosevelt (his one-time crony in civic reform movements) in his unconscious snobbery, his hectoring of the American people — he, too, hysterically insisted from 1914 on that America had to sacrifice its young men in the war, and when his son Victor died as an aviator with a French squadron, was able to write in the same letter that

. . . the consolatory feature of it is that the individual has so much power
— a few insuppressible individuals change the reputation of a hundred
millions. . . . The thing we need is depth of feeling, and this is religion.

Emerson has often been savagely criticized by traditionalists for
having helped to destroy formal religion in America, but he would
never have written anything so subjective and essentially incoherent
as "the thing we need is depth of feeling, and this is religion."

A phrase like "depth of feeling," calling attention to one's own
"spiritual" superiority in a period of great materialism, over and over
again reveals Chapman's personal priggishness. He has the quality
that one sees in Theodore Roosevelt's professional gusto and boy-
ishness — the mark of a gifted individual who cannot or will not
sacrifice the standards of his own particular clan and group and who
dramatically converts his guilt into a theatrical exuberance and
showmanship. Just as T.R. was always posing (and often just plain
lying) in order to give policemen, soldiers, settlement children and
other inferiors a touch of his showy "leadership," so Chapman was
always the would-be saint, the spoiled priest of his preparatory
school set, calling attention to himself as "religious" and "fiery"
when he plainly felt peculiar and inert. Chapman's letters, as one
reads them in Mark De Wolfe Howe's official biography, show a
man who more and more was content to be the "wild man" of his
clubby, chummy, smug little group. His utter hysteria about the
First World War, like his later hysteria about Jews and Catholics,
shows a man whose eye is not really on the ball, who devotes himself to causes but who is not really absorbed by any subject, who is
constantly posing, "shocking" his little group, flitting from enthusiasm to enthusiasm.

In part this is the tragedy of a certain lack of *profession.* Admittedly, he was no more of an amateur than Emerson was, or
than many American critics have been. They have all been commentators at large. But it is not his little plays and poems, his
selective little translations of Dante, his presumption in writing a
book on Lucian, that make him so irritatingly the pretentious
country squire, the intellectual Boy Scout or T.R. of the period; it
is his self-consciousness.

From Emerson to Mencken, we have always had a great tradition of the critic as iconoclast and reformer. But even Mencken, with his personal smugness, makes you feel that when he is lambasting the booboisie, he is really writing about *them*, not saving himself from them. And just as Emerson had this gift for raising his discourse above himself, so one feels about Chapman that he is always a little too conscious of being "mad Jack Chapman," the *enfant terrible* of his circle, the only man in it who *thought* it required great courage to speak out against President Eliot.

It is typical of Chapman's essential incoherency and complacency that when, in his old age, a friend urged him to "save" the Episcopal Church, he answered "there must be some things for which I do not agitate."

But, typically enough, it was middle-class Jews in Atlantic City that offended him, not the Sacco-Vanzetti case; it was Al Smith daring to run for the Presidency, not the smugness of Herbert Hoover, or the horrors of mass slaughter in the First World War. And the Chapman who hobnobbed with Nicholas Murray Butler at Fred Vanderbilt's party was the same man who could attack Whitman as a "tramp" and applaud Santayana only when the latter attacked German philosophy in the First World War; who was proud of being considered "mad" and "bad," but was simply the pet bulldog of his clan and, even more egregiously than Shaw, the pet entertainer of the group he was always pretending to defy, no danger to anybody. It was Chapman, ironically enough, who said of certain writers and painters of the Nineties that they were . . .

. . . O my! all amateur. Neither John Sargent nor Whistler nor Henry James had the attitude of workaday artists toward their work. They were each doing a stunt. . . . And all these people gas and talk and attitudinize. As for Shaw, he's the caricature of a caricature — the monkey of the show.

But if these things are true of Sargent and Whistler and Henry James, what — O my! — should be said of John Jay Chapman, who never did a book that was a solid contribution to the subject, and who spent so much of his life evading any test of strength with his gifted contemporaries?

The truth is that John Jay Chapman is significant not for what he wrote but for what he was. He is the symbol of an ordeal —

the ordeal of the gifted and sensitive individual, almost crushed by an inimical setting, who no longer has a *subject* to turn to. Despite the many books that Chapman wrote, his life gives out an unmistakable suggestion of idleness and personal embarrassment. He knew how he wanted to live, not what he wanted to live for. When he writes that "All life is nothing but passion," he is of no interest. When he relives Garrison's life and flames out again, he is significant and moving because, in writing about Garrison, he dramatizes the plight of the individual conscience in his own time.

But unlike Garrison and Emerson, who actively disturbed the peace, who determined the history of this country, Chapman's importance is symbolic, circumstantial. What he wrote matters far less than what he represents in our modern history and the fact that he knew this himself explains not only his suffering, but — what I have not even touched on here — his extraordinary intelligence. In the last analysis, Chapman's bond with other great historical actors of this period — Roosevelt, William James, Shaw — is not his gift of "passion," but of intelligence. No one can read his work, as in this fine volume of selections, without realizing how much more Chapman could have given us, if he had not had to spend so much of his energy in saving himself.

[1957]

And The War Came

THIS YEAR we begin to play Civil War. On February 12, in Montgomery, Alabama, the bells "opened a week of pageantry commemorating the beginning of the Confederate nation and the Civil War that followed." In the State House of Representatives Chamber, where the Confederate convention met, legislators re-enacted the secession debates that took Alabama out of the Union "To make the celebration as realistic as possible," it was announced that "men would walk the streets wearing Confederate beards, top hats, and string ties. Their womenfolk have forsaken formfitting dresses for the ankle-length hoop skirts of Civil War days." In Atlanta *Gone*

With the Wind has been "screened again to kick off Georgia's centennial observation of the War Between the States."

A more somber note was struck in Charleston, South Carolina, where it was firmly announced that a Negro member of the New Jersey Civil War Centennial Commission, which had planned to attend the ceremonies marking the firing on Fort Sumter, would not be allowed to stay at the hotel with other members of her state group. Major General Ulysses S. Grant III, chairman of the National Centennial Commission, seemed puzzled by the disturbance over one Negro lady. When Allan Nevins, in his official capacity as adviser to the national commission, also protested, the general said to a reporter, "Who's Allan Nevins?"

In Virginia, opening *his* state's commemoration of the great event, Governor J. Lindsay Almond, Jr., drew a parallel between the present conflict over what he called states' rights and the "unhappy difficulties" of the nation on the eve of the Civil War. He lamented, "It has unfortunately been the course of our history that men have raised false issues which could influence the minds and stir the emotions instead of exercising constructive leadership in the effort to mold common opinion in support of that which is best for the nation and the world." And in a special series of articles called "The Needless War" for the *New York Herald Tribune*, Bruce Catton (the last survivor on either side) pointed out that the war need not have happened at all, and would not have happened if responsible leaders North and South had been less emotional. By 1861, says Mr. Catton, it could be seen "that the very cause of the dispute was itself dying and would, if men approached it reasonably, presently reduce itself to manageable size . . . The American Civil War . . . settled nothing that reasonable men of good will could not have settled if they had been willing to make the effort."

But the war did take place. As Lincoln said in his second inaugural, looking back to that anxious day in 1861 when, taking the oath for the first time, he had pleaded with the South to stave off the war: "All dreaded it, all sought to avert it. . . . Both parties deprecated war, but one of them would *make* war rather than let the nation survive, and the other would *accept* war rather than let it perish, and the war came." The war came, and to read about it now — in the superb history of *The Ordeal of the Union* by Nevins, in the chronicles of the antislavery movement, in the great debates in Congress, in the novels and poems of the time, in the memoirs of Grant, in the wartime diaries of Whitman, in the letters and articles of foreign observers on the battlefields, in the inflamed and exacerbated writings of abolitionists, slaveowners, ex-slaves, politicians, soldiers — is to realize at once the frigid emptiness of all this current play-acting, with its characteristic suggestion that the war would have been averted if only people had been sensible.

The inescapable fact is that if you look at the passionate writing that helped to bring the war about, that in turn came out of the war, and that, among Southerners at least, has never ceased to come out of the war, you can see why even the endless debates between American historians as to the causes of the war seem dry and inconclusive by contrast with the torment of principle, the convulsion of experience.

« 2 »

A civil war is terrible — so terrible that perhaps only an irrepressible conflict of interests and principles can explain it. It is as terrible as the murder of brother by brother described in the Old Testament, of mother by son in Greek tragedy. The very foundations of the human family are ripped asunder, and that is why such wars are never forgotten and perhaps never quite end. They show us a side of human nature that we can never forgive. When you read in *The Personal Memoirs of General Ulysses S. Grant* of Confederate raiders killing stragglers and then of being caught and lined up in the town square to be shot, the fact that these men all spoke the same language, were usually of the same stock, may even have come from the same towns in Kentucky, Maryland, and Missouri, gives these scenes the same quality of elemental bitterness that you recognize in the quarrels between the Greek chiefs in the *Iliad*. And equally, when Grant describes how, immediately after Lee had signed at Appomattox, members of his staff asked permission to go into the Confederate lines to greet old friends from West Point or the regular Army, the scene calls up images on a frieze of Trojans and Greeks going off the battlefield arm in arm.

But when the war itself broke out, nearer than such elemental feelings were the widespread anger and disgust over the danger to what had been until then the world's most advanced political experiment. There had been a prophecy of this by Jefferson in a letter of 1820, in which he said that the "momentous question [the Missouri Compromise], like a firebell in the night, awakened and filled me with terror." The passionate indignation that could be aroused by the steady weakening of national unity is heard in Lincoln's complaint that year by year the eighteenth-century spirit of free discussion was being narrowed. "Little by little, but steadily as man's march to the grave, we have been giving up the old for the new faith. Nearly eighty years ago we began by declaring that all men are created equal; but now from that beginning we have run down to the other declaration, that for some men to enslave others is a 'sacred right of self-government.' These principles cannot stand together."

Lincoln cited a Southern senator's statement that the Declaration of Independence was "a self-evident lie," and broke out: "Fellow-countrymen, Americans, South as well as North, shall we make no effort to arrest this? Already the liberal party throughout the world express the apprehension 'that the one retrograde institution in America is undermining the principles of progress, and fatally violating the noblest political system the world ever saw.' This is not the taunt of enemies, but the warning of friends. Is it quite safe to disregard it — to despise it? Is there no danger to liberty itself in discarding the earliest practice and first precept of our ancient faith?"

Earlier Lincoln had written to his friend Joshua Speed: "Our progress in degeneracy appears to me to be pretty rapid. As a nation we began by declaring that 'all men are created equal.' We now practically read it 'all men are created equal, except Negroes.' When the Know-Nothings get control, it will read 'all men are created equal, except Negroes and foreigners and Catholics.' When it comes to this I shall prefer emigrating to some country where they make no pretense of loving liberty — to Russia, for instance, where despotism can be taken pure, and without the base alloy of hypocrisy."

The peculiarly biting quality of this is the other side of Lincoln's gift for invoking "our ancient faith." In a country like the United States, ceremoniously founded on certain propositions of political theory, effective political utterances have naturally tended to invoke principle for purposes of common rhetoric. It was agreement upon a common basis of political aspiration, not the common experience of a "folk," that in one sense held the country together — this consensus was, indeed, the country's only real tradition. All political speeches had to attach themselves to '76, the Constitution, the Founding Fathers, the great and noble experiment in liberty and self-government that was the United States. Even the most extreme proslavery arguments, so reactionary in their views of human nature, appealed to the Constitution and to the enlightened political theory behind it. It is always this profound commitment to the Republic as his absolute political standard that gives Lincoln's writing its assurance.

As Allan Nevins says so tellingly in the volumes of his history that deal with *The Emergence of Lincoln*, Lincoln's mind was distinctly a "countryman's" mind — slow, deep, and careful. But the peculiar passion of Lincoln's greatest utterances stems from the belief, natural to his generation, that America was the greatest step forward that political man had yet taken. And since his own position, in regard to the Negro and slavery, was at once firm and moderate — slavery was to be kept out of the territories, but not molested in the Southern states — Lincoln's style itself expresses the patient hope for the future that was the essence of his position. In 1858, debating with Douglas, he made it clear: "I say in relation to the principle that all men are created equal, let it be as nearly reached as we can. If we cannot give freedom to every creature, let us do nothing that will impose slavery upon any other creature."

That is of a piece with the moral distinctness that runs through many of the great utterances on slavery before the Civil War. The extraordinary hold of the images and rhythms of the King James Bible, the constantly growing sense of crisis in the air, the peculiar assertiveness of strong-minded and highly articulate men, some of whom on the Northern side felt that they were battling for the Lord, not for the country that had betrayed "His poor," some of whom on the Southern side proved by the Bible that He had ordained the blacks forever to be hewers of wood and drawers of water for His elect — all this, symptomatic of the national excitement, gave an intensity to the great debates in Congress, in the newspapers, in the daily confrontation of Americans, that in our generation perhaps only a few Negroes and die-hard segregationists can understand.

One reason for this depth of feeling, on the Southern side, is suggested in a remark made by Kate Stone, a Southern woman who confessed after the war that she never regretted the freeing of the Negroes: "The great load of accountability was lifted." In a culture that took literally man's accountability to God, men might live with guilt but they could not deny it. They were creatures of passion who wanted to keep the Negro in his place so that they would know a higher place for themselves. The slaveowners used the Negro man in one way, and they were free to use the Negro woman in another. But however Southern ministers and politicians might explain slavery away, they had to work harder and harder at the job of explanation. They were accountable. And what they did not of themselves find to account for, the occasional atrocity at home and the unrelenting attack from the abolitionists pressed them to account for.

The high and moral style of the period came back to me in Russia, of all places, when I was looking over Tolstoy's study at Yasnaya Polyana. On the wall, big as life, was William Lloyd Garrison, and on the photograph of himself presented to his dear colleague, Leo Tolstoy, was the inscription in flowing hand, "Liberty for all, for each, for ever!" Think of Thoreau calling a meeting in Concord to commemorate the execution of John Brown and spitting out his bitterness at the American people: "You don't know your New Testament when you see it!" Only when you put together the constant pressure on the Southerner from his religion, his property, and his need to play the great lord can you begin to understand why Southern writers have always taken the opposite line from Thoreau's majestically simple rhetoric — why they have gone deeper, have been more subtle and complex in their rendering of human conduct than the abolitionist writers were. Hawthorne, the only great novelist that New England produced in its heyday, was a Democrat, a friend and biographer of the pro-Southern President Franklin Pierce, scornful of the extreme reformers and doctrinaires who surrounded him. Hawthorne died in 1864, and it has been said that he died of the war. He could not abide fanaticism of any kind, and when the qualities in American life that he had struggled against exploded into war, he collapsed first intellectually and then physically.

New England produced a kind of prophetic writer who thought of himself as the voice of the Lord. But the Southerners, some of them more detached about themselves, were wiser about human limitations. As that fine Southern historian C. Vann Woodward has said in his recent book, *The Burden of Southern History*, the South is the only section that has known the collective suffering and humiliation which most countries have experienced. In our own generation much the deepest kind of imaginative writing in this country has come from Southern writers. It is almost too easy for us to sympathize with the Lost Cause, to fancy the aristocratic party over what proslavery orators used to call the "mudsills" of the North. As millions know from *Gone With the Wind*, the South had all the romance and all the honor. As early as 1888, the carpetbagger writer Albion W. Tourgée admitted, "Not only is the epoch of the War the favorite field of American Fiction today, but the Confederate Soldier is the popular hero. Our literature has become not only Southern in type but distinctly Confederate in sympathy." Everybody today reproaches the abolitionists, everybody knows that John Brown had insanity in his family. In any event, if you want to write about the most dramatic event in American history, where else can you set it but where almost all the fighting took place, and who can your hero be but the man fighting for his home?

« 3 »

I still believe that Emerson and Thoreau, Garrison and Whittier, caught unforgettably the moral wrong of slavery. But it was Southern novelists and poets and diarists who came up against the complex human relationships of slavery. Inescapably the Civil War remains, so far as the war really was a tragedy and not a liberation, the Southerners' war. The worst things that could have happened happened to them. Look, for example, at the diary of Mary Boykin Chesnut, *A Diary from Dixie*, first published in 1905. Her husband, Senator James Chesnut of South Carolina, resigned his seat months before Lincoln took the oath in March; he joined the Confederate cabinet as Secretary of the Navy. South Carolina, which took the lead in secession, was a particular center of what used to be called "fire-eaters" — violently proslavery extremists eager for secession and war. The Chesnuts were big slaveowners. Yet Mrs. Chesnut, who from the beginning was in a central position to observe the highest councils of the Confederacy, made out of her diary a record which for its humor, detachment, patience, and dramatic interest is one of the most remarkable documents of the period. She is a diarist in the grand style, an observer of the most minute things; her writing has a candor about it that compels one to go on reading with the same fascination that one finds in great memoirs of Russian family life like Tolstoy's and Alexander Herzen's. She says of South Carolina's headlong secession from the Union: "South Carolina had been rampant for years. She was the torment of herself and everybody else. Nobody could live in this state unless he were a fire-eater. . . . South Carolinians had exasperated and heated themselves into a fever that only blood-letting could ever cure. It was the inevitable remedy. So I was a seceder." When her husband had taken office in the Confederate government, organized in Montgomery, Alabama, Mrs. Chesnut wrote with sly disparagement of the local inhabitants that when she discussed her recent experiences in Washington as a senator's wife, "These people — the natives, I mean — are astounded that I calmly affirm in all truth and candor that if there were awful things in society in Washington, I did not see or hear of them." She notes that her nephew has volunteered as a private, to be an example to his class, but that he conveniently has his "servant" (slave) with him, and she said to an Englishwoman as they were passing a slave auction, "If you can stand that, no other Southern thing need choke you."

There is a lightness of tone about Mrs. Chesnut's intimate records, a delighted interest in gossip, and a conscious artistry in the depiction of character that make particularly vivid the tragedy of the South. Just as we today cannot help noticing the contrast between the grand but often abstract principles announced by New England intellectuals and the concrete defiance, courage, and desperation of Southerners fighting on their home grounds, so Mrs. Chesnut's ingrained social sense, her ability to convey the concrete human style of the people she is talking about, above all her attention to the truth of any human experience apart from the cause in which it is enlisted, give certain passages in A Diary from Dixie the stamp of universal experience that we value most in literature. She says of a family named Middleton, "Their lives are washed away in a tide of blood. There is nothing to show they were ever on earth."

Southern writers, now as well as then, have insisted that the abolitionists and their sympathizers, concentrating on principle alone, were either hypocritical or fanatical, and in any case ignorant of what slavery was really like. The most striking thing about so many Americans just then, as we get a direct glimpse of them in their period, was their moral rigor, their direct knowledge of what the Lord had intended the relationship between white men and Negroes to be, forever. It is not easy to enter into the minds of people for whom the creation has a design which they alone are privileged to understand.

« 4 »

The cocksureness with which representatives of every opinion habitually spoke of the Lord's intentions finally aroused Lincoln, in 1862, to reply to a committee, representing religious denominations, that urged him to free the slaves immediately: "I hope it will not be irreverent for me to say that if it is probable that God would reveal His will to others on a point so connected with my duty, it might be supposed that He would reveal it directly to me; for, unless I am more deceived in myself than I often am, it is my earnest desire to know the will of Providence in this matter. These are not, however, the days of miracles, and I suppose it will be granted that I am not to expect a direct revelation. I must study the plain physical facts of the case, ascertain what is possible, and learn what appears to be wise and right."

Despite his habitual tentativeness and reticence in religious matters, even Lincoln's public utterances became increasingly more scriptural in tone as the killing went on. By the second inaugural, four years of war drove Lincoln to say that although neither side could claim that the Lord spoke through it alone, it was clear that "The Almighty has His own purposes. . . . If we shall suppose that American slavery is one of those offenses which, in the providence of God, must needs come, but which, having continued through His appointed time, He now wills to remove, and that He now gives to both North and South this terrible war as the woe due to those by whom the offense came, shall we discern therein any departure from those divine attributes which the believers in a living God always ascribe to Him? Fondly do we hope, fervently do we pray, that this mighty scourge of war may speedily pass away. Yet, if God wills that it continue until all the wealth piled by the bondsman's two hundred and fifty years of unrequited toil shall be sunk, and until every drop of blood drawn with the lash shall be paid by another drawn with the sword, as was said three thousand years ago, so still it must be said, 'The judgments of the Lord are true and righteous altogether.' "

For Lincoln, as Edmund Wilson has said, it was the American Union itself that became the sacred object of his religious mysticism. There is an unfailing moral exaltation in Lincoln's greatest utterances, riveting his arguments together like the linked verses of Biblical prophecy. The application of his Biblical metaphors and images to the very geography of America shows the ground of his feeling. "The Father of Waters again goes unvexed to the sea," he wrote to James R. Conkling, hailing the victory at Vicksburg that opened the Mississippi all the way down to the Gulf. And speaking of the part that so many sections of the country were playing in the great fight, he went on: "Thanks to all: for the great republic — for the principle it lives by and keeps alive — for man's vast future — thanks to all." In Lincoln's feeling "for the great republic" one sees the classical value of politics, loyalty to the commonwealth as the embodiment of general value above each sectional and class interest. Contrast this with the religious fundamentalism that justifies its special interests as God's providence and the Marxist belief that the state must represent one class or another. The historian David Donald, in an interesting recent article entitled "An Excess of Democracy: The American Civil War and the Social Process," argues that it was the pressure of so many self-proclaimed rights on the part of so many different elements of the population that helped to bring on the Civil War. Against what he calls "majoritarianism," Professor Donald cites Lincoln's appeal to the principles of the Declaration of Independence: "There are some rights upon which no majority, however large or however democratic, might infringe. Lincoln warned that the future of democratic government depended upon the willingness of its citizens to admit moral limits to their political powers. . . . Possibly in time this disorganized society might have evolved a genuinely conservative solution for its problems, but time ran against it." American society, as Professor Donald sees it, was so torn apart by competing interests that it had no resistance to strain.

Certainly nothing about the proslavery argument, as it hardened in the South in the 1850s, ending the comparatively tolerant discussion of slavery that had prevailed until then, now seems so presumptuous and so wrongheaded as the rationalization that what was good for the slaveowner had been fixed for all time by God. Alexander H. Stephens, who before the war had been one of the more moderate Southern spokesmen, announced as vice-president of the Confederacy that the new state rested "upon the great truth that the negro is not equal to the white man, that slavery — subordination to the superior race — is his natural and normal condition. This, our new government, is the first in the history of the world based upon this great physical, philosophical and moral truth." The peculiar irrationality of this insistence on the unchangeable nature of social relationships was to lead the Southern slaveowners to their destruction. Senator L. Q. C. Lamar of Mississippi confessed after the war that he had never entertained a doubt of the Southern system until he found out that slavery could not stand a war. As Lamar said, the fatal "mistake that was made by the Southern defenders of slavery was in regarding it as a permanent form of society instead of a process of emergence and transition from barbarism to freedom."

« 5 »

The rigid assurance that certain people alone knew what all human "destiny" was to be, the delusion that human experience could be fixed forever, was not, of course, limited to slaveowners. It was the mark of an age in which religion hardened in moral rigor as the direct sense of God's presence faded; without its original supernatural element, American Protestantism hardened into self-righteousness for its own sake. The obstinate belief in New England that America was the chosen land, and that here God's promise would be fully revealed again, turned the conflict over slavery into a holy war. With so much at stake in the vast new territories of the West, it was natural for Americans to believe that "man's vast future" lay in their hands. John Bown's favorite maxim was, "Without the shedding of blood there is no remission of sins," and it was of course for the Lord that at the Pottawatomie, in Kansas, Brown took five pro-Southern settlers out of their beds one night and murdered them. Even in his famous last speech to the Virginia court that condemned him for the raid on Harper's Ferry, Brown spoke of himself as having interfered "in behalf of His despised poor . . . Now if it is deemed necessary that I should forfeit my life for the furtherance of the ends of justice and mingle my blood further with the blood of my children and with the blood of millions in this slave country whose rights are disregarded by wicked, cruel, and unjust enactments — I submit; so let it be done!"

When Harriet Beecher Stowe showed her husband the single episode of Uncle Tom being beaten to death (she had conceived it during a communion service in church, in a kind of trance), he said: "Hattie, you must go on with it. You must make up a story with this for a climax. The Lord intends it so." In later life, after the extraordinary world-wide success of *Uncle Tom's Cabin*, she said many times, "The Lord himself wrote it. I was but an instrument in His hand." Yet the remarkable impression produced by *Uncle Tom's Cabin* was due in large part to the fact that until its publication in 1852, hardly anyone in the South had troubled to describe slavery in any detail. A Southern scholar, Professor Jay Hubbell, says that Southern writers were unable to meet the challenge of *Uncle Tom's Cabin* for this reason: "The South, content in the main to get its reading matter from the outside, now paid the penalty for its inability to convince the world that Mrs. Stowe's picture was a biased and distorted one."

As Lincoln is *supposed* to have said, Harriet Beecher Stowe was the little lady who started the great big war. One reason for her effectiveness is that the Southerners, though so much more social-minded and less doctrinaire, so much more fitted for literature, were in fact without much literature of their own. Southern plantation owners looked down on the native literature generally, and preferred to get their reading matter from England; they starved writers of their own like William Gilmore Simms, and when the fear of antislavery agitation finally turned the South into an authoritarian state, with vindictive penalties for anyone teaching Negroes to read and for the dissemination of forbidden literature, the hysterical

crisis atmosphere it developed was as injurious to literature as a to-
talitarian atmosphere usually is. While Simms was being snubbed in
Charleston for his lower-class origins, the fire-eater William Lowndes
Yancey boasted that the South did not need literature: "Our poetry
is our lives; our fiction will come when truth has ceased to satisfy us;
and as for our history, we have made about all that has glorified the
United States."

« 6 »

The Civil War was the greatest trauma that the American people
had ever known. For more than a decade it had been gathering itself up, threatening to descend; yet even now, as one reads the exhaustive account of the coming of war in Nevins's *The Ordeal of
the Union* and *The Emergence of Lincoln*, again following the bitter debates up and down the land, the violence in Kansas, the
submission of three weak Presidents to the slave power, one has
the curious sense that the outcome is still undecided, that the war
may yet not take place.

When the war did begin with the firing on Sumter, and Whitman,
staring incredulously at the headlines in the flaring light of a New
York street, realized that the unthinkable had happened, a wave of
horror and outraged patriotic emotion passed though the North. It
was then that Whitman became the national poet that up to then
he had merely claimed to be. In 1862, hearing that his brother
George was wounded, Whitman went down into Virginia and saw
the amputated legs and hands and arms on the tables, saw soldiers
staggering back into Washington after battle to collapse in the
streets. Now he was at last able to turn his songs of innocence into
his book of experience. There is no better book on the Civil War
than *Specimen Days*, Whitman's great diary of his observations and
experiences as a volunteer nurse in the hospitals of Washington; his
art here becomes a model of the rapid, casual brush stroke, the detached, consciously homely touch that was to characterize the new
realistic literature that came out of the war. It is strange how little
this great prose book of Whitman's is read, though in many respects
it has the virtues of Whitman's poetry without the false touches.
Specimen Days is a book that Whitman did not plan to write but
that chose him: its subject took him by the throat, rushed him along,

molded his style to perfection without giving him time to dawdle about style.

Out of his war experiences Whitman developed a new kind of impressionistic verse form whose very titles breathe the movement he described in these poems themselves — "A Sight in Camp in the Daybreak Gray and Dim," . . . "As Toilsome I Wander'd Virginia's Woods" — poems that preserve the freshness of Winslow Homer's classic pencil sketches done in the field. Whitman's own literary sketches, with their unforgettable ink-smudged description of Washington streets and hospitals, of Southern prisoners being marched up Pennsylvania Avenue, and of Union prisoners looking like concentration-camp victims as they came out of Andersonville, make up an incomparable document of the time.

Except for Whitman, none of the major American writers had any direct experience of the war. Henry James had incurred his mysterious back injury; Howells was in Venice as consul, and Henry Adams was secretary to his father, the ambassador at London. Mark Twain had the short and almost furtive experience as a volunteer in the Confederate militia that he later facetiously described in "The Private History of a Campaign That Failed." There are, of course, unforgettable passages on the war by Captain Oliver Wendell Holmes, Jr., who said that "In our youth our hearts were touched with fire. It was given us to learn at the outset that life is a profound and passionate thing."

Of the great American writers who lived through the war but did not participate in it, perhaps none has left a more touching record than Herman Melville, whose *Battle-Pieces and Aspects of the War* (1866), the poems of a great writer virtually retired from prose fiction, "originated in an impulse imparted by the fall of Richmond. . . . I have been tempted to withdraw or modify some of them, fearful lest in presenting, though but dramatically and by way of a poetic record, the passions and epithets of civil war, I might be contributing to a bitterness which every sensible American must wish at an end . . ."

One of Melville's least-known poems, describing the view from his rooftop over East Twenty-sixth Street, New York, during the terrible Draft Riots of 1863, brings home a despair of the democracy in which Whitman, at least in his published writings, never lost faith and which Lincoln recognized, in its promise for all men, as the root of war. Melville assailed as rats the rough street crowds who were burning and looting, and in the light of the flames rising over many streets in New York, he affirmed that stoic and classical distrust of human nature that is so familiar in his greatest writings. Yet Whitman, trudging through the hospitals with his little gifts of oranges and notepaper, felt that the war had somehow justified and vindicated the democratic dream, that the war had established forever the matchless reserves of courage and hope in the average man.

Slavery ended before the war did. Even in the Confederacy, Jefferson Davis recognized that slavery would have to be abolished, although, as Lincoln said in his second inaugural, neither side "anticipated that the *cause* of the conflict might cease with or even before the conflict itself should cease." Lincoln plainly named slavery as the cause of the conflict; he said that slavery was "the offense" through which the war had come. What other cause could there have been but slavery, the contradiction of democracy which made it impossible for other men to be free? In later times, as the heat of the war cooled down, it became easy for historians to argue that slavery was not the cause of the war, since most people, even in the North, had certainly not been against it. But if most people in the North were not against slavery, slavery was certainly against the freedom of most people in the North. There is a curious, statistical way of thinking today which claims that the cause of a conflict must be something that most people are consciously aware of and want to go to war for. But the deepest interests are often those which we are not entirely conscious of, issues we cannot escape.

The Negro was such an issue and he remains one. So long as he was a slave, no one else in America was really free. As soon as people even anticipated his freedom, they had to look further and anticipate his becoming a citizen like themselves. So Allan Nevins is right when he says, at the end of his conclusive review of the events leading up to the Civil War, that the war broke out over slavery *and* the future status of the Negro in America. Look around you.

[1961]

IV
Old Boys, Mostly American

Dreiser:
The Esthetic of Realism

THE NOVELS of Theodore Dreiser have survived sixty years of complaint against Dreiser. They have survived most of the novels published by the realists of Dreiser's own generation, and they have survived (this would not have seemed so easy a thing to do some years ago) almost all concern with Dreiser himself. They have even survived the epoch of rugged individualism and sexual squeamishness out of which they arose — both of which once seemed so inseparable from his novels that there are still many people who mistakenly believe that Dreiser's novels have lasted only as records of a vanished period.

But a new generation of readers — among them many college students who were born in the 1940s and so cannot remember the New Deal, much less a time when Americans were afraid that railroads might someday dominate the country — has been discovering that Dreiser is one of the few American novelists who have survived into the second half of the twentieth century. We now take it for granted that *Sister Carrie* and *An American Tragedy* stand with *Babbitt*; *The Great Gatsby*; *Winesburg, Ohio*; *The Sound and the Fury*. It is clear that Hemingway, though a far more delicate and accomplished artist than Dreiser, has never written a novel that has the objective power of Dreiser's best books. Dreiser has always stood high with his own. Faulkner has listed him as one of the four or five greatest contemporary novelists; Fitzgerald admired him deeply; even Allen Tate, who is not likely to admire Dreiser for his philosophy or his style, has listed Dreiser among the strongest talents in American fiction. Despite the storms over his books (*Sister Carrie* was kept back by its own publisher in 1900; *The "Genius"* was suppressed for a time) Dreiser has been steadily admired by novelists from Ford Madox Ford to Saul Bellow. Obviously Dreiser would not have survived at all, he would by now have been as dead a novelist as David Graham Phillips or Robert Herrick or Upton Sinclair, if it had not been for his genius. And now that the issues that raged around his books have changed, in some cases are even meaningless to a new generation, it is important to understand what Dreiser's "difficult beauty" consists in.

« 2 »

Dreiser is a particular example of the kind of mysterious strength, the strength with which a writer assimilates his environment, then recoils from it in order to tell a story, that makes the novelist's art possible. Although there were a good many possibilities in the novel that Dreiser never used and perhaps never understood, he grasped, in the symbol of his own drive for success and in the tragic careers of so many individuals in his own family, that the essence of narrative is the illusion of life, the suggestion of truth through the use of fact. However a novelist may create this illusion, it is indispensable. From his first novel, *Sister Carrie*, despite his *personal* commonness and proverbial lack of taste (we are told that Carrie "could scarcely toss her head gracefully" and that Hurtswood worked in "a truly swell saloon"), Dreiser was able to wheel into motion that enormous apparatus for suggestion and illusion that makes us lose ourselves in his books as if each were a profound and tragic experience of our own. The novel, as D. H. Lawrence said, is "the book of life." For more than two hundred years now it has been the only literary form able to suggest the ponderousness, the pressure and force, of modern industrial society. More significantly, it has been the only form, as we can see from novels that have externally so little in common as *Moby-Dick, The Brothers Karamazov, The Sound and the Fury,* that has been able to find objective symbols for that increasing alienation from himself which man has come to feel in a society that is insensitive to the individual and a universe that is wholly indifferent to him.

On both these issues Dreiser is immense. In the wholly commercial society of the early twentieth century, Dreiser caught the banality, the mechanical routine, the ignorance of any larger hopes, precisely because he was able to recognize the significance of his own experience. Dreiser was never a "realist" in the pseudo-objective style that has been developed by American muckraking, advertising and sociology. The facts dredged up by impersonal "research" are often dubious and quickly dated, whereas the sheer web of fact that Dreiser put together about clothes, house furnishings and finance fifty years ago retains its interest for us today. Dreiser was an artist who operated with the *facts* of a new era because he saw them as instruments of human destiny. He saw man, man naked as he essentially is, playing with skyscrapers, trains, stocks and bonds, the costumes that man wears in our time. Only an imagination which can see the circumstances of life as significant accidents, which can portray the vulnerability of the human person under the pressure of social fact, can really portray the limited but unmistakable area of determinism within which we operate. What makes Dreiser's novels so extraordinarily "real" is his ability to make us aware that the world was not always like this, that it is not entirely like this even now.

The sense for the hidden dimension with which a true imagination always sees the present fills Dreiser's first novels with unforgettable images of the rawness of Chicago on the eve of the twentieth century. A recurrent symbol in Dreiser's work is the prairie left on the outskirts of Chicago, where the few houses look like sentinels. This is the picture of Chicago in *Sister Carrie*, which opens with a young girl on a train coming into the city; this is the Chicago that is seen by the magnate Frank Cowperwood, the millionaire hero of *The Financier* (1912) and *The Titan* (1914), who, when he moves on to Chicago after his bankruptcy and imprisonment in Philadelphia, rises to the possibilities of the city with wonder and admiration. In *The "Genius,"* the dirty and tumultuous industrial scene around the Chicago River is the material which Eugene Witla discovers as a newspaper artist and which develops into his original and successful paintings of the modern city scene. This recurrent image of coming on the big city past lonely prairie houses has its most poignant expression in the second chapter of *Sister Carrie*, and expresses, in the innocence and awkwardness of its heroine, the experience of a whole generation. "The city had laid miles and miles of streets and sewers through regions where, perhaps, one solitary house stood out alone — a pioneer of the populous ways to be. There were regions open to the sweeping winds and rain, which were yet lighted throughout the night with long, blinking lines of gas-lamps, fluttering in the wind. Narrow board walks extended out, passing here a house, and there a store, at far intervals, eventually ending on the open prairie."

In such a passage we recognize that disproportion between man and his world which is one of the themes with which Dreiser is often able to create the sense of actuality. Only a writer who conceives of historical events in terms of personal sensation and emotion, who can describe the peculiar mercilessness of industrial society as an inarticulated experience in the human heart, can create for us a sense of the "times":

Carrie looked about her, very much disturbed and quite sure that she did not want to work here. Aside from making her uncomfortable by sidelong glances, no one paid her the least attention. She waited until the whole department was aware of her presence. Then some word was sent around, and a foreman, in an apron and shirt sleeves, the latter rolled up to his shoulders, approached.

"Do you want to see me?" he asked.

"Do you need any help?" said Carrie, already learning directness of address.

"Do you know how to stitch caps?" he returned.

"No, sir," she replied.

"Have you had any experience at this kind of work?" he inquired.

She answered that she had not.

"Well," said the foreman, scratching his ear meditatively, "we do need a stitcher. We like experienced help, though. We've hardly got time to break people in." He paused and looked away out of the window. "We might, though, put you at finishing," he concluded reflectively.

"How much do you pay a week?" ventured Carrie, emboldened by a certain softness in the man's manner and his simplicity of address.

"Three and a half," he answered.

"Oh," she was about to exclaim, but she checked herself and allowed her thoughts to die without expression.

"We're not exactly in need of anybody," he went on vaguely, looking her over as one would a package.

It is not Dreiser's laborious concern with external facts — the gas-lamps in the wind, the heaviness of clothes, the lights of the saloon in *Sister Carrie*, the brokerage business in *The Financier*, Chicago street-car franchises and big-city politics in *The Titan*, advertising and magazine publishing in *The "Genius"* — that creates this kind of "reality"; it is Dreiser's inability to take anything for granted: it is his usual sense of wonder at the dense, peopled, factual world itself. The great realists have always been those for whom the "real" world is always strange, who are fascinated by the commercial and industrial world because they know that this world is not *theirs*. For Dreiser the emotion of the provincial Carrie in the big city has become a powerful ingathering symbol of the interest and fascination of a society that, by reducing everyone in it to a feeling of complicity and powerlessness, makes *everyone* feel provincial. Only a writer like Theodore Dreiser, to whom success in the external world and some understanding of man's destiny were equal passions, could have created such unforgettable images of man's homelessness in both society and the universe at large as Dreiser did when he described Carrie rocking in her chair, or Cowperwood in prison looking up at the stars with a sense that he was no more strange to the world of infinite space than he felt himself to be to the conventional world of marriage and business. It has not always been noticed that it is precisely the imagination that sees modern society as a gigantic accident, as a paradigm of the infinite and indifferent universe, which creates, in the burning and vivid metaphors of Dreiser, Zola, Hardy, the feeling of truth about society. Without this necessary perspective, without some sense of wonder, or opposition, or fancy on the part of the realistic novelist, society gets so much taken for granted that it can no longer be fairly *seen*; and indeed this is exactly what has happened in many contemporary novels, where the concern with purely personal or sexual themes betrays a lack of perspective, of serious intention on the part of the novelist.

Dreiser's love of documentation, his naïve passion for "facts," recalls the poetic intent behind Whitman's "inventories" of modern city scenes. Dreiser attempts to create a sense of the material structure of modern life in much the same way that Whitman, in "Song of Myself," itemizes in quick detail the "blab of the pave, tires of carts, sluff of boot-soles, talk of the promenaders." As in Whitman, the external world is portrayed for its interest as *spectacle*, yet remains one to which man feels connected. Dreiser still writes in the spirit of the nineteenth-century discovery of evolution: nothing moves him so much as the realization that man has always been a part of nature. The concern with outward "reality" is one that contemporary novelists often reject in an age when the novel may seem as abstract as today's all-powerful science of physics. Dreiser was wholly under the influence of nineteenth-century biology and social philosophy. For him man is indissolubly part of the natural world itself: the order of nature reflects man's personal emotions in the same way that his fellow human beings, who belong to the same species as himself, reflect his longings and his weaknesses. Dreiser was able to portray modern society as an organism precisely because he recognized that although it did not always satisfy human aspirations, society itself was a natural growth: it expressed sexuality, greed, social ambition, in forms that are natural to man. In Dreiser's novels men like Drouet and Hurstwood, Frank Cowperwood and Eugene Witla can almost for the first time identify themselves with each other because they already identify themselves with plants and animals. And they make the identification in a way that conveys both the truth of the resemblance and the uncertainty about its purpose which plagues man's awareness of the natural process.

This sense of modern society as itself biological and evolutionary attains in Dreiser's novels a glow of romantic exaltation, a suggestion that everything in the universe is alive and seeking new shape. It is hard to think of other American novelists who have described this as powerfully as Dreiser does when he introduces Carrie to Chicago, Eugene Witla to New York, and Clyde Griffiths to Kansas City: the sense we carry away of infinite reverberations in society is the greatest achievement of *The Financier* and *The Titan*. The bias of Dreiser's fellow "naturalists," as we can see in Stephen Crane's masterpiece, "The Open Boat," and in Frank Norris's best book, *McTeague*, was in favor of the *reductio ad absurdum*: life must be portrayed in such strong terms as to seem positively hostile to man. Dreiser, who shares their philosophy, nevertheless identified the world with his own ambition and his compassion, and this is why one recognizes a maturity of involvement in Dreiser's work that is very different from the self-conscious stylization in Crane and the essentially patronizing and abstract manner of Norris. The truth is that for many writers, the philosophy of naturalism was a way of rationalizing their own indifference and apathy, their typically modern sense of alienation. For Dreiser, on the other hand, this "scientific" philosophy actually played the role that evolution had for romantic pantheists like Emerson and Whitman: naturalism provided a way of binding himself more firmly to the world.

Dreiser sees the modern scene much as did the tender realists of the "ash-can" school of painters who discovered the beauty of the big city; he is not one of the pseudo-Nietzschean naturalists, like Jack London or Frank Norris, who mixed their toughness with romance; nor is he in the least a crusader, like Upton Sinclair and many proletarian novelists of the 1930s, for whom a novel was a description of things to be eradicated. Dreiser's loving realism is directed toward an urban world that is always various and colorful. Even Frank Norris's *McTeague* ends in a scene of such melodramatic claptrap — the hero in Death Valley chained to the enemy he has just killed — that we can see that for Norris the height of feeling was to show the world as the ironic enemy of man's hopes, tricking him. Dreiser, on the contrary, writes as a contemplative, one who finds the significance of the external scene through his personal attachment to it.

« 3 »

The nearest analogy to Dreiser's "personal" realism is to be found in the painter Edward Hopper, who shares Dreiser's passion for transcendentalist writers, for images of trains and roads. Despite his similar choice of "ordinary" subjects, Hopper has written that his aim "has always been the most exact transcription possible of my most intimate impressions of nature." One critic has said that Hopper's pictures — a silent city street early on a Sunday morning, a Victorian house by a railroad track, an usherette musing in the corridor of a movie theater — are astonishingly poignant "as if they were familiar scenes solemnly witnessed for the very last time." One feels in the awkwardness, the dreaming *stillness* of Hopper's figures, the same struggle to express the ultimate confrontation of men and things that one does in Dreiser's reverent description of saloons, street-cars, trains, hotels, offices. The beauty of such realism, which contrasts with the photographic exactness of a Charles Sheeler, is inevitably allied to a certain pathos. Just as in *An American Tragedy* one feels about Clyde Griffiths's exultant discovery of hotel luxury the pitiful distance between the boy and the social world of tawdry goods that he is trying to win, so in Hopper's street scenes and lonely offices one can visualize the actual unrelatedness between men and the objects they use every day. It is one of the paradoxes of modern art that the more "external" and ordinary the object portrayed — a city street in Hopper, the complex record of a stock deal in Dreiser — the more personal is the emotion conveyed. The emotion consists in exactly this surprise of attachment to the world that so often dwarfs us. *An American Tragedy* begins unforgettably with a picture of a small missionary family in a big city, engulfed by the tall walls in its commercial heart; Sister Carrie is stupefied by the immensity of Chicago, and, when she asks for work at Speigelheim and Company, is looked over by the foreman "as one would a package"; even Cowperwood, magnetic and powerful as he is, is surrounded by "the endless shift of things," first in Philadelphia, then in Chicago. But it is the haunting feeling for objects that the hero of *The "Genius,"* a painter, conveys in his pictures of the Chicago River, the muddy industrial stream that significantly moves Witla to a "panegyric on its beauty and littleness, finding the former where few would have believed it to exist." Later in New York, Eugene does a picture of Greeley Square in a drizzling rain, catching "the exact texture of seeping water on gray stones in the glare of various electric lights. He had caught the values of various kinds of lights, those in cabs, those in cable cars, those in shop windows, those in the street lamp — relieving by them the black shadows of the crowd and of the sky." This might be a picture by Alfred Stieglitz. Despite the personal vulgarity and tinsel showiness in Dreiser's style, his fundamental vision of things is always the artist's.

Yet beyond this sensitivity to the once realized beauty of the modern city, Dreiser's greatest strength is as a dramatist of human relations. Although his narrative technique, especially in chronicle novels like *The Financier* and *The Titan,* often becomes mechanical, in alternating chapters describing Cowperwood's love affairs and business deals, Dreiser's curiously unconscious masterliness is emphasized by the way he virtually devours a subject. When Dreiser is bad, it is never because of the slowness or literalness of his technique; it is because of the imposition of a purely subjective emotion, as in parts of *The "Genius."* In Dreiser the writer was *always* wiser than the man. When his instinctive transformative powers fail him, when he imposes on the reader great blobs of incoherent personal emotion, one recognizes how silly the man Theodore Dreiser could be. An example is the tasteless endearments that Eugene Witla addresses to young Suzanne Dale. What made Dreiser powerful in *Sister Carrie* and *Jennie Gerhardt*, where he used the stories of his own sisters, was his ability to see his own family in historic and histrionic roles, exactly as if he had visualized them in dreams. In the Cowperwood novels, it was his candid self-identification with massive creatures of power, who represented the fulfillment of his own social yearnings to be, in twentieth-century terms, a hero. Even more, Cowperwood, of all Dreiser's many sensuous heroes, was able to convey best the humanity of Dreiser's own feeling for women, his exalted sense of their beauty — which Dreiser represented equally in Cowperwood's love of painting. In *The "Genius,"* however, Dreiser was writing too close to the bone of his marital troubles; the objective sympathy that had been available to him in describing his heroines, or in modeling Cowperwood on an American magnate of the period, Charles T. Yerkes, broke down because of his own notorious lack of humor. It is an interesting fact that one of the most powerful scenes in *The "Genius,"* the birth of Eugene Witla's child, seems to have had no parallel in Dreiser's life. On the other hand, Dreiser's maudlin descriptions of Eugene in love, even of Eugene's earlier breakdown and his odd success in advertising and publishing, *are* all based on Dreiser's life, and it is these scenes that are handled with that showiness of emotion which afflicted Driser's writing whenever he moved out of his natural orbit as a storyteller into too personal and confessional a tone.

It is this clumsiness in *The "Genius"* that explains why Dreiser's work is so often identified with pedestrian novelists of his own generation. Yet the theme of the book is significant, for Dreiser is always concerned with eroticism. Despite the many attacks on his books, this side of Dreiser's work is undervalued, for in his old-fashioned way Dreiser connects sex with money and social ambition. It is this connection that leads Clyde Griffiths to his death in *An American Tragedy*, as it is this that leads Hurstwood in *Sister Carrie* to rob his employer; one can see the connection even in Frank Cowperwood, who despite his immense personal authority, his fortune, his undeviating attraction to so many women, must himself go from woman to woman in a yearning for that "refinement," that ultimate "spell of beauty," which would represent a social victory higher than anything in Philadelphia or Chicago. The fact is that Dreiser is one of the most cogent novelists of sex we have had — so long as he sticks to the inescapable involvement of women, money and power, or can reveal a compassion for women that shows us such very different victims in Carrie, Jennie Gerhardt, and the utterly innocent Roberta Alden. In Dreiser compassion is as strong an emotion as lust. Compassion as a source of sexual emotion is so rarely expressed in contemporary novels that it is important to emphasize how different Dreiser is in this from the aggressive realists of our day. (John O'Hara in books like *A Rage to Live* imposes a masculine psychology on his women characters.) It is Dreiser's compassionate sense of what women themselves are likely to feel that explains why Carrie, who has seemed commonplace to many unsympathetic readers, and whose perverse success in life enraged old-fashioned moralists, figured for Dreiser himself as a true heroine of the modern world. "In your rocking-chair, by your window, shall you dream such happiness as you may never feel." Dreiser was able to portray not only the kind of woman who was the "prize," the "lure," for a man making his way up (Suzanne Dale in *The "Genius,"* Sondra Finchley in *An American Tragedy*), but he was able to show that a woman like Carrie could dazzle an ambitious man like Hurstwood and yet within herself remain a solitary and bewildered child still trying to understand the world that looked so inhuman when she first had come on it in Chicago.

« 4 »

The real objection that must be considered against Dreiser's work refers to more than his occasional vulgarity of style or to the naïveté with which he often furnishes a room. The force of the objection lies in the contrast between unassimilated actuality — the purely personal-historical portrait that Dreiser so often achieved — and what Henry James, who insisted on the novel as a wholly realized art form, called a "situation." James unfavorably compared fiction which gives us a "case" with fiction that presents a "situation," where the novelist can display so many connections with life at large that the form of the novel becomes a "reflection . . . to one's sense of life in general." Dreiser certainly does think of each of his novels as a "case." *Sister Carrie* is so rooted in reminiscent emotion, one critic has commented, that Dreiser wrote it as if he were taking down a vision; "it was something like translating the Golden Plates." *The Financier* and *The Titan* naturally became the case history of an individual in the setting of time which the hero helped to make. *The "Genius"* is again the portrait of a single man, and even *An American Tragedy*, though it is the one Dreiser title that might be taken to refer to more than an individual, is essentially the "history" of Clyde Griffiths. Henry James would not, in theory, have objected to Dreiser's material, or even to the style of a writer he might conceivably have accepted as "our American Balzac" — a type of which he saw the necessity, and from which he sadly excluded himself because of inadequate knowledge of American business. James's objection would have been that all of Dreiser's work, to use the titles of two books of Dreiser's stories, is either a gallery of men or a gallery of women. We feel the "case," the individual within the drama of history; the individual is surrounded by the actuality of experience, but we do not find the well-made novel that was James's ideal: one in which the plot and the subtlety of its development give us the sense that the situation is primary, and that everything which gives us pleasure in a novel — place, character, action — has been joined to bring about a singleness of effect.

Dreiser does not meet these specifications. When we read him, we are aware not only of the unevenness of style and intelligence that we get even in so strong a book as *Sister Carrie*, but we also discover that Dreiser's interest is in the individual within the immense struggle and pathos of historical circumstances. Sometimes, as in the Cowperwood novels, the individual has the strength to rise above these circumstances; usually, as in *An American Tragedy*, he falls entirely out of life. When we read Dreiser we are also aware of "extricable" meanings; we never forget the underlying pressure of life on him: there is always a sense of issues, of historical personages thinly disguised, of an actual murder trial and the newspaper reports of it, as in *An American Tragedy*. By the time we finish any Dreiser novel, the grit of actual life has got into the fine machinery of the novel, and we are left not with the worked-out "situation" but with case after case — Carrie, Hurstwood, Jennie Gerhardt, Frank Algernon Cowperwood, Eugene Witla, Clyde Griffiths, Koberta Alden. . . . In the end, the supposedly "pessimistic" novelist of determinism, of the ruthless social process, has really given us an extraordinarily large gallery of individuals who are symbolically divided from their society and who in one way or another evade its claim to full domination over them.

It is this essential solitariness that lingers in our imagination, and that gives us our conviction of Dreiser's lasting value. Undeniably, it is not the "situation" of art but the "case" of history itself, as it afflicts the individual, that is the ruling image in Dreiser. In fact, we cannot help admiring Dreiser for exactly those insights that James suggested were fundamental to the novel, when he said early in his career that the novelist succeeds to the "sacred office" of the historian. We think of Dreiser's work as a series of indelible episodes in the moral history of twentieth-century man; we cannot help being aware of an interest outside of the novelistic "situation" itself. But more than this, we are aware that we feel this historical interest because, when we read Dreiser, we are directed to it by his art. In the classic way of art, the issue, the moment, the historical drama, all have been fused to give us an image of the human person that has outlasted the issues themselves. Without the "case," we would by now have little sense of the times themselves; these individuals are by now out of time precisely because they have been caught so well in time. May it be, then, that the real objection we feel to the "case" technique is that Dreiser makes us feel the solitude of the individual even in society, the individual ultimately undetermined by "forces," outside the net of facts? May it be that in Dreiser we see the human soul, though almost crushed by circumstances, nevertheless irreconcilably free of them, its own freedom made clear in the light of inarticulate longing?

The truth is that Dreiser's books belong to a period of literature in which the individual is still large, epochal, heroic — not crushed. What gives his characters stature is not what *they* accomplish in history (only Cowperwood has creative force, but his actions are morally dubious) but what one may call their innocence: they can never become nonentities, for as provincials in the city they have too much to think about. More and more the contemporary novel is stocked with individuals who have nothing to think about except themselves, and who in their dullness justify the mechanical psychology with which they are conceived. They are engulfed, they have been taken over, they hardly exist. Dreiser's individuals are *large* because they still have an enormous capacity for suffering — and for realizing their suffering. In their defenselessness they recapture the reality of the human person. They are so alone that we watch with awe what is happening to them. We are entranced, because we are watching a social process that in Dreiser's novels, despite what he *says*, is not yet finished, that may turn out another way. We watch with admiration because we know that despite Dreiser's philosophy, Dreiser's novels prove that history does not simply ride over man but is in some sense an expression of him. In creating history, in suffering it, man becomes vivid; there, however we may change, is the unmistakable light of reality itself.

[1959]

The Mystery of Gertrude Stein

YEARS AGO in Italy, I met Gertrude Stein's brother Leo, a vividly eccentric man as interesting for his many crotchets as he was on the subject of his sister. She had died the year before, but he still talked about her with lively resentment. Leo Stein was fascinating to be with, one long day in Settignano and Florence, for he had known many of the painters and poets who created "modern" art in the great years just before the First World War, and he was flavorsomely himself — honest, cranky, neurotic, gossipy, and above all ruminative. To meet him was to be given instant access to everything he was thinking at the moment. He not only shared his meditations with you; he made you feel like a psychoanalyst and brain surgeon invited to poke at his mental insides. He was such an original that you couldn't help wondering what it was that had held him back so long, that had kept him at seventy-five so bitterly jealous of his famous sister.

Afterwards, when I turned to some of Leo Stein's critical essays,

The Third Rose, by John Malcolm Brinnin. Boston: Little, Brown and Company. An Atlantic Monthly Press book.

I discovered that it was almost impossible to read him. A desperate juvenile conceit shone out of everything he said, and I remembered his hints that privately he had hit upon many of the most influential insights in contemporary psychology and esthetics, but that he had lacked the concentration — or narrowness of interest, as he allowed you to infer — that had permitted others to make their fame out of such discoveries. The trouble with Leo Stein, I discovered, was that although, in the course of his long self-analysis, many fleeting glimpses of higher things than himself had crossed his mind, he did not know how to work up these ideas, for they were too much attached to himself. Like everyone who is really outside of things, he could function only on the single plane of logicality. He was like Robinson Crusoe stolidly piling one piece of driftwood on another to make a habitation; he thought that he could reason himself into self-confidence, into greatness — in any field. And operating in the same way, he reasoned himself into the belief that not only was he stupendously intelligent, and so could have been a great painter, a great philosopher, a great scholar, but also that other people (like sister Gertrude) were just dumb.

Now sister Gertrude was anything but dumb, and unlike her brother Leo she did not (at least not with strangers) show so many cracks in her armor. She achieved for herself the fame of mental independence, of leadership in the world of art and intellect, that Leo Stein always dreamed of. He must have realized that but for her he would have been overlooked. Yet his real bitterness — that someone as endlessly analytical as himself should have succeeded in one field where he failed in all — was surely misplaced. For if anything is clear about Gertrude Stein's work today, it is that in the great mass of her work she, like her brother, is unreadable; that her work is now a curiosity, and has no part in our thinking. Mr. Brinnin's book is the best proof of this, for though he has written a book on Gertrude Stein, I cannot see that he gets any more out of her work than most people do. He is engaging and informative on the external social facts of a life lived so much in the creative stream of twentieth-century literature and art, and he is perceptive and deft in his handling of Gertrude Stein's complex personal character. But whenever Mr. Brinnin comes up against her work, it seems to me that he dodges a fundamental problem in connection with it —

whether there is something there that people can read and use; whether the work truly *exists* or not.

In writing about Gertrude Stein it is possible to overlook the possible final significance of her work even when one seems to be writing about the work itself. She figured importantly (and often just self-importantly) in the best writing of the 1920s, and right now can symbolize our nostalgia for past greatness. Mr. Brinnin writes, "Beyond the luster that poets continue to give this literary age, the excitement of books written thirty, forty and fifty years ago are, sad to say, still the only excitements." Say "Gertrude Stein" to a literary intellectual, and he automatically thinks of Hemingway and Picasso. He may keep thinking of Hemingway and Picasso even when he *reads* a little of Gertrude Stein — so fervently has the record of her associations and teachings impressed itself upon everybody, which is what she tried to do by deliberate lucidity in *The Autobiography of Alice B. Toklas* and *Everybody's Autobiography*. And it is perfectly possible to analyze Gertrude Stein's intentions as a writer, to trace the history of her work, without ever coming to grips with the actuality or lack of it in her work. Since she was one of the first to buy Picasso and among the first to appreciate Cézanne, and, as everybody now knows, tried to reproduce in writing certain values of postimpressionist painting, it is possible to discuss her vision, her mode, her intention, as if certain famous pictures themselves gave reality to her work. Mr. Brinnin explains that Gertrude Stein composed her most famous book, *Three Lives*, beneath Cézanne's portrait of his wife — a picture in which the subject is seated in a red chair and wearing a blue dress. Mr. Brinnin, describing her intention, explains that "by a ceaseless flow of half-articulated thoughts, worn phrases of speech and homely inflections from domestic life, she would match Cézanne's iterations of the qualities of light."

Now Mr. Brinnin does not deny that her work is often unsatisfactory. He clearly communicates his exasperation with those lesser works, like *Brewsie and Willie*, that convey her enthusiasm at having been taken up by so many G.I.'s who sought her out in France. Throughout the book he is careful to distinguish between her abstract intentions and actual achievements, and his account of her limitations is certainly correct. As he says, "Perhaps never in all the long association of poets and painters in the same creative climate has a writer attempted with such unabashed literalness to adopt methods springing from the theory and practice of painting. . . . The only course open to literature that would emulate painting was that of contemplating its own structure and image." My objection to his book is not that he overrates her work but that I cannot see a motivating reason for his own book. To write about Gertrude Stein without justifying her work is, at this stage, simply to recall her fashionable doings. Mr. Brinnin manages not only to say all the right things about her work but to hold it at a distance, to make us feel that the work is not pressing, of secondary importance.

One can deliberately understress a writer's work in a biography; it is easy to imagine a romantic biography of F. Scott Fitzgerald that does not discuss his work at all. But the importance of Fitzgerald's work would always be in our minds, would alone justify a biography at all. What, without the same mental weight given to her work, justifies a biography of Gertrude Stein? What is the real interest behind it? Partly, no doubt, it is the record of her associations in Paris before and after the First World War. Familiar as much of this material is, Mr. Brinnin makes a fluent social chronicle out of 27, rue de Fleurus, when Picasso came to call, and Matisse and Hemingway and Fitzgerald and Glenway Wescott and Sherwood Anderson and Virgil Thomson and Thornton Wilder. There is still something glorious and incomparably free about that early period — above all, about the years before the First World War, when modernism had not yet lost its connection with revolutionary thinking in all social and ethical fields, had not yet taken on the desperation of the late 1920s, was a long way from the safe investment in established taste that it has become today.

Yet by now the record of Gertrude Stein's influence on so many famous writers is not only familiar but mysterious. Consider how much she is supposed to have done for others, and how little she ultimately achieved for herself! I would suggest that one reason for her influence is the fact that these writers were usually men, and that despite her spectacular outward lack of female charm, it was as a woman with a deep rudimentary common sense that she influenced so many male writers. Whatever the sterilities and the self-infatuations in her work, she was a woman of extraordinary insight. She understood men who were writers, she understood fellow minds. Her influence was enormous because writers could pick up extraordinary suggestions from her thinking. She studied the world, from her mind as its center, with an intensity that literally made her a stream of consciousness, and writers could find particles of thought anywhere in this stream. Because of her quickness and her social sense, she was able to size up people quickly, and many of her verbal judgments on people — carefully repeated in her more popular books — are unforgettable. She said of a well-known novelist who had been "promising" all his life — "He has a certain syrup, but does not pour."

But if Gertrude Stein herself has become finally unreadable, it is because she did not think in terms of books at all but in orphic sayings, sentences, rhythmic paragraphs that brought home the sound of herself thinking to herself. She was fascinated by ideas, the outlines of things, the possibilities inherent in all subjects, the hidden voice of the individual beneath his social personality. Unlike so many writers today, who see their opportunity only in the generally accepted, she was utterly fearless and tried everything; there was nothing she ever found in her own mind that seemed alien to literature. If courage were the same as creativity, Gertrude Stein would have been Homer. But creativity is a matter of achieving whole works, not of ideas for books or brilliant passages in books. Gertrude Stein could make a Hemingway or Anderson or Fitzgerald — at times even a Picasso — glow with ideas. But when she sat down to write, she let the stream of all her thoughts flow as if a book were only a receptacle of her mind. One came to suspect that her wisdom was more in the realm of theory than of actuality.

Gertrude Stein's genius for suggestion actually stays more with poets than it does with novelists. Poetry, by its very character, deals with a world of essences that can be intimated but not always communicated, and the critical writing of poets is always essentially philosophical. It is noteworthy that Mr. Brinnin, a poet himself, thinks that the only luster today in literature comes from poets, and that in writing about Gertrude Stein's work he communicates

more enthusiasm for her intentions — which are pure literary ideas
— than for her books, which are usually dead novels. Gertrude
Stein may have tried to inject into the novel as a form some of
the power that poetry always exerts on the unconscious. So did
Joyce and Proust. But both these writers were able to carry through
epic works. Even *Finnegans Wake*, though often termed a failure
except as "poetry," exists as a shape, is connected from the first
word to the last, in the way that Gertrude Stein's works never
were.

Both Gertrude and Leo Stein were remarkable people. They were
remarkable because they visualized for themselves a power that most
people never dream of: they saw themselves as conquerors through
thought, through pure thought. Leo Stein hoped, by coming to the
root of his difficult personality, to unlock his hidden genius as a
psychologist and esthetician; Gertrude Stein dreamed of finding the
formula that would put all other modern writers behind her. She
thought she had found it, and she went on writing with the imper-
turbable smile on the face of a Buddha; she trusted in her thoughts
as if she were Moses tuned in to the Almighty. But the trouble with
these pure thinkers in art, criticism, and psychology is that the mind
is always an instrument, not its own clear-cut subject matter. No
one, not even a Freud, has ever been really sure just what pure
mind is; Freud had too much respect for the truth to think that he
had found a realm absolutely detachable from everything else. Gertrude Stein's error was not that she thought of herself as a "genius"
— who can say what that is? — but that she identified this genius
with pure intellect. She even defined a genius as a representative of
the human mind, partly because he understands, without submitting
to, the force of human nature. Artists, she thought, are slaves to
human nature, are bound by resemblances, subject to sorrow, disappointment, and tears. But "the human mind writes what it is . . .
the human mind . . . consists only in writing down what is written
and therefore it has no relation to human nature." There is the root
of the conceit that unheedingly drove her work into a cornet.
Gertrude Stein had a very good mind. But it was not as good
as she thought it was, or else she would not have assumed that
literature can be written about nothing but the mind itself.

[1960]

Lady Chatterley in America

RECENTLY Grove Press of New York sent me a copy of *Lady Chatterley's Lover*, the unexpurgated text of Lawrence's third and final version, with an introduction by Mark Schorer and a preface by Archibald MacLeish; on the jacket were admiring testimonies to the book's nobility and lovingness from Jacques Barzun and Edmund Wilson. I hadn't looked at Lawrence's book or thought of it particularly since 1956, when I had bought a copy of the unexpurgated edition in a Stockholm department store, and I was pleased that a young American publisher devoted to twentieth-century literature had had the imagination and the courage to bring out the book in this country for the first time.

I had an errand to do, and was not able to turn to the book immediately. I live in a vaguely middle-class neighborhood of New York, though, in the fashion of middle-class neighborhoods in New York, it is getting slightly "beat," and so I was irritated not more than usually when a group of mingled white and Negro young men, wearing earrings, very tight narrow trousers, with hair greased back into ducktails, swished past.

At the corner newsstand, where I stopped to pick up my afternoon paper, I could hardly see the papers for the sex magazine covers. There were at least a dozen females in languishing poses, so hugely uddered and yet so coyly draped that I marveled at the enormous effort it must take to play peekaboo with curtains, aprons, and blouses. While remembering a friend of mine who writes "serious" stories for one of these magazines and who sent me one, to the inexpressible delight of my eleven-year-old son, who hadn't thought he could decently get to see so much, I noticed that there are now as many homosexual smut magazines as there are heterosexual ones; the number of heavily muscled young men, occasionally arrayed against a Grecian background with hands on their waists, made me wonder what my dour newspaper vender thinks of it all.

But I didn't ask him; I was too busy thinking of some of the contemporary novels I had looked at that week. One was about necrophilia, another on sodomy between priests, a third on incest. Although I had discharged my ideas on the subject in a review of John O'Hara's *From the Terrace*, I was still angry about the misuse of his social talent on idolatrous descriptions of sexual intercourse. However, thinking of some equally talented but much younger writers, I had to admit that in his old-fashioned way O'Hara was still romantic about sex; like Scott Fitzgerald, he thought of it as an upper-class prerogative! By contrast, I recalled Norman Mailer, whom I had seen on television some weeks before explaining, in a discussion with Dorothy Parker and Truman Capote, that the aim of life should be "personal growth," that he admired Fidel Castro for looking "beat," and that it was important to be "good" in bed.

Well, I thought to myself, Lady Chatterley *is* out of date. Wasn't it Kinsey who managed to amass statistics on the number of ejaculations certain men have a week, and to sell this stuff to the public as scientific information? I remembered my students — the Smith sophomore who, in a discussion of Hemingway's characters, tossed her young head contemptuously and announced in a shrill piping voice that they were "afraid of sex." At Amherst, I had discovered, eighteen-year-olds would discuss the homosexuality of Whitman or Hart Crane as soberly and clinically as psychiatrists at a convention.

In England, during the war, I had heard of an American bureaucrat still old-fashioned enough to turn his wife's picture to the wall whenever he brought a girl back for the night; but, standing on Broadway and Eighty-sixth Street on a beautiful April day, I remembered how much my friends and I in college had loved Lawrence, I recalled Blake's insistence,

> What is it men in women do require?
> The lineaments of Gratified Desire.
> What is it women do in men require?
> The lineaments of Gratified Desire,

and I felt unbearably nostalgic, middle-aged, passé. O Lord, I thought to myself, is there no room for old-fashioned rebels who still love Lawrence and Whitman and William Blake and Sigmund Freud? Have the yahoos taken over here, as everywhere: the beatniks with their infernal smirks of frankness, the chorus girls who just adore *Lolita* — it's so cute — the sexologists?

I recalled the *New York Times Book Review* some weeks before, when I had seen ads for half a dozen manuals on "how to achieve sexual competence," and, thinking of the ex-leftist fanatics turned superanalyst wise guys, of all the sniggers, the sex manuals, the dirty magazines, the self-infatuated homosexuals, the incest, the necrophilia, the call girls and their businessmen, I not only felt *démodé*, but glad of it. To hell with sexual "competence" and hurray for the lineaments of gratified desire, for Whitman's "the sweet hell within." Down with competence and up with passion!

Is there anybody, I wondered, hurrying back to my first edition of *Lady Chatterley's Lover*, is there *anybody* in America who could still think of this book as immoral, who could miss Lawrence's romantic-religious, antinomian, ecstatic faith that sex is holy? Is there some police chief in Boston or Sioux City, some postal official in Washington, who, though he may know little enough of Lawrence's seriousness as an artist, may know even less of the actual effect of such books on the mind and think it dangerous? Undoubtedly, I had to admit. Just as the beatniks at one extreme personify the ridiculous ideal of sensation for its own sake, of freedom for the sake of sensation, so there is something about the legal or judicial or clerical mind which assumes that one person can be corrupted by one book — while overlooking the growing development in our culture toward a sexual permissiveness hard to tell from personal desperation, the desperation of juvenile delinquents for whom sex means the thrill of violence. And what would these custodians fix on in this book but certain four-letter words which — while they represent exasperated failure for the unquiet desperation that masses of men feel, lodged together in armies, prisons, ships — represented to D. H. Lawrence, born in 1885 and brought up in the Congregationalist Church, his wistful and hoped-for symbols of a new loving frankness between men and women? Despite the external smut — or rather, because of it and the divisions which it symbolizes in ourselves — there is something about the American mind that is quick to identify what it is afraid of or just ignorant of as "immoral."

Some years ago there came to America a mildly touching Italian film about a weak-minded peasant girl who was seduced by a stranger whom she thought of as "Saint Joseph." The protest line in front of the New York theater carried placards; one of them, never to be forgotten, read: "We give Europe our wealth and they reward us with filth." Was it possible that the same people could identify Lawrence's "daring," his Derbyshire-miner's-son horror of English gentility, with filth — only because he had used certain words, because he believed that "the holiness of the heart's affections" (Keats's phrase) could be realized in sexual intercourse? That *this* would at last be the path of freedom, of sacredness, of a new communion which would give men and women their only refuge from the hated abstractions and constant meddling of modern industrial society? The usual objection to the book, in more genteel times, had been conventional responses to Lawrence's romantic defiance, his cult of love. Was it possible that in our increasingly closed-up world there would now be a serious political objection to human beings who pursued sexual love too strenuously for its own sake? The crime of hero and heroine in Orwell's 1984 was literally that they ignored the state, devoted themselves entirely to each other. So the real crime of Lady Chatterley and her gamekeeper, in 1959, could be that they were not sufficiently "adjusted to the group," that they ignored their "social responsibility," that in devoting themselves wholeheartedly to the act of passion, they were making a contemptuous and unforgettable comment on the triviality and fanaticism of their times.

This "crime" is one of the few lessons of love in contemporary fiction; nowadays a man and a woman meeting to make love make a political criticism which is far more trenchant than the old radicalism. The contempt for ideology that can be expressed by passion, I discovered, is the real sense of *Lady Chatterley's Lover* in 1959. Yet how ironic this could be, the unintended fruitfulness of Lawrence's intelligent genius, since the whole purpose of Lawrence's tract-novel is to establish sexual love as a revolutionary weapon *against* our industrial society! Thus far have we traveled in the West, all of us, in the thirty years since Lawrence finished the final version of his book. Before the hardening pattern of our society set in for good with World War II, men still hoped to change our society, not to escape it. Lawrence is in the great tradition of English and American literary radicals, with Emerson and Thoreau and Whitman as surely as with Blake and the young Wordsworth and Shelley, in his belief that "the holiness of the heart's affections" can revolutionize society, can transform "the mills of Satan," the hated cities, the industrial reek and blackness which Lawrence saw as the enemy of the free human spirit.

« 2 »

This call to the higher powers as revolutionary instrument is indeed the great purpose of *Lady Chatterley's Lover*. It is a novel in praise of love, of physical love's exaltations, that symbolizes the union of the old yeoman stock, personified by Mellors, the gamekeeper, with the best of the English liberal intellectual class. Lady Chatterley was originally Constance Reid, daughter of a Scottish painter and herself a Fabian, and her passion for Mellors is a protest against the incapable and despotic upper classes, in the person of her husband Sir Clifford, who comes back from the war paralyzed from the waist down. Not only is he unable to give his wife a child, but he becomes increasingly selfish, querulous, "proper," as his paralysis comes to include, as a natural part of his experience, the meanness and helplessness of the old English upper classes. For Lawrence's most subtle and penetrating perception (Mark Schorer remarks in his introduction), "the knowledge that social and psychological conflicts are identical, is so firmly integrated in the structure of his book that it is almost foolhardy to speak of his having two themes when in fact he had one vision."

Lawrence is still in the great tradition of the English and American Romantic poets, those Protestant radicals for whom the "living intuitive faculty," the wild and irrepressible call of the spirit, made church authority unnecessary; they automatically interpreted all experience by that belief in the ideal unity of man's faculties which is typical of the religious imagination. Lawrence's novel was an effort to give religious value to relations between the sexes; so the sympathy born of sexual happiness would work itself into every part of life, would militate against the purely external relationships, the increasing deadness, of industrial society.

It is because Lawrence's supreme subject is love, not sex, that he is, in the Romantic tradition, political. His argument, like those of all religious reformers, is personalistic; nothing in the image of society avails against it, for it absorbs and grows on everything like itself. The external side of life in our time is too fierce, heavy, hard; when Lady Chatterley motors through town, the darkness of the industrial Midlands has crept into everything: "the brick dwellings are black with dust, the black slate roofs glisten their sharp edges, the mud is black with coal-dust." Yet life, in its vulnerability, like the newborn chick which the gamekeeper showed his lady — "there it stood, on its impossible little stalks of legs, its atom of balancing life trembling through its almost weightless feet into Connie's hands" — is the only measure of the value that one must preserve; above all, that one can respect. Mellors, who looks so much like Lawrence in his last racked years, fragile and dead-white of body, also represents the physical fragility of man in the present era; he gives himself wholly to passion, but he is also sorely hurt by life and often grumbles at how little passion can do against all those "mental states" absorbed from punishing labor, from the increasing lack of contact with his fellow men, from the habit of separateness and the ease of vice.

Yet Mellors accepts the risks of passion, the beautiful and terrifying involvement to the depths that comes with carnal knowledge, as opposed to the mythomania, the acting out of fantasies, that goes with casual amours and prostitution and smut: "It's life. There's no keeping clear. And if you do keep clear you might almost as well die." He knows, above the harried tenderness that is the message of the novel (and Lawrence's first title for it was *Tenderness*), that an even worse time is coming, that society will never get away from its compulsive outlet in war.

Reading the book in 1959, I recognize the political moral of tenderness, present to Lawrence's mind in 1928, as an alternative still present to us. With all the despondency Lawrence felt in his last illness, he still believed that honest human realization of man's physical needs, a resolute struggle against the spite and hatred that he identified with the purely mental life, could make people freer and more loving in a society visibly corrupted by suspicion and distrust. Yet at the same time every new development in Western industrial society, every ebbing away of the strength and sweetness of the old country life, was proving too much for the individual. The note of quiescence, the drooping away at the end of *Lady Chatterley's Lover* as the lovers, temporarily separated, await their divorces and the birth of their child — this is the natural intermittency of passion. But the long letter from Mellors on which the book closes also brings home to us, as much in Lawrence's novel does, the final insufficiency of a language too strained for the feelings. Lawrence once wrote that "We have no language for the feelings, because our feelings do not even exist for us." That is the measure of his original effort, his stand for integral human nature. Yet it is also true that the increasing sense of love as escape, from the all-enveloping society and passionless conformism, gives *Lady Chatterley's Lover* that slightly hysterical edge which results from too determined an effort to capture the feelings.

Lawrence wrote always with passionate urgency; he succeeded in giving his style the quickness of life, the immediacy of breath, the aroused physical rhythm of passion itself. But the more his fatal illness pressed on him, the more he tried to evoke in language those states of feeling, of sexual arousement and ecstasy, which are more successfully revealed by indirection and compression. It is folly to think that words, even D. H. Lawrence's words, can ever get to the heart of passion. The language of mystics is often unbearable in the tension, the verbal effort to tear through the external surface; if words could even begin to suggest the Divine Presence, the mystic would not have to work so hard at language.

Lawrence's rushing, swift, extraordinarily keen language for sensations often creates a splendid reality in language, the reality of a poem, which is parallel to the love-making ecstasy it seeks to describe and actually conceals from us. The more one studies art, the more one recognizes that it is not an imitation of life, that it never comes close to actual human experience, but is an independent creation, an addition to nature rather than a description of it. Language so passionate and breathless as Lawrence's ultimately describes the ecstasy of art, not of passion. To the ultimate of passion — fortunately! — there is no bridge in the language of mental consciousness.

Lawrence is not pornographic, as snoopers and censors and moralists would charge; in one sense he is not even "real." The excitement of the best scenes in *Lady Chatterley's Lover*, and these are not always the love scenes, lies in the beauty with which life is praised. Lawrence is so naturally religious about experience, his motivating purpose is so naturally the Protestant's exultant identification of his single consciousness with life itself, that behind the flowing freedom and ease of his prose is the stirring of language itself, the individual's embrace of life as he extends his private feelings to external nature. It is an ironic and beautiful fact that the very excess of religious spirit that led Lawrence to identify sex with the Holy Ghost exposed him to the hostility of moralists who believe that sex should be kept in its place. Of course Lawrence made too much of sex, as he made too much of life; we do not have the same keen sense of value. In an age when most writers lack that overwhelming responsibility for the whole human community which Lawrence had, it is Lawrence's overinsistence, his inability to think of sex as partial or furtive, that is likely to produce the characteristic response today that he is naïve rather than dirty.

In this sense, *Lady Chatterley's Lover is* out of date, for Lawrence's last great effort to establish love as a counteravailing power in our society offers us a conception of the novel, as of the sacred symbol of love-making, that is too much for the diminished individual, too lyrical, too unabashed, too free. The external niceness that we have come to value ever since Henry James put the seal of "form" on the contemporary novel militates against Lawrence. So does our belief in psychology as determinism, since to us love is helpless and compulsive. So does the sheer lack in America of that rural mystery, the old English wood in which the lovers make love. Lawrence's exultant, almost unbearably sensitive descriptions of the countryside can mean little to Americans, for whom the neighborhood of love must be the bathroom and the bedroom, both the last word in sophisticated privacy.

Lawrence's descriptions of the naked lovers gamboling in the rain, his ability to describe a woman's sensations and a man's body with feminine sureness — all this belongs to another world. *Lady Chatterley's Lover* brings back memories of a time when men still believed in establishing freedom as their destiny on earth, when sex was the major symbol of the imprisoned energies of man, for when *that* castle was razed, life would break open and flow free.

[1959]

The Youngest Man Who Ever Was

IMAGINE that you have just entered college, that you were born in 1941 or 1942, and that you have never or just barely heard of Ezra Pound, an elderly American poet who now lives in Italy. The text-book assigned to you in freshman composition is the present collection of documents — "The Case Of Ezra Pound: Pro And Con Selections Intended to Be Used as Controlled Source Material for the Freshman English Course." It is a remarkable collection; there is nothing like it anywhere else, for here you can read even the citation of his alma mater, Hamilton College, when it gave Pound an honorary degree. Included are newspaper and magazine stories on the case, the official medical report of 1945 by psychiatrists at St. Elizabeth's Hospital in Washington declaring Pound "insane and mentally unfit for trial," a reminiscence by a former editor of *Poetry* magazine on listening to Pound's broadcasts in England while waiting for D-Day, a remarkable memoir by a soldier who was one of Pound's guards when he was kept in a special wire cage in disciplinary barracks near Pisa, the statement of the judges who awarded Pound the Bollingen Award for the best book of poetry published in 1948, a sampling of the literary controversy, observations of Pound in the mental hospital, documents and statements on Pound's eventual release last year and return to Italy.

Now, students, when you have read the documents in the case you will of course write a paper, and in the back of this excellently arranged and thoughtful book you will find "Topics for Research Exercises." The editors explain that "All the topics below can be developed in 300-1000 words from the documents in this volume, but students should be encouraged to extend their investigations with the resources of the library." By all means extend your investi-

A *Casebook of Ezra Pound*, edited by William Van O'Connor and Edward Stone. New York: Thomas Y. Crowell Company.

gations! Still, only a few of you freshmen will actually extend them, and it is only these rare ones who will be puzzled or made unhappy by the case of Pound; the more you look into it, the more puzzled you will be.*

All other students, being clever enough to get into college anyway, will recognize this book as another aberration of the middle-aged professors who have unbelievable and inaccessible memories of the revolutionary 1930s and apocalyptic 1940s. Being sensible boys and girls, you will read the documents in the case as if you understood them, and on the basis of this one book you will write your little research papers, report your own opinions pro and con as if you knew all about the case, and drop Pound just in time to become sophomores.

History, someone said, is written by the survivors, but it has to be arranged so that freshmen can come to grips with it. In an "American problems" course I once taught, apple-cheeked youngsters, after listening to a few outside lectures on transcendentalism and after reading one pamphlet made up of highly selected passages on and about Emerson and Thoreau, had to write a paper defending or attacking the actual course of opinion that these writers followed. Of course most students had no real opinion, just as they had no direct knowledge; but I remember with admiration how well they impersonated understanding.

So the case of Ezra Pound, poet and madman, the author of some of the most beautiful lyrics in twentieth-century English poetry, who celebrated Nazi massacres as "fresh meat on the Russian steppes," becomes a research topic for kids who were just getting born when Pound was broadcasting his useless, idiotic, unintelligible, and often obscene messages to the great democracy "held captive" by Franklin D. Roosevelt. It is not a fault that these kids were born in 1941 or 1942, or that these days in America it is often unfashionable for young

---

* Ezra Pound could be a beautiful poet, in dribs and drabs of isolated lyric pieces. His real gift is for pastiche. He has imitated the Greeks, the Chinese, and finally his own youth. But he has always been obsessed; for a number of years he was clearly insane, and what makes him puzzling — if you really look into him — is his manic oscillation between savagery and tenderness, between real insight and phony scholarship. Any man of good will *must* be divided about Pound. For myself, surrounded as I am by inexpungible memories of the millions of dead, I cannot think of the purely literary case made out for Pound without horror.

people to have a normal share in the memories of older people. Young people have learned that the 1930s were seditious and the 1940s a mistake, and they have conveniently developed amnesia about dangerous times. (But it is amazing how quickly their *feelings* can be stirred on issues, like the New Deal, on which they are supposed to have no data.) Nor can we criticize Messrs. Stone and O'Connor for drawing up so useful a collection of documents — on the contrary! But it is worthwhile to remember, while a few of us are still around to oppose the truth to the "facts," that these documents cannot convey the anguish and folly of the "Pound case" to freshmen. And oddly enough, for all the students who will be mystified by Pound the dogged Bohemian and official traitor, there will be many more, missing the real shame and horror of the case, who will be delighted with his example of manic courage, his jazzy directness, his frenetic style.

To many young people Pound could re-emerge as an aged hipster and clown, a man who all his life has defied conventional authority and been agin the government. I once discovered in a Southern college that from the hospital Pound kept up a constant correspondence with the literary set. His notes, always referring to himself as "Ez," written in his well-known telegraphic style, full of obscene puns and heavy attacks on their teachers and the ruling literary scholars of the day, delighted these students. What a change! They were excited by his sauciness, his freshness, his profane and nervous style. From one point of view, "Ez" was someone who had never grown respectable, who had kept all his life the perpetual air of defiance that is so necessary to young people. Both as a poet and teacher, Pound has always, on principle, been against everything in sight. It is interesting to note that the famous beard which in the early 1900s got him fired from his teaching jobs for being "too Latin Quarter," the beard which at one time seemed the very flag of the *avant-garde*, has in our time become the symbol of pseudo-orphic jazz musicians and the beatniks.

Pound was the youngest young man who ever was; Nathaniel Weyl reports that shortly after Ehrlich discovered the "magic bullet" — 606 — Pound wanted to take his old friend William Carlos Williams with him to the North Coast of Africa. "He thought there were enough syphilitic chieftains there so that they could both make a fortune and retire within a year to write poetry. Nothing came of the scheme." Even at sixty, when he gave himself up to the American authorities in 1945 and was kept in the disciplinary barracks near Pisa, he made a particular appeal to young soldiers. They recognized him as a fellow victim of the brass, and a regular fellow. Probably the most interesting single document in the *Casebook* is the account by a highly literate soldier, Robert Allen, of Pound's early captivity. Pound himself said later: ". . . They thought I was a dangerous wild man and were scared of me. I had a guard night and day and when they built a cage out of iron mats from airplane runways and put me in the cage for the merriment of all, they posted a guard outside. Soldiers used to come up to the cage and look at me. Some of them brought me food. Old Ez was a prize exhibit."

Allen himself quite obviously shared the admiration of Pound's courage, openness, daring, that he reports among the troops. He writes: "Pound, always spoken of as 'Ezra,' became sort of a hero among the trainees when word was spread that he had 'made a dummy of the psychiatrist' — that he had turned questions around so that even the psychiatrist became confused. In the end, the unofficial opinion of the psychiatrist was that Ezra Pound was sane, although perhaps 'a little exotic,' as one of my friends put it." The trainees marching by or working in the area considered Pound with awe, "taking the reinforced cage as evidence that he was a particularly tough customer." Another guard in the disciplinary training center remembers that Pound was so much admired that one young prisoner risked his chance for clemency by making a rough table for him.

« 2 »

Even the usual literary case for Pound, the claim that Pound's *Cantos* (an epic poem saturated in history) can be treated as "pure poetry," always implied that Pound's personality, his political and social opinions, were too violent and uncontrolled to be judged. Professor Ray West, whose unimportant personal record of the Pound controversy is characteristic of the anxious sophistication that has replaced scholarship among literary professors, says nervously that "No one that I know considers Pound correct in his thinking."

John Berryman, in a *Partisan Review* essay on Pound's poetry — an essay cited but not reproduced in this book — romantically compared Pound to Sir Roger Casement. Dwight Macdonald, who as a journalist has always been uncontaminated by any conventional opinion, even if it makes sense, went into ecstasies over the Bollingen Award because it showed what a free country we are compared with the Russians.

Time and again the feeling for Pound was that of young people or middle-aged people still young who, with typical heartlessness or lack of imagination, thought that Pound's most disgusting statements were simply not serious. Just as the art-worship of our time is a symptom of perpetual youth, for we excuse any daub as self-expression, so some of the sympathy for Pound came, very naturally and understandably, from people who want art to be "pure," to control it, to keep it for a world removed from real human suffering, belief, entanglement. Professor West, lamenting Pound's most unfortunate anti-Semitism, said that "I should prefer to have the anti-Semitism of our age (and who will deny that it exists?) written from a point of view contrary to Pound's, just as I should have preferred it if Eliot had not joined the Church, if Huxley had not been converted to mysticism, if André Malraux had not become a De-Gaullist, if Breton had not become a communist, and if William Faulkner had not so bitterly resented the Civil Rights bill."

In short, Professor West doesn't like writers to think of anything but writing. His students, however, may see things a little more mischievously; they may welcome in Pound exactly those qualities which older poets like Yeats and Robert Frost have always deprecated. Though it was Frost, in gratitude for Pound's early help, who finally got Pound off (and Pound snarled that Frost had waited long enough to do it), Frost's disapproval of Pound is no secret. Yeats, whom Pound also befriended, nevertheless described Pound's cantos as ". . . nervous obsession, nightmare, stammering confusion; he is an economist, poet, politician, raging at malignants with inexplicable characters and motives, grotesque figures out of a child's book of beasts."

Young people find just this exciting. The more inexplicable the world becomes to them, the more they feel it necessary to lash out at wrongdoers, and since they can't locate the culprits any more, they find admirable the exasperation, the undirectable nervous force that became more and more characteristic of Pound's personality. T. S. Eliot remembers that even in Pound's early days "he seemed always to be a temporary squatter," he had "a kind of resistance against growing into any environment." In a world that seems to be hardening into collective mankind, it is ironic, amusing, and terrible to think that Pound — the poet as permanent revolution, the literary rebel incarnate, the Pound whose manic screeches and ugliest writings have always been particularly shocking because of the peculiar tenderness of his best work — might become the very type of the hipsters' hero. *Any* cause will do for some people nowadays, so long as it is "agin" something still left to be "against." Some of the most bizarre material in the Ezra Pound casebook deals with the maniacs and fanatics who hung around him when he was in the mental pokey. Among his visitors was "David R. Wang, a member of the Dartmouth class of 1955, distinguished as being the only Chinese poet of record who devotes himself to the cause of white supremacy. Since graduation, the *Dartmouth* reports, Wang has been touring the Ivy League colleges with the purpose of setting up White Citizens' Councils on the campuses. He has characterized Secretary of State Dulles as a 'wishy-washy Socialist.' "

Crazy, Man! Crazy!

[1959]

William Faulkner:
The Stillness of Light in August

LIGHT IN AUGUST begins unforgettably with a pregnant young woman from Alabama sitting beside a road in Mississippi, her feet in a ditch, her shoes in her hand, watching a wagon that is mounting the hill toward her with a noise that carries for a half-mile "across the hot still pinewiney silence of the August afternoon." She has been on the road for a month, riding in a long succession of farm wagons or walking the hot dusty roads with her shoes in her hand, trying to get to Jefferson. There, she firmly expects, she will find her lover working in a planing mill and ready to marry her, and there — that is the big city — she will put her shoes on at last.

This opening chapter, so dry and loving in its pastoral humor, centering on the picture of Lena and her precious burden being carried in one wagon or another, by one farmer after another, to her hoped-for destination in a husband, ends sharply on the outskirts of Jefferson, from which she can see smoke going up from a burning house. It is the house of Joanna Burden, who has just been murdered by Joe Christmas. And the images that have been crowding us with the dust and the heat of the unending road — with Lena continually amazed at how far a body can go, the serenity of the deserted young woman whose face is "calm as a stone, but not hard," the "sharp and brittle crack and clatter" of the "wagon's weathered and ungreased wood and metal," the identical and anonymous wagons, the mules plodding in a steady and unflagging hypnosis, the drowsy heat of the afternoon; with Lena's faded blue dress, her palm leaf fan, her small cloth bundle in which she carries thirty-five cents in nickels and dimes; with the shoes that she takes off and carries in her hand as soon as she feels the dust of the road beneath her feet — all provide us with that foundation in the local and the provincial, the earth and the road which man must travel on it, against which are set images of fire and murder, of aimless wandering and of flight, embodied in the figure who soon enters the book and dominates it in his remorseless gray anonymity. Joe Christmas does not even have a name of his own, only a mocking label stuck on him at the orphanage where he was deposited one Christmas Eve. "Joe Christmas" is worse than any real name could be, for it indicates not only that he has no background, no roots, no name of his own, but that he is regarded as a *tabula rasa*, a blank sheet of paper on which anyone can write out an identity for him and make him believe it.

It is the contrast of Lena Grove and Joe Christmas, of the country girl and the American wanderer, who is a stranger even to himself, the ultimate personification in modern loneliness, that frames the book — literally so, since Lena Grove begins and ends it, while Joe Christmas's agony and crucifixion are enacted as within a circle round which he runs in an effort to catch up with himself. When he finds that he cannot run out of this circle and stands still at last in order to die, the book comes back to Lena Grove and ends on her ritualistic procession up the road with her baby and Byron Bunch — Faulkner's version of the Holy Family. By the time we have finished *Light in August*, we have come to feel that the real greatness of Faulkner in this book (and indeed of his extraordinary compassion) lies in the amazing depth which he brings to this contrast of which American writers are so fond, particularly in Southern writing, between the natural and the urban, between Lena Grove's simplicity and the forces personified by Joe Christmas's walking all smooth city pavements with the same isolation and indifference, eating at the coldly smooth wooden counter, and murder. Faulkner even leads up to a strange and tortured fantasy of Joe Christmas as Lena Grove's still-unnamed son. There is virtually an annunciation to Lena, in the moving last phase of the book when Lena, delivered of her child just as Joe Christmas is running for his life, hears Mrs. Hines, Christmas's grandmother, calling the baby "Joey" — he who is a "nigger" murderer, and whom Lena has never seen. The reader comes to this with a shock, only because of Faulkner's reckless, desperate eagerness to wrest all the possible implications from his material, to think it out interminably, since there is no end to all one's possible meditations round and round the human cycle. One of the conflicts of which the book is made — between life and anti-life, between the spirit of birth and the murderous abstractions and obsessions which drive most of the characters — is in Faulkner himself, in his attempt to will his painful material into a kind of harmony that it does not really possess.

But in any event, it is Lena who opens the book, Lena's world, Lena's patience, that set the ideal behind the book — that world of the permanent and the natural which Joe Christmas seeks all his life without knowing that he does, and, seeking it, will run full tilt into the ground. "Light in August" is itself a country saying: Light as a mare or a cow is light after delivery.* And it is this world of Lena Grove from Doane's Mill — the tiny hamlet which was too small for any post-office list; yet even Lena, living in the backwoods, had not seen it until her parents died — with the sound of the wagon wheel taking her away from it, that remains in the book not merely a world

* Faulkner now denies this, and claims that the title just came to him because he liked the phrase. [1961.]

that Faulkner celebrates but a mythic source of strength. As indeed it is. For it is this intense sense of itself, it is this superb registering of country sights and sounds as the stillness is broken by the creaking and lumbering wagon coming up the hill, that is the secret of Southern writing. In his attachment to the irretrievable, in his obstinate feeling for the earth, the good Southern writer makes so much writing in America seem as shallow as if it had been composed by a young instructor in English sitting in his study surrounded by manuals on the great novels. Albert Camus, talking appreciatively about Southern novelists, once remarked to a friend of mine that what he liked about their books was "the dust and the heat." And to the man from North Africa, with his memories of that blazing world described in *Noces*, that world into which Paris can never enter, Faulkner's sense of local color must be especially moving. But after all, it is this sense of place that is the great thing about all American writing. It is the "mossy scabs of the worm fence, heap'd stones, elder, mullein and poke-weed" in "Song of Myself"; the landscape that in *Walden* seems always to be reflected in water; the strong native sense of the here and now that is the basis of Emerson's esthetic; the edge of the world seen from Hemingway's Michigan woods; "reading the river" in *Life on the Mississippi* and *Huckleberry Finn*; the "snow, the real snow" seen only beyond Chicago that Scott Fitzgerald described so rapturously in his memories of Midwesterners in Eastern colleges going home for Christmas. And if we ask what is so remarkable about that sense of place, which is, after all, essential to imaginative writing, the answer is that we Americans are in fact just the opposite of the homogeneous mass we are always trying to be, and that what distinguishes American writing is exactly the fact that we are strange to each other and that each writer describes his own world to strangers living in the same land with himself.

Now of all parts of the United States the South is certainly the strangest to the others; it is, in fact — or used to be — a separate nation. And almost all the good Southern writers have this sense of local color to an extreme, for to the same degree that the South is what it is because of its rural background, its "backwardness," its isolation, its comparatively homogeneous white population, to this same extent does the American need to value and venerate one's own region or place as the only escape from American bigness, American smoothness, American abstractness, American slogans, the juggernaut of American progress, find (at least it used to find) its deepest expression in the South. Even poverty, which in America certainly is a disgrace, becomes in Southern writing a sign of the natural man (Huckleberry Finn) or the earth-mother (Lena Grove). And, as so often happens in Southern writing — for the sensitive Southerners are likely to feel that they are lost in the modern industrial world and, in mourning their traditional homeland, to see the immediate world around them as damned — Faulkner's pictures of the impersonal modern world, the opposite of Lena's sacred grove, are lurid. As Lena is all fertility, the others are all barrenness. Destruction, fire, obsession, inhumanity, anonymity, the "friction-smooth" wooden counter at which Joe Christmas eats, the hard cold eyes of Bobbie the prostitute and Mame the madam and Max the pimp: set these against the images of locality, the farmers in their faded and patched but clean overalls, and of time, the wagon along the road and the "heelgnawed porch" of the country store around which the farmers sit. As soon as we get to Jefferson, we catch the typical dialectic of life and anti-life, the contrast of birth and destruction on which the book is founded, in the fact that the slow patient rhythms of Lena, the wagon, the road, are immediately followed by the whine of the saw in the planing mill, the reiteration of *smooth*. The world is narrowing down to the contest between the good Christian laborer, Byron Bunch, the very essence of the common ordinary good man, and those, like Lena's seducer, who have either taken on a name which is not their own, "Brown," a name too conventional even to be *his* name, or who, like Joe Christmas, have no name to begin with.

« 2 »

This contrast is familiar enough in Southern opinion, and one can find the same horror of miscegenation, of uprooting, of the city man's anonymity, in any expression of Southern agrarianism. But Faulkner does not stop at the abstraction of the alien: he carries it on, he carries it out, to astonishing lengths. And it is this intensity of conception that makes the portrait of Joe Christmas compelling rather than believable, makes him a source of wonder, of horror, yet above all of pity, rather than of pleasure in the creation of a real human being. For Joe Christmas remains, as he is born, an abstraction; from the moment he appears, "there was something definitely rootless about him, as though no town nor city was his, no street, no walls, no square of earth his home." He comes to work in the only clothes he has, a serge suit and a white shirt; and Byron Bunch, watching him, knows that Joe Christmas "carried his knowledge with him always as though it were a banner, with a quality ruthless, lonely, and almost proud." So from the moment Joe Christmas appears, he is seen as what others say about him, he is only a thought in other people's minds. More than this, he is looked at always from a distance, as if he were not quite human, which in many ways he is not.

We see Joe Christmas from a distance, and this distance is the actual space between him and his fellows. It is also the distance between the name "Joe Christmas," which is clownish, and the actual suffering of someone who has to live up to the nonhumanity of his name, to the obsession (founded on hearsay, not on actual evidence) that his father had "some" Negro blood in him. Joe Christmas, then, is really "Man" trying to discover the particular kind of man he is. He is an abstraction created by the racist mania of his grandfather, a former preacher whose tormented life is spent insisting that Negroes are guilty in the eyes of God and must serve white men. When his daughter ran away with a "Mexican" circus hand, Doc Hines not merely killed the man, and, after his daughter died in childbirth on Christmas Eve, left the baby on the steps of an orphanage, but later took a job as a janitor in the orphanage in order to make sure that his "nigger" grandson would never be allowed to contaminate anyone. This obsessiveness about race goes hand in hand with a Calvinist obsession of the elect and of the hopeless sinfulness of others, an obsession which is found both in Joe Christmas's rigidly doctrinaire foster-father, Calvin MacEachern, and in Joe's future mistress, Joanna Burden, a descendant of New Hampshire Puritans who remains in the South though she is the sworn enemy of its ways. All these obsessions about purity and guilt are, Faulkner indicates, the remnants of an inhuman religion that has added bigotry and arrogance to the curse of slavery. They are the symbols of a church that has lost its spiritual function, and that has been deserted by the Reverend Gail Hightower, who spends his days in endless reveries of the South's irretrievable glory. The obsessions are all summed up in the fate of Joe Christmas, who is trying to become *someone*, a human being, to find the integrity that is so ripely present in Lena Grove. Lena does not have to try; her symbol is the wheel on the road. Joe Christmas's is flight: flight on the same road, but flight toward himself, which he cannot reach, and away from hatred of himself, which he cannot escape. Only his pursuers catch up with him, to murder and to castrate him.

Joe Christmas is an abstraction seeking to become a human being. In the race-mad South, many a Negro — and Mexican, and Jew — is turned into an abstraction. But this man is *born* an abstraction and is seeking to become a person. He is an orphan, brought up in a foundling home, who in earliest childhood is watched by his own grandfather as if he were a caged beast. He is then bribed by the dietitian, whom he has heard making love with the intern, as if he knew enough to betray her. He is adopted by a farmer who renames him, lectures him, starves him, beats him for not memorizing the catechism. He is robbed and beaten by the pimp of the prostitute with whom he has fallen in love. He is constantly treated by his Negrophile mistress, Joanna Burden, as if his own personality were of no account, and is beseeched in her sexual transports as "Negro." And finally, after being starved, betrayed, flogged, beaten, pursued by bloodhounds, he is castrated. The essential picture behind Joe Christmas is that of his grandfather carrying him to the orphanage and then from it in a savage parody of loving care. Joe Christmas is nothing but the man things are done to, the man who has no free will of his own, who is constantly seeking a moment of rest ("When have I ever eaten in peace?") and who looks for an identity by deliberately provoking responses that will let him be *someone*, if only as a white man among Negroes, or as someone calling himself a Negro in an effort to shock the white prostitute he has just slept with. His passivity, his ability to lend himself to situations and to people who will "carry" him for a while, is immense and pitiful.

Joe Christmas is the most solitary character in American fiction, the most extreme phase conceivable of American loneliness. He is never seen full face, but always as a silhouette, a dark shadow haunting others, a shadow upon the road he constantly runs — a foreshadowing of his crucifixion, which, so terrible and concentrated is his suffering, already haunts the lives of others like a black shadow. For, almost *because* he does not look it, he becomes the "Negro," or the thought of, the obsession with, Negroes in the minds of those who, looking at Joe Christmas, can think of nothing else. And Joanna Burden, whose abolitionist grandfather was murdered in the South, whose whole life has been an obstinate carrying-on, deep inside Mississippi, of her family's coldly abstract espousal of Negroes, shows us how much of an abstraction Joe Christmas is when she makes love crying to him "Negro! Negro!" Whether the "Negro" represents the white man's guilt or the white man's fear, he is always a thought in the white's mind — and in the South, an obsession. So Joanna Burden, who befriends him, and Doc Hines, who hates him, come to see in him the cause of guilt that is finally the image of guilt. "I thought," Joanna says to her lover,

. . . of all the children coming forever and ever into the world, white, with the black shadow already falling upon them before they draw breath. And I seemed to see the black shadow in the shape of a cross. And it seemed like the white babies were struggling, even before they drew breath, to escape from the shadow that was not only upon them but beneath them, too, flung out like their arms were flung out, as if they were nailed to the cross.

And she quotes her father: "In order to rise, you must raise the shadow with you. But you can never lift it to your level. I see that now, which I did not see until I came down here. But escape it you cannot. The curse of the black race is God's curse. But the curse of the white race is the black man who will be forever God's chosen own because He once cursed Him." The grounds of this obsession, then, can be a compassion for the Negro that is as profound as hatred, and equally removed from brotherhood. This compassion seems to me the essence of Faulkner's approach to Joe Christmas, and the triumph of the book is Faulkner's ability to keep his leading character a shadow, and yet to make us feel all his suffering. Compare Joe Christmas with the types of the Northerner, the city man, the "stranger" in Southern writing, to say nothing of the Negro, and you realize that where so many neo-orthodox Southern literary critics are hysterically fearful of the "stranger," Faulkner, by a tremendous and moving act of imagination, has found in Joe Christmas the incarnation of "man" — that is, of modern man, reduced entirely to his unsupported and inexplicable human feelings. There are no gods in Faulkner's world; there are only men — some are entirely subject to circumstances, some protest against them, some are even moved to change them. The hero of *A Fable* is of the last; Joe Christmas is of the first. He is human to us because of the experience he undergoes, but his passivity is so great that he is finally a body castrated, a mere corpse on a dissection table — or someone whose body has been turned into the host, material for a ritual, so that his last agony will earn him the respect he never earned while he was alive. He is not, like the Christ of *A Fable*, a man who gives new meaning to life; like Benjy in *The Sound and the Fury*, he is an incarnation of human suffering, unable to speak — except in the tremendous action near the end of the book when he stops running from his pursuers and waits for them, and attains, in this first moment of selfhood, the martyrdom that ends it.

« 3 »

We see Joe Christmas always from a distance. This distance from ourselves to him seems to me the key to the book, for it explains why Joe exists for us principally as a man who is described, not seen. He is so far away that we cannot see him; he is reported to us. And this distance is filled with the stillness of a continuous meditation. *Light in August* tells a story of violence, but the book itself is curiously soundless, for it is full of people thinking to themselves about events past. As soon as Lena Grove arrives in Jefferson, at the end of the first chapter, the story of Joe Christmas comes to us through flashbacks, through talk by the other men at the planing mill, through a whole chapter of summary biography, through rumors and gossip by the townspeople, and at the very end, when Joe Christmas's whole story is put together for us, by Gavin Stevens's telling a stranger about the grandparents. Almost everything we learn about Joe Christmas comes to us in the form of hearsay, accusation, the tortured memories of others; even his death is told as an incident in the life of his murderer, Percy Grimm. All these reports about the stranger sufficiently suggest his alienation. But in themselves they also create that stillness, that depth of meditation into which all the characters are plunged.

This meditation begins in Joe Christmas himself, who in his distance from other men is constantly trying to think himself back to life, and who, without knowing exactly how his ordeal began — and certainly not why — finds himself like a caged animal going over and over the same ground. We hear him talking to himself, and we follow his slow and puzzled efforts to understand the effect of his actions upon others. We see him as a child in the orphanage, eating the toothpaste, frightening the dietitian out of her wits because he is staring straight at her, trying to understand what she is accusing him of. We watch him walking the path between his cabin and Joanna Burden's house for his meals, thinking out everything he finds between the four walls of her kitchen. Finally we watch him running, and thinking deliriously in his flight, until, in that magnificent and piercing scene near the end of his flight, he falls asleep as he runs. The pressure of thought, the torture of thought, is overwhelming — and useless, since Joe Christmas does not know who he is, and so cannot locate the first cause of his misery. But still he thinks, he broods, he watches, he waits. And it is this brooding silence in him, fixed in attention over he does not know what, that explains why he is so often described in the book as looking like a man in prayer — even like a "monk." There is a strange and disturbing stillness about him that eases him, more swiftly than most men, into the stillness of nonbeing.

The stillness of the book has, of course, an immense reverberation within it. Describing Doc Hines, Faulkner notes about him "a quality of outworn violence like a scent, an odor," and the actual violence of Joe Christmas is always felt about him even when he sits rigidly still at counters like a man in prayer. When Joe's back history is run off in the rapid newsreel style of Dos Passos, one feels not only his personal insignificance, but the just-leashed violence of American life of which Joe is, in his way, completely the creature:

He stepped from the dark porch, into the moonlight, and with his bloody head and his empty stomach hot, savage, and courageous with whiskey, he entered the street which was to run for fifteen years.

The whiskey died away in time and was renewed and died again, but the street ran on. From that night the thousand streets ran as one street, with imperceptible corners and changes of scene, broken by intervals of begged and stolen rides, on trains and trucks, and on country wagons with he at twenty and twentyfive and thirty sitting on the seat with his still, hard face and the clothes (even when soiled and worn) of a city man and the driver of the wagon not knowing who or what the passenger was and not daring to ask.

Yet it is a stillness of thought that generally pervades the book, in the form of enormous meditations by which Faulkner tries to lift his material into place. The stillness is interrupted by shooting, burning, beating, the barking of bloodhounds and Percy Grimm's mutilation of Joe Christmas, which interrupt like the sound which nails must make when they are driven into wood through human flesh. Yet, just behind this obvious figure of the Roman soldier torturing Christ, there is a pastoral world. As Irving Howe has noted, the arrangement of the book "resembles an early Renaissance painting — in the foreground a bleeding martyr, far to the rear a scene of bucolic peacefulness, with women quietly working in the fields." Despite its violence, *Light in August* is one of the few American novels that remind one of the humanized and tranquil landscape in European novels. Its stillness is rooted in the peaceful and timeless world which Lena Grove personifies and in which she has her being. It is the stillness of the personal darkness inside which Joe Christmas lives. But this stillness is also the sickly, after-dark silence of the Reverend Gail Hightower sitting in his study, with his stale clothes and stale thoughts, going over and over the tragedy of his life, his grandfather's "glorious" death, his wife's desertion and suicide — and finally and typically summing it all up into a stale round of human illusion and defeat. Faulkner wishes us to understand that Hightower finally cuts the Gordian knot of his thoughts when he delivers Lena's baby and is finally struck down by Percy Grimm as he stands between him and Joe Christmas. But Hightower, whether brooding out upon the street from behind the study window, or sitting behind the green lamp in his parlor when he receives Byron Bunch, his only visitor, enlarges the stillness, increases its weight, by personifying what is immediately present in the book and throughout Faulkner's novels — the Southern effort to explain, to justify, and through some consummation in violent physical action even to lighten, the burden of this obsession with the past.

Hightower, by general consent, is one of the failures of the book: he is too vague, too drooping, too formless, in a word too much the creature of defeat and of obsession, to compel our interest or our belief. But this is so partly because Hightower is both a surrogate figure for Faulkner's meditations and a kind of scapegoat on whom Faulkner can discharge his exasperation with Southern nostalgia and the endless searching in the labyrinths of the past for the explanation of the Southern defeat and of the hold it keeps on the descendants of the Confederate aristocracy. Hightower is a failure because Faulkner both uses and parodies him. Because of the absurdly literal symbolism of his name, his constant watchful position behind the green lamp, his useless reveries, he is never on the same scale as the other characters, who are equally obsessed by the past, but who function on the plane of some positive action. Hightower not only lives by his thoughts; he has no life but his thoughts. We miss in him the lifelike element of violence (the only possible end to characters so entirely formed of reverie) that we find in Joanna Burden's degeneration, in Joe Christmas's hatred, in Percy Grimm's fanaticism, in Doc Hines's mania. Hightower, acting in various sections of the book as a foreground observer, brings to them not merely a stillness but a deadness which intervenes between us and the other characters. This shapeless, ghostly body of thought has its symbolic place in the mind of Hightower. For just as his life is over, and he has no function but to brood, so Faulkner has signified in Hightower that wholly retrospective, watchful concern, not with the past but with their bondage to the past, that seems to me the essence of what Faulkner's characters are always thinking about.

Joe Christmas, Joanna Burden, Gail Hightower — each of these is the prisoner of his own history, and is trying to come to terms with this servitude in his own mind. That none of them can ever lift himself out of the circumstances that enclose him, Faulkner sees as the condition of man. Man is engulfed in events that are always too much for him. Hightower, listening to Byron Bunch make plans for Lena's confinement, thinks: "It is because so much happens. Too much happens. That's it. Man performs, engenders, so much more than he can or should have to bear. That's how he finds out that he can bear anything. That's it. That's what is so terrible. That he can bear anything, anything." Endurance, as we know, is the key word in Faulkner's system of values. At least this was so up to *A Fable*. There, Faulkner himself has told us, the highest value is represented not by the young Jewish pilot officer who said, "This is terrible. I refuse to accept it, even if I must refuse life to do so"; not by the old French quartermaster general who said, "This is terrible, but we can weep and bear it"; but by the English battalion runner who said, "This is terrible, I'm going to do something about it." *Light in August* does not arrive at this step. Man never thinks of changing the world; it is all he can do to get a grip on it, to understand some part of what has happened to him and to endure all of it. Any release that occurs is a purely individual one, as when Hightower finally frees himself, in the one profoundly unselfish act of his life, by delivering Lena's baby. In the freshness of the early morning, after Lena has given birth, Hightower feels that he is in touch with the earth again — the symbol throughout the book of rightness, authenticity, peace. But the earth is not his life, as it is Lena Grove's. Man's highest aim in this book is to meet his destiny without everlasting self-concern. Yet this profoundly tragic cast to *Light in August*, so much like a Hardy novel in the implacable pattern that unrolls against a country background and in the inarticulate stillness of its leading characters, is matched by Faulkner's ironic awareness that man, even in his endless brooding over the event, can never stop, that the event is nothing compared with the speculation that follows and in a sense replaces it. One of the most revealing phrases in Faulkner's rhetoric is "Not that" — it is not peace, not an end, that his people ever want. The violence may be "outworn," but it is the human passion. He describes his chorus, the townspeople, scurrying around Joanna Burden's house after her murder, looking "for someone to crucify":

But there wasn't anybody. She had lived such a quiet life, attended so to her own affairs, that she bequeathed to the town in which she had been born and lived and died a foreigner, an outlander, a kind of heritage of astonishment and outrage, for which, even though she had supplied them at last with an emotional barbecue, a Roman holiday almost, they would never forgive her and let her be dead in peace and quiet. Not that. Peace is not that often. So they moiled and clotted, believing that the flames, the blood, the body that had died three years ago and had just now begun to live again, cried out for vengeance, not believing that the rapt infury of the flames and the immobility of the body were both affirmations of an attained bourne beyond the hurt and harm of man. Not that.

We can never let the event go, for that would mean an end to the human history that is lived in retrospection. Just as Faulkner's language is full of words, like "avatar" and "outrage," which are really private symbols left over from his unceasing meditation, and just as his style is formed from the fierce inner pressure of problems which give no solution, so the actual texture of *Light in August* suggests, in the tension and repetition of certain verbal motifs, that man can never quite say what the event originally meant, or what he is to think of it now. Language never quite comes up to the meaning of events. To adapt Faulkner's phrase, it is not that, or that. The townspeople exist in *Light in August*, as in so many Faulkner novels, to ask questions whose very function is to deny the possibility of an answer. Faulkner's grim sarcastic asides show that he views language as in some basic sense unavailing. The astounding repetition of certain key phrases and verbal rhythms in his work signifies his return back and back on the question.

Call the event history, call it the Fall: man is forever engaged in meditating, not the past itself, for that would bring knowledge, but man's guilt, for that may bring freedom. Guilt, not history, is the nightmare from which all of Faulkner's deepest characters are trying to escape. The guilt arises from man's endless complicity in his own history, as when the innocent, gravely staring child that Joe Christmas was, ate her toothpaste and listened to the dictitian making love. Hightower is guilty because his sickly, foolish nostalgia for his grandfather's one day of glory made him unavailable to his own wife, who committed suicide; Joanna Burden feels so guilty that she has remained an alien in the Southern town in which she was born, accepting her isolation as the price of her identification both with her abolitionist forebears, who were shot down in the South, and with the Negroes, on whom a curse must have been laid. Even Doc Hines and Percy Grimm murder in order to "clean" life of the stain that Negroes have put on it, for as the Negroes were cursed by God, so they have cursed life, and the maniac "saviors" of Southern racial purity have to save their hallowed country from contagion. But just as no one of them can really distinguish the hate they feel for others from self-accusation, so no one can say with whom guilt began, where the ultimate human crime was committed. The paths which lead back to the human past are endless through the human brain, and sitting at his study window after he has gained new self-respect by delivering Lena's baby and by standing up to Percy Grimm, the dying Hightower still ruminates, goes over and over the past, as "the final copper light of afternoon fades" and "the world hangs in a green suspension in color and texture like through colored glass." The everlasting reverie begins again, but now the wheel of life that brought Lena Grove to Jefferson begins to slow down, runs into sand, "the axle, the vehicle, the power which propels it not yet aware." These memories are endless, and the style in which they are described is overcolored in a way that shows how static action often becomes in Faulkner's work, how much it serves as the raw material for reflection, which is why he can lavish so many Joycean compound words on objects which do not seem to move of their own accord, but to be rallying points in Faulkner's tortured concern with guilt.

Guilt is endless; in the labyrinths of the mind, there is turning but no deliverance. Like T. S. Eliot, Faulkner is a favorite today because he takes his stand on human guilt; this is the side of ourselves that we can recognize and, curiously, stand by; for in this alone, as we feel, is the possibility of our freedom. When men feel so wretchedly small before their own past, they must be guilty. So runs the legend. This is the argument behind Faulkner's novels: of the God who made Yoknapatawpha County. In the beginning, life was free and good and natural; but something inexplicable, a curse, was put on it. Perhaps the curse is nothing more than man's effort to get the better of events that are "too much for us"; the evil lies in arrogance. Doc Hines hears God addressing him personally, ordering him to act for Him. Calvin MacEachern, Joe Christmas's adopted father, starves and beats him because he cannot memorize portions of the catechism on order. "He asked that the child's stubborn heart be softened and that the sin of disobedience be forgiven him also, through the advocacy of the man whom he had flouted and disobeyed, requesting that Almighty be as magnanimous as himself, and by and through and because of conscious grace."

Even Joanna Burden tries to play God to her Negro charges. *Light in August* is one of the sharpest criticisms of Calvinism ever written, but unlike so many Southern writers on Puritanism, Faulkner knows that the same religion is found in Doc Hines and Joanna Burden. The guilt that is the mainstay of their faith is embodied in the assumption of excessive authority by fathers, lawgivers, teachers, ministers. Everyone wants to play God to the orphan Joe Christmas. In Faulkner's eyes, life is an ironic and tragic affair that is beyond human rule and misrule; but Calvinists like Doc Hines and Calvin MacEachern, or the children of Calvinists like Joanna Burden, even murdering simon-pure "patriots" like Percy Grimm, take life in their hands, they dominate, and they murder. Joe Christmas is their favorite charge; he is the man "things are done to." His final ignominy comes when his mistress, Joanna Burden, regarding him in her new phase as a Negro charge to be "brought up," tells him that she wants him to go to school so that he can become a lawyer. And it is at this point that he breaks. It is this point that has always been the signature of the everlasting victim. Other men are the lawgivers; the law is passed out to him, through him, inflicted on him. And so finally he murders and dies, a pure victim, shot, castrated, treated like a thing. It is the final ignominy. But in the very unattainability of his suffering, in its inexpressibility, is the key to his healing power over others. For where life exists so much in the relation of master to man, of the elect to the sinner, the only possible consummation man can ever reach, for Joe Christmas as for Uncle Tom, is in the final consistency of his suffering, in a fate so extreme that it becomes a single human word which men can read. This is what Faulkner means in that exalted passage after Joe Christmas's immolation:

. . . when they saw what Grimm was doing one of the men gave a choked cry and stumbled back into the wall and began to vomit. Then Grimm too sprang back, flinging behind him the bloody butcher knife. "Now you'll let white women alone, even in hell," he said. But the man on the floor had not moved. He just lay there, with his eyes open and empty of everything save consciousness, and with something, a shadow, about his mouth. For a long moment he looked up at them with peaceful and unfathomable and unbearable eyes. Then his face, body, all, seemed to collapse, to fall in upon itself, and from out the slashed garments about his hips and loins the pent black blood seemed to rush like a released breath. It seemed to rush out of his pale body like the rush of sparks from a rising rocket; upon that black blast the man seemed to rise soaring into their memories forever and ever. They are not to lose it, in whatever peaceful valleys, beside whatever placid and reassuring streams of old age, in the mirroring faces of whatever children they will contemplate old disasters and newer hopes. It will be there, musing, quiet, steadfast, not fading and not particularly threatful, but of itself alone serene, of itself alone triumphant.

Joe Christmas has attained the stillness that will finally allow us to see him. Of sufferings alone is he made, and in this sense, and in this sense alone, is he a figure whose condition is so total that he reminds us of Christ in the sense of Christ's integrality. That tortured and would-be Christian philosopher, Simone Weil, understood this when she found in *malheur*, affliction, that it could become so much in itself that she felt riven to the universe by bonds of pain. The archvictim may not be a "martyr," as students of modern totalitarianism have noticed, but there is a kind of suffering in our time which is so extreme that it becomes an integral *fact* of the human condition. Father Zossima bowed down to Dmitri Karamazov because of all the affliction he would undergo. So marvelous is Faulkner's compassion, he can visualize in the man who was nothing but a victim the shadow thrown from the Cross of Christ, who was nothing, as it were, but Himself. Men are men because events are always "too much" for them; Joe Christmas became one with his life in that extreme moment when even he had no longer to search out the past. The figure on the Cross is the most tremendous interventive symbol in history; the castrated man on the floor has only one free power in his life — to stop running at last and to face his murderer. Faulkner intends no parody; he is moved by the likeness of totality to totality. But neither is he a Christian. There is no redemption; there is not even in *A Fable* — but there man has the courage to redeem circumstances by denying their fatality. In *Light in August* the past is not merely exigent; it is even malicious, the spirit of pure bad luck, a godlike force that confronts man at every turn with everything he has been, and so seems to mock and to oppose him. This is called "The Player": Lena's seducer, "Brown," still running away from her at the last, sends a Negro boy to the sheriff for the reward money he has earned in informing on Joe Christmas, but knows despairingly that he will never see the money.

"He wont do it. He cant do it. I know he cant find him, cant get it, bring it back." He called no names, thought no names. It seemed to him now that they were all just shapes like chessmen — the negro, the sheriff, the money, all — unpredictable and without reason moved here and there by an Opponent who could read his moves before he made them and who created spontaneous rules which he and not the Opponent, must follow.

This is the Opponent that Joe Christmas decides finally not to elude again, the "Player" who moves Percy Grimm unerringly from position to position:

He was beside the ditch now. He stopped, motionless in midstride. Above the blunt, cold rake of the automatic his face had that serene, unearthly luminousness of angels in church windows. He was moving again almost before he had stopped, with that lean, swift, blind obedience to whatever Player moved him on the Board. He ran to the ditch.

All things are fated; man is in any place because the Player moved him there. Our past sets up the positions into which we fall. This is why Joe Christmas's grandmother, Mrs. Hines, utters the most significant lines in the book when, at the end, she pitifully cries out:

"I am not saying that he never did what they say he did. Ought not to suffer for it like he made them that loved and lost suffer. But if folks could maybe just let him for one day. Like it hadn't happened yet. Like the world never had anything against him yet. Then it could be like he had just went on a trip and grew man grown and come back. If it could be like that for just one day."

And it is in these terms that we come to understand why Joe Christmas, in running away from a past that he cannot escape, seems constantly to be looking back as he runs. Not only is no one free of his past; he even has, at the most critical moments, the sense not of moving at all, but of being silently lifted from position to position. It is because of this curious effect of immobility in Faulkner's characters as they run (as if they were held up in the air by wires) that Faulkner can lavish such idle poetic largesse upon them, can see in a Percy Grimm that "serene, unearthly luminousness of angels in church windows," and at various points throughout the book emphasize Joe Christmas's rigid likeness to a man in prayer. Even the countrymen in overalls move at one point "with almost the air of monks in a cloister." The reason is that all these characters are lost in contemplation as they are moved here and there by the Player. There is no free action for anyone: everyone is carried, as Lena Grove was carried to Jefferson in a whole succession of farm wagons, by the fate that was and so shall be.

« 4 »

Faulkner's world is grim — a world in which the past exerts an irresistible force, but against which there is no supernatural sanction, no redeeming belief. He believes in original sin, but not in divine love, and he is endlessly bemused by the human effort to read fate or to avoid it. The highest reach of his belief is the effort to become "a saint without God" (Albert Camus), but this is a point not yet tried for in *Light in August*. Correspondingly, there is great power in his work, but little color, and *Light in August*, for all its brilliance, somehow wears the lackluster look of the year in which it was published, 1932. It is a grim book, and the countryside described in it already has the pinched, rotted look that one sees in so many depression novels about the South. The greatest fault of the book is its overschematic, intellectualized cast. Although Faulkner himself has lived more like Joe Christmas than like the Sartorises, he is socially far from the world of Joe Christmas and Lena Grove, and there are telltale signs in the novel that it is written *down* — for Faulkner, too much from his head down, and about people whom he tends to generalize and to overpraise, as if he saw them only as symbols rather than as entirely complex beings. And it is a simple fact that the opening of *Light in August* is so beautiful that nothing else quite comes up to it.

On the other hand, it is one of Faulkner's greatest books, and although it does not have the blazing directness of *The Sound and the Fury* (a book written more directly out of Faulkner's own experience), it has much of the creative audacity which is Faulkner's highest ideal in art. With this book, published in 1932, Faulkner completed a period of extraordinary fertility. He was only thirty-five; since 1929, he had published, in rapid order, *Sartoris, The Sound and the Fury, As I Lay Dying, Sanctuary,* and *Light in*

August. It was a period of tremendous creative power. When he was recently in Japan, Faulkner said of this time: "I think there's a period in a writer's life when he, well, simply for lack of any other word, is fertile and he just produces. Later on, his blood slows, his bones get a little more brittle, his muscles get a little stiff, he gets perhaps other interests, but I think there's one time in his life when he writes at the top of his talent plus his speed, too. Later the speed slows; the talent doesn't necessarily have to fade at the same time. But there's a time in his life, one matchless time, when they are matched completely. The speed, and the power and the talent, they're all there and then he is . . . 'hot.' "

Light in August comes out of that "one matchless time." The only possible objection one can have to the book is the number of implications which Faulkner tries to bring out of his material — for just as the characters' own lives are "set" for them to mull over, so Faulkner constantly mulls over them, wringing a poetry that has grandeur but also an intensity of contemplation that is sometimes more furious in expression than meaningful in content. If we see Faulkner's narrative method as essentially recollective, in the form of individual meditation over past events, we can recognize the advantage he has over most "naturalistic" writers and we understand why Faulkner refers to himself as a "poet." For what makes the portrait of Joe Christmas so astonishing is the energy of imagination lavished upon it, the consistency of texture that derives from the poet's sense that he has not only to *show*, in the modern realistic sense, but to *say* — that is, to tell a story which follows from his contemplation of the world, and which preserves, in the nobility of its style and in the serene independence of its technique, the human victory over circumstances.

It is this that makes us hear Faulkner's own voice throughout the book, that allows him to pull off the tremendous feat of making us believe in a character who in many ways is not a human being at all — but struggling to become one. And this, after all, is the great problem of the novelist today. Joe Christmas is an incarnation not only of the "race problem" in America, but of the condition of man. More and more, not merely the American novel, but all serious contemporary novels, are concerned with men who are not real enough to themselves to be seriously in conflict with other men. Their conflicts, as we say, are "internal"; for they are seeking to become *some-one*. Joe Christmas lives a life that is not only solitary but de-tached. He lives in society physically, but actually he is concerned only with the process of self-discovery, or of self-naming, even of self-legalization. This is a fate which, as we know, can be as arduous and deadly as that of the classic heroes. But in Joe Christmas's case, there is no conflict from positions of strength, no engagement be-tween man and man — only the search of the "stranger," *l'étranger*, to become man.

[1957]

William Faulkner: More Snopeses

IN THE COUNTRY of William Faulkner's imagination — Yoknapa-tawpha County — the Snopes clan plays a role that is by now wholly symbolic. The Snopeses are not like the Compsons, the Mc-Caslins, the Sartorises, the De Spains (and the Faulkners), who were the ruling class of this highly stratified society — and with whom Faulkner so naturally identifies that his greatest works, like *The Sound and the Fury* and *The Bear*, come out of his anguished sense of decline. They are not like the Negroes, whom Faulkner also knows intimately, and from whom he has often drawn his no-blest and most significant characters. The Snopeses, at least in origin, are poor whites, "peasants," with a genius for trade, for sharp deal-ing. They are rapacious and grotesque-looking, impassive, inhuman and unbeatable. By applying an extreme shrewdness and an un-sleeping eye to every situation in life that can possibly be turned into cash, they always come out on top. In Faulkner's eyes, they are the great symbol of what has happened to the old order in the South. They are the fixers, the termites, the outsiders, the Neander-thal men of the new age who, by cunning alone, with an utter lack of tradition and culture, have stolen in from their corner in Mis-sissippi, Frenchman's Bend — see *The Hamlet* (1940) — and, taking every possible advantage, are now winning over the "town," Jeffer-

The Town, by William Faulkner. New York: Random House.

son, where they prepare the way for the final downfall of Faulkner's own class.

Symbolically, the principal Snopes, Flem, is impotent; symbolically, he wears, every day of his life, a nastily impersonal little metallic black bow tie. Symbolically, Snopeses are named I. O., Eck, Mink, and name their children Vardaman and Bilbo, after the more extreme racist Mississippi Senators. Other children pop up as Montgomery Ward Snopes, Wallstreet Panic Snopes, Admiral Dewey Snopes. Symbolically, the Snopeses now own the hotel; and Flem, the most ignorant of men, appears as superintendent of the municipal power plant — his wife is the mistress of Mayor De Spain. Faulkner even makes a pun on the strongest element in Flem's nature by having him steal the brass safety valves off the boilers. Symbolically again, Flem soon becomes vice president of the old Sartoris bank of which his wife's lover, the Mayor, is president.

When one Snopes goes to France in 1917, he not only spends his time behind the lines running a soldiers' canteen but turns it into a brothel; when he returns home, he rents a store and makes money projecting dirty postcards on an illuminated screen. One Snopes deliberately tempts kids to raid his watermelon patch so that he can shoot at them. And I have forgotten to add that I. O. Snopes hired a man to tie up his mules on a railroad track so that he could collect indemnity from the railroad company after the train killed them, and that when the man himself also got killed, this Snopes thought that, as the man's employer, he deserved a share of the widow's life insurance.

The Snopeses certainly are a symbol, and they are so inhuman in their effrontery, coldness and greed that they seem to do nothing all their lives but to work up some still more outlandish swindle. Episode after episode, each one weirder and more fantastic than the other, with Faulkner constantly outguessing the reader as to what possibly can come next from the unbelievable and innumerable tribe of Snopes. When he runs temporarily out of episodes, he just brings in more Snopeses. At the end of the book, one is not surprised to find a whole new generation of Snopeses, the products of an alliance between Byron Snopes and a "Jicarilla Apache squaw in Old Mexico" — all of whom carry knives, never use words at all, and are portrayed simply as wild prairie dogs with very sharp teeth.

Wildly extreme and insanely grotesque as many of these Snopes antics are, they do not make up comic episodes any more; they are synthetic jokes. The truth of the matter is that Faulkner does not believe the Snopeses are human enough to be taken seriously, and by now the "symbolic" pattern that you are supposed to see in the very name of Snopes has become a weak rubber stamp. I don't even believe that Faulkner sees the Snopeses as a causative agent in the decline of the old order; "Snopes" has become just a trade-mark, like the crazy family names in comic strips. The two Snopes brats who trick their grandfather back into the watermelon patch are simply the Katzenjammer kids.

The book is a string of anecdotes, some of which are worked up from old short stories, and it is dramatically so loose that it is plain that Faulkner himself has tired of the Yoknapatawpha saga. He does something here that he never did in any book before — he coyly serves up whole summaries of the saga to link this book with the others. In the past, he would offer such material not as "information" to the reader, but as the compulsive repetition of certain themes. And everybody out of his old books comes on stage in this one, as in the grand finale of a revue. It is a striking example of the loose, improvised, sometimes gagman quality of the book that the county attorney, Gavin Stevens, who figures so importantly in other Faulkner novels, here becomes a completely silly character, is constantly out of focus, and at times sounds more like a parody of Quentin Compson, the romantic intellectual in *The Sound and the Fury*, than like the sage, wise conscience of the old order that he was in other books.

And yet — tired, drummed-up, boring, often merely frivolous as *The Town* is — you can never forget that it comes from one of the most astounding literary imaginations in the modern world. As so often happens with a Faulkner book, one is conscious of Faulkner's own voice, of his unflaggingly passionate mind, above all, of his intense and brooding grief, as the most lifelike element in the book. The truth is not merely that *The Town* is a bad novel by a great writer, but also that Faulkner has less and less interest in writing what are called "novels" at all. It is significant that, despite his enormous influence on intellectuals, he means very little to many practicing novelists, and that professional storytellers often look upon him as a very queer duck indeed. Nor is it an accident that, of all the noteworthy American novelists of our time, the one most admired by Faulkner should be the self-centered Thomas Wolfe, who took the most "chances," or that Faulkner should constantly describe himself by the old-fashioned and generic name of "poet."

A better word for it would be soliloquizer. Just as one hears, louder and firmer than anyone else's, Faulkner's own voice, and with it those highly abstract words like "impervious" and "outrage" and "intractable" that flood into this book as regularly as the waves of the sea, so the episodes, the anecdotes, the jokes, even the characters, figure in *The Town* never as themselves but as devices to make points with. They are the dots and dashes, the punctuation marks, in his private unending soliloquy on the past. He is a man possessed, possessed not so much with his characters and incidents as with what they symbolize in his vision of things.

When he knows these characters well, or when he feels profound compassion for them, then he is magnificent; when he is concerned only with the symbol, his talk is abrasive and hysterical. And just as he can describe things only as a function of his own brooding meditation, so, in this book, the story is told by a succession of witnesses for whom everything is an illustration, a symbol, an example. He even needs two foreground observers, Gavin Stevens and the itinerant sewing-machine agent, V. K. Ratliff, to keep reporting to each other on the Snopeses, to keep outguessing each other on what Snopeses will do next, in order to retain the interminable brooding that is the very essence of Faulkner's mind and of the grief that fills it.

The grief is not over what the Snopeses have *done*. It is over a Southerner's constantly unavailing effort to make sense of history, to come to terms with the unexplained failure of the past. The Snopeses do not mean to Faulkner what they do to certain genteel Southerners who think of the past as "ruined" by a discernible lower-class enemy. Faulkner is not sentimental about the old order, and he shows, in this book, how the De Spains, the Stevenses, the Mallisons, the "old" families, have been only too eager to accommodate the Snopeses. But if the Snopeses do not figure in his mind as the devil in Southern history, they do indeed figure as the grotesque, the subhuman men, which his impatient, angry, irritable mind lights on as the generic illustration of what the South has come to.

One of the really compelling anecdotes in the book tells of the time that Flem Snopes had a whole house of furniture moved in on the promise that it would be fit for the "vice president of a bank." Flem didn't know anything about furniture, but the dealer understood him perfectly and shipped a whole house of furniture suitable to a vice president. It is no wonder that the Snopeses remind one of the freaks in comic strips: they have the same indistinguishable grotesqueness, the same horrible reality of modern men. They are symbols all right, not of a class but of a condition.

And the less Faulkner is able to understand this condition, the more he piles up the grotesqueness. He is talking to himself, trying to reason it all out. This is why, even when incidents are dragged out of old books, the characters renamed and the jokes refurbished, one feels, despite Faulkner's relaxed weariness with so old a tale, the immense, the still unspent, the inextinguishable power of his brooding concern. I am not saying that this power is enough to change *The Town* into a good novel. I am saying that it is a book with Faulkner's stamp and brand and fire all over it. One can be irritated with it, but not indifferent.

[1957]

William Faulkner: The Short Stories

FAULKNER's short stories are not of the kind that has made the *New Yorker* famous; they are not even the stories of a writer who often writes stories; many of them are not really "short stories" as that peculiarly contemporary branch of literature has been invented, patented, and mechanically imitated in the United States — tight, deft, wholly dramatic and polished fables of social life that present symbols rather than characters whose uniqueness is the prime concern of the writer. So little is Faulkner a short story writer, in fact, that several of these stories — and by no means the best! — were

Collected Stories of William Faulkner. New York: Random House.

written for the slicks: something that could never be done by the kind of short story writer who specializes in the art of the miniature, and for whom each short work has to be perfect.

Faulkner has often turned to the short story in order to relax. There is a hammy and grandiloquent side to his imagination — as well as to his rhetoric — a kind of sodden and mischievous looseness of manner that easily spills into his stories. It reminds me of W. C. Fields presiding over a banquet. One side of Faulkner's literary manner is that of the temperamental impresario presiding over his created world — a manner that recalls the gigantic confidence of Dickens and Balzac working away at their great blocks of marble. The fact that there is no other American novelist today who suggests such impressions to the reader is an instance of the power and breadth of Faulkner's imaginative world. Faulkner has an abiding sense that the whole human race can be fitted into his own native spot of Mississippi earth, no larger "than a postage stamp." The characters in these stories range from Indians on the old Mississippi frontier, who had *their* Negro slaves, down to Midwesterners who have been transplanted from their frontier into houses, in Southern California, backed "into a barren foothill combed and curried into a cypress-and-marble cemetery dramatic as a stage set and topped by an electric sign in red bulbs which, in the San Fernando valley fog, glared in broad sourceless ruby as though just beyond the crest lay not heaven but hell."

As such fiercely inimical phrases suggest, Faulkner pays out steady moral judgment on all that has unfolded in his *comédie humaine* of American life. Moving from the Indian swamps to Hollywood (past the South before and after the war, the clash of the poor Snopeses with the haughty De Spains and Sartorises, the young aviators in the Royal Flying Corps, traveling air circuses in the 1920s), the reader has a constant sense, in Faulkner's work, not of "America" but of world history on this soil, from the time when "New Orleans was a European city." A whole procession of races, clans, tribes, and classes moves through these stories, and you sense that you are reading not from story to story, from "gem" to "gem," as they say of collections by Katherine Anne Porter or J. D. Salinger or Hemingway (these are really virtuosi of the short story and perhaps exclusively of the story), but from anecdote to anecdote fallen from the novels that are themselves recurrent stories of what has happened on this "postage stamp" of land in Mississippi.

Of course there are stories in this collection, like "A Rose for Emily," that are famous anthology pieces — stories that show all too clearly how airily Faulkner can reproduce the manipulation of the reader's emotions that is the real aim of the commercial short story. "A Rose for Emily" is the story of the old maid who fell in love with a Northerner but resisted being jilted once too often; only after her death, when the curious townspeople were able to enter her house at last, did they discover that she had kept her dead lover in the bed where she had killed him after their last embrace. But even in "A Rose for Emily," the intended Gothic touch of horror counts less with Faulkner than the human drama of the Southern gentlewoman unable to understand how much the world has changed around her. And in a far greater story, "That Evening Sun," in which the characters are the Compson children from Faulkner's great novel, *The Sound and the Fury*, the emotion of the Negro servant, Nancy, who is pregnant by another man and lives in terror of being killed by her husband, is built up with such skill and communicates so well the bewilderment and anxiety of the children themselves (Quentin, the oldest, is the narrator) that the terror of the woman becomes the atmospheric center of the story, communicating itself to the children as the first absolute fact they must learn to recognize.

"That Evening Sun" begins with a description of "old" Jefferson in the days when Negro laundresses still walked about carrying baskets of wash on their heads, and were able to stoop under fences without dropping their load. And the use of this opening comes back to us when young Quentin describes Nancy telling a story to him and the children — ". . . like she was living somewhere else, waiting somewhere else. She was outside the cabin. Her voice was inside and the shape of her, the Nancy that could stoop under a barbed wire fence with a bundle of clothes balanced on her head as though without weight, like a balloon, was there."

This concern with emotion as a fact in itself, virtually an absolute, that stands apart from history and survives it — this is nowhere more pronounced than in "Red Leaves," probably the high point of this collection. An Indian chief has died, and his Negro slave, knowing that by custom the dog, the horse, and the body servant of a chief must be buried with him, runs off to the swamp. Faulkner indulges in a certain amount of mischievous humor, Southern white man's humor, at the expense of Negro slaves. With his marvelous sense of costume, he describes an old Indian, barefoot, in a long linen frock coat and a beaver hat, busily complaining that "This world is going to the dogs. It is being ruined by white men. We got along fine for years and years, before the white men foisted their Negroes upon us. In the old days the old men sat in the shade and ate stewed deer's flesh and corn and smoked tobacco and talked of honor and grave affairs; now what are we to do? Even the old wear themselves into the grave taking care of them that like sweating." And the torpid, tubby Indians go after the runaway with a kind of sadness — they are vaguely sorry for him, but sorrier that he cannot understand and accept fully the ritual that obliges him to be buried with his master, thus putting Indians to exertions that are undignified and useless. These Indians are philosophical-minded, yet they are so detached in their fatalism (the world moves as it must and men must die) that they can insist on their ritual without, as it were, having to respect it. The Negro slave, by contrast, is portrayed as *misunderstanding* his proper function as a man; he seems to find satisfaction in the exertion of flight itself (as does Joe Christmas in *Light in August*). When he gets panicky, he identifies himself with the animals in the woods, and all in all is shown operating on a level that causes the Indians to shake their heads. Yet as in his great novel, *Light in August*, Faulkner rises above these reflections on the race his own class so long held in servitude; the story ends on a concentrated image of the slave, begging for water before his end and unable to swallow it. On capturing the slave, who had nowhere to run but back home again, this Indian had said, "Come. You ran well. Do not be ashamed." Now he simply says, in a final, not unkindly order — "Come." It is a marvelous story, and not the least for the sense of fatality in human affairs that unites the Negro and Indian at last; this sense of what *must be* is always the deepest element in Faulkner's imaginative sense of things.

Perhaps it is this quality that interests me in a story, "Beyond," that is admittedly slight and even a bit forced in emotion. But Faulkner, portraying a dead father who in a brief interlude of consciousness after death has been searching for his son, who died at ten, has the man say, ". . . anyway, there is a certain integral consistency which, whether it be right or wrong, a man must cherish because it alone will ever permit him to die." At times, as in the story "The Tall Men," this classical understanding in Faulkner, his insistence on the supremacy of character over everything, tends to get propagandized. In this story an old Southern law officer says to a stranger: "Yes, sir. A man gets around and he sees a heap; a heap of folks in a heap of situations. The trouble is, we done got into the habit of confusing the situations with the folks." And Faulkner practically smirks as the old fellow says it. Still, the fact remains: it *is* "folks," not "situations," that make up the real life of fiction. "Situations" make short stories, but "folks" make life. Faulkner is interested in "folks." No wonder that his interest sometimes gets too big for the mold to which stories are fitted.

[1961]

Graham Greene and the Age of Absurdity

IN 1943 I saw a draftee, in a long line of men waiting in their underwear for an Army physical, reading Graham Greene's *The Confidential Agent*. It was a perfect book for the occasion, since it is possible to ignore almost anything while reading it; and since it deals with a much-troubled Loyalist agent in England during the Spanish Civil War, it was still highly suitable to the times. Graham Greene's "entertainments," as he now calls books like *The Confidential Agent* and *The Ministry of Fear*, to distinguish them from his later "serious" novels, reflected perfectly the pervasive anxiety of the Hitler-Mussolini age. In these thrillers the average man, the muddled and anxious man who usually appears in Greene's fiction as if he had stepped in a grimy mackintosh out of a London tube station, personified everyone's feeling of dread before the inhuman monsters of Nazism-Fascism. At the same time, the Greene hero personified that acute and enigmatic sense of guilt, usually arising

Our Man in Havana, by Graham Greene. New York: Viking.

from some surprising passion in his personal life, which so often made one irrationally feel that Hitler-Mussolini expressed the dark side of *everyone's* nature.

The sense of guilt is the essential theme of all Greene's fiction. It explains the chase after the hero in his "entertainments," and as the aftermath of adultery it results in the inner struggle on the brink of damnation that is the stuff of supposedly more "serious" books like *The Heart of the Matter* and *The End of the Affair*. The protagonists in both the entertainments and the novels are essentially decent and haunted human beings who are led into sins of violence and despair by the unexpectedness of some human attachment. They are fools, martyrs and clowns of love, and through their love we see parallel lines — love for a human person, love of the divine law — that cannot meet in time. In the nightmare world of the 1930s and 1940s, a man had good reason to connect his personal guilt with the even now incredible sadism of Hitler. When governments can turn civilized society into a literal hell on earth, it is hard for the average man, with his conventional share of original sin, not to feel that the world has been turned, in a bad dream, into the ministry of fear.

The Hitler period marked the high point of Greene's entertainments and concealed, because of its psychological pressure, the essentially hysterical personal emotions that Greene was able to whip up. He was able to find dramatic symbols for states of anxiety and dread because of his concern with plot, a neglected element in contemporary fiction. The Hitler age made for melodrama, the spy chase. In his later "serious" novels, Greene betrayed the subjectivity of his thinking by trying to make plots out of the complex moral dialectic of sin itself — the non-Catholic reader of *The Heart of the Matter* and *The End of the Affair* is embarrassed as well as baffled to find himself being invited to take points of doctrine as if they were universally accepted dramatic actions. As George Orwell complained, Greene, "by trying to clothe theological speculations in flesh and blood," produces psychological absurdities. Nevertheless, the plight of husbands and wives who fall passionately in love with people they are not married to furnishes in Greene's "serious" books the same authentic sense of imminent damnation that Hitler and Mussolini did in his scary "entertainments."

With *Our Man in Havana*, which is advertised as a new entertainment, we can see that the Khrushchev-Dulles age lends itself not to dread but to farce. Our plight is now so universal and at the same time so unreal that the age of anxiety has turned into the age of absurdity. The Greene hero has not changed. He is still defeated, sad, and the clown of love: an Englishman who sells vacuum cleaners in Havana, he was deserted by his wife and left with a young daughter to bring up. Like all true Greene protagonists, he feels guilty because *he* was deserted. That is the characteristic bit of adult psychology that one always finds in a Greene novel.

But otherwise, what a change is this! The engrossing nightmare thrillers of the 1930s and 1940s have turned giggly and empty. Formerly, a man became a spy for a cause he did not *quite* believe in because he was trapped by his own guilt, his sense of his human inadequacy. But now, Mr. Wormold (Worm-mold? — the average man and his destiny couldn't be more explicitly conveyed) accepts an invitation from the British secret service in order to accumulate a dowry for his pretty daughter. Our anti-hero is recruited in the men's room; the code book is Lamb's *Tales from Shakespeare* (the director for the Caribbean couldn't find duplicate copies of anything else except *Uncle Tom's Cabin*). Mr. Wormold industriously goes to work, collecting wages and expenses from London for wholly fictitious agents and for reports largely rewritten from the Latin-American section of *Time* and information bulletins put out by the Cuban government. In a rare moment of inspiration, Mr. Wormold thinks up and draws the plans of a superbomb that reminds his chief in London of a vacuum cleaner, but of course he cannot get away with it. This is not because London doubts him but because rival spies also take him seriously. This leads to murder, a chase, and to the final clinch between Mr. Wormold and the assistant sent out from London — a lady who left her husband because he was permanently in conference at UNESCO. When she discovers the deception Mr. Wormold has practiced on the British government, she realizes that he is priceless. "Do you think that I would ever have left Peter if once — just once — he'd made a fool of UNESCO? But UNESCO was sacred. Cultural conferences were sacred. He never laughed."

You are all expected to laugh with *Our Man in Havana*. But Mr. Greene still has strong feelings. The wicked police chief in Havana, who carried a cigarette case made of human flesh, "squeezed out a smile. It seemed to come from the wrong place, like toothpaste when the tube splits." The preposterous secret-service chief in London wears a black monocle over a glass eye. The eye itself is "pale blue and unconvincing; it might have come out of a doll which said 'Mama.'" These feelings are directly expressed in his lady's tribute to Mr. Wormold. "I don't care a damn about men who are loyal to the people who pay them. . . . There are many countries in our blood . . . but only one person. Would the world be in the mess it is if we were loyal to love and not to countries?" This is significant doctrine, but to use it against material — the cold war — that is portrayed as essentially meaningless can be dangerous. Mr. Greene has never believed that anything but love is significant. Once the times concealed this from him — from us — by lending him something really terrible to write about. In the age of terror, melodrama made sense. In the age of absurdity, a farce like this is just petty. It hardly exists.

[1958]

Edward Hopper

IN THE DAYS when Manhattan Bridge was still open to pedestrians, when you could make your way across the great central promenade of Brooklyn Bridge without being taken hostage, when nothing in this world was such a gift as the light over the East River bursting into a BMT car and breaking up the boredom, I would regularly make my way from "New York" to Brooklyn with the feeling that these halves of my life were joined not by ceaseless daily travel but by images drawn from New York paintings.

I did not know I loved New York, I did not know there was a New York to love more than a neighborhood, until I saw it in museums. The trouble with growing up in a Brooklyn tenement was not so much that you were poor — there was nothing but other people's poverty to compare yours with — but that the struggle for existence made everything else seem trivial, unworthy. The city fell on me every day like so much rain, but I was unconscious of the subtler impressions it was making. Why was the dome of a certain savings bank — it bulked on the horizon like a cathedral as the subway moved into the open across Manhattan Bridge — so dramatic? Why, long before I saw the photographs of Alfred Stieglitz and Joseph Stella's clotted bridge portraits, did the crisscrossing supports of Brooklyn Bridge haunt me? Why did the rows of brownstones just south of Washington Square and west of Fifth Avenue seem to me more healing and comforting than any image of green fields?

I had no positive city images of my own until I discovered John Sloan in the old American Wing of the Metropolitan, Reginald Marsh in the old Whitney Museum on Eighth Street, forgotten old prints of Columbia Heights in the Brooklyn Museum. New York painters seemed to love the city more than New York writers did; they were as romantically tuned into the passing show as fashion photographers. Fondly colored impressions of the crowds at rush hour under the old El. Brownstones and the old, low, red-brick storefronts. Decorative stone, wire, glass whose actual weight in the city had always hit me like a blow. The rooftops where the toughies in my neighborhoods trained racing pigeons, and where undernourished Jewish featherweights sparred on the gravel before they got knocked out in the ring at Canarsie. The roof edges across which I had actually seen cops chase robbers. The air shafts and chimney pots that were so "pictorial" in paintings, but sweetly overlooked what I knew as the subway huddle, the heat, the reports by terrified storekeepers of being threatened by Lepke Buchalter and Gurrah Schapiro of Murder, Inc. The unheard scream in the crowd when city marshals threw furniture out on the street during an eviction.

New York painters brought my chaotic secret impressions into the light. An unconscious watcher came to life one day and began to describe the city of his endless prowling. But of course these middle-class painters bravely facing the commonplace and the ugly were as sentimental about the city as our early painters were about mountains. They thought the grimy cheap-dress emporium Klein's on Union Square was so picture-worthy that it was almost beautiful. My favorite memory of Klein's was a crude drawing just inside the store of a weeping girl behind bars: "Don't Bring Disgrace to Your Family by Shoplifting!" I was amused by Reginald

Marsh's bouncy ballets of shoppers along Fourteenth Street. Someone had actually painted Fourteenth Street instead of just barely surviving it — as my father did when at his local of the Brotherhood of Painters and Decorators he once in his life voted against the union despot — a charmer known even to his family as "Jake the Bum."

John Sloan blissfully reported Greenwich Village backyards neighborly with cats and laundry drying on the line, little boys building snowmen; a shadowy woman in the stern of a ferry boat; full-figured secretaries in red hats just released from the office and rollicking under the curve that the Sixth Avenue El made at Third Street. There was a certain hastiness to urban American painting that no doubt reflected the excited discovery of New York as a subject. Such paintings were humanly skimpy, broad in outline, easy to take. Even George Bellows's 1924 painting of Dempsey knocking Firpo out of the ring was as pleasant in its way as the Soyers paintings of meltingly lovable New York girls of the thirties sitting around an employment agency.

None of the people in New York paintings ever seemed to me more than a symbol, shakily sketched in with other symbols to afford you recognition. You know, the New York crowd! Like so many American social novelists, New York painters were more at home with a sweating muscle than with the puzzle of existence. But I was grateful for Henri, Glackens, Bellows, Luks; for the technical sophistication of Reginald Marsh and the idealism of John Sloan — they gave dignity to a New York I knew as harsh, merciless, exhausting. Time after time I would stand amazed, especially at the Metropolitan's old American Wing, by what a picture would bring home to me. Someone had seen a design in New York bridges and rooftops that locked my whirling city into frame after frame. A charm essentially wistful softened even the stabbing outlines of New York skyscrapers, made familiarity an esthetic fact. What the "Ashcan" fellows saw, now I could remember having seen.

There was one exception to all this cozy, picturesque, and literary painting of New York: Edward Hopper. Unlike so many American painters before and after World War II, "realist" and "abstract" alike, his work was not slapdash, hurried, theatrically self-conscious. The immensely tall, immensely quiet man I often saw walking in the Village and in the moors of South Truro on Cape Cod seemed tensely alone; he reminded me of Virginia Woolf's impression of Robinson Crusoe — "a man staring at a pot."

Hopper for me was like his unexpected paintings of solitary figures staring at the glass in New York bedrooms, coffee shops, offices. Perhaps he
had taken the advice of the philosopher Wittgenstein: "Don't think!
LOOK!" Yet you could not have guessed what he was looking at as the tall,
handsome, very North-European-looking man edged his way through
Washington Square Park. His figures never looked *through* the glass they
were facing. Their masked, identical, hawk-like faces were concentrated in
thought unavailable to everyone else, perhaps especially to themselves.

Hopper and Hopper's work lacked the audience-grabbing extremism that
disconcerts me when I enter any exhibition of late twentieth-century
American painting. "Hey Castelli! Hey Clem! Look what I'm into *this*
week!" The solidity of objects in his paintings was in contrast with the
evanescence of so much in urban *and* rural America; only Hopper could
have lived and worked in the same walkup on Washington Square for fif-
ty-four years. Yet he was hardly under the illusion that what he liked would
stay around. What saved him from the jitters of incessant replacement —
of people even more than of one's favorite buildings — was his not being
topical. He was not a "social" painter or thinker; he was happily free of
"ideas." What absorbed him in the course of a long life and arduous career
was concentrated on certain repetitious themes — a single figure in a bare
room, office, restaurant, theater; the shock of the Cape Cod light on white
shingled boards; bridges and roofs in the city without any figure in the picture to recall the unseen watcher brooding over the thickness and hardness
of these building materials. It was all beautifully "personal." As this most
unwilling talker among American painters admitted for the 1933 retrospective at the Whitney Museum — "My aim in painting has always been
the most exact transcription possible of my most intimate impressions of
nature."

This sounds like Emerson or Robert Frost, two of Hopper's favorite
writers. In the light of what Hopper actually achieved in such still reverberating works as *House by the Railroad* (1925), *Automat* (1927), *Chop
Suey* (1929), *Railroad Sunset* (1929), *Early Sunday Morning* (1930),
Room in Brooklyn (1932), *Nighthawks* (1942), *Sea Watchers* (1952), *Office
in a Small City* (1953) — among other works that show no essential difference in style or interest from 1924, when he was finally "recognized," to
his death in the late 1960s — it has to be said that, for once, a painter's
"big" statement describes exactly what this painter sought in the realm of
his own mind — and achieved.

Gail Levin, the Hopper curator at the Whitney Museum, says in her new book, *Edward Hopper: The Man and the Artist**, that Hopper carried in his wallet this quotation from Goethe: "The beginning and the end of all literary activity is the reproduction of the world that surrounds me by means of the world that is in me, all things being grasped, related, re-created, moulded and reconstructed in a personal form and an original form." This is the kind of high-flying claim for one's own sacred Me that is Emerson's bequest to American writers and painters. From Thoreau, who lived this, to Clyfford Still, who just talked it, Americans have never been able to resist the transcendentalist religion. But Hopper, as the haunting expressiveness of *places* in his work reveals (the people are something else), achieved a personal transaction with the exterior American world that everyone who looks at *Early Sunday Morning* or *House by the Railroad* or *Office in a Small City* can take back as an equally personal experience.

What happens in these paintings, what is *still* happening when I look at them, is that Hopper's mind has incorporated something "outside" into itself. And in such a way as to make one's intimate thinking, this sense we have of being occupied by nothing but our own consciousness, dominated and concentrated by a particular image in all the solidity and exactness available to our senses. Everything happens within and because of our single consciousness. What makes *Early Sunday Morning* or *House by the Railroad* "unique," "memorable," "haunting" is that the binding between Hopper and certain houses has become restrictive of everything else. Why, in *Early Sunday Morning* (Hopper did not call it that, but you can see why the absolute silence of the street would lead other people to think of Sunday in certain parts of New York), does the hydrant, the barber pole, the *row* of low red-brick houses that Hopper saw on lower Seventh Avenue have such depth? Why does the *bulk* of these humanless houses rivet us, finally tell us what the unseen watcher has so long, and unconsciously, seen in them? Why does that ornate, complicated Victorian house "by the railroad" so fascinate us? It is not because the thing is "typically American"; Thomas Benton, John Steuart Curry, even the more interesting Charles Burchfield whom Hopper typically admired, never painted anything with this thoroughness. The fascination of the best Hoppers is that in each work something outside of him has come to seem the style of his own perception. Just as philosophers discovered the nature of thinking

*New York: W.W. Norton and the Whitney Museum.

by realizing that we do not really "see" anything that does not resemble the innate form in which we think, so achievement in any art lies in the ability to recreate the "world" into something that the mind totally feels at home with — that it ultimately welcomes as a further aspect of itself.

The shining new American Wing at the Metropolitan Museum of Art contains Hopper's *Office in a Small City*. There is the usually decorous taut American figure in an office; the face gives away nothing of what it may have absorbed from its surroundings. I suspect the man has absorbed nothing. Hopper was an indifferent psychologist, far more interested in architecture than in the human drama contained in offices as well as bedrooms. (Even his bedrooms often show only one figure.) The figure in *Office in a Small City*, like so many of Hopper's duplicate figures, is there to stiffen the already tight concentration with which a section of the external building frames the office box and the man at his desk. The most remarkable detail in this picture is the great white rectangle into which the outside of the building has been concentrated, illuminated, purified. It bestrides the office itself with marvelous force.

The caption to this picture in the Metropolitan informs us that Hopper achieved "purely objective presentations of people and places, with no traces discernible of the way they made him feel. His observations are as impersonal as those of a camera lens. . . ." Of course no one, least of all the eye perched over a camera, achieves "purely objective presentations." Even painters who tried for the impersonality of a diagram or blueprint, like Charles Sheeler, were as personal as the rest of us. What is poignant in the caption is the typical American confusion between the personal in feeling and the personal in thought. Very few painters and writers and scientists get down to the irreducible and untranslatable experience of their own thought — of being able to keep what they alone have thought. Emerson wrote that in the works of others we recognize, too late, our own rejected thoughts. The only meaning of "originality" can be a mind that, like Hopper's, is unable to dodge the overwhelmingness of that white rectangle in *Office in a Small City*. In *Early Sunday Morning* Hopper could not rest with the amazement of total silence on lower Seventh Avenue. Hopper had to put that silence back into the hydrant, the barber pole, the horizontal low-lying bulk of that dark red row of houses.

For years after the war, walking every day past a certain stretch of dark red houses on Fulton Street in Brooklyn Heights, I was convinced that here and nowhere else was the street wrapped in early morning shadows that Hopper had seen. Even when I learned that Hopper had found his subject on lower Seventh Avenue, I claimed his wonderfully strong, concentrated mass of New York silence for Brooklyn and myself. *Early Sunday Morning* convinced me that there is telepathy between a picture and its viewer. The passage from Hopper's street to my mind moved me more than any other image of New York. It was the silence that got me, for it is just silence that a writer or painter, that unseen watcher, will live in for years — not even knowing all that he is thinking about when he is alone with a street.

Edward Hopper was an extraordinary event in this now feverish, overstimulated American art world. He was the real thing, the artist who becomes nothing but his vision of things. Scott Fitzgerald said that "taking things hard" gave him "the stamp that goes into my books so that people can read it blind like Braille." Hopper took things hard. I saw him without ever thinking to talk to him. He looked concentrated on his thought, working things out in the slowness and privacy of his mind; it seemed absurd to confront that tall, utterly reserved figure sitting with his wife Jo over a hamburger in Riker's on Seventh Avenue near Barrow Street. Hopper was never easy with himself and the American world that he made a piece of himself. He was in his early forties before he began to sell, was able to give up illustrating and to marry. To the end of his life in the walkup at 3 Washington Square North, where he doggedly carried up the coal to heat the potbellied stove in his studio, he remained the laborious, taciturn, frugal fellow from Nyack whose father was in dry goods and who had started out in Robert Henri's classes at the old New York School of Art. Hopper hated having to earn his living for so many years illustrating advertisements and magazine fiction when "what I wanted to do was to paint sunlight on the side of a house."

Eventually he became famous, a particular favorite of the Whitney Museum, where Lloyd Goodrich did so much to present and explain Hopper until the art world was ready for him. Hopper was shown at the Whitney Studio Club even before there was a Whitney Museum on Eighth Street. There was a whole series of one-man shows and retrospectives; a great new exhibition of Hopper opened at the Whitney in September 1980 based on Mrs. Hopper's bequest to the museum.

Jo Hopper died in 1968, a year after her husband; she kept a careful record of his work and she is very much in his work, for I learn from Gail

Levin's book that Jo insisted on posing for every female figure in his paintings. Theirs was a long, close, difficult marriage; Jo was a fellow-artist not
so talented and successful as her husband. She hated to cook, which is why
one so often saw the Hoppers in Village coffee shops and cheap restaurants. The tall, vaguely melancholy man preferred not to talk at all unless
he absolutely had to; the little woman with the ponytail never stopped.

What first startled me more than anything else in Hopper was the absence of the superficially drawn crowd that New York romantic realists
went in for. Even when a man and woman were shown together (and this
was Hopper's idea of a crowd), there was some unexplained tension between them. The couples in *Room in Brooklyn* (1932), in *Office at Night*
(1940), in *Hotel by a Railroad* (1952), in *Cape Cod Evening* (1939), are
joined only by a mysterious silence. Whether they are in bed *(Excursion
into Philosophy*, 1959), or in a theater virtually empty but for themselves
(Two on the Aisle, 1927), or seemingly relaxed with their dog *(Cape Cod
Evening)*, or grimly looking at the sea *(Sea Watchers)*, they are together
only in being stiffly alike. *Excursion into Philosophy* shows a man, dressed
and disconsolately sitting on the edge of a bed with a book, while behind
him the figure of a woman, outstretched with her back to him, indicates
some disappointment and rejection.

But most often in Hopper there is that famous single figure, often a nude
or partially undressed female, that has imposed on Hopper's work so many
associations with "loneliness." Apparently to be alone for a minute in this
country is to seem "lonely" — to others. Hopper complained that the
"loneliness thing was overdone." What obviously obsessed him was not
"loneliness" but the tautness (on the outside) of some deeply engrained
solitude. That taut single figure is a great theme and structural mystery in
Hopper's work; I have never been able to determine what the stiffly posing
figure and hooded face are expressing. Do they express solitude as an emotion in itself? Yet even the lovely pictures of a woman alone rejoicing in
Cape Cod sunshine are as facially inexpressive — or taciturn — as the
supposedly troubled woman in *Eleven A.M.* (1926). Hopper's self-portraits
are so warm and even buoyant that I suspect that in painting women he di-
luted his sympathy with old-fashioned decorum. *Everyone* in a Hopper
painting has decorum, even when alone.

Hopper's pictures have often been compared to stages: something is
about to happen. But he was no dramatist. What he generally gives us is a
repetition of bleak psychic exchange. I know that in *Office at Night* the

secretary standing in front of the file cabinet and her employer woodenly seated at his desk (she is looking straight at him but he is immersed in his papers) are supposed to be emotionally involved. But the involvement, if it exists because they are together after hours, does not get beyond some elementary tension. As in so many "dramas" in Hopper, they are silent and mysteriously grumpy. The rooms and the building and the roofs talk more than the people do, and talk *for* them.

This lack of plausible, interesting, or extensive human drama in Hopper is not a failure but it is a limitation. Hopper is a truly good painter, but no more than any other American painter is he a great one. His emotional world is too anxiously at a standstill. How often do we see his people looking at a window without our being able to say what they are looking for, or whether they are "looking" at all. The window is more interesting than they are. And through the window, beyond the building, the light is magnificent. O that Hopper light! He caught the peculiar need of it in the crowded city; he caught the relief of all that light when he got out of the city to Gloucester, Maine, and especially the Cape.

Looking at the happy shock of all that light at the water, we find ourselves thirsting for light as if it were water. Hopper is in an old American line — he is the poet-painter of our total physical environment, the immediate skin next to our own skin of habitations and weather. The people moving about in those buildings and in that weather are really part of them. They have no life apart from these "forces"; they are wholly submissive to their material lives. And that is an American story.

[1980]

The Happy Hour

MY CLASS in modern poetry meets in a classroom so noisy that it could just as well meet on the street corner outside in midtown New York. And it meets at the cocktail hour, or what other people enjoy as the "happy hour" — which means that students going straight from job to class stave off hunger pains with pretzels, coffee, pizza slices that invariably muck up *The Norton Anthology of Modern Poetry* and in the heat of class discussion often fall to the floor.

So what with the pounding from the dance class just over our heads, the screeching of ambulances down Lexington Avenue, and the almost desperate nibbling from six to eight, our weekly journey into the grand and haughty world of T.S. Eliot, Ezra Pound, Wallace Stevens may be a great experience in the end but on the spot feels hot, bothered, tense.

Poetry is not prose, so most people do not read it at all. Poetry is not prose, so it gets itself not so much read as studied: something special, formal, complex, and highly ordered, like one of the ancient languages. The more you go back in time, the more complex and difficult the structure of language becomes. Poetry is really an ancient language. Like other languages, it is even special to itself. Young people who are likely to become poets — they will be reading poetry for themselves, which is even more unusual than writing poetry — find themselves, as T.S. Eliot remembered about being a boy in St. Louis — "communicating" with a poem in a language they can't yet read. Real poetry is highly structured even in what is called free verse — poetry without a definite metrical arrangement. If there is no inner structure to the poem but just a typographical arrangement on the page, you get pseudo poetry. Robert Frost defined it as playing tennis without a net. Structure can be as different in its order and as subtle as the poet wishes. The essence of a poem, where it is deeply felt as a poem and not something that just looks like one, is the beat, the ongoing rhythm to the whole. This begins in the condensation, the marvelous compressiveness, that makes words in poetry stand, by their sheer sound, for more than words do elsewhere. When you put together the beat, the tight metrical frame, the rhymes, the parallelism of letters beginning on the same word, the repetition and echoing not only of word endings but of vowel sounds in the middle of words, you realize from these formalities how old poetry is, how long the art of poetry has been practiced by the human race.

The emphasis on an elaborate pattern of sound tells us that poetry was recited long before people could read it. It is more natural to remember poetry than it is a piece of prose, for the mind falls into the pattern. The art of memorizing often depends on turning a piece of technical information into rhythm and rhyme. Poetry always begins in some state of inner awareness that asks for public expression. So the arrangement and repetition of sounds in poetry even correspond to our awareness of the heart thudding, our lungs expanding, the different ways in which when walking, dancing, jogging, climbing, making love, we move our hands and feet in a pattern that is somehow expected. To satisfy that expectation gives us pleasure. The most elemental things in life — poetry may be just that — are more formal, more elaborately designed, than we are aware of as we perform them.

Poetry is old, so old that a poem written today may recall stages of human growth that the individual can hardly remember in himself. Poetry is a sense in the body, like music and dance. Poetry is positively physiological at times, as a famous physician and poet, Oliver Wendell Holmes, showed in the connections between the stress of traditional iambic (tee TUM) and the binary rhythm of the heart. Poetry can have such emotional effects that sudden tears, twitching, even momentary disorientation, are associated with certain poems. The poet A.E. Housman said that "Experience has taught me, when I am shaving of a morning, to keep watch over my thoughts, because, if a line of poetry strays into my memory, my skin bristles so that the razor ceases to act. . . . The seat of this sensation is the pit of the stomach." Emily Dickinson said: "If I read a book and it makes my whole body so cold no fire can ever warm me, I know that is poetry. If I feel physically as if the top of my head were taken off, I know that is poetry. These are the only ways I know it. Is there another way?"

Yes, Emily, there is another way of reading poetry. Especially by people who have never read poetry for pleasure, poetry by themselves, and so are as afraid of it as if it were a totally foreign language. And then there is the problem of "modern" (meaning deliberately obscure) poetry. Although Shakespeare is far more brilliant, subtle, and complex than any mod poet, people lightly assume that Shakespeare, being over three hundred years dead, is more "regular" than, say, E.E. Cummings. The people who now automatically accept the distortion of the human face and figure in a Picasso will frown and suffer at encountering in E.E. Cummings lines like

my father moved through dooms of love
through sames of have through haves of give. . . .

Cummings is just being witty — which poetry is particularly good at — about the obvious fact that loving can be suffering. But the more you love (or so he says) the more you have. Cummings is consciously mod, innovative, provocative. He means to startle you; so the reader who *thinks* that Shakespeare is as familiar to him as the American flag cries out that Cummings is a bad boy, is "fresh," is something new. In fact, most of

Cummings is sentimental, and the "something new" is on the same order as an advertising copy writer's trying by some desperate arrangement of lines to get your attention.

Another and unexpected difficulty in the reading of "modern poetry" is that writing the damned stuff is now often more popular than reading it. Poetry has become a favorite nostrum or therapy in this narcissistic age. I have looked into the matter carefully and can report that there are now 2,578,000 more poets in the United States, Argentina, and the Western Isles of Scotland than there were thirty-five years ago. The poet Philip Levine, who teaches the writing of poetry, read a famous English poem to his class and was reproached by a student: "I paid to have my own poetry read." I discovered in the Soviet Union amiably undistinguished fellows who called themselves "poet" on their visiting cards.

Although my students get a furrowed, bothered look of anxious attention each time a new poem comes up by a famously "difficult" poet, it is also true that modern poetry is "in." Certain poets are legends, as famous and as public as the Beatles. By now E.E. Cummings's typographical funnies are as well known as Doonesbury. Dylan Thomas as public performer, public drunk, and interloper in many a faculty bedroom was an even bigger media event that the Bob Zimmerman who in homage to the poet became Bob Dylan. Robert Frost, a "failure" and virtually unpublished until he was forty, became so famous and domineering that he publicly stamped on other people's books. "Everybody" knows by now that T.S. Eliot's first wife was unstable, that Ezra Pound broadcast incoherent anti-Semitic tirades on the Italian Fascist radio, that Wallace Stevens was the vice-president of a Hartford insurance company. In the sixties Allen Ginsberg and his slovenly beard decorated more posters and were featured at more youth rallies than now seems believable. I once heard James Dickey talk — mostly about his Harley Davidson motorcycle — to an audience of college girls who squealed all through the performance as if they were being hopped up by a rock band.

But is the *poetry* of certain poets as well-known as their faces, their marriages, their drinking? Often the poetry is (in the sense of being identified with a point of view, a certain glamour) the legend of the poet's intellectual difference from ordinary mortals. But the poem alone, the poem in itself, is often mysterious. *April is the cruelest month*, the first line of *The Waste Land*, is now as much a part of the language as *Four score and seven years ago*. By the 1940s a boy-meets-girl movie actually had the boy saying *April is the cruelest month* as if he had thought of it himself. But is *The Waste Land*, that famous poem of our human climate published almost sixty years ago, a poem which has been explicated, discussed, taught, wrung dry for every possible symbol and meaning as if it were the Bible or the dark soul of Richard Nixon — is *The Waste Land* read for itself alone, is it faced head on? *Can* the poem alone be approached and enjoyed with the same confidence with which we make ourselves familiar with T.S. Eliot the famous poet? T.S. Eliot the legendary American expatriate who became a British subject — and an Anglo-American institution? T.S. Eliot without whom no anthology of modern poetry could exist? The T.S. Eliot whom until very recently every "English professor" in the country dreamed of night and day because ELIOT had, simply, become the biggest name in the business?

The Waste Land is easy to read but hard to follow. Eliot did not mean it to be so hard to follow. He did not mean it to be particularly anything but the poem it eventually became. But he alone did not make it what it eventually became. When Eliot wrote it he worked at Lloyd's Bank in London; he was an exhausted, anxious man; anxious about his difficult wife Vivienne, anxious about his own sexuality. He had cut himself off from his very proper parents in St. Louis; or rather his father had cut him off for marrying an English girl of doubtful sanity. In addition to all these personal stresses and family estrangements, Eliot was an overworked reviewer, he had the beginnings of lung disease, and he suffered from what he himself called mental blackouts. While still in England, he had tried to join the U.S. Navy and was rejected for medical reasons. At war's close he was in such a bad way that Ezra Pound in London raised money to send Eliot to a Swiss sanitorium. He came back with a long, rather indiscriminate manuscript which Pound (a great critic and always shrewder about other people's poetry than his own) edited with such perfect instinct for the emotional suffering that is the real burden of the poem that *The Waste Land* as we know it has been taken ever since as a masterpiece of form, compression, subtlety.

Now Eliot was anything but a "confessional" poet in the style to be made famous after another war by Robert Lowell in *Life Studies*, Allen Ginsberg in *Kaddish*, Sylvia Plath in *Ariel*. Eliot (already famous as a critic for advocating an "impersonal" anti-Romantic poetry) managed with a lot of highfalutin notes and quotations to persuade his baffled audience that *The Waste Land* was the same nihilistic postwar landscape that Hemingway

was writing about in *In Our Time* and Spengler in *The Decline of the West*.
In point of fact Eliot was writing about his own troubled self as one version
of a half-destroyed and increasingly meaningless civilization. The
"dryness" that is an obsessive refrain in the poem is sexual, sterile, and yet
a dryness of the heart, a lack of feeling, that is reflected generally in the indifference of the urban mechanism that is one setting of the poem. Eliot
was writing about a fragmented world, one that has divided man from his
past, from his God, from his deepest instincts for union and continuity. At
the center of the poem was the troubled mind and heart of an expatriate
American made rootless against his will and against his deepest beliefs —
but cut off from country, family, and from an unstable wife whose staccato
reproaches, we know now, can be heard in such haunting passages as

"My nerves are bad tonight. Yes, bad. Stay with me.
Speak to me. Why do you never speak. Speak.
What are you thinking off? What thinking? What?
I never know what you are thinking. Think."

   The Waste Land is a great poem, an unforgettable reading experience, a
symphony of assorted human sounds, references, quotations from classical
literature, French, Italian, old English plays, all pressed out of Eliot's
mind. The poem works on us as some irresistible discord — a succession
of fragments that becomes a mysterious striving within ourselves to elimi-
nate fragmentation, to reach the unity we also despair of. There is a chorus
of different voices within ourselves: that is the life of the poem. Out of
these many voices and what is seemingly the most scattered materials we
get a fascinated sense that something is happening to us, *in* us as we read.
What is happening recurs within the larger context of human memory and
dissolution. Something great and yet awful is happening; whole worlds of
experience are turning over in our heads. The prime image may be dryness, desolation; but what presses on us as we read, what creates the experience of *The Waste Land* is not sadness at all but the sense of a procession. We are on our way elsewhere. We are being moved to that other land
where we will feel, yes, positively redeemed because this poetry will show
us, as only poetry can, that our feelings are significant because they express
so much more than ourselves.

What are the roots that clutch, what branches grow
Out of this stony rubbish? Son of man,

You cannot say, or guess, for you know only
A heap of broken images, where the sun beats,
And the dead tree gives no shelter, the cricket no relief,
And the dry stone no sound of water. Only
There is shadow under this red rock,
(Come in under the shadow of this red rock),
And I will show you something different from either
Your shadow at morning striding behind you
Or your shadow at evening rising to meet you;
I will show you fear in a handful of dust.

What happens in following the procession of these lines is a return to a past that is less our individual past than it is some haunting memory of the race. Rilke said that poetry is the past that breaks out in our hearts. No individual secret is revealed here; no preceding tension is unloosed. But it is "a heap of broken images," the words and then the lines in series, the cumulative voice of their steady tread, that brings us back. The effect is enchantment, an unloosening. We *have* somehow made our way to another land. And we move about in this land to the irresistible rhythm that is the life of poetry.

Enchantment: to get away, to move, to escape into. Only this world is our inner world. In some way we have connected with our own "stream of consciousness," as William James first called it, through the rapidly alternating voices, the shifting metaphors. *Metaphor* literally means "transfer." And as the words transfer, shift the same *emotional* "message" from image to image, we are not only turned back into an inner world of dryness, lament, and striving but we have the happy sense of being able to hold many things in our minds at once.

A narrative in prose can't help being as straight ahead as a ruler: word after word, sentence after sentence, scene. Writing fiction, Saul Bellow once lamented, is like pushing a peanut up a hill with your nose. Poetry is more a matter of condensing words, packing each one in, then laying them out in a pattern that will have the rhetorical effect that comes from such intense compression and arrangement. Words as pattern are what immediately structure a poem. But what makes the accumulating *lines* in *The Waste Land* so effective is that the rhythm they start up in our minds gives us a terrific sense of mental power and freedom. Springing up with these words, we accomplish many different experiences; we move at ease through many echoes and issues.

The Waste Land is a successful epic poem. There is the marvelous sense in reading a real epic of moving through unexpected space, of being a con- quistador of new worlds. This feeling was put gloriously by Keats in his gratitude for discovering Homer even in translation:

Oft of one wide expanse had I been told
That deep-brow'd Homer ruled as his demesne;
Yet never did I breathe its pure serene
Till I heard Chapman speak out loud and bold:
Then felt I like some watcher of the skies
When a new planet swims into his ken;
Or like stout Cortez when with eagle eyes
He stared at the Pacific — and all his men
Looked at each other with a wild surmise —
Silent, upon a peak in Darien.

During the "happy hour" my students may not be drinking anything stronger than Coke. But the effect on them of certain lines in *The Waste Land* is sometimes stronger than a joint:

The river's tent is broken: the last fingers of leaf
Clutch and sink into the wet bank. The wind
Crosses the brown land, unheard. The nymphs are departed.
Sweet Thames, run softly, till I end my song.
The river bears no empty bottles, sandwich papers,
Silk handkerchiefs, cardboard boxes, cigarette ends
Or other testimony of summer nights. The nymphs are departed.
And their friends, the loitering heirs of city directors —
Departed, have left no addresses.
By the waters of Leman I sat down and wept.
Sweet Thames, run softly till I end my song,
Sweet Thames, run softly, for I speak not loud or long.
But at my back in a cold blast I hear
The rattle of the bones, and chuckle spread from ear to ear.

Elsie the brown-faced refugee from "mainland China" confesses herself at this point to be "shook." Dominic from Staten Island says "I feel it right here" and admits to being a little "scared." Why scared, Dominic? Shakes his head; this has become a matter too personal to discuss with Teacher. Myra, who teaches English in a Bronx high school and is taking "my

Master's" so that she can get a needed "augmentation of income" (Myra talks very genteel) knows that these lines contain quotations from 1) a marriage hymn by Edmund Spenser, 2) the Old Testament, 3) an address to his "coy mistress" by Andrew Marvell. Myra points out to the class that *But at my back in a cold blast I hear* is a parody of Marvell's *But at my back I always hear/Time's winged chariot hurrying near.*

And why, dear students, is parody not funny but indeed "scary," especially when Mr. Eliot goes on to say

But at my back from time to time I hear
The sound of horns and motors, which shall bring
Sweeney to Mrs. Porter, in the spring.
O the moon shone bright on Mrs. Porter
And on her daughter.
They wash their feet in soda water.

Are you a bit "scared" because the passage has something underhand to say about some worsening in your lives, some subtle falling off? As when you wake up in the morning after a night of vague heavy dreams, then feel yourself unable to throw off this mood for hours? In the night your mind went on some mysterious back road. Now you are in the "ordinary" world, as they call it. But Eliot reminds you that *your* world is never ordinary. All your life, whether waking or asleep, you have been besieged by dreams, fragments of popular sayings, memories, griefs, stifled outcries pasted chaotically together in no discernible order. In fact, the faces look like cutouts. In fact, so much has happened to us all, is happening right now, is forever going on, that without the compression and positive implosion that are the life of poetry, we overburdened but all-too-distractible creatures would not be able, ever, to do justice to the actual fury with which our minds work on our experience.

A famous French scholar said "words are poetic insofar as they condense their own history." Most people use words as if they were currency — and devalued at that. Here is a word, give me *that* in exchange! To a real poet like Eliot words are not giveaways, not transferable like dollar bills. They have an independent power. The source of that power, of the mysterious ability of words to break up what Kafka called "the frozen sea within us"? Words accomplish transaction with another mind. We somehow *know* by unconscious signals from Eliot what is in his mind. We read him with emotional comprehension because we share certain states of feeling. These "states" chime and *reverberate* in us when certain words are short or long enough, when certain sounds echo each other irresistibly in rhyme —

After the torchlight red on sweaty faces
After the frosty silence in the gardens
After the agony in stony places
The shouting and the crying
Prison and palace and reverberation
Of thunder of spring over distant mountains

In the end, *The Waste Land* is a poem about "history" as well as a poem that issues from the "agony in stony places" of T.S. Eliot. And what is astonishing to my New York class is that Eliot the famous and indeed immaculate reactionary who detested Jews and probably did not worry over blacks should make himself so satisfactory to them. Certain emotions make us kin. What troubles my class is not Eliot's views but the fact that they themselves come with such difficulty to the ancient language of poetry. With little Latin and less Greek, no real knowledge of history, no foreign languages to speak of, my students have to grope their way to knowledge. A great poet makes them feel uneducated; poetry beckons them to itself, will ultimately make them feel right at home. But just now, they tend in poetry's ceremonial presence to feel that with so much to learn about art, art does not care for them, does not need them. And so they definitely, oh my yes! feel "alienated." And are ideological as hell.

You would think that this makes them suckers for some simpleminded populist poet, some ranter of slogans like Carl Sandburg or Le Roi Jones. Or that a poet like Eliot, evidently tortured by guilt and impotence, should be boring or contemptible to youngish people for whom the sexual revolution is the only real revolution that ever was or ever will be. Not a bit of it! Eliot speaks to them not because they know his "politics" or care a hang about his "racism," but because *The Waste Land*, written out of some immense personal desperation — "To me it was only the relief of a personal and wholly insignificant grouse against life; it is just a piece of rhythmical grumbling" — is in fact an evident link to the mayhem, murdering, and terrorizing that scream at us every day from every headline.

Why the connection Eliot makes between me and the fragmented world outside (of politics, religion, every traditional loyalty)? Why, when I distrust his snobbery and resent, even fear, so many of the formal opinions he expressed in his lifetime, should I (like my students) tremble a little when we come to Part V of *The Waste Land*, "What the Thunder Said":

What is that sound high in the air
Murmur of maternal lamentation
Who are these hooded hordes swarming
Over endless plains, stumbling in cracked earth
Ringed by the flat horizon only
What is the city over the mountains
Cracks and reforms and bursts in the violet air
Falling towers
Jerusalem Athens Alexandria
Vienna London
Unreal

"Hooded hordes swarming" could indeed be those Iranian masses howling in unison and stabbing their arms up to the sky who turned my heart to jelly when I watched them every evening on television. The world *has* turned flat. We can now see so much of it at once, too much! *What is the city over the mountains/Cracks and reforms and bursts in the violet air?* That is us! And the Western world we have depended on without thinking that it could fail — that world is indeed now one of "falling towers." How clever of Eliot to call the roll of the great and falling cities without naming New York, the city that is the supreme marketplace of Western culture, but is increasingly full of people for whom the city at large is not their city, for whom the country surrounding the city does not exist, who live like animals tied up in a cage, staring at the people staring at them?

Something is definitely wrong. It is a wrongness that makes us tired, connects with the many ambulances outside, to Dominic from Staten Island, to Elsie the brown-faced refugee from "mainland China," to the black lady who comes to class all the way from Paterson, New Jersey, to the little lady so heavily lipsticked that the stuff has swallowed up her buttoned-up mouth.

Something is wrong with our culture, and therefore wrong in ourselves. Exactly what is wrong Eliot will not tell us. As Othello said so wildly as he entered Desdemona's bedroom to strangle her, "It is the cause, the cause." *What* is caused is a heavy consciousness, a sense of being in the wrong. The heart beating in us is one that we alone hear; the world that is so fantastically different for each one of us — if we only knew this! — makes each of us a different world. Poetry is one of the few things by which we enter, really enter, into the mind of another.

> I have heard the key
> Turn in the door once and turn once only
> We think of the key, each in his prison
> Thinking of the key, each confirms a prison...

Yet if each is a prison and we are all so different, why do we respond to Eliot so much the same way, virtually in chorus when the evening really gets going! Why, once we get some lines under our belts, do we feel so relieved of one world and so charged up with another? We are happy as the class ends, we are excited and tired, we are strangely together —

Gaily, to the hand expert with sail and oar
The sea was calm, your heart would have responded
Gaily, when invited, beating obedient
To controlling hands...

And fragment for fragment that we are, living in fragments, we also know, after *The Waste Land,* that some things will never be the same.

[1980]

V
Famous Since the War

The Southern "City of the Soul"

FAULKNER once wrote that "For every Southern boy fourteen years old, not once but whenever he wants it, there is the instant when it's still not two o'clock on that July afternoon in 1863, the brigades are in position behind the rail fence, the guns are laid and ready in the woods . . . and it's all in the balance, it hasn't happened yet." But after he has passed fourteen, a Southern boy who is unusually sensitive and intelligent and lives in an age like ours may find it impossible to dream back to that moment when it was all revocable. The legacy of the war has become all too real, and the contrast with what Southern hotheads once hoped for it can be torturing. No wonder that, like Faulkner's greatest characters, so many honest and intelligent contemporary Southern writers seem to be engaged in a wrathful quarrel with themselves — as if, with their moving sense of responsibility, they were both the past and the present, both the South that they love and the North that as intellectuals they find it easier to live in. No longer is it possible for *them* to pretend that "it's all in the balance, it hasn't happened yet." For Southern writers with this painful attachment to the past, all too much has happened, and the attempt to be morally equal to the present can be wearing. Sometimes the only way out of the circle of defeat, disillusionment, and guilt is a certain mordancy about human nature in general, an impatient cry that one should not have expected too much of people anyway.

An active sense of disillusionment, an insistence that human nature is flawed, endlessly paradoxical, and in a very real sense untrustworthy, recurs rather insistently in Robert Penn Warren's novels and poems and essays. Both in the character and in the political philosophy of Willie Stark, governor of a state very much like Louisiana, it became the theme and furnished the plot of Warren's best-known work, *All the King's Men*; even the title, *Brother to Dragons*, of Warren's book in verse about the sickening butchery of

The Legacy of the Civil War: Meditations on the Centennial, by Robert Penn Warren. New York: Random House.

a slave by a Virginian related to Thomas Jefferson told of his quarrel with Jefferson's eighteenth-century "illusions" about human nature. To judge from the recurring scene in Warren's novels of
lovers guiltily expecting to be discovered, his harsh concern with guilt
seems to be psychological as well as historical — and in fact
Warren's more recent novels have replaced with "Freudian" explanations what in his first and perhaps best novel, *Night Rider*,
was presented in theological terms.

But whatever changes of philosophical emphasis Warren has made
over the years — in this new book he conveys his own belief as
"pragmatism" — the theme of his work always comes to me as a
complaint against human nature. So much do I hear it as a complaint rather than as a positive point of view that I associate it
with some cherished innocence that has been destroyed. Just as
Warren has written one of his most famous poems directly about
original sin, so all his work seems to deal with the Fall of Man.
And if in reading Warren's books I have come to be more and
more wary of his handling of this theme, it is because of the
nostalgia that it conveys, the strident impatient language with which
it is expressed, the abstract use to which it is put. To complain in
every book that man is a brother to dragons, that "it's human to
be split up," that human nature is full of "bitter paradoxes" — this,
though not for me to disprove in our baleful times, seems to me not
the attitude of an imaginative artist. My objection is that Warren
tends to make rhetoric of his philosophy, as in Governor Willie
Stark's well-known saying, so much admired by American undergraduates, that "Man is conceived in sin and born in corruption
and he passeth from the stink of the didie to the stench of the
shroud." Whatever human nature may or may not be, Warren tends
more and more merely to *say* these things about it, often in bombastic language. The effect of these hotly charged statements is
curiously to make him sound sentimental about his own theories
and impatient in applying them to his analysis of events.

« 2 »

In a sense all of Warren's work could be called *The Legacy of the
Civil War*. This little book has the honesty and intelligence and
nervous force one expects of Warren's writing. But I must confess

that I am baffled by the enthusiastic reviews it has been receiving from distinguished historians. Can it be that there is now so little to say about the Civil War that this very slight essay, thoughtful and unexceptionable as it is, seems of importance because it has been written by Robert Penn Warren? I will admit that I turned to it myself because of my interest in Warren, but despite his verve as a writer, I cannot see that it contributes anything new to the subject. So far as the Civil War itself is concerned, I wonder that Warren can take up so cursorily a subject that requires more detailed handling. After all, this "legacy" is nothing less than the emergence of the modern United States.

Yet Warren can take on the subject because it is this legacy that he has had to face all his life. By now he tends to state it with abrupt positiveness. The truth is that despite Warren's enormous production of fiction and poetry and his influence on the teaching of literature, his habit is to sum things up rather than to portray them for their human interest. And since he is also a powerful and impulsive rhetorician, with a great tendency to use words for the pleasure he himself gets out of using them rather than because they are the most suitable words, his writing is often impatient in tone. Readers of *All the King's Men* will remember how much Warren hung on the expression "the Great Twitch" to denote modern deterministic philosophies (and on Willie Stark's litany about sin, corruption, and the didie). In this book he likes to call the Abolitionists "Higher-Law Men," as if that phrase took care of them all, and he writes, "The philosophy of the Southern apologists did, however, offer space in its finely wrought interstices," that ". . . we should seek to end the obscene gratifications of history . . ." And he speaks of "charismatic arithmetic." This language seems to me abstract, curiously excessive, and hurried. Yet this tendency to write in emotional shorthand can also put him right on the mark, as when he notes of the Abolitionists that they thought they had "a treasury of virtue" and that Southerners have used the war as "the Great Alibi." "By the Great Alibi the South explains, condones, and transmutes everything. By a simple reference to the 'War,' any Southern female could, not too long ago, put on the glass slipper and be whisked away to the ball. . . . By the Great

Alibi the Southerner makes his Big Medicine. He turns defeat into victory, defects into virtues."

Warren's main point, of course, is that the war showed that North and South were more alike than they had thought. As he says of the argument over slavery between the extremists on both sides, "If in the North the critic had repudiated society, in the South society repudiated the critic." For every Southern failing, he has a Northern one to match it; for every glorious achievement on the Northern side, he can cite one equally glorious among the Confederates. The war did away with the inhuman abstractions of the Abolitionists as well as with the inhuman fantasies of unlimited power held by the slaveowners. The North was not for the Negro but for the Union; the South was full of people who felt more loyalty to the Union than they were able to avow. Human nature was the same on both sides, and the final outcome was to produce on both sides a society in which people would not demand the impossible of themselves.

Warren's impartiality of analysis, I must say, interests me more for what it reveals about a Southern writer arguing with himself than for what it reveals about the war. He quotes an unreconstructed Southerner who prayed "to feel different, but so far I can't help it." Warren says that "Even if the Southerner prays to feel different, he may still feel that to change his attitude would be treachery — to that City of the Soul which the historical Confederacy became, to blood spilled in hopeless valor, to the dead fathers, and even to the self. He is trapped in history." The last phrase (it recurs in Warren's writing, like the words "obscene" and "vicious" he applies to experience) conveys a good deal of anguish to me. The war is of course analyzed by Warren as the great school of experience in our history. But even when he shows the lessons it brought, you feel that it figures for him as the event which more than any in our history symbolizes the loss of innocence. He notes that Washington and Jefferson can never interest us now as do Lincoln, Lee, and Stonewall Jackson; the latter we see as "caught in dark inner conflicts." And in an eloquent yet tremulous passage, Warren comes closest to revealing the nature of his own attachment to the subject when he says: "A civil war is, we may say, the prototype of all war, for in the persons of fellow citizens who happen to be the enemy we meet again, with the old ambivalence of love and hate and with all the old guilts, the blood brothers of our childhood. In a civil war — especially in one . . . when the nation shares deep and significant convictions and is not a mere handbasket of factions huddled arbitrarily together by historical happenso — all the self-divisions of conflicts within individuals become a series of mirrors in which the plight of the country is reflected, and the self-division of the country a great mirror in which the individual may see imaged his own deep conflicts, not only the conflicts of political loyalties, but those more profoundly personal."

What is new in Warren's book is his use of the term "pragmatism," which he seems to have taken on not only as a corrective of the abstractions and fanaticisms that prevailed before the war but as a personal philosophy that accepts our split-up, contradictory human nature and that views life as a matter of endless experiment. What Warren means by pragmatism, I would guess, is the symbol it furnishes of the American mind's usual opposition to dogma and fanaticism and the excessively theoretical. Perhaps it simply means to be skeptical. But can an imaginative artist really proclaim himself a pragmatist in this purely critical and even negative sense of the term? Can pragmatism — not as a philosophy in law or economics, such as came out of the Civil War — serve a novelist applying its lessons negatively to human nature? In reading these references to "pragmatism" as an outcome of the war, I automatically nodded agreement; but in Warren's sudden enthusiasm for the term, I saw what it is about his novels and poems that so often bothers me.

The truth is that no matter what philosophy of life a novelist may claim, no matter how astringent or realistic or "pragmatic" he may set himself up to be, literature itself consists in saying "Yes" to life — not just to the "open" life that Warren praises, but to the life in every man, whether he is an Abolitionist or a slaveholder. Warren shows us the lessons that Americans learned from the Civil War, that we can learn still; one reads these pages in full agreement. But should *theories* of human nature interest a novelist this much? Don't all these "pragmatic" lessons show up our own superficially questioning attitude toward life as shallow and smug? Whatever it may be in general, life, perhaps for the artist alone, is life in particular, the life that in some deep sense never can disillusion or dismay.

Good-by to James Agee

JAMES AGEE, who died in 1955, was a writer who gave all of himself, and often it was himself literally that he gave, to every medium that he worked in — poetry, fiction, reportage, criticism, movies, television. He was not only one of the most gifted writers in the United States, but such a natural as a writer that he found a creative opportunity in every place where drearier people pitied themselves for potboiling.

He was the only writer on *Time* who could reduce a managing editor to humility; the only critic who could ever conceivably write about movies for the *Nation* with love; the only documentary reporter for *Fortune* who could make a wholly original book (*Let Us Now Praise Famous Men*) out of an assignment to cover sharecroppers. He wrote two of the best and funniest movies of recent years, *The African Queen* and *The Bride Comes to Yellow Sky*. He wrote the commentary for that tender movie about a little Negro boy, *The Quiet One*. He did a series on Lincoln, for Omnibus, that has been called the most beautiful writing ever done for television; and John Huston thought that Agee was the best screen writer "we have."

In themselves, such distinctions can be meaningless, since not even the serious writers who work for movies or television always take them seriously. But Agee was a writer who actually did better

A Death in the Family, by James Agee. New York: McDowell, Obolensky.

in popular and journalistic media — where certain objective technical requirements gave him a chance to create something out of his immense tenderness and his high sense of comedy — than when he let himself go in purely speculative lyricism. He was a natural literary craftsman, not a literary intellectual, and it was only *avant-garde* associations that ever misled him. His most beautiful poems — like the title poem of his first book, *Permit Me Voyage* — are those which are most traditional in form.

Like so many Southern writers (he came from Knoxville, Tennessee), he had such an immense capacity for feeling and such easy access to the rhetoric of English poetry that when not taken in hand by his medium, he could oppress the reader with merely beautiful words. His almost ecstatic feeling for music itself led him to seek unexpected dimensions in prose, and extraordinarily like Thoreau in this, he tried, in *Let Us Now Praise Famous Men*, to convey his feeling for the American land in highly charged rhythms that would stick close to the facts. Still, it is easy to overrate *Let Us Now Praise Famous Men*, for so many other books of the 1930s now seem unbelievable. Agee wrote of the sharecroppers with such love and rage that it is impossible to read the book without sharing his suffering. But despite its overpowering beauty of language and its immense personal nobility, the book is a turbulent preparation for a work of art that was not achieved.

Agee published in 1951 a short novel, *The Morning Watch*, and at his death he left a virtually complete manuscript which has now been published under Agee's own title, *A Death in the Family*. To anyone who knows how introspective and self-accusing Agee's less successful work could be, both these books show a disciplined control of his narrative material which, if anything, went too far. In both, Agee worked from his earliest memories in order to show the impact on a child of what was plainly a major factor in Agee's own life — the death of his father in the early Twenties.

A Death in the Family is worked out with the most immense care and slowness, showing the effect of the father's death upon a family in Knoxville — on the mother, Mary; on the six-year-old Rufus and his sister Catherine; and on the circle of the mother's close relatives. There are several scenes in it that are really hair-raising — especially one where the family, sitting together, concertedly feel the spirit of the dead father coming into the room; and one where little Rufus, too young to realize the immensity of his loss, argues with the kids on the block that he now has a special distinction.

Yet what makes the book so significant is actually not the dramatic qualities of a novel, but a universe of feeling, of infinitely aching feeling, which is built up so thoroughly, with meticulous truth to the agony of bereavement, that we finally have the sense of a wholly tangible sorrow, a materialization of human grief. The book is remarkable as a literary performance because, although obviously written from within — almost as if in obedience to a hallucination — it tries entirely to describe it as an objective situation. The little boy is an unconscious participant in what will hit him only later; unlike his older self in *The Morning Watch*, here he is not old enough to be aware or "interesting."

The trouble with the book as a novel, however, is that although Agee wrote with an almost unbearable effort at objectivity, one feels from the writing that this effort was made to externalize a private grief, not because he thought of the characters in the book as outside himself. The personality of the dead father actually comes through better than any of the living, for he is the single fact outside them to which they all respond as one.

To speak of faults in a book by James Agee is to point up the absurdity of literary comparisons. Agee's book cannot be judged as another novel-of-the-week; it is an utterly individual and original book, and it is the work of a writer whose power with English words can make you gasp. A brother-in-law, looking at the dead man, feels that he is looking down "upon a horned, bruised anvil; and laid his hand flat against the cold, wheemed iron; and it was as if its forehead gave his hand the stunning shadow of every blow it had ever received." The sense of the father in this book, of both the place he filled in life and of the emptiness created by his death, is one of the most deeply worked out expressions of human feeling that I have ever read. And to think of Jim Agee, with his bad heart, writing with such fierce truth so soon before his own death is to marvel, all over again, how literally it is himself that a writer will give to his task.

[1957]

The Posthumous
Life of Dylan Thomas

DYLAN THOMAS's posthumous life began before he died. Before he died, before he lay for days in a coma in St. Vincent's Hospital, New York, while the literati, literary hostesses, patrons, and others milled around the hospital — one lady even came into his room and stared at him for half an hour while he lay trussed up in an oxygen tent, with tubes is his mouth and nose — anyone up and down the broad literary-academic acreage of this country who heard him read, or watched him drink, could have said to himself (more usually herself): "That man is great, that man is disturbing, nothing so exciting has happened to me since I passed my Ph.D. orals, I am going to remember this; he will soon be dead."

He will soon be dead. The legend of the poet-dying-young is based not merely on the opposition between poetic idealism and a materialistic society documented by Chatterton, Keats, Shelley, Hart Crane, but on the romantic faith that true poetry is of a shattering intensity that destroys the poet even as it brings out of him, in letters of fire, the poetry itself. And the expectation is superstitious. What is peculiarly dear to us, what really transports and charms us, what brings new life to us from the hero, the poet, the great man — this, by an automatic human discount, is vulnerable and frail. But beyond these general considerations was the overwhelming single consideration of Dylan Thomas, who not only seemed more gifted, more eloquent, more joyous than any other poet of his generation, but was peculiarly available to all and everyone, so utterly without pose and literary pomp — he was always ragging his own poetry and, as he beerily filled out, the little barrel figure he made — that, alive, he was already "Dylan" to every casual pub-mate and literary pick-me-up, with the impending appeal, winsome and rakish, of a Frank Sinatra.

It was this combination of genius and plainness, of force and sweetness, that made so many people write him off from the living before he was dead. He had an old-fashioned "big" gift that made people identify him with the "big" tragedies of old-fashioned poets. Just as many people in England and America who had no contact with advanced poetry read him with a puzzled but obstinate sense that he was important, while foreigners in Germany and Sweden, puzzling out his poems, would say with a sigh, "*This* is a poet," so they knew, they all knew, that he would "die soon." For beyond everything else — beyond the fact that he was endlessly available, that he conducted his life in public, so that everyone knew whom he loved and whom he drank with and how he had turned over a table full of food and drink at Sweet Thing College — lay the overwhelming fact that he was so obviously not in control of his life and did not pretend to be. Perhaps no one is in control any more and it is only in America that people still pretend to be. But the ruling fiction in government and philosophy and education, and even among writers, is that we must all know exactly where we are going and how to get there. As *Time* once noted admiringly about a suburban housewife, "she had life by the tail."

It was just the other way with Dylan Thomas. And it was because in an age full of supremely careful people searching for the "security" of personal happiness Dylan lived without sense, without a bank account, without an analyst, that he provoked the most tremendous astonishment and affection from people who had understandably forgotten what an enormous personal force can lie behind poetry. But he also aroused a certain fear, a fear for him and just as strong a fear of him, of all he could do to people's arrangements and engagements, and this often took the form of wishing "justice" to be done to him. He was so *outrageous*, as a student once complained, that in certain quarters his death aroused moral approval. And this belief in punishment, in righteous wrath against the outrager, was something that Dylan himself felt. When he first got the d.t.'s near the end of his life, he said that he had seen "the gates of hell." With his background in the shabby-genteel and the Nonconformist Welsh conscience, with his all-too-schoolteachery father and profoundly influential mother (to whom he paid dutiful daily visits at home), he not only felt at the end that he was in hell but that he deserved to be.

Of course he felt this — nobody brought up in our Hebraic-Anglo-Saxon-Puritan tradition ever sins carelessly, is ever totally apart from the sense of "sin." But the essential fact remains that Dylan Thomas didn't yield to that peculiarly American and modern folly of imagining that one can morally ensure one's destiny. As a poet and as a very canny observer in several countries, he felt that life in the twentieth century is peculiarly chaotic and measureless, full of desperate private rebellions and self-blame in a society which less and less gives most people any ideal to be faithful to. He felt that metaphysically we have no knowledge and no certainty — he said that his poems had been written "in praise of God by a man who doesn't believe in God" — and that only "the force that through the green fuse drives the flower," the life process from love to death, is real.

And since he lived what he believed, or rather what he didn't believe, it was quite clear — oh, terribly clear long before his death! — that Dylan Thomas was wonderful but extreme, and that he would die soon. It was not merely that he behaved badly, that he turned over the plate of canapés at one place and addressed ribald remarks to the pretty young dean of women at another. What made him outrageous to some — and exactly as challenging to others — was that he had, in the provocative sense, no hope.

He had no hope. I don't pretend to know exactly why this was, and it's too easy to say, as so many have, that he drank in order to recover the first excitement of his lyrical gift. I think that fundamentally his lack of hope came from the lack of ideas suitable to the boldness of his temperament and vocation. He had no philosophy or belief that could express for him, that could work for him, that could even explain the burden of love and terror before the natural world that is the subject of all his poetry. He was almost the pure type of the romantic artist in our world, determined to write only "happy" poems that would show life as joy. But he was unable or unwilling to bridge the gap between the splendor of his solitary conception and the deadness of the world without the poet's light on it. All of Thomas's poetry shows the profound romantic need to intensify existence, to make it all come alive as it is in personal consciousness. But where so many great poets — Blake,

Wordsworth, Keats, even Whitman — have recognized that their task is not to lose their new vision to the commonplace world but to explain and to unite it to human existence, Thomas felt absurd and histrionic, acted like a man who in his heart thought himself a fake.

He was too humble. It is a strange thing to remember of anyone whose gift was so personal and sweeping, but he regarded his own gift as slightly absurd; he sheltered it, wouldn't have his poems discussed, because he couldn't admit that poetry *is* thought, and that what he said in his poems many of his contemporaries really believed and were most deeply grateful to a poet for saying again. He was left with his fantastic linguistic gift as if it were something to read from, to entertain with, but not, in the artistic sense, to practice as a criticism of life.

But then, how could he have felt this in our age? The great Romantic manifestoes were charters of human liberation by poets who identified themselves with new classes and revolutionary new ideas in society. In the gray drab British welfare state, Dylan Thomas felt like a "spiv," a juvenile delinquent. Being an utterly accessible and friendly and idle-feeling man, he couldn't help seeing himself as a faintly comic version of that universally respected legend, "The Poet." The public entertainer in him exploited the miseries of that humble bloke, that rumpled and tired Welshman, Dylan Thomas, who had no trouble enjoying his gift but who sometimes looked on it as something that had oddly been given *him* — he couldn't say just why! About other poets he could be utterly conventional in his admiration; his BBC talks on poets of Welsh background are banal. He even read the poetry of others with steadier power than he did his own. But if he was more reserved with people and perceptive about them than anyone watching him would have guessed, he was, about himself, without hope in the sense that he had nothing with which to explain and to justify the utter naturalness and human application of his poetry.

He believed in himself as a poet, there is no question about that; what he didn't believe in was what it was peculiarly the task of someone with *his* genius to believe in: that his poetry gave us truth about life and was a judgment on all of us, not just on himself. When people say that he drank in order to recapture the old ecstasy, his first excitement, they forget that his problem was not merely to recover this ecstasy, which understandably flagged, but to believe in it. Only this would have shown that he was in fact as great as others knew he was.

But guessing at his vulnerability, people foresaw his early death; and observing his abandon, they mistook his hopelessness for confusion. Obviously no poet of such fierce perception can tidily put his life away when he is not writing. The poet lives the truth he has to write, and when he is not writing he may live it in a chaos of unorganized sensations, of an excitement throwing itself upon life, that can bound back and destroy him. And Dylan Thomas's lack of "hope," in the specific sense in which I have tried to state it, should not obscure the central fact that as a poet he was the very opposite of the anxious salvation-seekers who are so dear to contemporary poetry. The tremendous vogue of Thomas's poetry stems from the fact that after the era of would-be "hard," pseudo-Christian verse of T. S. Eliot's followers and the self-conscious ironies of Auden, Thomas brought back to poetry the resonance of feeling, the connection with nature, love, and death which is the peculiar power of poetry and which Rilke defined as "the past that breaks out in our hearts."

The deepest side of such poetry — and of such an attitude to poetry — is not merely that it rests on images which are to be accepted literally in their unmediated force, but that it represents an attitude toward life itself which is the opposite of control, complacency, and deliberation. In Thomas's poetry, life speaks *through* us:

> The force that drives the water through the rocks
> Drives my red blood;

man is an instrument of the energy that is divine; he is not, to use the American idiom, "structuring" life to make all things neatly realizable and containable. Ours is an irreverent culture. In the work of Thomas — and of Thomas's beloved Whitman — life, in the final vision, attains not a definite character but the quality of a worshiped and awesome natural force. It becomes a great fire, beyond man's ability to put it out, but to which he is glad, at most, to get near, still nearer, so as to be able to get down in words a breath of this radiant flame.

« 2 »

Obviously, then, Dylan Thomas represented for many Americans a rare touch of greatness, a relief from the ever-pressing success story. He embodied, without a word said to this effect outside his poetry, the pure romantic vision that is still admired in America underneath the automatic responses of our culture. No matter how fussily detailed and self-conscious our lives become, there is in our fundamental classlessness and our physical restlessness freedom from the frigid respectability that can be so depressing a feature of middle-class life in Britain. And Dylan was so friendly, in this respect so much like an American, so easy to call by his first name! He encountered a welcome here which made him feel as if he were free-floating in a sky made up of unlimited parties, girls, and liquor, and in the heady, inflated, overprosperous, overstimulated atmosphere of America since the war, this must have made him, with his peculiarly heightened capacities for life, feel that he had been sent spinning out of the damp, dark wrappings of seaside life in Wales and hackwork in London. The more uncontrolled he felt about life, the more he fell upon American parties, American excitement, American adulation, as if everything came from a rich, infatuated, always indulgent mistress. He drank here not like an alcoholic who enjoys his liquor, but like a fat boy gobbling down chocolate bars who can't believe that they make him fat. Inevitably, his death here made it seem to many glumly envious and depressed Britons at home as if Dylan Thomas had died of America as well as in America, and as soon as the news of his death at thirty-nine reached London, the word went out from his old literary pals that "America killed Dylan Thomas."

In a sense it was true. Just as many Americans die of the American way of life, of the American pace, of American traffic, so Dylan Thomas's end was certainly speeded by that unlimited supply of hard liquor without which nobody dares entertain any more, and which is not only more difficult to obtain in Britian, on British incomes, but which became to Dylan what poetry might have been if, in his own rueful words, he hadn't been flying over America "like a damp, ranting bird."

But it is also true that since the war a great many Britishers haven't needed to find in Dylan Thomas's death a reason for being exasperated with America: they already have so many. Any American who follows the British literary and highbrow press becomes hardened to the bitter and sometimes hysterical jealousy of this country — particularly from Marxists who can't bear to admit how much, in different fashions, Russia and the gray British welfare state have let them down — but it is ironic that Dylan Thomas's death should be blamed entirely on America. Like so many Romantic writers, he felt a natural affinity with this country, while in Britain, being utterly outside the "Establishment," he was regarded with a certain loving contempt by some of the snobs who so righteously gnashed their teeth after his death. Nevertheless, Thomas's death was a terrible loss to his own people, to his own kind, and it is really because the mediocrity of literature today is less cleverly concealed in Britian than it is in this country that the death hit so hard.

« 3 »

The posthumous life of Dylan Thomas as a legend and a symbol — the last Romantic poet in a conformist society, the Welsh lyric singer corrupted by the American fleshpots — became really intense when the personal rivalries between those who had loved Dylan came out into the open. Now that he was dead, many people felt an enrichment of their lives through their retrospective share in him. The fact is that Dylan Thomas was a peculiarly lovable as well as magnetically gifted person, that he inspired a great many gifted people with the sense of an unusual radiance in their lives. And just as the many elegies after his death addressed him with an intimacy that is inconceivable in relation to any other famous poet of our time, so the extraordinary agitation he inspired lives on after him in the fascinated reportage of every detail of his life by people who obviously preferred Dylan drunk to anyone sober.

John Malcolm Brinnin's *Dylan Thomas in America** was, of course, the principal tool in shaping the posthumous legend of Dylan Thomas. And it is a mark of Thomas's fantastic vitality in

---

* *Dylan Thomas in America*, by John Malcolm Brinnin. Boston: Little, Brown and Company. An Atlantic Monthly Press book.

death that a great many people who don't read his poetry, but who very properly see his life as a symbol of it, have found in Brinnin's book the documented record of what they regard as the very poetry of excess. They love this excess because it gives them a touch of the old romantic heedlessness and abandon, the price of which they do not have to pay, and which, as they read in Brinnin the account of Thomas's terrible last days, makes them shudder at an end so violently consistent with his life.

It is no accident that in our period the unconscious protest of so many young people against an overregulated but vacuous society is embodied in the admiration of recklessness which one sees in the cult of the young movie actor James Dean, who died speeding; and that among a great many of the young intellectuals there is a similar cult of "Dylan," whose extraordinary records are fancied by the same people who admire the new jazz and hot rods. In colleges all over the country, listening to Dylan's voice as, "crooning" his poems, he still tries to catch his breath between lines, young people get from him the same suggestion of pure feeling that they get from good jazz. The California poet, Kenneth Rexroth, has linked as heroes of "the beat generation" "two great dead juvenile delinquents — the great saxophonist Charlie Parker, and Dylan," and insists that "if the word deliberate means anything, both of them certainly destroyed themselves. . . .

"Both of them," Rexroth has written, "were overcome by the horror of the world in which they found themselves, because at last they could no longer overcome that world with the weapon of a purely lyrical art. . . . Both of them did communicate one central theme: Against the ruin of the world, there is only one defense — the creative act. . . . Dylan Thomas's verse had to find endurance in a world of burning cities and burning Jews. He was able to find meaning in his art as long as it was the answer to air raids and gas ovens. As the world began to take on the guise of an immense air raid or gas oven, I believe his art became meaningless to him." And in a violent but moving elegy to Thomas, "Thou Shalt Not Kill," Rexroth attributes the poet's death to the superficiality of his contemporaries:

> Who killed the bright-headed bird?
> You did, you son of a bitch.

You drowned him in your cocktail brain.
He fell down and died in your synthetic heart.

The bitterness in these lines is by no means unusual. All over
the country, often in isolated places, there are people, more especially young people, who look on Thomas as a rebel against mass
society and a victim of the organization man. It is in America, at the
antennae of the modern age, where the full force of technological
culture is felt, that the cult of Dylan Thomas has reached its peak
— documented, too often, from the remorseless day-by-day record
of Thomas the drunk and the wastrel which Brinnin put down with
so much fervor and unconscious resentment against the elusiveness
of this magnetic figure. So closely do people feel related to Thomas
that there are endless arguments still about Brinnin's book, for
people tend to identify with Thomas to the point where they resent its itemization of his "lapses." When Brinnin admitted that
he could not really account for Thomas's more extreme behavior, he
meant that he did not want to and was punishing him for being so
unmanageable. But to the "ardents," Thomas's life in itself, not in
relation to them, has a heroic significance quite the opposite of the
continuous disintegration that Brinnin leaves us with.

« 4 »

It was in protest against this impression that Dylan's widow,
Caitlin Thomas, offered a brief foreword to Brinnin's book. And
now that her own memoir, *Leftover Life to Kill*, has finally been
written, a most important word from the most intimate source of all
has been said.* In his posthumous life Dylan Thomas really speaks
now, through his widow. Caitlin Thomas's book is not the "answer"
to Brinnin — the mere justification of her husband — that had been
expected. It is better than that. It is an amazing duplication of
Thomas's own strength and recklessness and abandon by a woman
who obviously was the only person with a spirit equal to his and
who consequently fought him and hated him and loved him to the
point where their conflicting intensities almost killed each other. I
don't like the self-pity in the title and a would-be pathos, at the

* *Leftover Life to Kill*, by Caitlin Thomas. Boston: Little, Brown and Company.
An Atlantic Monthly Press book.

end as at the beginning; but the self-pity is utterly shown up and exploded by the fierce emotional charge of the book and a style which, once she gets control of it, gives one the same pleasant Celtic resonance from her careening Irish sentences that one gets from his tipsy Welsh ones.

The people who will be shocked by Caitlin Thomas's book would be shocked by Dylan Thomas if he were alive. A posthumous life is easy to take, for us who deal with it as symbol; Caitlin Thomas is so much alive that her book, which is as much about herself as about Dylan, never explains Dylan's directness and eloquence so much as when, with amusing honesty and perfect tenderness, she recounts her life on the Isle of Elba with a young Italian miner, surrounded by the hostile respectable.

There is about her, as about Dylan, a perfect genius for trouble. She is a born rebel who in today's situation doesn't know what to rebel against. She has her husband's instinct for extreme and desperate situations. But reading the account of her dismal life in Wales after Dylan's death, and of her flight to Elba with her five-year-old son, I could not help feeling that, given her temperament, she behaved with exemplary courage and humanity. What makes the book so remarkable is that, time and again, whether she is writing about Dylan, or herself, or her children, one hears the boisterous Thomas lilt, the authentic note, the lyrical cry from the heart that gives his style its force. And most unexpected and revealing, she makes it clear that in her, as in Dylan, is the fatal mixture, with her powerful temperament, of that intellectual frailty, that excessive availability and need to be loved, which so many pettier types have known how to protect themselves from.

The tragedy of Caitlin Thomas is not what she says it is — not entirely a matter of the tempestuous life with a genius as erratic as herself or of the subsequent loss which, frightful as it is, has obviously given her back to herself. The tragedy is in the excessive vulnerability, the constant readiness to be hit in the face, which, in a person with her insurrectionary heart, cripples her at the very moment that she can rise to her full strength. She tells us that she had a passion for solitary dancing à la Isadora Duncan, where she could feel the "flowing"; but "as soon as I spotted the 'glance' of an audience, I was finished: the brain on the alert, all suspicion again, put the pincers on, and the capricious flow stopped abruptly. . . .

"That was one reason, now I come to think of it, why Dylan found it so annoying: it is the direct opposite of words. . . . It may be one of the substances that poetry is made of; that words are formed from; but its elemental — right back, through the encumbering ages, to the creation, the planets, the dinosaurs; the skeletons and protoplasm — force is, above any other point of supremacy, *wordless*. . . ."

Actually, her sense of what art means to her — this elemental force, right back through the encumbering ages — is exactly what makes her husband's poetry so vivid. In her, as in him, there is this same exciting and disturbing combination of force without hope — without a meaning she can assign to her experience that would relieve her from emotional suffering. Her rule of life, she says, is "always be ready to clasp the impending disasters," and I believe her. So that despite the essential modesty that seems to me the key to the tragedy of Dylan Thomas and the long-delayed emergence of his wife, it is this elemental force for which one remains grateful in reading her book. It is so much rarer than a "defense" of Dylan Thomas — who needs none.

[1957]

Bernard Malamud:
The Magic and the Dread

THE STORIES of Bernard Malamud are a striking example of the opportunities — and hazards — that are faced these days by "minority" writers who have rejected special pleading in favor of modern art. Writers like Ralph Ellison and James Baldwin are no longer tempted to sing the chain-gang blues once favored by Negro writers in this country; originals like Saul Bellow, Daniel Fuchs, and Bernard Malamud are not likely to retrace the kind of sentimental or aggressive pathos that has afflicted so many recorders of Jewish experience in this country, from Fannie Hurst to Michael Gold — a style that has found its last haven in the Hollywood of Irwin Shaw and other nostalgic readers of *PM*.

The Magic Barrel, by Bernard Malamud. New York: Farrar, Straus and Cudahy.

The newer writers (who seem "new" not because they are young but because it has taken them so long to climb out of the depression and war and to discover themselves as individuals) have turned their backs on what James Baldwin has jeeringly called "everybody's protest novel" — Uncle Tom, the Negro or the Jewish Christ dead of American capitalism, the saintly victim. But agile and really gifted as these new writers are, they have been just as unwilling or unable as Jewish and Negro writers always have been to let their experience alone, to describe it as something that may be valued for its own sake. It is here that one sees the peculiar nemesis of writers who feel that they can fit themselves to American life only by trying to give universal meaning to each piece of their experience.

The patron saint of these writers is always Dostoevsky — the supreme example of the novelist whose characters must always search for meaning, who cannot for a moment allow life to exist without scrutinizing intervention. But where Dostoevsky had equal ability to embody the emptiness and sloth of nineteenth-century Russia, these new American writers itch with symbolism. They have been exposed so continually to modern literature and modern art that they find it hard to find their way back to what Herbert Gold has called the lesson of Balzac's "stupidity." Although these writers have produced a peculiarly penetrating kind of fiction, haunting as well as haunted, there is a certain overeagerness in them all to stand and deliver, to be freed of certain painful experiences through the ritualistic catharsis of modern symbolism. The Jewish or Negro writer, far from being mired in his personal pathos as of yore, is now so aware that his experience is "universal" that he tends to escape out of his particular experience itself, to end up in the great American sky of abstractions.

Of all these new writers, Bernard Malamud seems to me the most unnecessarily tempted by symbolism. For he is the most compassionate, the most concerned and involved of them all, and whenever I turn back to the best scenes in his fine novel, *The Assistant*, or to the little masterpiece about a rabbinical student in search of a wife who went to a marriage broker (the title story of this collection), I get something of the same deep satisfaction that I do from the great realistic masters of Yiddish literature.

Malamud's world has its own haunting archetypes: the desperate and sickly storekeeper, the refugee who turns up in Rome or New York to accuse his fellow Jews of heartlessness, the lonely student with ovoid eyes in staring search of love, the American intellectual abroad who finds it impossible to escape his Jewish past. The scene is always the down-at-heels grocery, the winter street, the irreversible hardness of the modern city. Malamud has caught as one the guttural toughness of big-city speech and the classic bitterness of Jewish dialogue. The remarkable story "Take Pity" contains the typical situation of all his work — a great love condemned to ineffectuality. A man who has committed suicide so that he can leave all his property to a widow who always refused to accept him during his lifetime sits in the other world telling a "census-taker" (his name is Davidov) how the woman's husband died. "Broke in him something. . . ." "Broke what?" "Broke what breaks. He was talking to me how bitter was his life, and he touched me on my sleeve to say something else, but the next minute his face got small and he fell down dead, the wife screaming, the little girls crying that it made in my heart pain. I am myself a sick man and when I saw him laying on the floor, I said to myself, 'Rosen, say goodbye, this guy is finished.' So I said it."

This is the talk of people who are not merely on edge but who really live on the edge. Their tense expressiveness is one of the cultural symbols of the Jews, in art as in religion; just as the great Rabbi Hillel could be challenged to give the whole meaning of the Law while standing on one foot, so there is a Doomsday terseness to Jewish speech — as if the book of life were about to close shut with a bang. Malamud has caught this quality with an intimacy of understanding that is utterly remarkable. But in their terseness, his characters fundamentally express despair rather than any spiritual refusal of the great world. His world is all too much an inner world — one in which the city streets, the houses, the stores, seem, along with the people who broodingly stand about like skeletons, some with flesh, always just about to fold up, to disappear into the sky. People talk to each other disbelievingly, as if each felt that the other was about to disappear, as if the world under their feet were itself unreal. People flit in and out of each other's lives like bad dreams.

It is a curious, almost uncanny transformation of the old Jewish mysticism, where earth is so close to heaven — or to hell — that the supernatural and the trivial jostle each other. From the historic standpoint of Jewish theology, of the seemingly incredible Jewish experience itself, everything is entirely real. Life is always strange and God always moves in unpredictable ways. In Malamud's stories everything real becomes unreal; we are under the sign not of theology but of surrealism. Sometimes this is unbearably effective; but when the symbols become too explicit, as in "The Lady of the Lake" or "Angel Levine," Malamud's own tone is undecided between the mysterious and the silly. In "The Mourners," an old man, suffering for the guilt of having deserted his family years back, is about to be evicted; the landlord is driven half mad trying to get the dirty old man out of the tenement. The old man begins mourning for him, the landlord, as dead — he is spiritually dead — and the landlord, staring in unbelief, is engulfed in the sudden upsurge of his own shame and becomes a mourner too. The symbolism here is not only explicit, it is positively allegorical. And indeed, Malamud explains, in his Hawthornesque touches, why Hawthorne and symbolist novelists like Kafka so often read alike.

But Malamud is at his best in those stories which depend not on surprise but on the moment of ungovernable human feeling. In "The Loan," an old friend turns up in a baker's shop to ask for a loan — to pay for a headstone for his wife's grave. The baker's wife, his *second* wife, steadfastly refuses to countenance the loan, and at the end of the story the two friends, each bereft in his own way, "pressed mouths together and parted forever." In the title story, Malamud's usual attempt to escape "realism" is brilliantly, triumphantly justified. It is the marriage broker's own daughter whom the rabbinical student falls in love with, from a photograph, and at the end of the story the ambiguities of life and death are so close that one has the sense of being caught in a dream. Life is never very solid for these Jews, these people "who live on air"; they are always on the verge of saying good-by and departing for the other world.

« 2 »

The otherworldly feeling in the great Jewish writers of the past was supported by a conviction that earth and heaven are connected.

Malamud captures the strangeness of Jewish experience brilliantly, but he relies on compassion, not on the covenant. He is so concerned with the dread, the flimsiness of the human material in our age, that he has to outwit his own possible sentimentality. This, as I see it, is why he so often turns to symbolic endings, goes through his material so quickly. The result is that while this book seems to me masterful and indescribably haunting, it is surprising to note, when one closes it, how many of the people fade indistinguishably into each other. What remains in the reader's mind is not a world, *the* world, but the spectral Jew in his beggarly clothes — always ready to take flight.

It is an extraordinary fact that although the great Yiddish writers in Czarist Russia could not call the country their own, they gave the earth of Russia, the old village, a solid reality, as if it were all the world they had left to cherish, like the Jewish graveyard that is lovingly kept up even when the houses decay. Malamud, the closest in wit and depth of feeling to the great Yiddish writers, nevertheless falls into the same abstractness that is the bane of so many new writers in America. Unlike those who are abstract because they have only their cleverness to write from, Malamud is abstract out of despair: despair of the world itself, which can no longer be represented.

In this one sees the curious danger of the American writer who has been influenced by Kakfa, Joyce, Eliot, *et al.* Life in America changes so quickly, and people are so quick to change into each other, that the everlasting thinness and abstractness of American writing, which comes from our lack of "society," of a solid core of leaders, manners, tradition, is likely to be intensified by our new writers, who have a society but don't believe in it enough to describe it — to deal with it not merely as it is but as something that *is.* One of the things we now long for in contemporary literature is escape from the tyranny of symbolic "meaning." We want to return to life not as a figure in the carpet but as life in its beautiful and inexpressible materiality — life as the gift that it actually is rather than as the "material" that we try to remake.

Malamud provokes these reflections because he is so gifted. There seems to me no writer of his background who comes so close to the bone of human feeling, who makes one feel so keenly the enigmatic quality of life. The only thing I miss in his work is a feeling for the value of life, for the body of this world — for that which cannot be explained because it is too precious to turn into symbols.

[1958]

The World of Saul Bellow

IN SAUL BELLOW's *Seize the Day* (1956) there is a scene in which the panicky middle-aged hero and a quack psychiatrist have lunch in a Broadway cafeteria. ". . . Dr. Tamkin came along with a tray piled with plates and cups. He had Yankee pot roast, purple cabbage, potatoes, a big slice of watermelon, and two cups of coffee." Mr. Brendan Gill of the *New Yorker*, in reviewing this book, warmly saluted Bellow's talent, acknowledged his pre-eminence among the younger American novelists, but shuddering at the sentence above, expressed his earnest hope that Bellow would drop such writing — which, I suppose, seemed a dull and gritty naturalistic catalogue.

I know that there are many people to whom Bellow's novels seem the familiar material of American naturalism, and who even think of him as a tough, aggressive writer. But I do not understand them. To me Bellow's world is far from being identical with the mass big-city America he writes about. It is distinctively a world of his own — in style, in speculative intelligence, in the anguish of its feeling and the conscious buffoonery of its wit. It as little resembles even the European tradition of the novel Bellow would like to follow as it does those young American novelists who have lately found in him the kind of strength they would like to capture. Bellow, even for a writer, is so much his own man that the various cultural labels that come with him — the Chicagoan, the Jew, the one-time anthropologist — figure more as themes in his work than they explain *him*. One of the key themes in his fiction, however, is the attempt of his protagonists to get a grip on existence, to understand not themselves (they know that this is impossible) but the infinitely elusive universe in which, as human creatures, they find themselves.

Yet at the same time Bellow is very much a novelist of the known, familiar surfaces. From the Chicago winters and boardinghouse blues of his first novel, *Dangling Man* (1944), to his latest, which begins with Henderson on his Hudson Valley farm, feeding his pigs, stripped to the waist like a convict, breaking stones with a sledge-hammer, Bellow has caught, particularly in the New York City scenes of *The Victim* (1947) and the unforgettable "grandeur of place" that informs *The Adventures of Augie March* (1953), the heaviness, the violence and the energy of American life. But Bellow describes the clammy big-city world as Hardy described Wessex fields, as the unconnected spectator of man's hopes; he never writes about these separate and cruel forces with the half-nostalgic feeling of earlier realists like Dreiser, or with the infatuation of "tough" sentimental reporters of the big city like Nelson Algren. There is no class for which Bellow has the proletarian novelist's political sympathy. The external world, for Bellow, is always the covering, not the home, of a spirit not so much disaffected as unattachable. He is a novelist who in this sense reminds one of "metaphysical" American novelists like Melville, for he identifies man's quest with the range of the mind itself. Even when he describes a sinister mountebank dismally carrying pot roast and purple cabbage to a cafeteria table, Bellow sees in him multiple aspects of the human condition.

What makes Bellow's work so unusual, and in its very sense of the extreme often so comic, is the fact that his characters are all burdened by a speculative quest, a need to understand their partic-ular destiny within the general problem of human destiny. This compulsion, even when it is unconscious, as is the case of Asa Lev-enthal in *The Victim* or Tommy Wilhelm in *Seize the Day*, or mocked in himself as it is by Augie March, is the motivating energy of his heroes. And in his latest novel, *Henderson the Rain King*, the cry "I want! I want!" forces the hero to desert his family for Africa.

« 2 »

The problem of destiny is the need to accept one's whole fate as a human being, to recognize the "axial lines" of life, as Augie March puts it. But to know whether the axial lines that we see, or think that we see, are what fate *had* to draw, is not merely the theme of Bellow's fiction, it is the overriding passion of his characters. And it is this extraordinary prominence of speculation in Bellow's novels that gives him his unusual, his involuntarily provocative, place in American fiction.

For the fact is that we do not like our novelists to be too intelligent; we like them to be tough, hard, external, concerned with "facts." And if the facts of life in a novel concern speculation about destiny as much as they concern money or sex or business or family? Then we say that the authors are not novelists but intellectuals. We will easily admit intelligence as manner, in the now-classic style of Henry James, but not life and death and destiny as passionate subjects in themselves.

Now, Bellow is anything but a "philosophic" novelist in the German style of mock-profundity. He is, like Augie March himself, Chicago-raised ("Chicago, that somber city") and the sharp, questioning, exultantly self-educated mind of the immigrant's son is on every page. But a novelist is defined not only by his mind, his style, his address; he is defined as well by his ruling subject, the idea of drama that is his obsession, by that point of view which is not only the content of his work but also its truly driving and unconscious side. Bellow's novels offer the deepest commentary I know on the social utopianism of a generation which always presumed that it could pacify life, that it could control and guide it to an innocuous social end, but which is painfully learning, as in *Augie March* and the end of *Seize the Day*, to celebrate life, to praise in it the divine strength which disposes of man's proposals.

It is this problem, first of representing all that a man intends and plans, and then of getting him not merely to recognize the countervailing strength of life but to humble himself before it, that is the real situation in all Bellow's novels. In *Dangling Man* young Joseph, caught in a legal tie-up with his draft board, unable to join the Army and unable to continue a normal life, calls himself "that creature of plans. He had asked himself a question I still would like answered, 'How should a good man live; what ought he to do?' Hence the plans. Unfortunately, most of them were foolish."

Yet Joseph's response is not one of cynical sophistication, for it is not the defeat of plans that concerns Bellow. It is the fact that in obedience to the external sophistication of society, one makes plans in accordance with conventional standards. Actually one's real plans, to discover all one's potential freedom as a human being, must yield with a kind of furtive reverence to the ultimate power which one can only call God. In all of Bellow's work man's realization of his illusions, of his greedy expectation, so deepens that Henderson asks, "Does truth come in blows?" He has learned to receive it on his body and in his face, to wrestle with it and to be humiliated by it; he has learned, as the profounder Jewish spirits have learned, that God is not easy, but must be fought with, as Jacob wrestled with the angel.

Man proposes and God disposes. Americans in particular propose a very great deal, but life always catches up with them — at least with the protagonists of Saul Bellow. But the way of Job, of ultimate tragedy and the high manner, is not the way of a novelist from Chicago. The other way, the Augie March way, is the longing to embrace in life itself, in its most commonplace texture, the actual miracle of existence, the great gift itself, conferred and confirmed and to be praised in every breath, richer than any man's words for it. Augie March praises life by learning to say *no* to men. In his elusiveness, he is faithful not to men and their schemes and plans for him — but to existence made manifest in himself. The plans of Augie's contemporaries — and it is to the point that the novel was originally entitled *Life among the Machiavellians* — betray not merely egotism but petty vision. They want, they want . . . to make the world like themselves. But as Augie says, "You do all you can to humanize and familiarize the world, and suddenly it becomes stranger than ever." To know strangeness is to recognize that fate itself is character. Or as Augie puts it in one of those monologues that bring home the sulphurous world of self-made intellectuals from Chicago: "I have a feeling about the axial lines of life, with respect to which you must be straight or else your existence is merely clownery, hiding tragedy. I must have had a feeling since I was a kid about these axial lines which made me want to have my existence on them, and so I have said 'no' like a stubborn fellow to all my persuaders, just on the obstinacy of my memory of these lines, never entirely clear. . . . Lately I have felt these thrilling lines again. When striving stops, there they are as a gift."

For Augie this wisdom resulted in an attachment to life itself, at every turn and in every breath of his monologue to the reader. The beauty and exhilaration of this novel showed that Bellow could turn the sense of destiny, his respect for what Henderson would call "blows," into comedy. Bellow's sense of comedy is always a human being's diffidence before the superior forces of life, a Chaplinesque sense of himself as the accidental and paltry vessel on which life has been conferred. Privately, Bellow has always had this humor to a surpassing degree. I've never known any writer who has more clearly both a sense of his destiny as a writer and a humorous self-deprecation before his fate. Some time ago, when a Fuller Brush man at his door who had got nowhere with him finally demanded, "Won't you even take it as a gift?" Bellow is supposed to have replied, "I've been given the gift of life, and it's more than I know what to do with."

From the ex-radical dangling man to the man who sees in himself the comic hero of destiny is a short step; the amazing relaxation of Bellow's work, from the anxious soberness of style in *Dangling Man* and the tight nightmare plot of *The Victim* to the rapturous ease of *Augie March,* has finally reached its climax in the open buffoonery and philosophical shenanigans of *Henderson the Rain King.*

Henderson is a work that does not really please me. Yet it is typical of Bellow's growing power as a novelist that he can now create a comic hero who is openly and jeeringly his own predicament, who feels the pang of the human situation in his six feet four, his 230 pounds, his millions, his pig farm, his two wives, his bad teeth. In Bellow's earlier novels the leading protagonists were gray, urban and dim, specters, *Luftmenschen,* who did not altogether convince me that they could put up much of a fight. They were almost too easily put upon. Even Augie, *picaro* and adventurer that he is, is too much a thought in Bellow's own mind to impress us with the weight that he can put into his plans to outwit life. But Henderson is from the beginning built to the size of the titans, the wrestlers-with-God, as the Russians used to describe the type. He is an American eccentric, a gentleman farmer, a war hero, a desperately unavailing husband and father, built to scale.

I gave up fishing and sat on the beach shooting stones at bottles. So that people might say, "Do you see that great big fellow with the enormous nose and the mustache? Well, his great-grandfather was Secretary of State, and his father was the famous scholar Willard Henderson who wrote that book on the Albigensians, a friend of William James and

Henry Adams." Didn't they say this? You bet they did. . . . In the dining room I was putting bourbon in my morning coffee from a big flask and on the beach I was smashing bottles. The guests complained to the manager about the broken glass . . . me they weren't willing to confront.

I came, a great weight, a huge shadow on those stairs, with my face full of country color and booze, and yellow pigskin gloves on my hands, and a ceaseless voice in my heart that said, *I want, I want, I want,* oh *I want — !*

With this one, then, the possible testing of himself against life offers new possibilities. The extraordinary freedom of style that Bellow learned with Augie has resulted here in an intimate connection of temper and thought, an ease and gaiety that gives the key scenes in the book with Dahfu the native king, a new sense of the laughter that Bellow can bring to intellect.

It is the kind of book that no one else could have written, and which is so much in the necessary line of his development that Henderson naturally takes his place alongside those other agonists, those constant strivers, who make up the significant gallery of Bellow's heroes.

My quarrel with the book has to do with my feeling, suggested to me even in so good a work of its kind as *Seize the Day,* that these Jacobs give up to life a little too eloquently, that they do not struggle enough with the angel before crying out in reverence and submission, "I will not let thee go, except thou bless me." In *Seize the Day* Tommy Wilhelm, after making a mess of things all day long and in every way, realized only by intercepting a funeral that there was something more than himself to weep for, that he could weep only in weeping for another. I was troubled by the excessive awareness of the submission, by the lack of someone big enough to fight with life. In *Henderson,* scene after scene is brilliantly inventive, but the spaces in between do not sufficiently convey the weight that the antagonists bring to the struggle. This Africa is still too clearly a further station along the way for the anxious pilgrim through life. The typical Bellow hero must travel not to struggle with the angel but in search of an angel or demon or God to submit to.

But the beauty of the last scene, when the hero, on his way home, steps off his plane at Newfoundland to run over the fields with a child — "I guess I felt it was my turn now to move, and so went running — leaping, leaping, pounding, and tingling over the pure white lining of the gray Arctic silence" — catches perfectly that sense of man in the middle of things, a joyous consciousness in accidental space, that gives us the abiding vision of Saul Bellow's novels.

[1959]

Gravity and Grace: The Stories of J. F. Powers

SOME YEARS ago Mr. J. F. Powers startled us with a book of stories called *Prince of Darkness*. They came out of the dry and vast plains of Middle Western boredom, and they were mostly about life in Catholic rectories. Remembering what James Joyce had said about his own first book, *Dubliners*, that he had tried for a style of "scrupulous meanness," I thought that Mr. Powers had managed with almost the same saturated plainness to draw just the opposite conclusions. Joyce showed his people in a limbo of cultured hopelessness, people who were moving from faith into the secular bleakness of the modern city. Mr. Powers showed in the Church the ferocious process of "Americanization," of "normalization," the world of utter mediocrity in which everybody's daily life is lived. And it made no difference. The spirit triumphed every time — but so quietly and unexpectedly that the effect was one of humor rather than zeal. "Grace," to use the formula of Simone Weil, won over the law of "gravity" that keeps *everybody* with his feet too much on the ground.

What made these stories so remarkable was maturity. American fiction is always striking an attitude or being "psychological" or just reporting the violence of some unusual experience. Mr. Powers's work was about a *world*; it constantly yielded literary vanity to the truth and depth of this world. He was subtle, funny, precise, and always unexpected. The book seemed to come out of a longer background than most young American writers of fiction ever own.

And now here is a new book, stories again, for Mr. Powers thinks

The Presence of Grace, by J. F. Powers. New York: Doubleday and Company.

in stories. He is a miniaturist, a close thinker, close as a chess player at times. When you take on a Powers story, you find yourself working hard from line to line, and constantly being outguessed. Nevertheless, the point is usually the same: the world falls at the feet of the spirit; the smart sophisticated young curate somehow gets his comeuppance, while the deaf impossible old coot he is trying to replace as pastor not only retains his post, but stands supreme in his dignity at the end, representing a truth, a charity, that makes him beautiful. Indeed, the usual situation in Powers is not even a struggle on equal terms between the world and the spirit; it is, more usually, the vain struggle of the ambitious young curate to make his place in the church through "realism," salesmanship. And in his constant defeat, we are expected, I suppose, to see that the wisdom of the Church is deeper than even it knows.

In story after story the space in which we move is one of "gravity," but the victory that is won is one of grace. Gravity not only holds us down to earth; it is the fatal ordinariness of life that brings everybody down, even priests. The humor is that ordinary American materialism can operate as a *means* to ends that are implicit in the faith. The point that he always makes so quietly is that clerical housekeeping gets as muddled as any other. The coffee, apparently, is a particular horror, and there is an obsessive amount of bread-pudding. Itchy; everything needs painting; the vow of chastity includes the usual absent-minded American overeating. Everybody's life in the morning, especially, is one of gravity, and these priests are no exception. The atmosphere Mr. Powers creates is exemplary in its suggestion of dyspepsia, overfeeding, and competitiveness. And grace? The point about grace is that it is always mysterious. Its presence is a gift. In the title story, there is even a complicated pun on the word, for the lady named Grace is a gossipmonger, a horrid Pharisee who has broken with her best friend, a middle-aged lady who has taken in an eligible widower for a boarder. The presence of grace nevertheless makes itself felt — or rather, the intimation of it is felt as possible — when Grace's gang of ladies are stopped by an old priest who in all other respects appears incompetent.

I admire Mr. Powers very much — story after story is worked out to the finest possible point; this is work that manages, by fusing intelligence and compassion, to come out as humor. There is real love in his heart, but he knows that the *heart* does not write short stories, and that the beauty of grace can appear only against the background of the horrid daily element, which is gravity. Gravity and grace are the *only* possible elements in which a true imagination can work. The one stands for "reality"; the other for ideal beauty. Most American writers don't even know that they are necessary to each other. Their world has no background, nothing by which to judge the pitifulness of our daily actions.

But may I, very softly, complain? Mr. Powers has fallen into a rut, he now works too much by formula, and the deplorable cuteness into which he sometimes falls is there because he knows too well in advance what his material "means," so that we find him looking for situations with which to "handle" his material. Two stories here are told by cats; one would have been enough. Mr. Powers offers us so "shrewd" an outcome, in story after story, that by now it is clear not only that he is writing about life in the Church, but that he is dramatizing the Church itself, constantly pointing to the unpretentious means by which it wins its true ends. There were several times when I definitely saw Bing Crosby and Barry Fitzgerald in this collection as the lovable priests. Like any other fictional "world," Mr. Powers's scenes from clerical life have become, from too close exploitation, rather obviously picturesque.

But I must not close without saying again what an original Mr. Powers is, and what a true writer he seems on the immature American scene.

[1956]

In Praise of Robert Lowell

ROBERT LOWELL's poetic style has been marked by a peculiar force, one that might well have been called violence but for its learning, bookishness, and nostalgia for traditional order. In the book that made him famous, *Lord Weary's Castle,* he wrote with the precision of passion, he cut his phrases as fine as Braille; but between the

Life Studies: New Poems and an Autobiographical Fragment, by Robert Lowell. New York: Farrar, Straus and Cudahy.

elegantly turned tumult of style and the invocation of Catholic glory and order, he was saved not only from violence but also from confronting his own past too directly, from getting too close to rude experience. The formal beauty of his style was extraordinary. Yet shaken as I was by *Lord Weary's Castle*, I felt that Lowell had not only learned (or intuited) a style from reading many books, but that this same rapid and mountainous eloquence had kept him chaste before life, had saved him from some more necessary and desperate encounter with himself. There was something clingingly literary about the tone of these strong poems, as there was about his going to prison during the war as a Catholic conscientious objector. He seemed to be more intense about life than intimate with it.

Life Studies is a remarkable book precisely because Lowell has had the wit — or is this simply the virtue of his imagination? — to face his past and to strip his style without sacrificing its native elegance. It is the book of an absolutely first-rate talent; and, what is so rare, it is a *book*, not an arrangement of poems. It includes a prose autobiography, "91 Revere Street," that presents all the personal themes developed in the poems, and in itself is the vividest example that I have seen in years of how witty, light, seemingly negligent, and always controlled the prose of a really gifted poet can be.

Robert Lowell is a . . . Lowell, and comes out of the heart of Lowell country — Beacon Hill. His memoir, though acerb and wise and tender, has above all that extraordinary subtlety of upper-class commentary on itself (something you don't find in so good a book as *The Late George Apley*) that is possible to Americans who don't really know anyone beyond themselves but who have the gift of experiencing and expressing their own situation to the depths. It is this that made Henry Adams, with all his pretentiousness, such a marvelous autobiographer; Robert Lowell has only, poker-faced, to write "In 1924 people still lived in cities" for us to know exactly where we are. The Lowells bought 91 Revere Street ("looking out on an unbuttoned part of Beacon Hill . . .") because the poet's mother wanted to get her husband out of the Navy, and a civilian address was the opening wedge, since the commander of the Boston Navy Yard disapproved of his officers' living in town. "My mother felt a horrified giddiness

about the adventure of our address. She once said, 'We are barely
perched on the outer rim of the hub of decency.' "

The portraits of Lowell's parents are superb in their ease and sug-
gestiveness. The mother "was hysterical even in her calm, but like a
patient and forbearing strategist, she tried to pretend her neutrality."
The father, a kindly and dim naval engineer, seems always to have
been under attack by forces more articulate than himself. "By the
time he graduated from Annapolis, he had a high sense of abstract
form, which he beclouded with his humor. He had reached, perhaps,
his final mental possibilities. He was deep — not with profundity,
but with the dumb depth of one who trusted in statistics and was
dubious of personal experience." The hand of conventional expectation in Boston was heavy on Brahmin boys enrolled at birth in St.
Mark's. "We were darkly imperiled, like some annual bevy of Athe-
nian youths destined for the Minotaur. And to judge from my father, men between the ages of six and sixty did nothing but meet
new challenges, take on heavier responsibilities, and lose all freedom
to explode."

« 2 »

The poems open with a meditation on Rome in 1950 that catches
the nervous sense of other people's grandeur that the American is
likely to feel in Europe — and that also catches the poet's romantic
disillusionment and Boston self-enclosure:

> There the skirt-mad Mussolini unfurled
> the eagle of Caesar. He was one of us
> only, pure prose. I envy the conspicuous
> waste of our grandparents on their
>   grand tours —
> long-haired Victorian sages accepted
>   the universe,
> while breezing on their trust funds
>   through the world.

The regret that Mussolini was "one of us/only, pure prose" seems to
me a revealing expression of that overliterary inflation which Lowell
learned from Ezra Pound along with Pound's dash and speed. But
the conscious wit of the poem is remarkable, far more controlled and

poised than such set pieces in Pound's *Cantos.* Just as Pound so often reminds one of Browning, so Lowell seems, through Pound, to have gone straight back to Browning.

It is 1950, the year of the dogma of the Assumption, and Lowell catches the excitement and density of the Roman crowds, the memory of the dead idol:

> The Duce's lynched, bare, booted skull still spoke.
> God herded his people to the *coup de grâce* —
> the costumed Switzers sloped their pikes to push,
> O Pius, through the monstrous human crush.

It is this vividness, the energy and texture of each image, that is Lowell's distinct achievement. He specializes in place, in eloquent vertigo, in stylizing the communion with self that is the essence of dramatic monologue, and I can't think of any poet of his generation who has polished the dramatic sense, rare enough, to such acuteness. One of his favorite words is *jack-hammer*, and there is a similar intimation of strength in all his language, like the lash of the sea images in his earlier book, that comes through even in isolated bits. Marie de Medici speaks after the assassination of her husband, Henri IV:

> And so I press my lover's palm to mine;
> I am his vintage, and his living vine
> entangles me, and oozes mortal wine
> moment to moment.

The poem on Eisenhower's first inauguration reproduces the leaping style of Hart Crane:

> The snow had buried Stuyvesant.
> The subways drummed the vaults.
>   I heard
> the El's green girders charge on Third,
> Manhattan's truss of adamant,
> that groaned in ermine, slummed
>   on want . . .

but ends with a steely passage that Crane could never have held up:

> Look, the fixed stars, all just alike
> as lack-land atoms, split apart,

and the Republic summons Ike,
the mausoleum in her heart.

But beautiful as these opening poems are — the soliloquy of Hart
Crane, the address to Santayana in the Protestant Cemetery in
Rome, and others — my greatest pleasure in this book is in the "life
studies" proper. Here Lowell has achieved the nakedness toward
which all good poets yearn — freedom from the suffocating traditions of fine style that in our day have again overcome poetry. When
I first saw these intensely personal, brilliantly candid poems about
mental breakdown and marital dolor, I was not able to imagine
how natural the whole group of them would look in a book. Any
good writer will learn to trust his inner impressions, but in a relatively minor poem like "Memories of West Street and Lepke," it is
the cross-stitch and variation of line that gives Lowell's "new" simplicity its exhilaration. As a conscientious objector in jail, Lowell
saw the "T-shirted back" of Lepke, the Czar of Murder, Inc.

> there piling towels on a rack,
> or dawdling off to his little segregated cell full
> of things forbidden the common man:
> a portable radio, a dresser, two toy American
> flags tied together with a ribbon of Easter palm.
> Flabby, bald, lobotomized,
> he drifted in a sheepish calm,
> where no agonizing reappraisal
> jarred his concentration on the electric chair —
> hanging like an oasis in his air
> of lost connections . . .

The vividness, picture after picture, is striking. Lowell describes
his father, who, leaving the Navy, drifted from job to job, and every
time he lost a job bought a better car:

> but his best friend was his little black *Chevie*,
> garaged like a sacrificial steer
> with gilded hooves,
> yet sensationally sober . . .

Lowell's mother died in Italy, and he relates how the body was
taken home for burial in the States. "Mother travelled first-class in

the hold;/her *Risorgimento* black and gold casket/ . . . In the grandiloquent lettering on Mother's coffin/*Lowell* had been misspelled LOVEL./The corpse was wrapped like *panetone* in Italian tinfoil." Even a poem about life in a mental hospital has this typical wit, the ease and neutral tone with which Lowell speaks of "These victorious figures of bravado ossified young." But the poem ends, unforgettably, on the lines "We are all old timers,/each of us holds a locked razor."

In these poems twentieth-century poetry comes back to its great tradition as plain speech; comes back, in Pasternak's phrase, "to its sister, life."

[1959]

J. D. Salinger: "Everybody's Favorite"

THE PUBLICATION of his two well-known stories from the *New Yorker* in book form, *Franny and Zooey*, brings home the fact that for one reason or another J. D. Salinger now figures in American writing as a special case. After all, there are not many writers who could bring out a book composed of two stories — both of which have already been read and argued over and analyzed to death by that enormous public of sophisticated people which radiates from the *New Yorker* to every English department in the land. Yet Salinger's fascination for this public is so great that although he has refused this book to every book club, it may yet sell as if it were being pushed by book clubs. Since 1953, when *The Catcher in the Rye* was reprinted as a paperback, it has become the favorite American novel on the required or suggested reading lists of American colleges and secondary schools, and it has sold well over a million and a half copies. Yet no less unusual is the fact that the *New Yorker* — which if it did not originate certainly brought to perfection the kind of tight, allusive, ironic story with which Salinger's earlier stories (reprinted in *Nine Stories*, 1953) felt so much at home — published in

Franny and Zooey, by J. D. Salinger. Boston: Little, Brown and Company.

"Zooey" (41,130 words) the longest story it had ever published, and a story for which the *New Yorker* obviously felt personal affection and some particular intellectual sympathy.

In one form or another, as a fellow novelist commented unlovingly, Salinger is "everybody's favorite." He is certainly a favorite of the *New Yorker*, which in 1959 published another long story around the Glass family called "Seymour: An Introduction" (almost 30,000 words), and thus gave the impression of stretching and remaking itself to Salinger's latest stories, each of which has been appearing, like a visit from outer space, at two-year intervals. But above all is he a favorite with that audience of students, student intellectuals, instructors, and generally literary, sensitive and sophisticated young people who respond to him with a consciousness that he speaks for them and virtually *to* them, in a language that is peculiarly "honest" and their own, with a vision of things that captures their most secret judgments of the world. The only thing that Salinger does not do for this audience is to meet with them. Holden Caulfield said in *The Catcher in the Rye* that "What really knocks me out is a book that, when you're all done reading it, you wish the author that wrote it was a terrific friend of yours and you could call him up on the phone whenever you felt like it." It is well for him that all the people in this country who now regard J. D. Salinger as a "terrific friend" do not call him up and reach him.

A fundamental reason for Salinger's appeal (like that of Hemingway in the short stories that made *him* famous) is that he has exciting professional mastery of a peculiarly charged and dramatic medium — the American short story. At a time when so much American fiction has been discursive in tone, careless in language, lacking in edge and force — when else would it have been possible for crudities like the beat novelists to be taken seriously? — Salinger has done an honest and stimulating professional job in a medium which, when it is expertly handled, projects emotion like a cry from the stage and in form can be as intense as a lyric poem. A short story which is not handled with necessary concentration and wit is like a play which does not engage its audience; a story does not exist unless it hits its mark with terrific impact. It is a constant projection of meanings at an audience, and it is a performance minutely made up of the only possible language, as a poem is. In America, at least, where on the whole the best stories are the most professional stories and so are published in the most famous magazines, "second-rate" stories belong in the same limbo with unsuccessful musical comedies; unless you hit the bull's-eye, you don't score.

This does not mean that the best-known stories are first-rate pieces of literature any more than that so many triumphant musical comedies are additions to the world's drama; it means only that the story has communicated itself with entire vividness to its editor and its audience. The profundity that may exist in a short story by Chekhov or Tolstoy also depends upon the author's immediate success in conveying his purpose. Even in the medieval "tale" which Tolstoy in his greatest stories seems to recapture in tone and spirit, the final comment on human existence follows from the deliberate artlessness of tone that the author has managed to capture like a speech in a play.

« 2 »

What makes Salinger's stories particularly exciting is his intense, his almost compulsive, need to fill in each inch of his canvas, each moment of his scene. Many great novels owe their grandeur to a leisurely sense of suggestion, to the imitation of life as a boundless road or flowing river — to the very relaxation of that intensity which Poe thought was the esthetic perfection of a poem or a story. But whatever the professional superficiality of the short story in American hands, which have molded and polished it so as to reach, dazzle and on occasion deceive the reader, a writer like Salinger, by working so hard to keep his tiny scene alive, keeps everything humming.

Someday there will be learned theses on *The Use of the Ashtray in J. D. Salinger's Stories*; no other writer has made so much of Americans' lighting up, reaching for the ashtray, setting up the ashtray with one hand while with the other they reach for a ringing telephone. Ours is a society complicated with many appliances, and Salinger always tells you what his characters are doing with each of their hands. In one long stretch of "Zooey" he describes that young man sitting in a bathtub, reading a long letter from his brother and smoking; he manages to describe every exertion made and every sensation felt in that bathtub by the young man whose knees made "dry islands." Then the young man's mother comes into the

bathroom; he draws the shower curtains around the tub, she rearranges the medicine cabinet, and while they talk (in full) everything
they do is described. Everything, that is, within Salinger's purpose in
getting at such detail — which is not the loose, shuffling catalogue of
the old-fashioned naturalists who had the illusion of reproducing
the whole world, but the tension of a dramatist or theater director
making a fuss about a character walking just so.

For Salinger, the expert performer and director (brother Buddy
Glass, who is supposed to be narrating "Zooey," speaks of "direct-
ing" it and calls the story itself a "prose home movie"), gesture is
the essence of the medium. A short story does not offer room enough
for the development of character; it can present only character itself — by gesture. And Salinger is remarkable, I would say he is almost frenetically proficient, in getting us, at the opening of
"Franny," to *see* college boys waiting on a train platform to greet
their dates arriving for a big football weekend. They rush out to the
train, "most of them giving the impression of having at least three
lighted cigarettes in each hand." He knows exactly how Franny
Glass would be greeted by Lane Coutell — "It was a station-platform
kiss — spontaneous enough to begin with, but rather inhibited in
the follow-through, and with something of a forehead-bumping aspect."

And even better is his description of the boy at a good restaurant taking a first sip of his martini and then looking "around the
room with an almost palpable sense of well-being at finding himself
(he must have been sure no one could dispute) in the right place
with an unimpeachably right-looking girl." Salinger knows how to
prepare us with this gesture for the later insensitivity of a boy who
is exactly one of those elaborately up-to-date and anxiously sophisticated people whom Franny Glass, pure in heart, must learn to tolerate and even to love in what she regards as an unbearably shallow
culture.

But apart from this, which is the theme of *Franny and Zooey*, the
gesture itself is recognized by the reader not only as a compliment
to himself but as a sign that Salinger is working all the time — not
merely working to get the reader to see, but working to make his
scene itself hum with life and creative observation. I don't know
how much this appearance of intensity on the part of Salinger him-

self, of constant as well as full coverage, is due to *New Yorker* editorial nudging, since its famous alertness to repetitions of words and vagueness of diction tends to give an external look of freshness and movement to prose. Salinger not only works very hard indeed over each story, but he obviously writes to and for some particular editorial mind he identifies with the *New Yorker* — look up the stories he used to write for the *Saturday Evening Post* and *Cosmopolitan*, and you will see that, just as married people get to look alike by reproducing each other's facial expressions, so a story by Salinger and a passage of commentary in the *New Yorker* now tend to resemble each other.

But whatever the enormous influence of any magazine on those who write regularly for it, Salinger's emphasis of certain words and syllables in American speech and his own compulsiveness in bearing down hard on certain details (almost as if he wanted to make the furniture, like the gestures of certain people, tell *everything* about the people who use them) do give his stories the intensity of observation that is fundamental to his success. Lane Coutell, sitting in that restaurant with Franny and talking about a college paper on Flaubert he is horribly well satisfied with, says: ". . . I think the emphasis I put on *why* he was so neurotically attached to the *mot juste* wasn't too bad. I mean in the light of what we know today. Not just psychoanalysis and all that crap, but certainly to a certain extent. You know what I mean. I'm no Freudian man or anything like that, but certain things you can't just pass over as capital-F Freudian and let them go at that. I mean to a certain extent I think I was perfectly justified to point out that none of the really good boys — Tolstoy, Dostoevski, *Shake*speare, for Chrissake — were such goddam word-squeezers. They just *wrote*. Know what I mean?" What strikes me about this mimicry is not merely that it is so clever, but that it is also so relentless. In everything that this sophisticated ass Lane Coutell says, one recognizes that he is and will be *wrong*. Salinger disapproves of him in the deepest possible way — he is a spiritual enemy.

Of course it is a vision of things that lies behind Salinger's expert manner. There is always one behind every manner. The language of fiction, whatever it may accomplish as representation, ultimately conveys an author's intimation of things, makes us hear (not in a statement but in the ensemble of his realized efforts) his quintessential commentary on the nature of existence. However, the more deliberate the language of the writer, as it must be in a short story, the more the writer must convey his judgment of things in one highlighted dramatic action, as is done on the stage.

At the end of "Franny," the young girl collapses in the ladies' room of the restaurant where she has been lunching with her cool boy friend. This conveys her spiritual desperation in his company, for Lane typifies a society where "Everything everybody does is so — I don't know — not *wrong*, or even mean, or even stupid necessarily. But just so tiny and meaningless and — sad-making." Her brother Zooey (Zachary Glass), at the end of the long second story, calls her up from another telephone number in the same apartment and somehow reaches to the heart of her problem and gives her peace by reminding her that the "Fat Lady" they used to picture somnolently listening to them when they were quiz kids on the radio — the ugly, lazy, even disgusting-looking "Fat Lady" who more and more typifies unattractive and selfish humanity in our day — can be loved after all, for she, too, is Jesus Christ.

‹ 3 ›

In each story, the climax bears a burden of meaning that it would not have to bear in a novel; besides being stagy, the stories are related in a way that connects both of them into a single chronicle. This, to quote the title of a little religious pamphlet often mentioned in it, might be called "The Way of a Pilgrim." Both Franny and Zooey Glass are, indeed, pilgrims seeking their way in a society typified by the "Fat Lady" and even by Lane Coutell's meaningless patter of sophistication. No wonder Franny cries out to her unhearing escort: "I'm sick of just liking people. I wish to God I could meet somebody I could respect. . . ."

The Glasses (mother Irish, father Jewish) are ex-vaudevillians whose children were all, as infant prodigies, performers on a radio quiz program called "It's a Wise Child." Now, though engaged in normally sophisticated enterprises (Franny goes to a fashionable woman's college, Zooey is a television actor, Buddy a college instructor), they have retained their intellectual precocity (and indeed their precocious charm) and have translated, as it were, their awareness of themselves as special beings into a conviction that they alone can do justice to their search for the true way.

The eldest and most brilliant of the children, Seymour, shot himself in 1948 while on his honeymoon in Florida — this was the climax of Salinger's perhaps most famous story, "A Perfect Day for Bananafish." And it is from Seymour's old room in the Glass apartment that Zooey calls up his sister Franny — on a phone that is normally never used, that is still listed in the name of Seymour Glass, and that has been kept up by Buddy (who does not want a phone in his own country retreat) and by Zooey in order to perpetuate Seymour's name and to symbolize his continuing influence on them as a teacher and guide. It is from reading over again, in Seymour's old room, various religious sayings from the world's literature that Seymour had copied out on a piece of beaverboard nailed to the back of a door that Zooey is inspired to make the phone call to Franny that ends with the revelation that the horrible Fat Lady is really Jesus Christ.

This final episode, both in the cuteness of its invention and in the cuteness of speech so often attributed to Seymour, who is regarded in his own family as a kind of *guru* or sage, helps us to understand Salinger's wide popularity. I am sorry to have to use the word "cute" in respect to Salinger, but there is absolutely no other word that for me so accurately typifies the self-conscious charm and prankishness of his own writing and his extraordinary cherishing of his favorite Glass characters.

Holden Caulfield is also cute in *The Catcher in the Rye,* cute in his little-boy suffering for his dead brother Allie and cute in his longing for his sister, "Old Phoebe." But we expect that boys of that age may be cute — that is, consciously appealing and consciously clever. To be these things is almost their only resource in a world where parents and schoolmasters have all the power and the experience. Cuteness, for an adolescent, is to turn the normal self-pity of children, which arises from their relative weakness, into a relative advantage vis-à-vis the adult world. It becomes a "role" boys can play in the absence of other advantages, and *The Catcher in the Rye* is so full of Holden's cute speech and cute innocence and cute lovingness for his own family that one must be an absolute monster not to like it.

And on a higher level, but with the same conscious winsomeness, the same conscious mournfulness and intellectual loneliness and lovingness (though not for his wife), Seymour Glass is cute when he sits on the beach with a little girl telling her a parable of "banana fish" — ordinary-looking fish when "they swim into a hole where there's a lot of bananas," but "after that, they're so fat they can't get out of the hole again. . . . They die." His wife, meanwhile, busy in their room on the long-distance phone to her mother in New York, makes it abundantly clear, in the hilariously accurate cadences and substance of her conversation, why her husband finds it more natural to talk to a four-year-old girl on the beach than to her. Among other things, Seymour expects not to be understood outside the Glass family. But agonizing as this situation is, the brilliantly entertaining texture of "A Perfect Day for Bananafish" depends on Seymour Glass's conscious cleverness as well as on his conscious suffering — even his conscious cleverness *about* the suffering of "ordinary-looking" fish who get so bloated eating too many bananas in a "hole" they shouldn't have been attracted to in the first place.

In the same way, not only does the entertaining surface of *Franny and Zooey* depend on the conscious appealingness and youthfulness and generosity and sensitivity of Seymour's brother and sister, but Salinger himself, in describing these two, so obviously feels such boundless affection for them that you finally get the sense of all these child prodigies and child entertainers being tied round and round with veils of self-love in a culture which they — and Salinger — just despise. Despise above all for its intellectual pretentiousness. Yet this is the society, typified by the "Fat Lady" (symbolically, they pictured her as their *audience!*), whom they must now force themselves to think of as Jesus Christ, and whom, as Christ Himself, they can now at last learn to love.

For myself, I must confess that the spiritual transformation that so many people associate with the very sight of the word "love" on the printed page does not move me as it should. In what has been considered Salinger's best story, "For Esmé with Love and Squalor," Sergeant X in the American Army of Occupation in Germany is saved from a hopeless breakdown by the beautiful magnanimity and remembrance of an aristocratic young English girl. We are prepared for *this* climax or visitation by an earlier scene — the Sergeant comes upon a book by Goebbels in which a Nazi woman had written, "Dear God, life is hell." Under this, persuaded at last of his common suffering even with a Nazi, X writes down, from *The Brothers Karamazov*: "Fathers and teachers, I ponder 'What is hell?' I maintain that it is the suffering of being unable to love."

But the love that Father Zossima in Dostoevsky's novel speaks for is surely love for the world, for God's creation itself, for all that precedes us and supports us — that will outlast us and that alone helps us to explain ourselves to ourselves. It is the love that D. H. Lawrence, another religious novelist, spoke of as "the sympathetic bond" and that in one form or another lies behind all the great novels as a primary *interest* in everyone and everything alive with us on this common earth. The love that Salinger's horribly precocious Glass characters speak of is love for certain people only — forgiveness is for the rest; finally, through Seymour Glass's indoctrination of his brothers and sister in so many different (and pretentiously assembled) religious teachings, it is love of certain *ideas*. So what is ultimate in their love is the love of their own moral and intellectual excellence, of their chastity and purity in a world full of banana fish swollen with too much food. It is the love that they have for themselves as an idea.

The worst they can say about our society is that *they* are too sensitive to live in it. They are the special case in whose name society is condemned. And what makes them so is that they are *young*, precocious, sensitive, different. In Salinger's work the two estates — the world and the cutely sensitive young — never really touch at all. Holden Caulfield condemns parents and schools because he knows that they are incapable of understanding him; Zooey and Franny and Buddy (like Seymour before them) know that the great mass of prosperous spiritual savages in our society will never understand them.

This may be true, but to think so can lead to a violation of art. Huckleberry Finn (so often cited as a parallel to the hero of *The Catcher in the Rye*) was two years younger than Holden, but the reason he was not afraid of an adult's world is that he had respect for it. He had never even seen very much of it until he got on that raft with a runaway Negro slave he came to love and was able to save. It was still all God's creation and inspired him with wonder. But Holden and, even more, the Glass children are beaten before they start; beaten in order not to start. They do not trust anything or anyone but themselves and their great "idea." And what troubles me about this is not what it reflects of their theology but what it does to Salinger's art.

« 4 »

Frank O'Connor once said of this special métier, the short story, that it is "the art form that deals with the individual when there is no longer a society to absorb him, and when he is compelled to exist, as it were, by his own inner light." This is the condition on which Salinger's work rests, and I should be sorry to seem unsympathetic toward it. It is an American fact, as one can see from the relative lack in our literature of the ripe and fully developed social novel in which the individual and society are in concrete and constant relationship with each other. But whatever this lack, which in one sense is as marked in the novels of Scott Fitzgerald as it is in Salinger's emphasis upon the short story, it is a fact that when Fitzgerald describes a character's voice, it is because he really loves — in the creative sense is fully interested in — this character. When Salinger describes a character's voice, it is to tell us that the man is a phony. He has, to borrow a phrase from his own work, a "categorical aversion" to whole classes and types of our society. The "sympathetic bond" that Lawrence spoke of has been broken. People stink in our nostrils. We are mad with captious observation of one another. As a friend of mine once said about the novels of Mary McCarthy, trying to say with absolute justice what it was that *shocked* her so much in them — "the heroine is always right and everyone else is wrong." Salinger is a far more accomplished and objective writer of fiction than Mary McCarthy, but I would say that in his work the Glass children alone are right and everyone else is wrong.

And it is finally this condition, not just the famous "alienation" of Americans from a society like our own, that explains the popularity of Salinger's work. Salinger's vast public, I am convinced, is based not merely on the number of young people who recognize their emotional problems in his fiction and their frustrated rebellions in the sophisticated language he manipulates so skillfully. It is based perhaps even more on all those who have been released by our society to think of themselves as endlessly "sensitive," spiritually alone, gifted — and whose suffering lies in the narrowing of their consciousness to themselves, in the withdrawal of their curiosity from a society which *they* think they understand all too well, in the drying-up of their hope, their trust, and their wonder at the great world itself. The worst of American sophistication today is that it is so bored, so full of categorical aversion to things that writers should never take for granted and never close their eyes to.

The fact that Salinger's work is particularly directed against the "well-fed sunburned" people at the summer theater, at the "section men" in colleges parroting the latest fashionable literary formulas, at the "three-martini" men — this, indeed, is what is wrong. He hates them. They are no longer people but symbols, like the "Fat Lady." No wonder that Zooey tells his sister: *Love them, love them all, love them anyway!* But the problem is not one of spiritual pride or of guilt: it is that in the tearing of the "sympathetic bond" it is not love that goes, but the deepest possibilities of literary art.

[1961]

How Good Is Norman Mailer?

PERHAPS more than any other book since Scott Fitzgerald's *The Crack-up*, this book reveals how exciting, yet tragic, America can be for a gifted writer. It is a remarkably full book; all of Mailer up to now is in it; and that is exactly what is wrong with it. For at thirty-six, after following up *The Naked and the Dead* with an artistic failure, *Barbary Shore*, and one ambiguous *succès de scandale*, *The Deer Park*, Mailer (now embarked on a very long and extremely ambitious novel that may take many years) has obviously been hungry to make his mark again in one big smashing outrageous way. He has put together an anthology of all his works, from undergraduate short stories to two sections of the novel in progress, that

Advertisements for Myself, by Norman Mailer. New York: G. P. Putnam's Sons.

includes his columns from a Greenwich Village weekly, social and political comment, his now famous essay on "The White Negro" and other socio-sexual themes, stories, spoofs, interviews, poems, and some shrewd but essentially subjective evaluations of his literary generation. In the "advertisements" to the different works he talks about himself and Hemingway, himself and marijuana, himself and sex, himself and Eisenhower's America. By the time you get through what is often a very brilliant if screamingly self-conscious book, you feel that Mailer has worked so hard to display everything he has done and everything he knows that it has all collected on the surface. Mailer's performance here reminds me of the brilliant talker who impresses the hell out of you at a cocktail party but who, when he turns his back to go home, seems vaguely lost.

« 2 »

Yet *Advertisements for Myself* is a remarkable performance, and it is clearer to me than ever that Mailer is a powerful, courageous talent admirably provoked by our culture. I admire him because he is naturally a radical, strong, and exuberant talent; this book is full of more penetrating comment on the America of Eisenhower, television, suburbia, and J. D. Salinger than anything I have seen in years. But as Mailer says, "I have been running for President these last ten years in the privacy of my mind," and he is probably the only Jew who has been. He wants to be not just a good novelist but the Hemingway of our period. Hemingway obsesses him (and ignores him); Faulkner once made fun of him for saying that whites are always jealous of Negro sexuality; the publisher who made so much out of *The Naked and the Dead* finally turned down *The Deer Park*; there are actually good writers in America who pay no attention to him.

In short, like many another American radical, desperado, Reichian stalwart of sexual frankness, Norman Mailer has been driven crazy by an affluent and greasily accommodating society which not only doesn't oppose him but which turns even his disgust and frankness into a form of literary capital. Just as the hipsters, whom Mailer admires, are not outlaws, not radicals, but the slobs and remittance men and spoiled brats of a society so wasteful and indulgent and satiated with normal sex that it has to discover new thrills all the time, so the secret burn of Norman Mailer is that a book like this, which is meant to slap respectable America in the face, may not sell as much as it could. Like every American writer whose name is an instant password, who can support himself by his writing, who knows himself a celebrity because he moves largely in the company of celebrities, Mailer can no more stay off television or move back to Brooklyn than, being an honest and intransigent spirit, he can admire television or sentimentalize the Brooklyn which, as he says, is not the center of anything. Anyone who reads this book with as much attention and admiration as I have just done can, nevertheless, see that what obsesses Norman Mailer is not just the swarminess of our culture, the repressiveness of our official morals, the flabby gentility of our ruling intellectuals, but the fact that this same America is itself constantly coaxing Norman Mailer to share in the take and join the fun.

What makes this society so marvelous for the gifted rebel, and so awful, is that, lacking all standards by which to counter or to question the new, it hungrily welcomes any talent that challenges it interestingly — but then holds this talent in the mold of its own shapelessness; the writer is never free enough of his neighbors and contemporaries to be not simply agin the government but detached from it. Mailer, who like all his generation has had to work against the overpowering example of Fitzgerald and Hemingway and Faulkner, now thinks that these older fellows had it easier, that our society did not drag them into its maw as compulsively as it does present writers. When I recall how desperately out of fashion Fitzgerald and Lewis and Anderson and Cather felt at the end of their careers, I doubt that the literary competition has ever been less punishing than Mailer obviously feels it to be. What has changed since the 1920s is first that there are more and more writers, as there are more and more people. Even "advanced" literature is beginning to get as crowded as the mass media, and Mailer cannot be sure, now that he has dismissed Bellow, ignored Malamud, and ruled out all women writers as unreadable, that there isn't someone in South Dakota who may yet outdistance him.

More important, Hemingway (of whom Mailer seems constantly to dream and to curse in his dreams) was still based enough on the old "inner-directed" Protestant culture to measure his need of courage against the moral abstractions of courage, duty, grace, etc. Mailer measures himself against others. Symbolically, Hemingway got his great experience in the first world madness by volunteering for the Italian Army long before Americans were in the war. Mailer in 1943 had to keep from becoming a clerk, for only as a rifleman could he collect the experience for the great Hemingwayish novel about the war that he was already prepared to write. And only in the Pacific, as he brilliantly estimated again, would he be able to gather experience for a really provocative novel, since there the growing reactionary tendencies in American life would be manifest.

Without his egotism, no writer is likely to carry much weight. But granted that he must fight for himself and push himself, what reserves of thought and imagination are left? A writer is not only what he knows himself to be, what he consciously fights for and hates and loves — he is the book he makes, the book that must surprise him in the making, the book that somewhere within itself is always greater than he is. Scott Fitzgerald's *The Crack-up*, moving as it may be, has less of Fitzgerald than *The Great Gatsby*. The question all over this book is: How good is Norman Mailer? — and the trouble is that Mailer thinks that he can answer it in terms of available competition. Only a highly self-conscious and rather stormily competitive fellow would have tried so hard to win the prize by dismissing so many writers whose books he hasn't read. This performance calls up the comment on the famous French writer who boasted in his journal that sexually he was more gifted than other men: "How does he know?"

Still, *we* have a right to ask, How good is Norman Mailer? How good are his books? Quite apart from the deleterious influence of our government, our publishers, our official morals — and apart from all the obscene words about television and the cowardice of the "squares" and the marvelous sexuality of Negroes and the necessity of Hip — how good are Norman Mailer's novels? My answer would be that *The Naked and the Dead* is a good novel, though too literary, with worked-up army detail that is thin compared with James Jones's *From Here to Eternity*, and with only one real character in it, the General, who is too obvious a villain; that *Barbary Shore* is hysterical politically and a bad novel by a writer of obvious talent and guts, so that everything in it makes its mark, but not as a work of art; that *The Deer Park* is an extraordinarily uneven and somehow sick book with something peculiarly closed and airless about it. I felt this painfully when I read the novel, and Mailer says in *Advertisements* that he rewrote the novel under marijuana. I am neither shocked by this nor moved to admire Mailer because of it; I do think that *The Deer Park* is not what Mailer thinks it is. It seems to me ridiculous for. Mailer to push his novel so hard in this book, since the question is not what Rinehart or the critics did to the book but what Mailer did.

How good is Norman Mailer? The answer varies from work to work, sometimes from page to page. Some of his new work, particularly a torrid story wholly about sexual intercourse, "The Time of Her Time," seems to me remarkable; the opening of his new book, "Advertisements for Myself on the Way Out," a lot of wind. Not only can Mailer not know how good he is; he is himself one of the most variable, unstable, and on the whole unpredictable writers I have ever read. He has a remarkable intelligence, and this book shows it; a marvelously forceful and inventive style; great objective gifts as a novelist. On the other hand, his intelligence, though muscular, has no real ease or quietly reflective power; he is as fond of his style as an Italian tenor of his vocal chords, and he sometimes tends to overpower when the more manly thing — if I may touch on a major concern in this book — would be to convince; his sense of reality, though boldly critical, is often obsessive in its self-consciousness. On the whole, Norman Mailer is very, very good indeed — not better than ten million other fellows, as he thinks one has to be, but good.

But what will become of him God only knows, for no one can calculate what so overintense a need to dominate, to succeed, to grasp, to win, may do to that side of talent which has its own rule of being and can never be forced.

Truman Capote
and "the Army of Wrongness"

THE HEROINE of *Breakfast at Tiffany's* is of the type made famous by Christopher Isherwood's Sally Bowles. She is the adorable im-

Breakfast at Tiffany's: A short novel and three stories, by Truman Capote. New York: Random House.

moralist, the completely free spirit in a world whose dominating
types are usually disgusting; where her true friends — the narrator,
who speaks as Truman Capote himself, and a lovable old bartender
— can only watch in helpless admiration as she is whirled away from
them to one bed after another.

The lovable strumpet, as Isherwood showed, is a setup for a clever
novelist with a good ear and a flair for highly polished comedy, and
Capote's accurate sense of both the speech and the night life of
upper Bohemian New York shows itself in the way he combs in detail after detail of Holly Golightly's life against the background of a
fly-by-night apartment in the East Seventies. The time is 1943, not
because the war really enters into this society of fashion photographers, South American diplomats, degenerate millionaires, and an-
imal-like Hollywood agents, but because the date symbolizes a society wholly in flux. No one else, however, has the charm of the
lady of the story, who is nineteen, devastingly honest, and in this
cold, often phony world can find comfort only in Tiffany's. When
she gets the "mean reds," which are far worse than the blues, "What
I've found does the most good is just to get into a taxi and go to
Tiffany's. It calms me down right away, the quietness and the proud
look of it; nothing very bad could happen to you there, not with
those kind men in their nice suits, and that lovely smell of silver
and alligator wallets. If I could find a real-life place that made me
feel like Tiffany's, then I'd buy some furniture and give the cat a
name." She has steadily refused to give her cat a name. " 'Poor
slob,' she said, tickling his head, 'poor slob without a name. It's a
little inconvenient, his not having a name. But I haven't any right
to give him one: he'll have to wait until he *belongs* to somebody. . . .' "

This profound instinct for nonattachment, mixed with a certain
wry tenderness for those who would like to be attached (the cat, the
narrator, the elderly bartender), is the "serious" side of the book,
and one that ultimately raises doubts about Capote's ability to
bring off the story he intended to write. But the purely external
side of Holly's character, as seen before one gets to know her or by
those who never do, is skillfully done. Capote has caught perfectly
the professional accent of New York, the trigger-tenseness of a
speech that is always excited, declamatory, on the make. Miss Golightly alone seems to keep cool — Miss Holly Golightly, who can

never hold on to her key and, coming home in the dead of night with a new gentleman, cheerfully rings other people's bells so that they will let her in. She is impulsive, she is direct, she is generous — and while she does not get *paid* for anything, she judges a man by his "chic." "Any gent with the slightest chic will give you fifty for the girl's john, and I always ask for cab fare too, that's another fifty." When she discovers that the narrator is a writer, she is reminded that she has never been to bed with a writer, and demands the ages of the more famous. "I can't get excited by a man until he's forty-two. . . . I simply *trained* myself to like older men, and it was the smartest thing I ever did."

A horrible old Hollywood agent ("Tufts of hair sprouted from his ears, from his nose; his jowls were gray with afternoon beard, and his handshake almost furry") reveals that Holly gave up her big chance in Hollywood. "She says you got to want it to be good and I don't want it, I say Well, what the hell do you want, and she says When I find out you'll be the first to know." There is a cocktail party at Holly's. "Except for a lack of youth, the guests had no common theme, they seemed strangers among strangers; indeed each face on entering had struggled to conceal dismay at seeing others there." At the party is a pro-Nazi millionaire, and it is worth quoting the first description of him, for it conveys the acidulous, "social," and hard manner of Capote at his best:

He was a middle-aged child who had never shed its baby fat, though some gifted tailor had almost succeeded in camouflaging his plump and spankable bottom. There wasn't a suspicion of bone in his body; his face, a zero filled in with pretty miniature features, had an unused, a virginal quality: it was as if he'd been born, then expanded, his skin remaining unlined as a blown-up balloon, and his mouth, though ready for squalls and tantrums, a spoiled sweet puckering.

This is good writing, and — what one should not miss in Capote when he has his eye on a character, not on his own "style" — it is angry writing. For as the narrator reflects, "If Holly could marry that 'absurd fetus,' then the army of wrongness rampant in the world might as well march over me."

Holly doesn't marry him, but the end of the story is as inconsequential as its background. It turns out that Holly is really a hillbilly who was married to a Texas farmer at thirteen or so and played stepmother to his many children before she ran away. The hoped-for tenderness that Capote tries to build up as a significant part of her life fails, and because of this failure the story turns sentimental when it is no longer clever. The fact is that it is impossible to believe anything of Holly but what we can see before us. Without her patter, her legion of boy friends, her cat, and her guitar, she is nothing. And the failure to make her background convincing starts from the curious doubleness that afflicts Capote's writing. Either he builds up a witty line of social details, seen from the outside, or he collapses into tender and mawkish details that are really private symbols. As Holly herself says about the narrator, he does a lot of "Yearning. . . . He wants awfully to be on the inside staring out," and she pictures him with his "nose pressed against a glass."

The lovable old bartender in the story, the narrator's fellow in respectful admiration of Holly, insists that it is possible to love a woman without sex. "You can love somebody without it being like that. You keep them a stranger, a stranger who's a friend." Yet *Breakfast at Tiffany's* is a love story; the point of the story lies in the narrator's attachment to one who can be attached to nobody, and who, when she gives up her cat in the end, suddenly realizes how frightened you can get from "Not knowing what's yours until you've thrown it away." The trouble with the narrator's kind of love is that it is too easy; it presents us with an image of the loved one that cannot be proved; it gives us the outline without the woman, a "character," not a person.

Whenever Capote tries to suggest the inner life of his heroine, the writing breaks down. The image of the starving hillbilly child never comes into focus behind the brightly polished and eccentric woman-about-town in her black dress, pearl choker, and sandals. The reason is that the narrator can show us only his "admiration," not his passion, and one of the serious faults of the story is that we are meant, for the explanation of certain passages, to think of the narrator as Truman Capote the author, the sad little devil whose picture is always so prominent on the back of each book. This kind of extraliterary reference violates the imaginative unity of the story; yet in one sense the story has never been unified at all, for the emphasis has been alternately on Holly as a town character and Holly as a Southern waif — never on Holly as a woman. This double vision was a limitation of Isherwood's portrait of Sally Bowles, but what gave *Good-bye to Berlin* its lasting quality was the documentation of Germany on the eve of Hitler, and the humility with which Isherwood recorded the oncoming disaster. For Truman Capote the "armies of wrongness" are indiscriminate: the "absurd fetuses" are really everybody. They are the enemies of those who are truly poor in spirit, like Holly. But we cannot take these "armies of wrongness" too seriously, for between Capote's pity for the hillbilly child and his instinct for the smart Madison Avenue manner, some deeper tone than either — the tone of actuality, which comes from the portrayal of people in truthful relationship with each other — has been lost.

It is a great pity, for Capote is not only a writer of admirable talent, but he has an eye for human weakness, a feeling for those who really are oppressed, that could be devastating. He is not a superficial writer; no one should miss how much he has aimed for in this clever book. But he is a writer for whom the world is all society or all self, public vice or private tears.

[1958]

The Essays of James Baldwin

RECENTLY, a scholar investigating the Negro novel in America discovered that of sixty-two Negro novelists writing between 1853 and 1952, forty published only one novel; eleven published only two; only eleven published more than two. Certainly one reason for this situation is the economic difficulties that so many Negro writers have had, a lack of encouragement from publishers and a lack of audience among Negroes as among whites. But surely another reason is that too often a writer turns to the novel not because his talent lies in fiction, not even because he wants to write fiction, but because he hopes to make his experience seem as individual and artistically realized as possible. To many writers in this country the novel seems the only badge of "creativity," and it is understandable

Nobody Knows My Name: More Notes of a Native Son, by James Baldwin. New York: Dial Press.

that a Negro would aim for the novel as a way of gaining distinction for his individual experience.

This is a kind of thinking that operates among many minorities in this country, for one of the incidental blows to a writer's self-respect is the belief that everybody knows about his background anyway, and that the only way for him to get out of the rut of Harlem or the East Bronx is by transmuting his experience into a conscious work of art. But of course the deliberate transmutation of one's own experience into "fiction" works badly. The book doesn't really hang together on its own terms, as the novel of a genuine novelist does. So after the first, transparently autobiographical novel, the second requires a wholly imaginative conception that often isn't there. And even among the pros, those who write novels because they think in narrative, there is often a strained and "hypothetical" quality, to adapt the title of one of James Baldwin's essays, that suggests the writer is trying to do certain things in and with the novel to show that he can do them. Baldwin himself, who is certainly a good novelist and is likely to become an even better one, nevertheless strained pretty hard in *Giovanni's Room* to show that he could write a novel entirely about a sexual conflict among white people. That was a "hypothetical" situation, and in some respects the novel remained hypothetical too.

When I read Baldwin's first collection of essays, *Notes of a Native Son,* I realized that the tortured intellectual consciousness I felt behind his fiction could be turned into the self-representation of an absolutely first-class essayist, reporter, and social critic. *Notes of a Native Son* is one of the two or three best books ever written about the Negro in America, and it is the work of an original literary talent who operates with as much power in the essay form as I've ever seen. I'm sure that Baldwin doesn't like to hear his essays praised at the expense (seemingly) of his fiction. And I'm equally sure that if Baldwin were not so talented a novelist he would not be so remarkable an essayist. But the great thing about his essays is that the form allows him to work out from all the conflicts raging in *him,* so that finally the "I," the "James Baldwin" who is so sassy and despairing and bright, manages, without losing his authority as the central speaker, to show us all the different people hidden in him, all the voices for whom the "I" alone can speak.

Each of his essays in this new book is a facet of this different experience, each is a report from the battlefield that is himself, that he sometimes feels may be *only* himself: he is in Paris as an American writer, he attends a congress of "Negro-African" writers where he certainly doesn't feel altogether at home, he indignantly describes a slummy housing project in Harlem, he speaks up for the Negroes who broke up the U.N. meeting by protesting against Lumumba's murder, he goes South for the first time in his life, he is in Stockholm to interview Ingmar Bergman. No doubt other writers could have done all these pieces coolly, as correspondents from another shore to us; for Baldwin, each of his subjects represents a violent conflict in himself.

The extraordinary thing about these essays is that he can give voice to all his insights and longings and despairs without losing control — indeed, without ever missing his chance to dig in deeper. Speaking now with the moral authority of the future, now with the bitterness of Harlem, now with the sophistication of the perennial American abroad, now with the toughness of the adventurer who knows the slums and messes of Paris, now as the dopester on Gide's marriage, now as the literary celebrity moving in the company of other celebrities, he somehow manages never to enjoy things so well that he will get heedless, never suffers so constantly that he will lose himself. He is bitter yet radiantly intelligent as he seizes the endless implications in the oppression of man by man, of race by race. To be James Baldwin is to touch on so many hidden places in Europe, America, the Negro, the white man — to be forced to understand so much! He has a relatively weak essay on Norman Mailer and other white friends who romanticize the Negro sexually. But Baldwin himself, in what is probably his best piece, "Fifth Avenue, Uptown," can say: "The Southerner remembers, historically and in his own psyche, a kind of Eden in which he loved black people and they loved him. Historically, the flaming sword laid across this Eden is the Civil War. Personally, it is the Southerner's sexual coming of age, when, without any warning, unbreakable taboos are set up between himself and his past. Everything, therefore, is permitted him except the love he remembers and has never ceased to need. The resulting, indescribable torment affects every Southern mind and is the basis of the Southern hysteria."

The humiliation and worse that the Negro remembers can also become an issue of hysteria — and it is extraordinary how Baldwin can manage so often to suggest both the Negro's impatience for the future and his own despair in the present, both the understanding made necessary by despair and the futility of intelligence in the face of so much despair. What the "Negro-African" writers in Paris "held in common was their precarious, their unutterably painful relation to the white world." This is often the endless subject of the American Negro's life. But powerful and lashing as Baldwin can be when he accuses the white man, he also knows that oppression has worked its way into his own character. What ultimately makes these essays so impressive and moving is not merely the *use* Baldwin makes of his conflicts but the fact that this personal form is an urgent necessity. This is the book of a deeply troubled man, the spiritual autobiography of someone who hopes, by confronting more than one beast on his way, to see whether his fear is entirely necessary.

« 2 »

When one is a Negro always in the path of this juggernaut of hate and suspicion and exclusion, how can one say where the social cruelty ends and one's private weaknesses begin? Who can say just how much the Negro as actor, the Negro as dissembler in the white man's world — how much of this has been made by "society" and how much by family hatred, love, and jealousy? Of all the many things I admire about Baldwin's essays, I think what I admire most is this: more than any other Negro writer whom I, at least, have ever read, he wants to describe the exact place where private chaos and social outrage meet. He wants to know just how far *he* is responsible for his unhappiness. Of course he can sum up the social paranoia of Southern racists "who are quite incapable of telling you what it is they are afraid of. They do not really know what it is they are afraid of, but they know they are afraid of something, and they are so frightened that they are nearly out of their minds." But he can also say generally, remembering his experiences in Europe, that "In America, the color of my skin had stood between myself and me; in Europe, that barrier was down. . . . It turned out that the question of who I was was not solved because I had removed myself from the social forces which menaced me . . . The question of who I was had at last become a personal question, and the answer was to be found in me."

The answer, perhaps, but not the cause. Baldwin will face what has become a personal condition, but of course he will not let off history, society, man in general. He is too intelligent to rest on the soft and psychological cliché that allows so many middle-class white Americans to absolve the society that feeds them. He knows that in certain crucial areas we are all under the same pressures. "The one thing that all Americans have in common is that they have no other identity apart from the identity which is being achieved on this continent." And the fact that Baldwin, a preacher's son, ends every essay with a plea that something be done to make us more human, that this is the job for which we really and at long last must look to each other — this expresses the American hope about as obstinately as I've seen it done in our languishing time. And how funny and touching and like Baldwin it is that these sermony endings should follow on as ruthlessly deep an analysis of American incapacity as we are likely to get. "In short, I had become an American. I had stepped into, I had walked right into, as I inevitably had to do, the bottomless confusion which is both public and private, of the American republic." No wonder that the range of feeling, the vibration of so many conflicts, puts this book as close to us as any personal document can be.

[1961]

VI
The European Current

The Plant, Man, Is
More Robust and Large in Rome
than Elsewhere

FROM THE TIME he first saw the country, when he was seventeen, with Napoleon's conquering and liberating armies, until his last years, as French consul at Civitavecchia, Stendhal had so uncontrollable a passion for Italy that, as Benedetto Croce was to say, even Stendhal's dreams came dressed up as Italy. He constantly visited it, wrote about it, held it up as an example to France. Italy was the embodiment of his own passionate and romantic nature in a world that had forced him to disguise it, and it is this that explains the dominating role of Italy in all his work. Italy, for Stendhal, was more than a pleasure; it was an idea, and it was because of this idea that he enlisted himself in the struggle against the reactionary spirit in Europe after Napoleon's downfall.

The most obvious thing about Stendhal's strength as a novelist is that he always serves an idea. It would have seemed preposterous to him that a time would come when novelists would aim at "truth" for its own sake, as if they were laboratory technicians recording the behavior of another species. Stendhal, although one of the first consciously "psychological" novelists in history, would have suspected that it is only when novelists cease to believe in the importance of ideas, when they come to think of fiction — as so many young writers do now — as wholly psychological, that they become subjective and uninteresting. What saved Stendhal from the obsession with himself to which his erratic and emotional temperament exposed him was the historical fact that he belonged to a revolutionary generation that had come to life under Napoleon and, like Stendhal himself, in Napoleon's armies. After Waterloo — which for him signified the end of revolutionary Europe — Stendhal could never believe that conservatism in any field was anything but devitalizing. And in this drama of opposition between the spirit of Na-

A *Roman Journal*, by M. de Stendhal. Translated by Haakon Chevalier. New York: Orion Press.

poleon and the world that had so fearfully succeeded him, between the imperial tradition of audacity and those who tried to re-establish the *ancien régime* — "candle snuffers," as Stendhal called them — Italy was, to Stendhal, the most important part of the symbolic landscape of sensuousness, colorfulness, carelessness, joy.

It is this intense and brilliant appreciation of Italy that gives significance to Stendhal's old "guidebook," *Promenades dans Rome*, which has been translated into English by Haakon Chevalier under the title *A Roman Journal* and published by the Orion Press in a large and handsome edition sumptuously decked out with prints of the period. Although *A Roman Journal*, like so many of Stendhal's minor works on Italian subjects, would probably have been forgotten if he had not held a winning ticket, as he predicted he might, in the "lottery of fame," the book has a special interest for us, both because it is a portrait of Rome under the temporal rule of the Papacy and because of Stendhal's incomparable sassiness on this subject and every other. Stendhal could not sit down to any book, not even to a guidebook done purely for the money, without making his intelligence and verve felt on every page. The book was written in 1828 and 1829, in a hotel room in Paris, when Stendhal was at a low ebb, broke, and — as usual — at the end of a love affair. He thought a good deal about suicide, and in one year he made seven wills. But such was the hold Italy had on him that even though the book was an astonishingly personal exposition of Rome, it nevertheless served as a useful guidebook in an era when people traveled in Italy on the advice not of Baedeker but of travel books by Goethe and Mme. de Staël. The form of *A Roman Journal*, a fictitious day-by-day tour of Rome by Stendhal and a group of friends, is of no particular significance in itself, since Stendhal was the kind of writer who would have intruded his own personality if he had written the Book of Genesis. But it is an indication of Stendhal's longing for his other country that in grinding out his guidebook in Paris he wrote it as if he were actually walking about Rome.

Stendhal's passion for Italy was literally a passion, explicitly connected in his mind with women. Just as he attributed to Italian men a libertine boldness that, he felt, bourgeois morals and manners had checked in France, so he identified with Italian women in particular that perfect warmth and tenderness which all his life he sought in an unbelievable succession of love affairs. Stendhal's mother died when he was seven, and from the time he first saw Italy, a young officer excited by the brilliance of Milan, he seems to have personified the country as the face and body of that ripe older woman, permissive, loving, indulgent, whom he portrayed as the bewitching Countess Sanseverina in *La Chartreuse de Parme*. And in his other great novel, *Le Rouge et le Noir*, a dominant figure is an older woman, Mme. de Rênal, who extends to the young Stendhalian hero a protectiveness that enables him to pursue a woman of his own generation. It has been pointed out by Mr. Frank O'Connor, in a recent book on modern novelists, that if Stendhal associated the softness and ease of Italy with his mother, he identified with France his harsh and despotic father, whom, quite simply, he called "the Bastard."

The most peppery side of *A Roman Journal*, as in everything Stendhal wrote about Italy, is the contrast between that country and France, which for him was the contrast between the heart and the mind, between the pleasure principle and the repressive instinct. When he emphasizes "that passionate sensibility without which one is unworthy of seeing Italy," one can guess how many Frenchmen, in his eyes, lack it. He writes that "in Rome, clever people have *brio*, which I have observed only once in a man born in Paris. One sees that the superior men of this country despise affectation. They could well say, 'I am like myself: so much the better for you.' " He cites a cardinal in Italy who, aged ninety-two, is "constantly in society, busy . . . addressing subtle remarks to young women." In France, he complains, you have to be solemn in order to succeed, and while the country is moving toward liberty "along an extremely dreary path," there is "nothing of this kind in Rome; everyone is looking for a good time." Frenchmen are petty, care only for public opinion, bother their heads with political nonsense. Italians are bold, indifferent to opinion, swashbucklers — and besides, the country is full of real paintings, unlike the art shops of Paris, with their "painted curios." "An Italian who loves a painting hangs it opposite his bed so as to see it on awakening, and his salon remains without ornament. Here people want pleasures that are real, and *appearance* is nothing."

Such observations (or, rather, inventions) made up Stendhal's contrast between France, which oppressed him, and Italy, whose greatest charm was that he found it easy to adore what he did not respect. The effect of Italy on all travelers is the effect not merely of the climate and the physical beauty of both the country and the inhabitants, but of their supposed primitivism, which has enabled so many writers to describe the country as if they were on holiday from tiresome moral restrictions. Although Stendhal had a good deal of contempt for the ignorance in which the Italian people were kept, he was able to write with admiration, with relief, "What can one not dare in a country that has had only a glimpse of modern civilization from May 17, 1809 [when Rome was annexed by Napoleon], to April, 1814 [when it was restored to the Pope]?" That "what can one not dare" was especially exciting to Stendhal, who often wrote about Italy as if it existed chiefly to please his sexual imagination. Like a great many other writers, he openly enjoyed the violence of Italian life. He complained that Christianity had spoiled the "sweet delight" of sitting in the Colosseum and watching wild animals put to death, and that civilization, by "etiolating" the passion and poetry that had once distinguished martyrs in Rome, "will destroy cruelty." The more he despised the self-conscious prudence of so many people in the France of the 1820s who were afraid of risking further revolutionary upheavals, the more he delighted in the spectacle of the papal city, where corruption and indifference seemed to walk hand in hand. Everywhere else, people appeared to take politics too seriously, but in Rome there was not even a pretense that popular opinion mattered, and in such a climate people looked more colorful, more passionate, more truly alive. Nowhere in Stendhal's many pages on Italy did his admiration find better expression than in his "the plant, man, is more robust and large in Rome, than elsewhere."

From other books of his, one learns that Stendhal actually liked Rome far less than he did Milan, and he described the two cities as women — Milan his special love, Rome "her elder sister . . . a woman of grave, austere worth, without music." But in A Roman Journal he shows how much he could suspend his passion for the metropolitan gaiety of Milan and submit fully to Rome, a city so full of historical ghosts, the city that for Stendhal represented the violence and bloodiness of the Renaissance — and that was full of the Raphaels he particularly loved. Rome in the grip of the Vatican dramatized perfectly for Stendhal the extremes of Italian despotism and superstition that seemed to him in such colorful contrast to the self-satisfied common sense of the French. Rome was a city where the dead were carried down the main street late at night, with heads exposed — "an atrocious spectacle that I shall not forget so long as I live, but that makes one think of death, or rather that strikes one's imagination with it, and in this sense a spectacle highly useful to those who reign in this world by making people fear the other." In the leading churches of the city, there had been gravely shown to the faithful a portrait of Jesus Christ painted by the Saviour Himself, the ark of the covenant, Moses' rod, Aaron's rod, the marble table that had been prepared for the sacrifice of Isaac, one of the pieces of silver received by Judas. The Franciscan monks of the church of Santa Maria in Aracoeli, the famous church next to the Capitol, "have the power to attract to their church every year all the devout of Rome and the surrounding countryside by putting on view a doll that is called *il santo Bambino*. This child of olive-wood, magnificently swaddled, represents Jesus Christ at the moment of his birth. This is what is being done in 1829 to pick up a little money, on the spot once revered by the masters of the world as the center of their power."

No one loved the tale of a juicy Renaissance murder as did Stendhal. Although he was describing a tour of contemporary Rome, he reached for every bit of historical gossip or scandal. In the "heyday of poisoning," as he admiringly calls it, "about 1650, it was possible to cut a peach into two halves with a gold knife poisoned only on one side. This peach would be shared with the woman who had made one jealous; the half that had been touched by the sound part of the knife could be eaten without danger; the other half was fatal." Stendhal, who praised brigands and highwaymen for their defiance of society, found in authority a defiance of the people that excited him by its very outrageousness. He describes some of the treasures of the magnificent Vatican library, full of manuscripts that the Popes have collected because of their rarity but that at the same time are considered heretical, so in the Vatican library itself there are areas "into which one cannot enter without being excommunicated *ipso facto*." He reports with glee that among the paintings in the Vatican is one showing the assassination of Admiral de Coligny, the leader of the French Protestants who were slaughtered in the St. Bartholomew Massacre. No wonder that once Stendhal got into the swing of things in Rome, he wrote, "If I were not afraid of shocking moral people, I should confess that I have always thought, without saying so, that a woman really belongs to the man who loves her best. I should be inclined to extend this blasphemy to paintings."

The fact that the Pope had temporal as well as spiritual power seemed to Stendhal highly entertaining, an example of the unreal world that had been foisted on Europe by Napoleon's conquerors. But because it was unreal, it appealed to his sense of the absurd. He felt that in Rome he was watching an opera, and although he was an unrelenting critic of existing society, he had such misgivings about the onrush of the middle-class future that he decided to enjoy the revival of the past while it lasted. The antithesis to the squalid magnificence of Italy was the sterile virtuousness of Protestant England and America. One of the funniest things in the *Journal* is his campaign against the English, whom he has standing about Rome like morose savages, and he can never refer to the United States without attributing to all of it the frigid goodness of a Sunday school. Since the disorder and roughness of nineteenth-century New York might have stimulated him, it is entertaining to find him writing that although the country around Rome is infested with bandits and "this country could be civilized in eighteen months by a French or English general, [it] would thereupon be as estimable as it was uninteresting; something like New York. . . . In this highly moral country, boredom would put an end to my existence in a very few months."

In Rome, by contrast, even cardinals come dressed like Bartolo in Rossini's *Barber of Seville* — "a black habit with red braids and red stockings." He has the Pope attending Mass, sitting behind the altar on a throne, sucking at the Saviour's blood with a gold straw. He reports that from the upper stories of the Colosseum "one can look down on the arena and see the Pope's convicts working while they sing." He often describes "this Roman revery, which seems so sweet to us and makes us forget all the interests of active life," and he sees Romans spending "whole hours in mute admiration, leaning on a window of the Villa Lante, on Mount Janiculus." But sensitive as he is to these purely peaceful impressions of "Rome, where the dome of St. Peter's is outlined against the exquisitely pure glow of an orange-hued twilight surmounted high up in the sky by some star that is just appearing," he never allows the Eternal City to blunt his sensuality or to melt his anger at what the world has become.

[1958]

Sholom Aleichem: The Old Country

THE WAY TO READ Sholom Aleichem is to remember from the outset that he is writing about a people, a folk: the Yiddish-speaking Jews of Eastern Europe. There are a great many Jews and non-Jews who resent the idea that the Jews are a people, for they think this requires all Jews to speak the same language and to live in the same territory. But Sholom Aleichem's characters already are a people. They are a people not merely because they speak the same language, Yiddish, or because they live in the Pale of settlement that the Czarist government kept Jews in. They are a people because they think of themselves as a people. And what is most important, they are a people because they enjoy thinking of themselves as a people.

This is the great thing about the Jews described by Sholom Aleichem. They enjoy being Jews, they enjoy the idea of belonging to the people who are called Jews — and "their" Sholom Aleichem, perhaps more than any other Jewish writer who has ever lived, writes about Jewishness as if it were a gift, a marvel, an unending theme of wonder and delight. He is one of those writers whose subject is an actual national character, a specific type — the Jew as embodied in the poor Jew of Eastern Europe. In a way he does remind us of Mark Twain,* who was so entranced with a new character, the Western American, that he was always trying to weigh

* Sholom Aleichem was so often called "the Jewish Mark Twain" that Mark Twain, on meeting him, referred to himself as "the American Sholom Aleichem."

him, to describe him, as if he, Mark Twain, had discovered a new chemical element. When Mark Twain writes of "the calm confidence of a Christian with four aces," we know that the pleasure he gets in writing that is, in part, the satisfaction of knowing that no one but an American could have written that sentence. It is an artistic pleasure, not a chauvinistic affirmation or a defensive maneuver: it is the pleasure of presenting certain local traits, feelings, habits, jokes, even certain biological characteristics, as a physical *substance*, a living addition to the world of nature — something that you can smell and taste and enjoy. You find this kind of artistic substance in Shakespeare's presentation of a lower-class character like Pistol; in Dickens's Cockneys, who walk off the streets of London, delighting us with their pleasure in being Londoners, in their physical relish of their identity as people of that place and time (and who are proud that they spring straight from the imagination of Charles Dickens). Americans, in their attempt to endow a new country with a specific national type, have contributed very largely to this art of national character. But, generally, this kind of pleasure in one's own national being is, I should say, more European than it is American. I have often noticed the difference in the greater pride with which Europeans tend to project their own language, as opposed to our more functional and careless use of English. I have seen it particularly in the Neapolitan dialect theater of Eduardo de Filippo, and in Italian movies, where a type will appear that instantly captivates the audience because he is recognizable, a symbol of the country's human wealth, a tangible re-creation of the life of ordinary experience.

« 2 »

It is this European, seasoned, familiar pleasure in the national circle of one's own people, that lies behind Sholom Aleichem's stories. But what kind of enjoyment can these people derive from being Jews, since they are incessantly harassed by the Russian government and surrounded by peasants who are usually anti-Semitic and can easily be goaded, with the help of the usual encouragement from the government itself and a lot of vodka, into making pogroms? What is it, in short, that makes for *enjoyment* in these local terms? The answer is that one enjoys being a member of a people because one shares in the feast of their common experience. You share in something that is *given* to you instead of having to make every institution and every habit for yourself, out of nothing, in loneliness and with exertion. The secret of this enjoyment consists not so much in physical solidarity and "togetherness," in the absence of loneliness, as in the fact that a deep part of your life is lived below the usual level of strain, of the struggle for values, of the pressing and harrowing need — so often felt in America — to define your values all over again in each situation, where you may even have to insist on values themselves in the teeth of a brutish materialism. We enjoy things only when we can commit some part of our daily life to tradition, when we can act ceremonially, ritualistically, artistically, instead of having to decide in each case which act to perform and how to go about it and what we are likely to get out of it. What we enjoy is, in fact, nothing less than the unconscious wealth of humanity, which is its memory.

This is the fabled strength of "the old country," which deprived the Jews of Eastern Europe of every decency that we take for granted, but allowed them to feast unendingly on their own tradition — and even to enjoy, as an unconscious work of art, their projection of their fiercely cherished identity. The very pen name "Sholom Aleichem" is an instance of this. (His real name was Solomon Rabinowitz; he was born near Kiev in 1859 and died in the Bronx in 1916.) *Sholom aleichem* is the Hebrew greeting, "Peace be unto you," that is technically exchanged between Jews. It is said with more lightness and playfulness than you would guess from the literal translation. Its chief characteristic, as a greeting, is the evidence it gives of relatedness. Now Solomon Rabinowitz, who actually belonged to the prosperous and more "emancipated" middle class of Russian Jewry (he even married into its landed gentry), took this pen name precisely because he found in the phrase an image of the sweet familiarity, the informality, the utter lack of side, that is associated with the Yiddish-speaking masses of Eastern Europe. A Yiddish writer who calls himself *Mister* Sholom Aleichem tells us by this that he has chosen cannily to picture himself as one of the people and, modestly, to be a register or listening post for his people. Sholom Aleichem! The name's as light as a feather, as "common" as daylight, as porous to life as good Yiddish talk: it is the very antithesis of the literary, the mannered, the ornate. If you didn't know anything else about Mister Sholom Aleichem (several of his characters address him so when they bring their stories to him) you should be able to guess from the name the role that he has chosen to play in his own work. He is the passer-by, the informal correspondent, the post office into which Jews drop their communications to the world. All he does, you understand, is to write down stories people bring him. He invents nothing. And need one say — with that name, with that indescribably dear, puckish, wrinkled face of his — that you will never learn from him *what* he has invented, that he has all Yiddish stories in his head, that any one story people bring him will always be capped with another?

In the world of Sholom Aleichem, nothing has to be made up, for the life of the Jews, to say nothing of the Jewish character, is an unending drama. Nor can it be said of anything that it's never been seen or heard of before. The Jews have lived with each other for a very long time, and they know each other through and through — and this, often enough, is what they enjoy. Their history, alas, has too often been the same, and everything that you see in Kasrilevka (the little Jewish town which is all little Jewish towns) or Yehupetz (Kiev, the big city) can be matched from something in Mazeppa's time, which is late seventeenth century, or that of Haman, who tried to kill all the Jews in Persia in the fifth century B.C. Nor, indeed, is anything ever said just *once*. Everything is real, everything is typical, and everything is repeated.

You must understand, first, that Sholom Aleichem's characters possess almost nothing except the word — the holy word, which is Hebrew, and the word of everyday life, which is Yiddish. They are "little" people, not in the sense that they are poor little victims, but in the sense that they are unarmed, defenseless, exiled, not in the world, not in *their* kind of world. All they have is the word. They talk as poor people always talk — because poor people live near each other, and so have a lot of opportunity to talk. They talk the way the European poor always talk — Cockneys or Neapolitans or Provençals: they talk from the belly; they roar, they bellow, they grunt, they scream. They imitate the actual sounds that life makes, and they are rough and blunt. But most of all, they are poor Jews talking, i.e., they find an irony in language itself. Their words strive after the reality, but can never adequately express the human situation.

This sense that the letter strives after the spirit, but can never fully capture it — this seems to me the essence of the historic Jewish consciousness, with its devout and awestruck yet faithful obedience to some overmastering reality. We are all familiar enough with the Hebrew psalmist's despair that he can find the word, the deep, deep word still lacking to human speech, that will convey the bounty of God. But Yiddish, which is particularly the language of the exile, of the long Jewish wandering, is identified by these poor Jews with the contrast between the °Jewish situation in the world and the large and inextinguishable hope of another world which they profess. They do not "despise" Yiddish because it is the tongue of everyday life, and one which they themselves call a vernacular: they love it; it is theirs. But by identifying it with their reduced situation, with their exile, with their isolation, they embody in it a historical moment, the present and its desolation, rather than the world of eternity which is mirrored in Hebrew. Yiddish is the poor Jew's everyday clothes rather than his Sabbath garment, Hebrew. But in the Jewish consciousness it is precisely the life of everyday that is contrasted with the divine gift of the Sabbath, and it is this awareness of what life is actually like (seen always against the everlasting history of this people and the eternal promise) that makes the very use of Yiddish an endless commentary on the world as found.

And it is a commentary on the spirit of language itself. One of the things you get from Sholom Aleichem is this mockery of language, a mockery which — need I say it? — carries a boundless pleasure in language and a sense of the positive strength that goes with mighty talk. The mockery may indicate the inadequacy of words when describing the vastness and strangeness of Russia, in which Yiddish-speaking Jews felt lost: "They all began to tell each other stories about spirits and ghosts, incidents that had occurred right here in Zolodievka, in Kozodoievka, in Yampoli, in Pischi-Yaboda, in Haplapovitch, in Petchi-Hvost, and other places." It conveys, over and over, a mild, loving, but positive irony toward the Creator. "How cleverly the Eternal One has created this little world of His, so that every living thing, from man to a simple cow, must earn its food. Nothing is free." The mockery may indicate despair at reproducing a really odd face: "In appearance Shimmen-Eli was short and homely, with pins and needles sticking out all over him and bits of cotton batting clinging to his curly black hair. He had a short beard like a goat's, a flattened nose, a split lower lip, and large black eyes that were always smiling. His walk was a little dance all his own and he was always humming to himself. His favorite saying was, 'That's life — but don't worry.' " Sholom Aleichem leaves the rest to the imagination. Only the imagination can do justice to the rest.

Or the mockery may, as in a familiarly shrewish tirade by a wife or mother-in-law, mean not only the opposite of what it seems to mean (i.e., it may actually hide affection, though no one but the husband-victim should be expected to know this); but, even more, it will be a commentary — to put it gently! — on the world which a woman cannot always act in, but which, with tongue and blazing eyes, she implacably judges. The husband is always in a direct line of fire, since he is a ne'er-do-well, a *schlemiel*, a genius at bad luck, a *schlimazl*. But it is not the husband's failures alone that are scorned; it is the folly of the world itself — for daring to think of it as *the* world (i.e., a place where human beings can live). Thus Menachem-Mendel ("In Haste"), who tries his hand at everything in the big city and succeeds at nothing, and who, precisely because his ambition is exceeded by his innocence, illustrates the cruelty of the great world in which he naïvely tries to get a living. The particular joke just now is that he has become a professional matchmaker. Home for Passover, first off he sees in the yard his mother-in-law engaged in furious housecleaning for Passover:

When she saw me, she managed to control her joy. She kept right on with her work, muttering to herself:

"Well, well! You mention the Messiah — and look who comes! Here he is, my bird of Paradise. . . . If he doesn't spoil, he'll find his way home. Goats run away, chickens get lost, but men always come back. . . . The only place they don't return from is the Other World. Now I know why the cat was washing herself yesterday, and the dog was eating entrails. . . . Oh, Sheine-Sheindel, daughter, come here! Welcome your ornament, your jewel, your crown of gold and diamonds! Your holy of holies. . . . Quick, take the garbage away!"

At this point my wife runs out, frightened, and sees me. Her welcome is more direct.

"Tfui!" she spat out. "You picked just the right time to come. All year long you roam around that dirty city, lying around in all the attics, engage in every idolatry — and here you come fluttering in on Passover Eve, when we're busy cleaning up and there is not time to say a word to each other. . . ."

An irate man says of a stranger he doesn't like: ". . . comes all the way from Zolodievka and fastens himself to us like a grease spot." Sholom Aleichem says of Kasrilevka itself (the very embodiment of all little Jewish towns, the poor man's town): "From a distance it looks — how shall I say it? like a loaf of bread thickly studded with poppy seed." He remarks, in passing, that "the real pride of Kasrilevka is her cemeteries." The wonderful, the lovable Tevye, Tevye the dairyman, the poorest and most faithful and most touching of all Sholom Aleichem's poor Jews, remarks in passing: ". . . with God's help I starved to death." And when he comes through the woods from Boiberik to Kasrilevka, late, so very late that he has to say his evening prayers on the spot, the horse runs off and Tevye runs after his wagon — saying his prayers as he runs. Characteristically, he regrets that he cannot, now, enjoy saying his prayers. "A fine way to say Shmin-esra! And just my luck, at a moment when I was in the mood to pray with feeling, out of the depth of my heart, hoping it would lift my spirits."

In this world, the extreme is a matter of course — and yet, from a Jewish point of view, an understatement. For these people have much to think about, much to live with; much, much, to live through. In the lovely lyric story, "A Page from the Song Of Songs," which portrays the closeness to nature, to ordinary sensuous enjoyments that these Jews so rarely experienced, the boy cries out, in the rapture of Passover, of spring: "What delights the Lord has provided for his Jewish children." But Tevye the dairyman, who loves God with all his might, can still remember, as he runs after his horse — "chanting at the top of my voice, as if I were a cantor in a synagogue" — he can still remember to add private comments on his prayer. "Thou sustainest the living with loving kindness (and sometimes with a little food) and keepest thy faith with them that sleep in the dust. (The dead are not the only ones who lie in the dust; Oh, how low we the living are laid, what hells we go through, and I don't mean the rich people of Yehupetz who spend their summers at the *dachas* of Boiberik, eating and drinking and living off the fat of the land. . . . Oh, Heavenly Father, why does this happen to me?) . . ." And coming to the part of the evening prayer which asks, *Heal us, O Lord, and we shall be healed,* he cannot help adding under his breath: "Send us the cure, we have the ailment already."

For Tevye and his people the word is not the beginning of things, the foundation of the world; it is a response to the overmastering reality — to the world and the everlasting creation, the eternal struggle and the inestimable privilege of being a Jew.

[1956]

Thomas Mann:
or The German as Novelist

I ONCE SAW Thomas Mann plain. It was in Hollywood, of all places; and of all things, it was at a wartime rally of "progressive" movie stars and "united front" scriptwriters. John Garfield was an usher, and I found myself sitting next to Thomas Mann. He told me how much he liked movies, and I soon discovered that the culture lovers who produced pictures at Paramount and M-G-M would solicitously send new films out to his house in Pacific Palisades. Tall, inexpressibly grave yet unmistakably arch, he hid his thoughts behind his well-known disguise: the German professor. The contrast with himself and the scene in hand was delicious. The businessmen who made movies all talked like intellectuals and even tried to look like intellectuals, but the author of *Buddenbrooks, Death in Venice, The Magic Mountain,* and how many other lightly demonic works of creative intelligence looked like a highly patrician bourgeois or the scholarly chief of the German General Staff — anything, that is to say, but a "writer."

This contrast between the conservative social self and a mind so

The Ironic German: A Study of Thomas Mann, by Erich Heller. Boston: Little, Brown and Company. An Atlantic Monthly Press Book.

complex that his real opinions were always elusive — this was
Thomas Mann's situation, his strategy in human relations as well as
in his books, and often enough the very theme of his novels, which
in one guise or another are concerned with "ordinary," bourgeois,
conservative men rising to the challenge of an utterly unsettling
and unpredictable universe. Mann, the creative peer and contemporary of great experimental novelists like Proust and Joyce, is easier
to read but actually harder to grasp through the external conventionality of his form and the heavy load of German philosophic apparatus. He is so continuously double-sided, so "safe" in manner
and so subversive within, so much the pompous German pedant in
his literary manner and in his substance so representative of his
esthetic, nihilist, decadent generation, that it is almost impossible
to do justice to the range and elusiveness of his mind. Either one
makes too much of only one side of him or one imitates his own
tiresome Olympian irony, the suavely self-protective use to which he
put his doubleness by effectively concealing his real opinions.

Perhaps no one but a European critic could do full justice to the
complexity and genial deceitfulness of Thomas Mann's mind. American critics have often written acutely about him, but without full
awareness of his marvelous imposture, his self-referring irony. Yet
even European intellectuals, writing out of the full emotional vibration of what modern Germany has meant and done to the world,
have either celebrated in Mann the conservative German decencies
that Hitler hated, or attacked in him the German pretentiousness
that Hitler made use of. It is hard to see the many sides of Mann
without taking sides, and Erich Heller's book, which brilliantly does
the first, should interest American readers not only for its passionate
defense of Mann but also because its intelligence, its emotion, and
its learning represent unforgettably the debate of a cultivated European mind with itself.

Erich Heller, now a professor of German in Wales, comes from
Kafka's country — the German-speaking minority in old Bohemia
who once were Austro-Hungarian, then Czechoslovakian, then German, and who have lived inside such a maze of national contradictions, have seen so many artificial political constructions destroyed,
that the German language and the German intellectual tradition
have come to seem their only real fatherland. "The background to

my writing," Heller has said, "is the political and cultural catastrophes of this century, and my attachment to the things overtaken by them. My aims: to preserve the memory of the things I love, to be truthful to them. . . ." His first book in English, a masterly study of German literary thought, was significantly titled *The Disinherited Mind*; his second, *The Hazard of Modern Poetry*; a key chapter in this book on Thomas Mann is called "The Conservative Imagination." Heller is a traditionalist first because he is a literary scholar and critic, with a deep and urgent sense of the norm to which contemporary works are to be joined or compared; it is probably impossible to be a literary scholar at all — concerned with the development of literary forms, with the analogy between books — without a deep sense of tradition. But Heller is not a conservative in the native, deeply rooted sense in which Thomas Mann seems to him to be one: Heller is a writer who feels himself "disinherited," exposed to "hazard," looking for "order." And it is precisely this urgency, the civilized but remarkably intense commitment to "order" — which, he once wrote, "is neither behind us nor before us. It is, or it is not" — that gives his writings their extraordinary web of cultural detail, their moving quality of invocation, and, above all — remarkably so for a man writing in an adopted language — their pith and style.

« 2 »

The best side of Heller's writing is the fact that he recalls the essentially philosophical nature of literary criticism when it is not shop talk written by poets, dramatists, and novelists. Literary criticism is technical only when it illuminates a technique that one practices oneself; nobody can "explain" what makes a book good, or even what a book wholly is, least of all if he cannot write a book like it. A critic like Heller not only makes no pretensions to that phony *explication de texte* which has fooled so many half-literate American undergraduates into thinking that talk about "metaphors" gets into a "work of art," but, standing his own ground, he shows us that criticism is essentially speculative discourse concerned with ideas and values of life. The better the critic, the more he will contribute to our understanding of life in general; but he must do this in the critic's own way, solidly commenting on the text before him.

As a reader of Mann's works, Heller is superb. Anyone who appreciates criticism for the passionate intelligence it can display, who recognizes it as a classic form of literary activity, will derive great pleasure from this book. In its learning, its wit, its steadiness and ease of tone, in the gaiety and sharpness of its critical asides, it is not only exciting but, as only really seasoned and disciplined European writers can be, truly satisfying, for it stems from a European awareness of the difficulty and the tragedy — but also the satisfaction — of life when it is interpreted by the intelligence. Yet because Heller's book is written from so strong a personal emphasis on the importance of tradition, it seems to me to overvalue the externally "bourgeois," conventional *form* of Mann's thought over that purely mischievous and artistic side of him which represents the intelligence of Thomas Mann the novelist, not Thomas Mann the German thinker.

This is a book on a novelist that has nothing to say about the novel as a general form. Heller has much to tell us about Mann's relationship to Schopenhauer, Nietzsche, Wagner, *et al.*, but nothing about his lack of relationship to Joyce, Proust, Lawrence. After all, Mann interests us in the outside world because he was *not* simply another heavy German thinker but a superb novelist and storyteller. There have been so few writers in Germany wholly committed to the novel that Mann's genius in this form, though it can be demonstrably related to the dramatic side of Nietzsche or the literary side of Wagner, surely asks for some further explanation in itself. The "conventional" side of Mann's outward manner as a novelist (which he himself, no less than Dr. Heller, opposed to the great iconoclasts and experimentalists like Joyce) may be due simply to the lack of the novelistic tradition in German literature. Just as Kafka writes novels with the chilling simplicity of a man who has none to imitate, so Mann writes them with the ponderous complexity of a man imitating every literary form except the novel.

Mann's indebtedness to German philosophers and composers is indeed the story within the story of his life. To anyone brought up outside this German literary tradition, the fascination of Thomas Mann's career, ending in a whole series of extraordinary novels, is as complete as the sensation of being outside it. Just as German poets and composers seem to have more in common than, say, Beethoven has with Rossini, so in reading Heller's book our sense of this German tradition makes us feel that we are witnessing a cultural phenomenon that is not only complete in itself but which, in its union of philosophy and art, of religion and style, seems constantly to ache for the projection of its completed image.

Erich Heller's literary criticism is deeply grounded in the German tradition, even to the characteristic of being most deeply critical of it; he seems constantly to yearn for a world that no longer is, for "order" to be restored to a world that long ago lost it. This particular emphasis in Heller's work is not so very different from what one finds in German philosophy, music, criticism, and even fiction. In the German tradition, he seems to yearn for philosophical absolutes, he longs for "sense" to be restored to the world, though he bases himself entirely on a cultural (not a religious) tradition which is already full of the particular German sense of self-contradiction and inner conflict. In Heller's work there is a constant effort to reach beyond the "chaos" of modern literature to what, in the German tradition, is itself nothing but the felt "chaos" of modern thought, modern Germany. Perhaps it is this longing for an explicit spiritual solution, which reminds one of the entreaty in the last quartets of Beethoven and the last poems of Rilke, that explains why intellectuals in the German tradition find it difficult to take the novel seriously as a form in itself. For the genius of this form is precisely that it works against the explicit solution and even the "spiritual," when it is hugged too tightly.

My objection is not that Heller wishes so urgently to make sense of the world, to return to a spiritual order, but that he may possibly exaggerate Thomas Mann's own desire to do so. I have the impression that Mann, more solidly rooted in the nineteenth century and the old bourgeois way of life, may have been concerned with the mundane side of life more than is Erich Heller, who attributes to Mann a religious quest that tells more about Heller than about Mann. The fact is that Mann's famous "irony" is not only a matter of eating one's cake and of having it too — from the plaudits of Hollywood producers in 1944 to those of East Germany in 1954 — but it is typical of the kind of solid taste for the details of life from which one writes *novels*. There is a degree of spiritual urgency that novelists need not make explicit. In the same way, Germany as a country meant literal and material things to Thomas Mann that the literary tradition of the German language cannot mean to Erich Heller in Wales.

[1959]

Isaac Bashevis Singer: The Saint as Schlemiel

WHEN I first read "Gimpel the Fool" (in the quick and pungent English of Saul Bellow) I felt not only that I was reading an extraordinarily beautiful and witty story, but that I was moving through as many historical levels as an archaeologist at work. This is an experience one often gets from the best Jewish writers. The most "advanced" and sophisticated Jewish writers of our time — Babel, Kafka, Bellow — have assimilated, even conquered, the whole tradition of modern literature while reminding us of the unmistakable historic core of the Jewish experience. Equally, a contemporary Yiddish writer like Isaac Bashevis Singer uses all the old Jewish capital of folklore, popular speech and legendry, yet from within this tradition itself is able to duplicate a good deal of the conscious absurdity, the sauciness, the abandon of modern art — without for a moment losing his obvious personal commitment to the immemorial Jewish vision of the world.

Perhaps it is this ability to incarnate all the different periods that Jews have lived through that makes such writers indefinably fascinating to me. They wear whole epochs on their back; they alone record widely separated centuries in dialogue with each other. Yet all these different periods of history, these many *histories*, represent, if not a single point of view, a common historic character. It is the irony with which ancient dogmas are recorded, the imaginative sympathy with which they are translated and transmuted into contemporary terms, that makes the balance that is art.

Gimpel himself is an example of a legendary Jewish type — the saint as *schlemiel*. The mocked, persecuted and wretched people, who nevertheless are the chosen — chosen to bear a certain knowl-

Gimpel the Fool and Other Stories, by Isaac Bashevis Singer. New York: Noonday Press.

edge through a hostile world — are portrayed again in the town fool, a baker who is married off to a frightful slut without knowing what everyone else in town knows, that she will bear a child in four months. Gimpel is *the* fool of the Jews: a fool because he is endlessly naïve, a fool because, even when he does learn that he has been had, he ignores his own dignity for the sake of others. His wife's unfaithfulness, her shrewishness — these are not the bourgeois concealment, the "cheating" on one's spouse that it would be in another culture, but a massive, hysterical persecution. The child she already has she passes off as her "brother"; Gimpel believes her. When she gives birth to a child four months after the wedding, Gimpel pays for the circumcision honors and rituals, and names the boy after his own father. When he cries out that his wife has deceived him, she deliberately confuses him, as usual, and persuades him that the child is "premature":

I said, "Isn't he a little too premature?" She said that she had a grandmother who carried just as short a time and she resembled this grandmother of hers as one drop of water does another. She swore to it with such oaths that you would have believed a peasant at the fair if he had used them. To tell the plain truth, I didn't believe her; but when I talked it over next day with the schoolmaster he told me that the very same thing had happened to Adam and Eve. Two they went up to bed, and four they descended.

The humor of this is always very real, for these people are rough old-fashioned village types who know their own. The town boys are always playing tricks on Gimpel, setting him on false trails; he is mocked at his own wedding — some young men carry in a crib as a present. His wife, Elka, is a living nightmare, a shrew of monumental proportions, a Shakespearean harridan. Yet in Gimpel's obstinate attachment to her we recognize, as in his customary meekness, the perfection of a type: what to the great world is folly, in itself may be wisdom; what the world thinks insane may, under the aspect of eternity, be the only sanity:

She swore at me and cursed, and I couldn't get enough of her. What strength she had! One of her looks could rob you of the power of speech. And her orations! Pitch and sulphur, that's what they were full of, and yet somehow also full of charm. I adored her every word. She gave me bloody wounds, though.

One night, Gimpel comes home unexpectedly and finds another man in bed with Elka; this time he has had enough, and he separates from her. But the town mischiefs take her side and persecute him, while Gimpel worries whether he *did* see the man:

Hallucinations do happen. You see a figure or a manikin or something, but when you come up closer it's nothing, there's not a thing there. And if that's so, I'm doing her an injustice. And when I got so far in my thoughts I started to weep. I sobbed so that I wet the floor where I lay. In the morning I went to the rabbi and told him that I had made a mistake.

Elka has another child and "all Frampol refreshed its spirits because of my trouble and grief. However, I resolved that I would always believe what I was told. What's the good of *not* believing? Today it's your wife you don't believe in; tomorrow it's God Himself you won't take stock in."

Even his superstitions — Singer uses local demons and spirits as dramatic motifs — become symbols of his innocent respect for the world. One night, after covering the dough to let it rise, he takes his share of bread and a little sack of flour and starts homeward:

The moon was full and the stars were glistening, something to terrify the soul. I hurried onward, and before me darted a long shadow. It was winter, and a fresh snow had fallen. I had a mind to sing, but it was growing late and I didn't want to wake the householders. Then I felt like whistling, but I remembered that you don't whistle at night because it brings the demons out. So I was silent and walked as fast as I could.

He returns home to find his wife in bed with the apprentice. Characteristically, he suffers rather than storms; characteristically, "the moon went out all at once. It was utterly black, and I trembled"; characteristically, he obeys his wife when she sends him out of the house to see if the goat is well; characteristically, he identifies himself tenderly with the goat, and when he returns home, the apprentice having fled, the wife denies everything, tells him he has been seeing visions, shrieks prodigious curses. Her "brother" beats him with a stick. And Gimpel: "I felt that something about me was deeply wrong, and I said, 'Don't make a scandal. All that's needed now is that people should accuse me of raising spooks and *dybbuks.*'"

So he makes his peace with her, and they live together for twenty years. "All kinds of things happened, but I neither saw nor heard." When his wife dies, she tells him that none of their children is his, and the look on her dead face seems to say to him — "I deceived Gimpel. That was the meaning of my brief life."

Now Gimpel is tempted by the Spirit of Evil himself, who tells him that it is all nothing. " 'What,' I said, 'is there, then?' 'A thick mire.' " And, succumbing to the devil, Gimpel urinates into the risen dough. His dead wife comes to him in a dream — and, when he weeps in shame at his act, "It's all your fault," she cries — "You fool! You fool! Because I was false, is everything false, too?"

When the mourning period for his wife ends, he gives up everything to tramp through the world, often telling stories to children — "about devils, magicians, windmills, and the like." He dreams constantly of his wife, asks when he will be with her; in his dreams, she kisses him and promises him that they will be together soon. "When I awaken I feel her lips and taste the salt of her tears."

The last paragraph of the story, Gimpel's serene meditation before death, is of great beauty. It sums up everything that Jews have ever felt about the divinity that hedges human destiny, and it is indeed one of the most touching avowals of faith that I have ever seen. Yet it is all done with lightness, with wit, with a charming reserve — so that it might almost be read as a tribute to human faithfulness itself. "No doubt the world is entirely an imaginary world, but it is only once removed from the true world. . . . Another schnorrer is waiting to inherit my bed of straw. When the time comes I will go joyfully. Whatever may be there, it will be real, without complication, without ridicule, without deception. God be praised: There even Gimpel cannot be deceived."

« 2 »

Singer's story naturally suggests a comparison with I. J. Peretz's famous "Bontsha the Silent," who was offered everything in heaven, and meekly asked for a hot roll with fresh butter every morning for breakfast. One thinks also of Sholem Aleichem's Tevye the dairyman, who recited his prayers even as he ran after his runaway horse. But in his technique of ambiguity Singer speaks for our generation far more usefully than the old ritualistic praise of Jewish goodness.

While Bontsha and Tevye are entirely folk images, cherished symbols of a tradition, Gimpel — though he and his wife are no less symbols — significantly has to win back his faith, and he wins it in visions, in dreams, that give a background of playfulness and irony to this marvelously subtle story.

This concern with the dream, this everlasting ambiguity in our relations with the divine — this is a condition that our generation has learned to respect, after rejecting the dogmas first of orthodoxy and then of scientific materialism. This delicacy of conception unites Singer to the rest of imaginative humanity today: Man believes even though he knows his belief to be absurd, but what he believes represents a level of imaginative insight which shades off at one end into art, at the other into Gimpel's occasional self-doubt, the thought that he may be "mad."

It is the integrity of the human imagination that Singer conveys so beautifully. He reveals the advantage that an artist can find in his own orthodox training — unlike so many Jews who in the past became mere copyists and mumblers of the holy word. Singer's work *does* stem from the Jewish village, the Jewish seminary, the compact (not closed) Jewish society of Eastern Europe. He does not use the symbols which so many modern writers pass on to each other. For Singer it is not only his materials that are "Jewish"; the world is so. Yet within this world he has found emancipation and universality — through his faith in imagination.

His case is very much like that of Nathaniel Hawthorne, who also grew up in an orthodoxy against which one had in some sense to rebel in order to become a writer at all. Only a Jewish writer in the twentieth century could make one think of Hawthorne, who said that although his ancestors would have been shocked to see him become a writer of storybooks, his values would not have surprised them. Singer illustrates the extraordinary ubiquity of the Jewish writer in time: the demons, the spirits, even the fools belong to the woodland past, the dark mythological background of modern life. At least one of his stories, "From the Diary of One Not Born," could have come out of Hawthorne's stories, for Singer is concerned with the same theme of temptation that led Hawthorne to fill up New England woods with witches. But the positive way in which Singer makes one feel that he has a conviction (very different from Hawthorne and, indeed, from most Jewish writers today) shows the burden of spiritual responsibility that his work carries. The Jews have been so long kept from art that it is interesting to see, at least in Singer, how much respect there is for orthodoxy. For him, at least, it nourished the secret of art — the revelation of the truth that lies in imagination.

[1958]

A Condemned Man: Albert Camus

THIS SELECTION of essays, editorials, and manifestoes, made by Camus himself, represents in an oddly tragic way his last word. I don't mean that the selections are all from his last period — the book opens on his wartime editorials from the underground paper *Combat* and with his well-known "Letters to a German Friend"; no doubt there will be other books by him. But what the present selection conveys most of all is the last stand that Camus took on a whole variety of political and generally contemporary subjects that, like Algeria, divided him from others and from himself.

Often enough it is not the stand that he made but his attempt to fix a position in moral terms alone that makes the book dispiriting. It brings home the side of Camus's literary character that underlay the artist — and that outlasted the artist.

In the last years of his life Camus was at odds with both sides in Algeria, with Sartre, with the apologists of Soviet totalitarianism. Even his silences were recognized as evidence of his struggle with himself. As a child of the French working class in Algeria, he could sympathize neither with the Algerian nationalists nor with the reactionary *colons*; and long before the Algerian crisis had reached its present intensity, Camus had been involved in polemics arising from his criticisms in *The Rebel* (*L'Homme Révolté*) of the French revolutionary tradition. He was inevitably the victim of many malicious literary attacks after the Nobel Prize award in 1957. In addition to the independent, wholly moral "third force" position he took

Resistance, Rebellion and Death, by Albert Camus. Translated by Justin O'Brien. New York: Alfred A. Knopf, Inc.

on so many political issues dividing French opinion, he talked of a moral "renaissance" vaguely based on solitary inspiration like his own.

Intellectual polemic is, of course, more familiar in France among imaginative writers than it is in this country — where a Hemingway derides a Melville for caring about ideas. In itself, there was nothing unusual about the fact that during the war Camus wrote his first novel, *The Stranger*, along with many noble editorials for *Combat*; after the war, the author of *The Plague* also wrote editorials commemorating the Spanish Republic, pleading for an end to capital punishment, denouncing Eastern Europe's "socialism of the gallows." But step by step he became almost wholly a moralist, a definer and upholder of *formal* values.

Looking back on his work as a whole, one can see that even his fiction consists of short moral anecdotes. The extraordinary success of his first "*récit*" and most unqualified artistic success, *The Stranger*, surely rests not on the kind of powerfully sufficient image of life that is the imaginative artist's challenge and delight, but rather on an explicit idea of life. *The Stranger*, in itself Camus's one "nihilist" work of fiction (and succeeded by the antinihilistic *The Plague*), owes its great popularity to the fact that it speaks for widespread feelings of alienation from social cant. Vivid and acridly ironic as many details in the book are, the hero of *The Stranger* represents the bitterness of the early Camus rather than the bewildered and self-pitying clerk that Meursault is supposed to be. The beautiful last pages, in which the condemned man welcomes death as freedom, can only be read as Camus's own austere philosophical testament. The very titles of his books — *The Stranger*, *The Rebel*, *The Fall* — denote stages in one man's struggle for moral clarity, while the curt simplicity and tense balances of his style represent, in fact, that need to embody a position, to fix a value, which is typical of those for whom a moral, once defined, is a lesson to be followed. It is typical of Camus, who, I think, did not read English, that he was instinctively drawn to Emerson, the author of so many moral "gems" and epigrammatic conclusions about life, and that he was always quoting Emerson's admirer Nietzsche, whose writing is probably the most brilliant example of this genre that we have had in modern times.

The moralist is always one who tries to prescribe for life, for whom man has a destiny that he can put into words. The background of Camus's concern with this is significant: it is his awareness of death, of war, of the afflictions rained on our generation by totalitarianism. All the finest essays in this book, like the famous wartime editorials on man's duty to the spirit of life, the lament for a poet-friend shot by the Germans, the magnificent attack on capital punishment, the rage against Kadar and his hangmen — all these reflect the writer who was one year old when his father was killed at the Marne, who from a very early age saw the human violence as well as the natural beauty in North Africa, who thought that he would himself die young of tuberculosis, whose most famous story describes the senseless killing of a native by a "Stranger" who at the end of the book awaits his own death. All his life Camus felt himself surrounded by death — his death and that of a whole generation. As he said so movingly in his debate with left-wing intellectuals, each of us today can expect some day to be condemned to death for political reasons, "whereas that eventuality would have seemed ridiculous at the beginning of the century."

Camus was aware of death at home, death in the verminous hovels of Algeria and on the beaches, death in Spain during the Civil War, death in France itself from the Nazis, death in Poland, Hungary, East Germany. At the end of his life, when he was so exhausted and driven by the effort to be "reasonable" on Algeria (for him hardly an "objective," political question), he wrote hopelessly, like a man engulfed by the unreasonableness of politics. Finally it was Algeria itself, with all its memories for him, that he might also have to lose. It hardly needs to be emphasized that the violent death that Camus anticipated all his life, the death that seemed to glare out at him from every political crisis of his time, finally did find him — in an automobile accident as violent and yet as "absurd," as typical of man's uncontrol over his mechanical creations, as any of the larger defeats that Camus brooded over in our era.

« 2 »

Albert Camus wrote like a condemned man. To me, it is this desperate emphasis on the value of life that is the key to his moral urgency. In his best essay, the one against capital punishment, he felt no complication in his way; he had nothing to plead for but life itself. The key images in all his best books are of "strangeness," death, violence to the human person. Like his adored Dostoevsky, he was haunted by the scaffold. And like all people who feel themselves condemned, who look to a new teaching to lead them back into life, Camus, with his shattering background in working-class poverty and family misfortunes, in political defeat and intellectual isolation, came to identify life with certain values alone. It was this that made him, even when he became world-famous, preach before non-Communist workmen on the "union of labor and culture"; he could not bear to divorce himself from the experience in which he had first come to his values. The more genuinely philosophical radicals like Sartre, now implacably opposed to Camus's "soft" principles, seemed to isolate Camus from the class he came from, the more Camus, in calling attention to Soviet totalitarianism, tried to create a "moral" solidarity. The more he fell away from fashionable left-wing ideologies, the more he had to explicate and to reason and to prove what his own particular values were. The life that Camus had so painfully grasped from death he had to reestablish as absolute clarity about life.

This clarity is the great value of Camus's essays — as, indeed, it is the great thing about the ending of *The Stranger* and of key passages in his plays, novels, and essays. It is the quality of the man who has set his teeth, as it were, in the face of the absurdity that overhangs life in the shape of death. It is the "Spanish" quality (his mother was Spanish) of grace under pressure. It is the style of the man who has set his focus on what is possible, on the portion that belongs to man, on man's consciousness of himself, and on man's duty to himself. Although Camus was careful to declare himself in principle an atheist, he rejected even the fashionable term "humanism" for his personal philosophy. It is this grim wariness at the expense of every illusion but hope itself that gives Camus's essays the fundamental quality of French moralism — which is to recognize a limit, to define a need, to posit some small specific hope. Clarity of this kind is clarity won for oneself and out of oneself, the clarity that helps one to live. This is seen in the terse, true exactness of many passages in these essays. Camus, in his wartime

"Letters to a German Friend," speaks of them as "a document emerging from the struggle against violence." Of the new French militancy in the Resistance, he says, "In order to face up to you, we had first to be at death's door." And shrewdly, to his friend turned German nationalist: "What is spirit? We know its contrary, which is murder. What is man? There I stop you, for we know. Man is that force which ultimately cancels all tyrants and gods. He is the force of evidence. . . . Man must . . . create happiness in order to protest against the universe of unhappiness."

Camus's essays are full of aphorisms, and they make one wonder if the truest monument to Camus would not be one of those collections, such as has been made from Proust, which convey the French *moraliste's* sense of fact. "Nothing is given to men, and the little they can conquer is paid for with unjust deaths." Speaking at a Dominican monastery: "If Christianity is pessimistic as to man, it is optimistic as to human destiny. Well, I can say that, pessimistic as to human destiny, I am optimistic as to man."

Yet precisely because this is such arduous knowledge and has been won with such desperate honesty, because it is so grimly self-created and forever self-conscious, because it is so unsure of everything but what man can discover moment by moment, it is somehow without avail. It is rhetorical. The only thing you can do with a principle, in this kind of writing, is to repeat it. And Camus does, in lecture after lecture, in interview after interview. The liberty, ease, and joy — of either a great belief or a great imaginative talent — are denied him. We are left with the impression of a painful sincerity and of a nobility that expresses itself only in definitions, not in the activity of imagination. The secret of conquering a greater world than himself is not known to him.

I read these essays with constant agreement and respect and yet with pity, for Camus's life was harder than even he thought it was. Camus thought that truth will live for man if only he defines it closely and truly enough. But truth is never something that man controls. And the very closeness with which Camus tried so hard to condense the truth is one of the most poignant things about his life. There was a fundamental distrust that he could not conquer, a space across which his imagination could not carry him. He hugged life close, as he hugged his style close. And so the felicity and brilliance of these essays remind one all too sadly of the world that has to be conquered with each sentence — but which, with each sentence accomplished, is as quickly lost.

[1960]

The Least of These

OF ALL THE CRIMES by the Nazis, surely the most unforgivable is the internment and murder of so many children. It has been calculated that a million Jewish children perished during the war. Yet many children managed to survive years in the death camps, and now, only in their late twenties and early thirties, have turned out to be the most effective personal historians of life under the Nazis. This is the generation of Anne Frank (who would now have been thirty-one), and the young Spaniard Michel del Castillo, who in that unforgettable memoir *A Child of Our Time* described what it was like to be a child in Buchenwald.

Children who went through such experiences and survived have more than anyone else been able to express the fundamental violation of human dignity committed by the Nazis. The battle-weary soldiers, the superficially experienced journalists, the hardened politicals — none of these has been able to convey, with the same innocence, the full atrocity of the camps. And perhaps only a few of the children themselves felt innocent enough, after constantly being told that they were guilty of being outside the German law, to resent the Nazis at all. But what has made a few good books possible is the fact that some of these children were still so impressionable and trusting that the terrible experiences of the camps were stored up subconsciously in their minds. Only now, in our relatively "peaceful" period, have such memories risen to the surface. Yet such experiences can become curiously unreal even to people constantly obsessed by them, and remarkably vivid as these memoirs are, they often betray the writer's fear that he may be describing a hallucination.

Night, by Elie Wiesel. Translated from the French by Stella Rodway, with a foreword by François Mauriac. New York: Hill and Wang.

The author of this piercing memoir of life in Auschwitz, Birkenau, and Buchenwald was only sixteen when the war ended for him in April, 1945. By that time he had been separated from his mother and sisters, whom he never saw again; he had seen his own father, after surviving so many "selections," smashed to death. He had lived in Auschwitz with the constant odor of burning human flesh; he had seen children, still alive, thrown into the crematoria; he had seen starving men, in the cattle cars transporting them from one camp to another, fighting each other to death over pieces of bread negligently tossed them by German civilians. There are details in his book which can be read only with fresh astonishment at the un-flagging cruelty of the Nazis and the peculiarly sadistic frivolity of those who directed this vast system of human extermination. The infamous SS doctor, Mengele, who quickly "selected" those who were to be gassed from the terror-stricken crowds running and stumbling before his eyes, would motion people to death with a conductor's baton! And there is one particular scene which has already made this book famous in Europe. A young boy, after days of being tortured in an attempt to make him reveal where a Dutch prisoner had hidden arms, was put up on the gallows to be hanged. His body was too light and so he kept strangling in front of the thousands of prisoners who had been summoned to watch the execution and who were marched past the gallows. As they went by, Wiesel heard a man asking, "Where is God now?" And he heard himself thinking: "Here He is — He is hanging here on this gallows . . ."

It is this literal "death of God" as absolute emptiness in the soul, the blackness that in his mind means that there is no longer any light from a divine source, that Wiesel experienced most in the end-less night of Auschwitz. What makes his book unusual and gives it such a particular poignancy among the many personal accounts of Nazism is that it recounts the loss of his faith by an intensely re-ligious young Jew who grew up in an Orthodox community of Transylvania. To the best of my knowledge, no one of this back-ground has left behind him so moving a record of the direct loss of faith on the part of a young boy.

Night is about a world so unreal that often indeed it reads like a nightmare. Wiesel would be the first to admit its seeming unreality; often enough it must seem unreal to him. But the book satisfies us as a human document; it brings us back to the world we all know, through the crisis of faith that it describes. The Book of Job is the most universally understood part of the Bible, and the young Wiesel's embittered interrogation of Providence unites, as it were, the ever-human Job to the history of our own time; it recalls that peculiarly loving and scolding intimacy with God which is the most powerful single element in the history of the Jews.

« 2 »

It was Wiesel's religious background that originally interested the French Catholic writer François Mauriac in this book. When Wiesel, now an Israeli newspaperman, came to interview Mauriac, the latter described the ineradicable impression that had been made on Mme. Mauriac as she watched the trainloads of Jewish children being deported from Austerlitz Station in Paris. When Mauriac spoke of how often he thought of these children, Wiesel replied, "I was one of them." Mauriac's preface to the book is singularly beautiful, and though a devout Christian, he describes the martyrdom of the Jews in terms reminiscent of the death of Christ. He too sees the Jewish experience under Nazism in Biblical terms. He describes young Wiesel as "a Lazarus risen from the dead," and, recalling Nietzsche's cry that "God is dead," expresses his compassionate understanding of why a boy in Auschwitz should have thought that "God is dead, the God of love, of gentleness, of comfort, the God of Abraham, of Isaac, of Jacob, has vanished forevermore, beneath the gaze of this child, in the smoke of a human holocaust exacted by Race, the most voracious of all idols." Mauriac's preface is written with that charity and intellectual passion which is the particular mark of French Catholic writers. The magnanimity and literary distinction of his few pages puts into relief the rather delicate literary achievement of Wiesel himself, who in recounting these atrocious early experiences makes one realize how difficult it is for a victim to do full justice to the facts.

Yet Mauriac's preface, beautiful as it is, misses the dramatic human element, the Job-like accusations that actually unite Wiesel to the religion of his fathers. On the Jewish New Year service in Auschwitz, when ten thousand prisoners said with one voice, "Blessed be the name of the Eternal," the young boy defied the Divinity, Whom he had come to think of as blind and deaf: ". . . but why should I bless Him? In every fiber I rebelled. Because He had had thousands of children burned in His pits? Because He kept six crematories working night and day, on Sundays and feast days? Because in His great might He had created Auschwitz, Birkenau, Buna, and so many factories of death? How could I say to Him, 'Blessed art Thou, Eternal, Master of the Universe, Who chose us from among the races to be tortured day and night, to see our fathers, our mothers, our brothers, end in the crematory?' . . .

"This day I had ceased to plead. I was no longer capable of lamentation. On the contrary, I felt very strong. I was the accuser, God the accused. My eyes were open and I was alone — terribly alone in a world without God and without Man . . . I stood amid that praying congregation, observing it like a stranger.

"The service ended with the Kaddish [prayer for the dead]. Everyone recited the Kaddish over his parents, over his children, over his brothers, and over himself."

To Mauriac, this loss of faith seems unnecessary as well as tragic, and he wishes, in effect, that Wiesel could see all these immense losses in our time from a Christian point of view. Mauriac feels that the deportation of children touches upon "the mystery of iniquity whose revelation was to mark the end of one era and the beginning of another. The dream which Western man conceived in the eighteenth century, whose dawn he thought he saw in 1789, and which, until August 2, 1914, had grown stronger with the progress of enlightenment and the discoveries of science — this dream vanished finally for me before those trainloads of little children." Mauriac is a great soul in our time. But less gifted, less hopeful, and even pathetic as the young Wiesel is, there is a positive strength to his complaints against God that Mauriac may have missed.

The accusation of God is of someone very real to Wiesel. The dialogue continues. It is exactly because of a child's demand for justice, because of his demand on God, because of his insistence that the consummation has not yet been reached and that history remains imperfect, that the book is so effective. Faith is often hard to talk about. Franz Kafka even said that he who has faith *cannot* talk about it. What counts may be not always one's explicit assent to faith or to non-faith, but the immense confrontation of history, the demand that we make of it as the only ground on which justice may yet show itself. I don't think that I shall soon forget the picture of this young boy standing on a mound of corpses, accusing God of deserting His creation.

[1960]

No Sky for Renaud

A YOUNG PARISIENNE is in a provincial town to claim an inheritance. At the hotel, she opens the wrong room and discovers a suicide attempt. The man is taken to the hospital in time, and the young woman, visiting him out of a sense of duty, finds herself physically so fascinated by a man who constantly spews out his contempt for everything and everyone that she moves him into her Paris flat, gives up her studies, and goes through most of her capital keeping him in drink.

Renaud is not just an alcoholic; he is a brilliant and devastating unbeliever who, brought back to life by Geneviève against his will, feels that it is up to her to keep him alive. If she doesn't, he will simply go under again, and without the slightest concern. And since he can barely be bothered to get out of bed, he is constantly accessible to the mistress in whom he has awakened a capacity for violent passion. Renaud jeeringly makes love to her as if anything else were too much trouble.

Suicidal, drunk, and cynically lecherous, Renaud is the "warrior" of the title — a warrior for the hard truth against the softening illusions, a warrior personifying the human condition in our day against those who would minimize its bitterness. And the real jolt of the story is that the warrior is brought low, brought to his "rest," by the mistress who despite all her abandon with him and her boundless sympathy for him cannot help but betray a skepticism she cannot share. This acidulous little novel, which was a best seller in France and has largely been ignored here, goes to the heart of a

Warrior's Rest, by Christiane Rochefort. Translated from the French by Lowell Blair. New York: David McKay.

quarrel that seems to be on in all countries just now, between the angries and the squares. In France this quarrel tends to dwell with more deliberate bitterness on the emptiness of contemporary life than it does in the United States — where Renaud would promptly be packed off to a psychiatrist and saved by the love of a good woman, or at least by a passionate one. In this book Renaud is not "saved" but surrendered; he even helps to surrender himself by falling in love with the woman when he can no longer keep up his anger with the world. After the last jolting paragraph, you are meant to go back to the book and to recognize that it is the woman's unwearying stress on love and desire that robs him of his anger, of his unwearying complaint against man's lot. "My love is stronger than you, Renaud. The finish line is coming closer and closer, and that's why you are so panicky, you're kicking out in all directions. Do whatever you like, you won't wear out my patience, and you'll consent to happiness at last; soon you and I will find peace, we'll rest. We'll rest."

There is no belief stronger in America just now than that love is best. In fact, there is virtually no other belief. But it is an old European conviction that what is decisive is man's relationship to transcendent truth — to the gods, when there are any — and not what Americans now value as the "security" of being loved. This first conviction (which may help to explain why current French novels, though not great, are so much more interesting than current American ones) makes Christiane Rochefort's novel particularly telling. For the warrior is as a human being utterly impossible, loathsome, and "difficult," yet you are meant to recognize what he is fighting for even when he seems just to be fighting everyone. The hypocrisy of our civilization on the brink of possible world disaster revolts him, but the increasing meaninglessness of a life lived in mindless self-absorption terrifies him. What makes the story so biting is the fact that the woman won to him by his very intransigence, by the immobility that expresses his contempt and despair, nevertheless destroys him with a love that is unconsciously selfish because she lacks his principles.

This is a brilliant novel rather than an important one; it is brilliant in the testimony given to Renaud, whose speeches denouncing contemporary life run away with the book, and brilliant in the rhythm and pace of the narrative. It is nimble, amazingly rapid and subtle in the way the story springs out of the heroine's thoughts; and because the hero is deliberately powerless everywhere but in bed, it brings much forgotten humor back to the act of sex. Artistically, it lacks extension, reverberation, the sounds of humanity moving about in the world; it is *small*, like so many good novels of today content to tell a single story well. But it is truly a contemporary novel, a novel that speaks to our condition — one might almost say to our hidden condition.

The difference between Renaud and those "beat" characters whom he would seem to resemble in being "difficult" is that Renaud is dying of what ails him. His intelligence has been stricken, one could say insulted, by the lack of significance, of depth in which to move — a lack covered up by a postwar generation anxious to swill up the brief moment of peace it may have. Renaud's mistress, telling the story, cries out: "Who ever heard of a madman with all his wits about him? I couldn't understand him. A man couldn't live that way . . . There was no sky for him, no outside. Time didn't flow, the days didn't follow one another, there was only one homogeneous, continuous day, one indefinite hour that wiped away everything as it passed; his life left no trail, he was always dying and forgetting himself along the way . . . I had him constantly, yet it seemed to me that I possessed nothing." He touches her, but she cannot help him. One day, when she allows him to walk out on her, she panics and finally catches sight of him at a crossing: "He'd stopped. He didn't know which of the four directions to take. He didn't know where to go. The earth was round. Round. He had nothing. He had no one. He stayed there. He might die there." Here is a woman utterly possessed by sexual passion for a man she has constantly but who tells her: ". . . Sex isn't important to me. Don't look surprised, it's obvious. If anything is absent from me it's sexuality. It means nothing to me. What matters in an orgy is the god, not the pleasure, and the god was always absent."

What makes the novel too tight, a brilliant demonstration rather than a moving narrative, is the fact that, since it is told by the woman herself, she can convey only her own changes of mood, of thoughts. She communicates her humanity but we see the leading character only through her — a woman voraciously in love — and so we miss his humanity and get only his intelligence. Once in a while the irony of her own eventual betrayal of him comes through, as when she complains that "he went on sinking as though I'd sacrificed nothing." For the rest, we see him from a distance; as if in his rages, his drunkenness, his sloth, he appeared improbable to us, an "idea" rather than a human being, an idea that she possessed and one that eventually she will crush. But the ideas themselves, as Renaud speaks them, are the passion of truth, and it has taken the fine French hand of Christiane Rochefort to find words for the complex disgust that may fill an intelligent man in this year of our Lord:

"Ah, snows of yesteryear that never were and never will be! The snow was warm in those days, I was there. But those days never were, and we won't go back to the source because there was no source; the rivers come from the sea and Bach is dead. I won't survive him . . . The whole conscience of the world is gathered here, but it's only useless love without an object, hopeless love, a drop of water in the desert, now do you understand at last why I get so thirsty? . . . I'm very tired. Rest me. You're the warrior's rest, the cowardly warrior's rest, the slacker's. . . . I want to sleep-die, and a woman is the best way to do that. Love is a kind of euthanasia . . .

". . . I'm resigning from the job of being an idealist in a vacuum. You can't keep grace without faith, my love, it was an illusion . . . hope can't be invented. . . . I'm tired of playing the part of a fugitive whose place is nowhere, I want . . . to enter the Great Washing Machine; help me, you know how it's done."

[1960]

From a Russian Diary

[1959]

OUR NEW INTERPRETER talks perfect American with a very slight, almost teasing Cockney accent, looks like a Brooklyn taxi-driver, and asks us to call him Georgie. Although he talks the lingo so well that he boasts of fooling American tourists at the Intourist hotels, he is 150 per cent patriotic, a true-blue Bolshevik, a model of the smiling, happy youth on the face of the Soviet calendar who used to cry, "Thank you, Comrade Stalin, for giving us such a happy childhood!" Georgie is the son of a Red Army colonel who fell in the Battle of Kiev. I have heard — not from Georgie, certainly — that the Red Army was wiped out at Kiev because Stalin obstinately, insanely insisted on the troops making a stand when the Nazis were already on the other side of the Dnieper. But when Georgie talked to me of Stalin's death in 1953, of the hushed and shaken crowds, he referred to him only as "the old man."

"Cried like a baby," said Georgie reminiscently. "Couldn't help it. What he meant to us!"

And at one point, when I asked him to tell me something about the "doctors' plot" and the open drive against Jews in Stalin's last days, I joked, "Don't worry, the chauffeur doesn't understand English." Georgie turned to me and said with hauteur: "Before 1953 I would not have talked to you *at all*; now I would not be afraid to talk to you about *anything*."

Georgie is a Jew. All our interpreters have been Jews, and unfailingly Jews pop up as assistants to the editor, translators, technical personnel in most of the literary establishments we are taken to. And since I seem to be one of those Jews whose very presence brings up discussion of Jews — if I ever touch at the North Pole, the first Eskimo running up to me will ask my opinion of Ben-Gurion — I am not surprised to have a disconcerting effect in a culture that is so notoriously and visibly nervous about Jews — no one more so than the "official" Jews here in Russia themselves. In Leningrad, I heard one of them mimic the "Jewish" accent of various writers we met, and in Kiev the Jewish writer Gregory Plotkin, who has written an unforgettable series of articles for Soviet papers about the coercion of Jews in Israel, explained that only a few "riffraff" Ukrainians participated in the Nazi massacres of the Jewish population of the Ukraine.

When I lectured before the "American literature specialists" in Moscow on our recent writing, the Jewish professors tore me limb from limb on the grounds that a book I had edited on Dreiser had no discussion of Dreiser's "Marxist" book of reportage on the Thirties, *Tragic America*.

The fact is unmistakable here: Jews embarrass. I am struck over and over by the extraordinary significance attached here to being a Jew, and I am almost ashamed to have to put down now what happened to me, at the hands of Georgie, when we were all in Tashkent.

It was a hot day, and coming out of the local park of "culture and rest," we hurried to the car to take us back to the hotel. The Oriental street was full of women in veils, vendors of *shashlik*, bazaars. The other members of the delegation were already in the car when I noticed with interest exactly such a glimpse of the Orient as I had dreamed of seeing all my life — an aged blind man with a magnificent Muslim beard, like a muezzin, being led along the street by a lady swathed in veils. "Ah," I said appreciatively to Georgie, "how Oriental they are!" He looked sour. "They're not Orientals," he said curtly. "They're Jews." When I expressed a desire to meet them, Georgie shrugged his shoulders and declined to assist me. I went over and introduced myself as an American and a Jew, and asked if they would be good enough to converse with me.

Would they converse with me! In the middle of the hot Uzbek street the old man let out a great cry, *"Blessed be the Lord!"*, threw his arms around me, and to my astonishment engulfed me in such a scalding, weeping, tumbling account of everything they had gone through since they had left Odessa in 1941, just ahead of the Nazis — he had been blinded by a machine-gun bullet from a Nazi plane that had shot up evacuation ships crossing the Black Sea — that I could barely keep up with everything he and his wife were trying to tell me. They spoke at once, they blessed me in Hebrew at every other sentence, they crowded the experiences of sixteen years into a few minutes, and they lost me altogether in an involved story of a Jewish leader in the Tashkent community of evacuees who had betrayed certain people to the police.

As I stood there, listening with the deepest emotion — after all, they could very well have been my grandparents — I felt someone pulling at my elbow. It was Georgie. Looking at the two wretched old people with what seemed to me appalling condescension, he informed me that my fellow delegates in the car wished to return to the hotel and that I was being asked to return with them immediately. Perplexed by this, I went back to the car, discovered that everybody else was asleep, and returned to the conversation. After a few minutes, Georgie pulled my sleeve again. Would I *please* terminate this interview *immediately*; my presence was most *urgently* requested back at the car. I waved him aside, and went on listening, and then to my amazement found Georgie pulling me to the car. The blind old man, who had already seemed mentally disturbed, took his wife's hand, and in the glaring sunlit street they took up their stand behind an old sentry post at the entrance to the park, trying to conceal themselves. I took my place in the car.

« 2 »

Surely I was here in a former life. There is so much that I recognize on sight — that bustling Russian propriety in offices and hallways, the pillows piled high on my bed, the flash of golden teeth, those square (yet somehow round!) Russian females, always in transparent blouses over pink slips, bodies into which have been poured tons of crusty yellow wheat bread, borsht, and kvass — bodies strong but agile on a concrete foundation that seems to say, *No nonsense here!* — bodies which say, Only a sincere Russian love could win *me*.

Always the smell of furniture polish, always the covers over the sofas and the chairs, always the many Russian readers. In the clean Russian parks — under the statues of Lomonosov and Lenin, Gorky and Lenin, Pushkin and Lenin, Lenin and Lenin — on the clean and dear Russian slat benches under which there is not a speck of old bourgeois dirt (for all day long old women in white aprons with white cloths tied around their hair walk about with brooms and scourges, as in a Russian bath, scouring our parks clean of all dirt) — in the dear and meditative Russian parks, sage and staid readers in crushy soft Panama hats sit reading Stendhal and Balzac, Tolstoy and Mark Twain.

"And in your country?"

Clean as clean as clean is our old dear Moscow with its many banners — *Forward in the Battle for Peace!* And at each Russian desk before the old-fashioned penholder and glass inkwell and curved blotter with a handlepiece, we sit at attention, serious and studious.

That Russian propriety, that Russian schoolmistressy exactness and solemnity, that Russian straightforwardness! Our own delegation shocks by its levity, its loud internecine disagreements, its unheard-of lack of interest in agricultural fairs, its interest in drinking vodka. Our official Soviet hosts, the Foreign Commission of the Union of Soviet Writers, should be an object lesson to us all.

Four Russians sit at one side of the greenclothed table and four Americans sit across from them. On the walls, pictures of famous writers — Anna Seghers, Martin Anderson Nexø, Pablo Neruda, Louis Aragon. Alexey Surkov, poet, formerly head of the Union of Soviet Writers and now head of its Foreign Commission — orients us. In the Soviet Union, literature is produced in some sixty languages — even more, perhaps. . . . Is sixty languages, is thousands of magazines, is hundreds of thousands of copies of any book, is millions and millions of readers! Is not printing enough copies of any book, so great is the demand! . . . Poetry! Long lines outside the dozens of bookshops the day the edition is coming out! We are honoring your great American writers, Jack London and Mark Twain . . . celebrating just recently sixtieth birthday of your great Ernest Hemingway!

"And in your country?"

Surkov is a man with a mighty voice, a great Russian wind instrument. Its boom effortlessly fills the room, and as he recites literary statistics I get the impression that he is as awed by the sound of his voice as we are. It is a great voice, an authoritative voice, rich and deep — it works with relish on the crunchy Russian consonants. It is the voice of the man born to be the branch chairman, the district organizer. He *knows*.

But he can be genial. When we ask to see Pasternak, he leans over to a colleague and grins — "Now it's out in the open!" — and then turns to us with the remark, "Between Pasternak and ourselves there is, as you might say, a state of peaceful coexistence." He laughs at the abstract paintings he has seen at the American exhibition. Maybe that contorted female depicted in the garden is the American woman! Hah! Hah! He will now imitate an American *avant-garde* painter at work. Closes his eyes, throws paint about. Grins. When we come back to literature, their treatment of Pasternak is up again — and the obvious contrast with our handling of Ezra Pound. Surkov explains that the psychiatrists who originally put Ezra Pound into St. Elizabeth's did so because they were all in sympathy with Pound's Fascist views.

‹ 3 ›

Tea with Ilya Ehrenburg and his wife at his *dacha* in the country. We had heard a good deal about Ehrenburg's "post-Stalin" novel, *The Thaw*, and about two long recent essays, one on Stendhal and the other on Chekhov; the latter has references to the Dreyfus affair which have been interpreted as a partly veiled defense of Pasternak; and Ehrenburg's recorded passion for both Stendhal and Chekhov has been taken as a stand against the crudities of official Soviet realism. On the way over, I remembered that Ehrenburg during the war became the most celebrated of the many Soviet writer-correspondents, and despite Stalin's dislike of Jews, one of his favorite writers. I had heard a good deal, too, about Ehrenburg's wealth — he is said to own a Rembrandt and in his Moscow apartment keeps a notable collection of modern French paintings — and so was rather startled, when we were welcomed at the large and splendid country house, by his lack of teeth.

Wrinkled, clever, haughty, sad face. They say that Ehrenburg has much to be sad about, for it was he who first signalized, with his attacks on "rootless cosmopolitans," the roundup of Jewish intellectuals slain in the madness of Stalin's last days. Ehrenburg is now in his sixties. But how many Ehrenburgs there have been already — the Ehrenburg who once wandered over Russia as a tramp, the Ehrenburg who fled the Revolution, the Ehrenburg who lived so long in Paris, the Ehrenburg who at one time thought of becoming a Benedictine monk, the Ehrenburg who returned to Russia in 1940, the Ehrenburg who is still faithful enough to his origins to speak out against certain well-known literary anti-Semites in Russia.

Which Ehrenburg sits before me now?

Exquisite wooden house, sturdy blond Russian wood, style severe and bracing. Rooms as thick with greenery as a jungle scene by Henri Rousseau. Outside, flowered terraces. There is an unmistakable atmosphere of civilized good living about the Ehrenburgs — cigars from Havana, cognac from Paris, and Madame has so obviously bought her dress in Paris rather than in Moscow that she looks like a visitor from another planet.

Conversation begins a little nervously, however, when my colleague from the *Atlantic Monthly*, taking out a memorandum book to make a note, is startled by a scream from Madame. She has seen her maiden name, Kozintsev, written in the book and now cries out, "Why have you my name written in your book? I ask you, why?" The name is that of a prominent Soviet film director whom we had met in Leningrad, and who turns out to be Madame Ehrenburg's brother. Perplexed by her suspiciousness but fascinated by her English, which she learned in India when her former spouse was attached to the Soviet Embassy.

Meanwhile, Ehrenburg opens up with a sharp attack on the mis-use of his recent books in the United States. I've never read *The Thaw*, but he loudly complains that the novel, after being turned down by his publisher, has been brought out by a right-wing house in Chicago, and that the edition includes an anti-Soviet post-script, added by the publisher himself, which puts Ehrenburg in a false position. By his account of the matter, he has been badly used; and we all agree that since the cold war, many of the best Soviet writers have been strikingly absent from the lists of American pub-lishers.

Ehrenburg becomes more and more cordial — perhaps because he is launched on a monologue that will outlast the rainstorm that drives us indoors from the veranda. Fascinating performance. Ehren-burg manages to run down most of his Soviet critics and to estab-lish his popularity with Soviet readers — especially the younger ones. His main point: "Today the grandfathers and the grandsons have more in common than either has with the fathers." Those who grew up with the revolution (like Ehrenburg himself) and those who have come of age since 1945 understand one another far better than they do those who grew up between the wars. (This is a point confirmed in conversations with young Soviet intellectuals, who are now undoubtedly more skeptical and easy than their Stalinist fa-thers.) Still, it is ironic to hear Ehrenburg belaboring this point, for he is reaping the advantage of survival. He has written from so many different positions, he has survived so many purges, that by now he has caught up with a Russia naturally evolving toward a more sophisticated culture. Actually, he has probably never been an ideological fanatic himself, and in his company, you know that you are not far from the cafés of Paris.

Yet how wily he is! He happens to be the only survivor of the Anti-Fascist Jewish People's Committee, organized after the Nazi in-vasion to enlist Jewish support for the Soviet war effort — all the other members were shot or disappeared. Apart from distrust of him inspired by his many shifts, Ehrenburg's literary reputation has suffered in recent years; I heard several of the younger writers here complain that his recent novels tend to make a topical point and then to peter out. But no doubt there is some resentment in everything said about him. Whatever his literary limitations, he understandably feels himself a man of the world and thus a cut above the party hacks and trained literary seals who unwearyingly chant the same slogans. Ehrenburg's scorn for the "rank and file" in the Writers' Union* is well known. To us, he pointedly emphasizes the work of some younger poets, and suggests that this turn to poetry is more significant than the novels of "Soviet construction" so much better known abroad. He makes many analogies between literature and painting. And unlike a more solidly talented and relatively uncomplicated realist such as Mikhail Sholokhov — still the most popular novelist in the Soviet Union and probably the best — Ehrenburg finds it necessary to demonstrate his popularity with young people.

This demonstration of the writer's audience is becoming tiresome, both as personal boasting and as a proof of the writer's national standing. "The people" are brought up again and again as the highest audience that a Soviet writer can reach — and as the only possible material for the writer. Soviet writers seem always to be dashing off to new industrial cities being built in Siberia, or staying at home engulfed in thousands of letters, suggestions, and criticisms from their readers.

> Dear Ilya Grigorievitch:
> We have read your last story, with its description of our cement factory, and want, in a comradely way, to tell you that your portrait of the foreman is lacking in Socialist verisimilitude! With love . . .

This insistence that the writer be constantly in touch with the people, always in tune with the national purpose — this is so dominating that even a foreign visitor finds himself feeling a bit heretical if he talks shop for a moment. Still, it is apparently easier in the Soviet Union than anywhere else in the world for a writer to know if he's made it or not. Like a television star in the United States, a Soviet writer always knows his rating. The people are always right — especially when they write letters!

I wonder if commonplace literature here does not have the role that advertising does with us. The good writers here, like good writers everywhere, probably work on a deeper level; but since the situations are often identical, it is hard, listening to Ehrenburg talk

---

* At the last Writers' Congress a delegate from Orel said that once there had been only three writers from Orel: Turgenev, Bunin, and Leskov. Now, however, there were seventy-nine members of the Writers' Union from Orel.

about how many letters he gets each week, to suppress thoughts of movie stars, and TV comedians, and other "personalities" equally beloved by the audience. Of course it was not wholly out of vanity that Ehrenburg dwelt so long on his popularity; there has always, in Russia, been a traditional image of the writer as the teacher of the people, a guide to the young. But it is also clear that every bushel of letters received by Ilya Ehrenburg helps to stave off the many grievances against him personally — to say nothing of complaints that his recent novels have been unsatisfactory.

When not engaged in special pleading, Ehrenburg's considerable intelligence has all the famous Russian bluntness. That old Russian alertness to the spiritual weakness of the West has become under Soviet Communism a hard and brilliant instrument of denunciation. Describing a visit by Alberto Moravia, Ehrenburg dwelt mercilessly on the morbidity of Moravia's fiction. (I wonder, however, if Moravia was pompous enough to say, "None of my characters is as intelligent as I am.") Ehrenburg has the easy raconteur's skill of a good journalist, and by the time tea was over I felt that I knew all his best stories. I can't see that these *always* point up the optimism of Soviet civilization and the corresponding demoralization of the West. Ehrenburg quoted his friend Picasso: "I do not search. I find." I believe Picasso does just that. But what is the bearing of this on Ehrenburg's own writings, on the immediate scene around us?

Later, he showed us around his gardens and told us something about the immediate district — Chekhov had practiced here as a young doctor, and across the plain stands the house of the millionaire Morosov, who had been the friend of Chekhov and Gorky and who had supported the underground Bolshevik paper *Iskra*. He eventually committed suicide. Grinning with pleasure at his own mot, Ehrenburg remarked that the history of the Morosovs was the history in brief of Russian capitalism — the grandfather a peasant, the father a magnate, the grandson (Chekhov's friend) a patron of arts. It occurred to me that this seemed to be the case with certain very wealthy American families as well, though perhaps the sympathy with the arts so noticeable in the more recent Guggenheims and Rockefellers did not, as a historical necessity, lead to suicide. Ehrenburg did not want anyone to take him up on this. He had made his joke. One does not discuss social analogies

between Russia and America; to do so might make us all a little
more forbearing with each other.

On the road back to Moscow, we stopped to see Chekhov's old
house. It had been burned by the Nazis, and the ruins have
pointedly been left by the Soviet authorities. A bust of Chekhov
stands before the charred door.

Pasternak's Wake
[1960]

BORIS PASTERNAK died on May 30. From Moscow, next day, the
New York Herald Tribune correspondent Tom Lambert revealed
that "neither the state-controlled Russian press nor radio has yet reported Mr. Pasternak's death. . . . Relatives, friends and admirers
of the kindly and talented writer — he still has many of the latter
despite the official attitude here toward him — will gather at his
house Thursday afternoon for the traditional Russian Orthodox
'Panikhida' (farewell to the dead) service. . . ."

One of the first friends to call, the correspondent continued, was
"Konstantin Paustovsky, a writer who was Mr. Pasternak's supporter
even when Moscow's Communist Party-directed writers were baying
his deportation abroad and the then chieftain of the Young Communist League was likening the great writer to a pig."

I had never heard of Konstantin Paustovsky until I went to the
Soviet Union last August with an American literary delegation to
meet Soviet writers. In the plane going over I read up on the
speeches that had been made at the recent Soviet Writers' Congress,
and was staggered to come across Paustovsky's hard, clear, contemptuous remarks on Soviet literary timeservers. Most literary pronouncements in the Soviet Union, as I was to discover even in personal
meetings with lesser writers, are composed in an officially correct
and fawningly patriotic style that seems designed to avoid saying
anything dangerous. No wonder that at the congress Khrushchev admitted his boredom with Soviet literature and contemptuously
told the writers not to take their "squabbles" (like the Pasternak
case?) to him.

Paustovsky's speech at the congress was about "Ideas — Dis-
putable and Indisputable." Since it is always in order in the Soviet

Union for a writer to write up a new tractor works in Sverdlovsk as
if the news story put him "in touch with every heartbeat of our
people," he began by saying that a writer never fools his readers,
and that they can tell instantly whether he is writing from "pureness
of thought or, on the contrary, timeserving adaptation, [from]
breadth of horizon or a sinister paucity of ideas . . ." The writer,
he went on, gets from the people the appreciation he deserves. "All
literary people and critics who take on themselves the right to speak
in the name of the people should keep this in mind. . . .

"We are lucky that Leo Tolstoy managed to write *Anna Karenina*
before [the current] tradition appeared. He did not have to make a
bow to anyone, even the publisher; he could allow Anna to break up
her family and pass out of life from purely private, and consequently
impermissible, considerations.

"It is not our custom to write of [Soviet] shortcomings . . .
without making in advance an apologetic bow and bringing to mind
our achievements. . . . One might think that one had to drive
home to every Soviet reader the advantages and superiority of our
system to the capitalist system — in the forty-second year of the
revolution, mind you!

"There is nothing so cruelly affronting as hypocrisy in a writer.
. . . Why do we tolerate . . . bureaucratic and Philistine language?
. . . Language is being turned into a bureaucratic jargon from top
to bottom, beginning with the newspapers . . . and ending with
every minute of our ordinary everyday life."

These are the words of a faithful, decent person — not a great
writer, I gather, probably not anywhere so accomplished and subtle
a writer as Pasternak was in his greatest poems, but at the same
time a less complicated, more open, and exuberantly generous
nature. Paustovsky is actually cherished in the Soviet Union for his
charm, and the same lady official of the Writers' Union who told me
out of a blue sky that Pasternak was "awful" pressed on me an English translation of Paustovsky's literary autobiography, *The Golden
Rose.*

Paustovsky is a descendant of Ukrainian Cossacks, and after early
schooling in Kiev worked as a laborer, sailor, and reporter, then
fought in the civil war. He has tramped all over Russia, and in
his almost sentimental ardor for the Russian land, and in his

loyalty to early associations, his book reminds me a little of Gorky's marvelous reminiscences of his life in the lower depths, *My University Days*. Paustovsky tends to be an impulsive, rambling writer, but his respect for the private human experience, for genuine feeling of any kind as opposed to official orthodoxy, is unmistakable.

One of his most charming stories is called "Loaf Sugar." A strange old man, a wanderer who has taken refuge for the night in a farmhouse far to the north, is asked to show his papers by a fat little bureaucrat carrying "a shabby briefcase . . . stuffed with reports and accounts." When the old man explains that he has papers "but they weren't written for you, dear man," the bureaucrat calls in a militiaman. The old man tells the story of *his* grandfather, whose famous singing voice the poet Pushkin loved so much that when Pushkin was killed in a duel, the grandfather sang over his coffin, in the freezing cold, until he lost his voice forever. His illiterate grandson, the old man of the story, goes about collecting folk songs and tales. The militiaman is so moved by the story that he presents some sugar for the old man's tea. "Ah, the pity of it," the old man says. "There's nothing worse than for a man to have an arid soul. Those kind of people make life wither as grass withers from the autumn dew."

Paustovsky's generous act of homage to Pasternak is liberating. It reminds me of the traditional respect that the great Russian writers and thinkers have always known how to show each other despite intense differences of opinion. (Paustovsky is unmistakably more in sympathy with the October Revolution than Pasternak was.) Paustovsky's gesture reminds me of the dying Turgenev writing to Tolstoy after years of estrangement: "I am writing to you particularly to tell you how glad I am to have been your contemporary." He calls up Gorky's unforgettable tribute to Tolstoy: "I am not an orphan on earth so long as this man lives on it." Even Lenin, the author of the system that finally outdid itself in calumniating, blackmailing, and isolating one introverted, highly literary symbolist poet, knew how to pay proper tribute to his Menshevik opponent Martov. As the old man in Paustovsky's story sang over Pushkin's body in the freezing cold until he lost his voice, so Pasternak was among the first to rush to Mayakovsky's flat when the poet committed suicide in 1930. So, in the steady Russian cold, many a Russian poet, many a Russian reader of poetry would, if he could, mourn over Pasternak today.

« 2 »

In Russia last summer, it was not the American visitors but the Russians who kept bringing up Pasternak. Every time they abused him in public, they would look around at each other as if to make sure that they were reciting their lessons well. The talented novelist Pavel Nilin gratuitously, at a public reception, told us not to be misled by the example of *Mister* Pasternak. The old Stalinist boss of the Writers' Union, Alexis Surkov, ranted that Pasternak had betrayed him personally by publishing *Doctor Zhivago*, and that the great aim of *his* life was now to write an "Anti-Zhivago." Even the charming and urbane novelist Konstantin Fedin, who had been made first secretary of the Writers' Union to replace the impossible Surkov, had to denounce the "traitor" during the campaign against Pasternak. Pasternak was Fedin's neighbor in Peredelkino. Last summer, four American writers had dinner with Fedin at his *dacha*, and we talked of many things. But Pasternak, who lived so near, was not mentioned. He could not be mentioned. Officially, Boris Pasternak was already dead.

Rome:
A Meditation on Keats

JOHN KEATS died in this house on February 23, 1821, aged twenty-five and four months. He had been here since November 1820, growing gradually worse after a debilitating journey from England that had taken almost three months and whose last stage, from Naples in a barbarous carriage, had further provoked and exhausted him as he jolted and bounced his way to Rome while his companion, the painter Joseph Severn, cheerfully grew healthier walking beside the carriage for the last part of the journey.

Dying in this house, knowing all too well that he was dying, having known since his hemorrhage just a year before that he was doomed — "I know that blood, it is arterial," he had said, recognizing his death warrant — Keats experienced an agony of total frustration, a sense of oncoming nullity as a man, a poet, a lover, whose stabbing despair in his last letters can still shake us with Keats's particularly rapid, gyrating expressiveness of sensations. "O for a life of sensations rather than of thoughts!" he had written in those early joyful letters of his violently accelerated self-discovery as a poet. Now he was dying by sensations, dying to sensations. With his great gift both for enumerating everything he felt, and for getting some general principle and aspect of human thought out of what he had learned about himself through his sensations, Keats felt as "annihilated" — to use one of his characteristic words — as a man can feel while still in the flesh.

To his distrusted friend Charles Brown, who had failed him at the last by not accompanying him to Italy, and whom he suspected of flirting cynically with Fanny Brawne, Keats wrote from Rome on November 30, 1820: "I have an habitual feeling of my real life having past, and that I am leading a posthumous existence. God knows how it would have been — but it appears to me — however, I will not speak of that subject . . . I am so weak (in mind) that I cannot bear the sight of any hand writing of a friend I love so much as I do you. . . . There is one thought enough to kill me — I have been well, healthy, alert &c, walking with her — and now — the knowledge of contrast, feeling for light and shade, all that information (primitive sense) necessary for a poem are great enemies to the recovery of the stomach. . . . I am well disappointed in hearing good news from George — for it runs in my head we shall all die young. . . ."

The seeming disjointedness of Keats when ill is of course very much like the headlong mental excitement of Keats's letters in the great years 1817-19 when he was striking off his great insights about Shakespeare, the character of genius, and Wordsworth to his brothers, to Woodhouse, to Benjamin Bailey, from the merest morsel of reading. But now, dying in Rome at twenty-five, his extraordinarily spontaneous, living, brilliantly abrupt way of dancing his way from item to item of his experience becomes the most chilling enumeration of his steady annihilation.

This was an avidly sensual young man — "Mister John Keats five feet high" — who made up for his five feet by his passionate eagerness to lap up all of life. Everything to do with the body was of special, sometimes morbid, importance to him. His mother, his brother Tom, and his brother George in America were all to die of tuberculosis; his father had died in the prime of life after an accident; Keats had been trained as a medical assistant, had performed dissections and operations. He had whored about in the company of exuberantly free, radical-minded litterateurs and editors in the still-heady air of pre-Victorian England. Wonderfully free to roam what were still country districts in and just out of London, to take enormous walking trips into the Lake Country and Scotland, to splash all his senses about, as he felt, in what was still England's green and pleasant land, he had become a poet in and through his senses — at the late age of nineteen — exactly with the emergence of his conscious sexual energy.

Keats the body poet, the sexual poet, opting for a life of sensations rather than of thoughts, moving between ecstasy and annihilation, seeking transcendence in and through the body, explains why his every mental adventure as a poet was a matter of feeling it, as he said, upon his pulses. The peculiar excitement of Keats's great letters and poems, even of the diffuseness in *Endymion* that he compares to a scattered pack of cards, is a sexual excitement made up even more of *wonder* at what he feels than of pleasure and pride. Geography for Keats has come down to the body rather than to the world. He reads the world *from* his body. Early, middle, and late, as we say so amazedly about a poet whose actual writing spanned less than six years, Keats was peculiarly vibrant. He clung to every possible reverberation in his own mind of the light and shade, heat and cold, manifested through *his* sensations. No wonder that Keats's total output can remind us of a fever chart in severe illness — with the slow rise to some frightening but totally expressive peak in the great odes — and then the dying away, literally, to the exhaustion of the body and the senses.

It is the physicality of Keats's poetry, the allegory it expresses of our own emergence, maturation, and decline, that explains why Keats has been important to our time as a life in poetry rather than as an influence on the practice of poetry. To this must be added his intense agnosticism. Keats's style was artificial even in his own time. It was disliked by Byron, patronized by Wordsworth and Shelley. Keats's adherence to what Gibbon had properly called "the thin texture of the pagan mythology . . . interwoven with various but not discordant materials," like his constant invocation of what he still called "poesy," stems not just from his casual reading, or an education entirely in English (and depending on hearsay), but from his ready skepticism as regards Christianity.

Blake's "paganism" — the word expresses his physicality rather than his brilliant philosophy of life realized exclusively through the self rather than from intellectual tradition — is amazingly deep-seated by contrast with the other great Romantics. Blake was an independent religious mind tortured by his need for a total new grammar of human history in its relation with the divine. Shelley was a natural and of course educated classicist who opted for the Devil's party and knew it — for Prometheus rather than Zeus. Wordsworth had a well-recognized genius for drawing a sustainedly general Christian pantheism out of every rock and rill in the Lake Country.

Keats was a libertarian radical who happened not to be that much interested in politics. His own philsophy is that "Essential Beauty," as he called it, drawn by art alone out of natural existence, is enough for him. Art, as many an early twentieth-century modernist would have said — but with not as much courage as Keats displayed in a more hidebound period — is what makes life tolerable tomorrow and tomorrow and tomorrow. At its best, like its obvious affinity in physical sex, it becomes a model of attachment and even of ecstasy.

Keats's theme of expressiveness, though it may call on the gods for inspiration and fortitude, is a world of forms, not of beliefs. Man is alone on earth with the resources allowed him by blind fortune. The poet or oracle of the new knowledge to be won by poetry is not a priest, as even the aboundingly physical Whitman thought, but, in Keats's marvelous image, like a soldier walking up to a battery. Keats of course shares in the romantic cult of genius that went on and on in the nineteenth century and became in Carlyle, Ruskin, Arnold, Shaw the typical idea of the writer educating necessary opinion by the irresistible momentum of his demands on the future. Without the belief in genius as repeating God's work on earth — the poet, as more than any king, the deputy of God in the endlessness of creation — this son of a livery-stablekeeper, a mere medical assistant far to the rear of English society — could not have come to his fiery greatness in one single year.

But Keats does not believe in traditional religion. He does not even believe that there is a tradition prior to and greater than each "individual Man of Achievement." Jesus, he says, was like the "seldom-appearing Socrates" — "a man by whose persistent endeavors mankind may be made happy — I can imagine such happiness carried to an extreme." There is a grand march of intellect, he wrote on May 3, 1818, and that proves "that a mighty providence subdues the mightiest minds to the service of *the time being,* whether it be in human knowledge or religion."

In the most famous of his self-discoveries through an act of criticism, he pronounced his ideal in Shakespeare's profusion, variousness, and inconsistency.

Hempstead, Sunday, 22 December 1818, My dear Brothers — Brown and Dilke walked with me & back from the Christmas pantomime . . . several things dovetailed in my mind, & at once it struck me, what quality went to form a Man of Achievement especially in Literature & which Shakespeare possessed enormously — I mean *Negative Capability*, that is when man is capable of being in uncertainties, Mysteries, doubts, without any irritable reaching after fact & reason — Coleridge, for instance, would let go by a fine isolated verisimilitude caught from the Penetralium of mystery, from being incapable of remaining content with half knowledge. This pursued through Volumes would perhaps take us no further than this, that with a great poet the sense of Beauty overcomes every other consideration, or rather obliterates all consideration.

Now it is possible to admit the rightness of this and nevertheless credit it to a young poet's realization of what is right for him and not for Coleridge — especially when it was also right for Shakespeare. But contracted as Keats's progress was into certain tearing moments of insight, we have to understand Keats's metaphysical courage, his grim refusal of religious consolation, in order to understand more fully why, when he was dying in this house, his greatest despair was that his full gift had not been and might not be recognized. Some writer once said ruefully that other people judge us by what we have written, while we judge ourselves by what we are planning to write. Keats, to adapt the extraordinary image used by Herman Melville about his own swift and somehow killing development in *his* twenties, had come to the inmost leaf — and was, like Melville, "ready to be annihilated."

But Keats was not morbid like Melville, who in any event lived into his seventies (probably because he never again tried anything on the order of *Moby Dick*). Keats was a casualty of tuberculosis, his guardian's financial selfishness, and mismanagement — and of his understandable fear of curtailment as a man and poet. He was held to this slender margin of existence. That is why his belief that genius does not so much instruct as "operate" is important to understanding his frame of mind at the end. To Benjamin Bailey, on November 22, 1817, he had written: "Men of Genius are great as certain ethereal Chemicals operating on the Mass of neutral intellect — but they have not any individuality, any determined Character."

The refrain that genius has no individuality is most vibrantly contained in the letter to Woodhouse of October 22, 1818: " . . . the poetical character is not itself, — it has no self — it is everything and nothing — . . . What shocks the virtuous philosopher, delights the chameleon Poet. —." This was crucial to Keats: identity came through the work, through repeated acts that had no significance except as the experience of renewal. No dependably continuous Christian or even classical tradition, no future life except as an image of oneself in the great body of memory — Keats certainly held out for that.

"That which is creative must create itself." And only this Shakespearean conception of a writer's career as a discontinuous series of creative acts can explain why Keats could have found faith and hope in so "personal" a philosophy of greatness. Matthew Arnold did not mean this when, at the height of Keats's rediscovery in the Victorian period, he piously breathed: "He is — he is with Shakespeare." Keats's own brinkmanship, his dominant trait of mobility, the courage to accept mobility, discontinuity, the great flashes of Essential Beauty as the truest life we have on earth — these must often have seemed not much to hold on to when he was losing life itself at twenty-five. And hence his bitterness of a kind unknown to the other Romantics, as sexual as it was fame-obsessed. To lead a "posthumous existence," as he vehemently put it, was nothing to a man whose first book had been savagely attacked in the quarterlies, and whose dramatic genius in his second — *The Eve of St. Agnes*, the great odes, *Lamia, The Fall of Hyperion* — would be far less appreciated than the pathos in his final struggle and his gift for inspiring Tennyson and Arnold with seemingly "divine" moments of realization.

Keats was indeed badly misread by his contemporaries. Even those to whom he felt closest for political reasons — the airily radical Leight Hunt, the Hazlitt obstinately pro-French Revolution and Napoleon — patronized him. The gorgeous mistake that made possible *Adonais* — the assumption that Keats had been destroyed by some critics — was again as patronizing as Byron's sneer in *Don Juan* that a fiery particle had been snuffed out by an article. Carlyle, born the same year as Keats, said with his usual brutal contempt for worldly failure that "Keats was a miserable creature, hungering after sweets which he can't get."

Yet even when Keats became an idol in the Victorian period that would have been his natural lifetime, he became an excuse for overromanticizing his own life, a figure in the Anglo-American literary opera in which the young hero chokes out his life in the last act, like Mimi or Camille — deserted by a faithless Fanny Brawne. To anyone who grew up on Eng. Lit.

— Amy Lowell's unconsciously indecent lust to possess helpless John Keats, some teacher's half-tearful recitation of *Beauty is Truth, Truth Beauty,* — *that is all/Ye know on earth and all ye need to know* as the ultimate wisdom — it was somehow no comfort that the next generation would see brilliant critical biographies and studies — Walter Bate, Aileen Ward, Robert Giddings, Christopher Ricks, Lionel Trilling. These somehow did not affect the practice and theory of contemporary *poets.* Eliot said wonderful things about Keats as a new stage in human consciousness, but Keats did not affect Hardy or Hopkins any more than he was to affect *Prufrock, Sunday Morning, Hugh Selwyn Mauberley, The Death of the Hired Man, Song of Myself,* or "Because I Could Not Stop for Death, Death Kindly Stopped for Me."

Where indeed *was* Keats in the modern poetry that began with the Romantics and, as we have never seen more clearly than today, is sustained by Blake and Wordsworth? The question was important because Keats, absent as he was from the later poetry, occupied so much of our consciousness; he *was*, he *is*, so much an active and continuing delight that it is startling to think that the dominating naturalness and even jauntiness of twentieth-century style might have found him luscious and stagy, the human stance in his poetry too passive, poignant, and exclamatory. Yeats said haughtily that Keats was "like a boy with his face pressed to a sweetshop window." It is possible that the several brilliant biographies of Keats in recent years, the emphasis on Keats's letters and on the active spirit of his short life, while correcting the bias against Keats's "softness," have also been ways of bypassing the problems presented to the practice of poetry by the artificality in Keats's poetic diction and by his reliance, even for his cast of characters, on a mythology both stilted and unsure. So much of modern poetry came out of the desire to redress the late Victorian fanciness in favor of a flat natural voice, that Keats's can still seem just too ceremonial — *How many bards gild the lapses of time! A few of them have ever been the food/Of my delighted fancy,* — *I could brood/Over their beauties, earthly, or sublime.* ... Or: *Spangling those million poutings of the brine/With quivering ore: 'twas even a awful shine/From the exaltation of Apollo's bow.* ...

This is early Keats. Even his mature style, mixed from the same gold leaf, can remind us of the grand style that Wordsworth, almost in the year of Keats's birth, had punctured for all time in the preface to the *Lyrical Ballads.* But the real problem for the modern poet is that Keats does believe that the task of the poet is to portray himself *mastering* his own experience. One great discovery of modern poetry is that the poet need not do anything of the kind. The poem must work, but it does not follow that the poet is or should be the hero of his solitary quest. Hardy — whose quiet, sometimes hopeless Dorset voice seems more and more essential than the strained brilliance of Hopkins — pointed the way in his love poems by commemorating a series of urgently disjointed encounters, of the human mind as a fluid corridor packed with couples who constantly failed to recognize each other in time. *Prufrock*, which far more directly expressed Eliot's real anguish, sexual sterility, than *The Waste Land*, remains sixty years later the archetypal poem of what Rilke called the past that breaks out in our hearts. Modern poetry, like modern painting, has for too long been influenced by itself. Long ago, Eliot's artfully broken voice, with its stealthy subconscious persona, became our academic tradition.

So Keats, who in poem after poem does indeed walk like a soldier up to the battery, and as regularly gets mown down, presents us with another, older idea entirely: the poet openly one with his life, style as affirmation, experience as a problem to be solved, life as full possibility, Homer and Shakespeare, Spenser and Milton looking down upon him as he writes, challenging him to join them in the company of the immortal dead. "Poesy" or ceremonial style translates everything into costume: bards, Apollo, Titans versus Olympians, a golden pen, a hymming angel.

Yes, I will be thy priest and build a fane
In some untrodden region of my mind . . .

As Byron said wickedly of even the great Nightingale Ode, why the *true* Hippocrene? How in the world, we ask ourselves when we read Keats through after having tasted him in our youth, did this skeptical medical student, this admirer of Hazlitt's fierce radicalism, come to rely on such a cast of outworn actors as Endymion, Diana, Hyperion, and even that Grecian urn?

But this was precisely the poetic machinery that was around for a radical empiricist who was a poet self-educated by poetry and whose gift for making the most of every experience was so intense that it mattered no more to him where he borrowed his characters and plots than it did to Shakespeare. He did, let us admit it, think that "poesy" required the poet to walk on his toes in court step. Suddenly discovering himself as a poet at nineteen, sometimes confused by histrionic characters like Leigh Hunt, distracted by his own powerful gift for sheer enjoyment, he is timid, playful, tentative. Pretending to be less serious that he is, he is self-conscious *eloquently*: one must be eloquent in every line and always at the same pitch. He has not grown up with poetry; he does not have a poetic tradition of his own, as even the totally idiosyncratic Blake did. Like a Sunday painter, Keats the beginner is intent on making beauty. He does not yet know what a secret and a surprise writing can be to the writer himself. But he is not long in finding out. "19 Feb 1818: Many have original minds who do not think it — they are led away by Custom — ... Now it appears to me that almost any Man may like the Spider spin from his own inwards his own airy Citadel. ... Man should not dispute or assert but whisper results to his neighbor." The key moment had come earlier, November 22, 1817 — "the simple imaginative Mind may have its rewards in the repetition of its own silent Working coming continually on the spirit with a fine suddenness."

From here on, the master words for Keats are *presses, seizes, abrupt, suddenness, draught*; or as he put it, the *authenticity* of the imagination. What the imagination seizes as Beauty must be Truth. The poet discovers that he can write, and write at any time, to any length, as in the four thousand lines and more of *Endymion*; that he can imitate, parody, extend himself in this rhetorical country of mythology because he trusts the sequences of his own mind. This is what moves his excited identification with Shakespeare's ability to create an Iago as gladly as an Imogen. Keats now has such self-confidence that he can rate Wordsworth over Milton because Wordsworth "thinks into the human heart," yet mock Wordsworth as "the egotistical sublime."

Now Keats comes into his own — and the drama of reading him emerges as Keats's mind working itself out through (and sometimes despite) the formal occasion set up by him. Formal indeed: the poet faces his theme as a priest the altar. There is invocation, high ceremony. But even more there is a contest of strength and wit, Jacob wrestling with the angel. The subject can be subdued but must not be absorbed entirely into the poet as his only protagonist. (So much "radical selfhood" is modernism.) Keats moves close to this in the identification with the nightingale. But the immense journey we take in reading that poem represents something else, classic in its own right. The stages by which we move from line to line keep their mystery every time we read the poem; we feel that there is a mind behind the mind, following the nightingale and tracing its echoes in the mind that presents itself to us as writing the poem.

April, 1819. We begin in the unexplained middle of things, in a complicated human heart that aches, whose sense is pained by a *drowsy numbness,* as though of *hemlock I had drunk,/Or emptied some dull opiate to the drains/One minute past, and Lethewards had sunk;/'Tis not through envy of thy happy lot,* he says to the nightingale, *But being too happy in thine happiness, — /That thou, light-winged Dryad of the trees,/In some melodious plot/Of beechen green, and shadows numberless,/Singest of summer in full-throated ease.* The physical exactness here keys us up even though the theme is aesthetic pain. "When I first heard two-part harmony in Bach," said Schweitzer, "I thought I would faint from excess of pleasure." The excess of pleasure is surely what accounts for the minutely tuned adjectives: *shadows numberless, beechen green, full-throated ease, drowsy numbness, dull opiate;* above all for the abrupt surprise and intermediacy of style — *But being too happy in thine happiness — /That thou, light-winged Dryad of the trees,/In some melodious plot/Of beechen green and shadows numberless,/Singest of summer in full-throated ease.*

In stanza 2, the sudden longing for *a draught of vintage, . . . /Cool'd a long age in the deep-delv'd earth,* shifts us into a dream fantasy of intoxicating plenty. The theme is the northerner's irresistible dream of the Mediterranean — *Dahin!* — and each line in itself expresses Keats's belief that he could identify with any object, even a billiard ball in its smoothness and roundness. *O for a beaker full of the warm South,/Full of the true, the blushful Hippocrene,/With beaded bubbles winking at the brim/And purple-stained mouth.* . . . But now the reversal into dream, into death as another existence: *That I might drink, and leave the world unseen,/And with thee fade far away into the forest dim.*

Death is the mother of Beauty, said Wallace Stevens in *Sunday Morning,* another poem of natural existence without illusion but on the margin of hallucination. I think of this as I come to the echolalic repetitions of *Fade far away, dissolve, and quite forget/What thou among the leaves hast never known,/The weariness, the fever, and the fret/Here, where men sit and hear each other groan.* . . . The firmness of style, the ringing alliteration, the luminous images of a whole cycle of life are in the most wonderful contrast to the exhaustion pictured.

And now the dream takes over — *Away! Away! for I will fly to thee —* the poet has willed his way into the dream *on the viewless wings of Poesy,* and *Though the dull brain perplexes and retards,* the growing faith that Imagination can be Truth has taken Keats into the heart of the mystery that had first seized him five years before: *Already with thee! tender is the night, /And haply the Queen-Moon is on her throne, /Cluster'd around by all her starry Fays....*

Here, he says, *there is no light /... I cannot see what flowers are at my feet, /... But in embalm'd darkness, guess each sweet /Wherewith the seasonable month endows /The grass, the thicket, and the fruit-tree wild....* The passage is into enchantment, onto a plateau of steady sexual delight. The sensations are of the world as another body. And they are all of a piece, without the breaking disillusion at the beginning of the poem and at the end. He has been carried over completely, and we are carried over by images that are not epithets for the things, as in *Endymion*, but are the thing itself — *The grass, the thicket, and the fruit-tree wild; /White hawthorn, and the pastoral eglantine; /Fast fading violets cover'd up in leaves; /And mid-May's eldest child, /The coming musk-rose, full of dewy wine, /The murmurous haunt of flies on summer eves.*

But from here on, Beauty becomes the mother of Death — as so often sexual repletion and depletion bring lovers a sense of death. *Darkling I listen ...* in those words Keats describes a fall into another consciousness, alone, the margin of annihilation that has been his demon, but now seems all too tempting: *for many a time /I have been half in love with easeful Death, /Call'd him soft names in many a musèd rhyme /... Now more than ever seems it rich to die, /To cease upon the midnight with no pain, /While thou art pouring forth thy soul abroad /In such an ecstasy!...*

Yet still he can pull back: for the song itself has become an absolute, a stunning transcendence of the mortal condition:... *No hungry generations tread thee down; /The voice I hear this passing night was heard /In ancient days by emperor and clown; /Perhaps the self-same song that found a path /Through the sad heart of Ruth, when, sick for home, /She stood in tears amid the alien corn....* The song is now openly seen as the voice of poetry alone — *The same that ofttimes hath /Charm'd magic casements, opening on the foam /Of perilous seas, in faery lands forlorn.* But now the song and the poet divide — poetry is an ecstasy that can enchant, drug, create, but cannot redeem our mortal condition. *Forlorn! the very word is like a bell /To toll me back from thee to my sole self! /Adieu! the fancy cannot cheat so well /As she is famed to do, deceiving elf. /Adieu! Adieu! thy plaintive anthem fades /Past the near meadows, over the still stream, /Up the hill-side; and now 'tis buried deep /In the next valley glades: /Was it a vision, or a waking dream? /Fled is that music: — Do I wake or sleep?*

No other Romantic poet was to go so far into the dream absolute on a purely natural basis — without Coleridge's drugs, without Blake's wholly spiritualized universe, without Wordsworth's natural piety, without Shelley's illusion that Prometheus will make war on Father Zeus for *our* sake. No other Romantic poet was to divide life from death, death from life, so absolutely *within* himself — and all this within the letters of fire that are the style of John Keats.

Rome, November 30, 1820: "Yet I ride the little horse — and, at my worst, even in quarantine, summoned up more puns, in a sort of desperation, in one week than in any year of my life. There is one thought enough to kill me — I have been well, healthy, alert, &c, walking with her — and now — the knowledge of contrast, feeling for light and shade, all that information (primitive sense) necessary for a poem are great enemies to the recovery of the stomach."   [1976]

Isaac Bashevis Singer:
God May Be a Novelist

EAST EUROPEAN JEWS have produced many stories, narratives, legends, but until our day, very little fiction. At a 1973 symposium in Jerusalem on "the sources of Jewish creativity" to which Isaac Bashevis Singer was not invited (he embodies so many "sources of Jewish creativity" all by himself), the orthodox Chaim Potok admitted that "It is not possible for an orthodox Jew who is committed to aesthetics to be honest to both traditions."

This should be obvious, but isn't to a great many Jews who still read novels but can't understand why, since as the one Jewish novelist who can write about the unchanging Jewish struggle through the ages, Isaac Bashevis Singer doesn't flatter them as their rabbis do. In any event, a good novelist is committed to more than "esthetics," and Isaac Singer is just as interested in truth as he was when he was a young Hasid in gaberdine and earlocks timidly looking at the street life in Warsaw.

The historic problem for Isaac Singer — as witness those other children of devout families, Hawthorne, Melville, James, Mark Twain, Stephen Crane — is that whereas the orthodox believe that truth is personified by God and God is the truth, the Jewish novelist who derives from orthodoxy

A *Crown of Feathers*, by Isaac Bashevis Singer. New York: Farrar Straus & Giroux.

may find truth always protean and amazing because this is the way God actually thinks and moves. God may even be a novelist ceaselessly creating characters who, as Melville said to Hawthorne, astonish Him as much as He astonishes us.

Isaac Bashevis Singer is an extraordinary writer. His stories represent the most delicate imaginative splendor, wit, mischief, and, not least, the now unbelievable life that Jews once lived in Poland. But Singer is also a rarity among Jewish novelists. Though necessarily secularized, he still has access to the mystical Jewish theology in which he was brought up by the rabbis who were his father, grandfathers, uncles. So the world to Isaac Bashevis Singer still represents the *mind* of God. Pious folk are obsessed with obeying the will of God. But God, the inexpressible Other, the unfathomable Father who dominates pious lives, is to Singer an endlessly surprising thinker whose unaccountable variables of creation are so many that Singer has an amused understanding of classical paganism, made up of irreconcilable spirits who were nevertheless behind every bush. And who rather crowded the world with their busy divinity. But who else would say in his own voice about Israel: "In the paper before me I read about thefts, car accidents, border shootings. One page is full of obituaries. No, the Messiah hasn't come yet. The Resurrection was not in sight. Orthopedic shoes were displayed in a shop across the way" and in the same story have a painter say about Israel:

Once I had a philosophy about indifference. But here one cannot be indifferent. At night, when the moon is shining and I walk through the narrow alleys, I am enraptured. If I moved to another country I would die from yearning. I stroll along the sea and literally hear the words of the prophets. It's in my imagination, I know, but I'm surrounded by the old Israelites and even the Canaanites and the other nations that preceded Joshua, the son of Nun. I've lived in both Algeria and Morocco. The ghosts there are wild apaches, murderers, maniacs. This land teems with saints and heroes. Although I do not believe in God, I hear His voice. An atavism has taken hold of us Jews and it is even stronger than the instinct for life. Don't you feel it?

The (mostly) Jewish characters who pass through Singer's short stories (not forgetting the thin unsaintly vegetarian who wrote them) do just that — they pass through. They are part of a mysterious creation that is the larger, more interesting part of themselves. Their notable temporariness in this world may express their flight through the mind of God. But this "passing through" is also a tribute to the larger body of believers, God's people living and dead, whom a Jew calls upon when he prays and who help make up the deeper existence of the individual Jew. But since Singer is the most unsentimental observer of his fellow Jews, this "passing through" is also seen as a desperate mutability. It is what his Polish Jews have built into themselves as a result of so much hatred. In their hearts, they believe the world to be unreal.

Singer's characters are vivid, vociferous, but they are not all-important to themselves any longer. Perhaps that is why there are so many of them. Yet they are not mere victims, either; they suffer from their own capriciousness (always a cardinal point with Singer), for they mean to do right, out of habit, but suddenly find their duty in this world indecipherable. And that is something they have against the world, which in their pious youth felt easier to the touch.

In "A Crown of Feathers" a beautiful and gifted young orphan, Akhsa, brought up by her wealthy, pious, and indulgent grandfather, hears the voice of her dead grandmother scorning the harshly pious suitor her grandfather has picked for her. Akhsa refused him, the grandfather is disgraced and dies. Akhsa, alone in the world, now hears her grandmother telling her that Christ *is* the son of God and telling her to look inside her pillow for the sign. It is a crown of feathers, topped by a cross. Akhsa is so impressed by this communication from the spiritual world that she becomes a Catholic, marries a Polish squire. Eventually she discovers that her "grandmother" is being impersonated by the devil. In the last and most remarkable section of this story, she returns to the Jewish community, searches out and marries her old suitor, a religious fanatic who has never forgiven her and who forces her to undergo a series of wild penances that finally kill her. Before her death she still longs for a sign, "the pure truth revealed." But though she guesses that there is another crown of feathers in her pillow and that this one bears the four Hebrew letters that stand for the unsayable name of God, Akhsa dies without the assurance that this crown is more a revelation of *the* truth than is the other. The townspeople who find bits of down between the dead woman's fingers can never figure out what she has been searching for, and "no matter how much the townspeople wondered and how many explanations they tried to find, they never discovered the truth."

For some reason Singer thought it necessary to add to this story the reflection that "if there is such a thing as truth it is as intricate and hidden as a crown of feathers." This is so much his faith as a novelist, and his practice, that I can only suppose that he wanted to admonish the Yiddish readers of the *Jewish Daily Forward*, where Singer's stories usually first appear, and who are now accustomed to more unctuous accounts of Jewish life and belief than they get from Singer.

I do not mean that Singer is a shrew about Jewish life, like certain American Jewish writers who cannot get over mama and can displace her only by reproducing her legendary force of invective. Singer swims happily in the whole ancient and modern tradition of the Jews — Jews are his life. But he would certainly agree with Mark Twain's reply to anti-Semites: "Jews are members of the human race; worse than that I cannot say of them." And he would also say, as Jews know better than anyone, that oppression does not improve the character.

In Singer's recent stories the Jews emerge on a world scale, yet remain parts of a distinctive Jewish environment: Warsaw when it was under Russian rule (the first time), Coney Island, Paris, Tel Aviv. They have been through Czarist pogroms, Nazi camps, Communist camps; their intimate family memories go back to the murdering, rampaging Cossacks of the seventeenth century who buried Jewish children alive. And here they are anywhere but in Poland, with the blue concentration camp numbers on their wrists, up to their lips in one mad love affair after another (Singer is among other things the most rueful and the funniest novelist of the erotic life in Yiddish literature), and above all, bemused by their own obsessions.

Singer describes old Kerenskyites in New York (some of them Russian aristocrats) hobbling around each other until one of them falls dead. "Bulov took the corpse's wrist and felt for a pulse. He made a face, shook his square beard from side to side, and his eyes were saying 'This is against all rules, Count. This is not the way to behave.' Skillfully, he closed the corpse's mouth." He describes a Warsaw mother, insanely vain, and her son, a self-destructive prodigy, who in their night clothes dance together in the middle of the night. They will die together in the Warsaw Ghetto. He describes a Yiddish writer so madly in love with a married woman that her enraged husband maliciously makes her pregnant. Now "her son" regularly comes for handouts to the lover, who supports him in memory of his beloved — and out of guilt for "causing" her pregnancy. He describes a woman who unaccountably, maddeningly is always losing things, and finally gets permanently lost herself. She just disappears, like one of her possessions.

Demons, it seems. Demons are a big thing in Singer's fiction, though many of his "first" readers complain to him that demons are not to be believed in — a strange complaint indeed when you consider Jewish experience. But on this point the husband of the wife who was always losing things has the perfect comment, addressed to Singer himself, who appears in a growing number of his stories in the most natural and anecdotal sort of way. Memoir here becomes story and story somebody's memoir.

You often write about the mysterious powers. You believe in demons, imps — what have you. ... Even if demons do exist, they are not in New York. What would a demon do in New York? He would get run over by a car or tangle himself in a subway and never find his way out. Demons need a synagogue, a ritual bathhouse, a poorhouse, a garret with torn prayerbooks — all the paraphernalia that you describe in your stories. Still, hidden powers that no one can explain exist everywhere. ... I have had an experience with them. The Yiddish newspapers wrote about it and the English ones too. But how long do they write about anything? Here in America, if the Heavens would part and the angel Gabriel were to fly down with his six fiery wings and take a walk on Broadway, they would not write about it for more than a day or two. If you are in a rush to go light candles and bless the incoming Sabbath, I will come back some other time, he said smiling and winking.

[1973]

VII
Freud and
His Consequences

Sigmund Freud, 1856-1956: Portrait of a Hero

THE FRONTISPIECE to Volume II of Ernest Jones's biography of him shows Freud in 1906, age fifty. With his arms militantly folded across his chest, the everlasting cigar in one hand, only one somber eye visible in this profile of his tensely reflective face, he sits for the photographer with such immense conscious self-possession that it is impossible not to see this calm but vibrant look of mastery as the goal of Freud's maturity and the manifestation of his intellectual authority. This, we say to ourselves out of the midst of Jones's almost thousand pages on Freud — this is what has persuaded so many who do not believe his science; this is the face of the founder, the father of his subject and the father in spirit to so many of his disciples; this is the face not of the pleasure principle but of transcendent consciousness; this is the man who in his dreams identified himself with Joseph, in his writings with Moses. This is the look that wins respect for the Jews and the deepest resentment — for this man lived apart from the greater world around him, and yet claimed to understand everything inside it. This is the look which I, living all my life among the Freudians, the disciples, have never seen in the flesh. For this is the face of a great man — a man who taught us not only to see, but, as he said, to "tolerate a piece of reality." This man transformed our sense of things. He is the only *kind* of man that ever works magic in our lives. By devotion to his task, he becomes the most aloof of men — the hero.

Ordinarily, the early life of a hero is not really significant. For what counts with him is not, as with us, the search for "maturity," for "integration," but the tales of his mastery over the secret and the forbidden, the recital of his ability to make nature yield up its secrets. The early struggles of the hero may have a purely dramatic element. For we who know what he must become can still watch with suspense as a Freud discovers cocaine and does not develop his

The Life and Work of Sigmund Freud, by Ernest Jones. New York: Basic Books.

discovery, or comes to the verge of discovering the neurone without fully realizing it. His destiny lies elsewhere, and generally these early struggles are decisive only as they lead to the discovery of his true vocation. But in a man like Freud, whose interest so peculiarly was the self, and who even formally documented his science from his own dreams and self-analysis, this early period becomes the very material which the hero will rework into the fully forged personality he needs for his appointed work. For this reason the intensely Jewish background of Freud did not, as critics of psychoanalysis often say, simply act to limit his knowledge to idle repressed ladies of the Jewish bourgeoisie in Vienna; it served (a Jewish background often does this for certain thinkers) as a microcosm of the world, a guide to that larger reality in which he did not share. Such confidence may not be valid. The point is that a Jew can think that it is, if he sees an essential unifying principle of identity running through human experience. The very mark of Freud's ability to speculate so largely on the basis of what would seem very restricted evidence is, indeed, a measure of his ability not merely to come to terms with himself — to suffer so many early anxieties and to rise above them — but to *use* these disabilities as a guide to the elucidation of many larger problems.

This, for me, is the fascination of Jones's first volume. And it is a measure of the unforced but remarkable artistic tact of Freud's biographer that even the second volume, which carries us to Freud in his sixties, should close so beautifully, like a musical *da capo*, on those probable childhood musings by the little Freud about his complicated family situation, which, Jones thinks, explains Freud's passion for the truth and his aggressive independence in seeking it out.

This link between early sexual curiosity and the passion for knowledge is, of course, standard Freudian doctrine. Freud applied it to the scientific side of Leonardo da Vinci, and Jones centers Freud's curiosity, finally, on his need to ferret out the truth about his half-brother Philipp, who was so much older and given to "joking" about the difference in their ages that he could be thought of as the mate of Freud's own mother. As Jones speculatively works it out, the little Freud thought that Philipp "evidently knew all the secrets," but that he could not be trusted to tell the truth about them. And so perhaps it was "this insignificant little man," Jones surmises, who "through his mere existence . . . fortuitously struck the spark that lit the future Freud's determination to trust himself alone, to resist the impulses to believe in others more than in himself. . . ." This explanation of Freud's inquisitive genius is something that one may be permitted to doubt in favor of the intrinsic gift of curiosity itself. And yet the decisive fact in Jones's account is exactly Freud's confidence that in his own situation he could find the nucleus of reality.

This kind of confidence reminds one of Thoreau's saying that a poet learns to watch his own moods as narrowly as a cat. It displays that gift for being convinced of the significance of one's experiences that seems to me the essence of being an artist. But this confidence may also signify that spiritual ability to generalize on the basis of restricted experiences which seems to be an essential of Jewish consciousness. Nothing is so astonishing in the history of the Jews as this disparity between their history of exile, of marginal existence, of worldly inexperience in the ghetto — which by contrast with Western civilization looks like a long sleep — and their belief that reality is consistent, all of one piece. Where *they* are is perspective enough on the "world," on the world's great, and on the issues of heaven and earth. Indeed, one might even say that one can measure the degree of originality one finds among Jewish intellectuals by this ability to trust themselves. Where this faith in the essential correspondence between themselves and the world is at once intense and yet clouded by self-doubt, as in Kafka, the effect in their work is significantly morbid even when the achievement is very great.

Now Freud would have assented to this "gift of conviction," as I call it, but would have located it not in the Jewish genius but in the scientific conviction of the biological identity of mankind. The mechanistic school of physiology in which he was trained under Brücke was the school that supplanted Schelling's romantic view of nature and established, in a succession of vital discoveries, basic examples of cause-and-effect in the body. Indeed, Freud was so wedded to positivism that in the absence of any empirical evidence he had to pronounce God an "illusion." But in point of fact this kind of empirical evidence is not always present in psychoanalysis either, for even where certain "confirmations" exist, they lie under the suspicion of being culturally instigated by psychoanalysis itself. The "proofs" that Freud found for his theories lay not so much in evidence — for some *part* of this evidence, by the very nature of the material, must always be beyond proof — *but in his way of reasoning solidly about material which only he could see.* It is precisely this enormous honesty and carefulness that make so curiously impressive a book like *Moses and Monotheism,* which is not merely unfounded on evidence, but at times preposterous because of Freud's suggestion that he may be just about to find evidence at any minute. Yet the book is anything but preposterous; indeed, it is strangely persuasive. The basis of this, I submit, is the wholly sane, orderly, scientific way in which Freud reasons, and which is so compelling in Freud's work that he convinces us of the reality of what he is discussing. When you look back, you can see that this air of leading us step by step to the truth, of considering all possible objections, is not always justified, for Freud often merely appears to consider objections. But the point is that Freud had an honest persuasion and that once he saw his subject, he opened up its possibilities honestly. Not everyone who is wedded to positivistic explanations has an instinct for the unexplored, and people who go in for Freud's kind of material rarely bother to reason at all. But he had the kind of mind that has both an instinct for the reality behind phenomena and a moral determination to find a cause for everything. And it is no accident that in him the wish for fame represents not only a hunger for success but a desire to find a reputation that will express the immense role he had to play.

Now this kind of mind, I feel, represents in Freud the Jewish belief in the essential logic of human experience, and it is this, as I see it, that enabled Freud to seize with such *conviction* — the essential mark of genius — on the basis of his early childhood experiences. Freud, by attributing inquisitiveness in general to early sexual curiosity, tended, if anything, to make this principle too hard-and-fast. For all biological explanations of human curiosity are too general to account for a Leonardo, a Newton, an Einstein, a Freud. But the sense of the presence of larger things within the restricted family circle, of things which we dare not think are real but which *are* real *to us* — this seems to me the essence of Freud's early struggles to accept his gift of divination. The drama, then, is not that Freud was eager for fame because he was "insecure," as so many people who in our age recognize only the "integrated," "well-organized" personality seem to feel, when they express their *surprise* that the great man had so many anxieties. Freud was indeed eager for fame, so much so that he was always looking for solutions in different fields that would make his name. (In the golden era of positivism, all subjects seemed to be laid out, so that it seemed that only keys were needed to the various locks; Freud characteristically inaugurated a new *field.*) The point about his early discoveries and near-discoveries, surely, is not only that Freud was trying desperately to become famous so that he could get some money to marry on and rise despite the usual restrictions against him as a Jew. He was so aware of his unfulfilled gifts that he was trying to find the occasions that would allow him to discover just what they could do for him. Hence, as we see in all these early scientific efforts, he was either too impatient, as in the cocaine episode, where he recklessly tried it out on everyone, or, as in the neurone episode, too cautious, for he missed out, says Jones, by "not daring to pursue his thoughts to their logical — and not far-off — conclusion." In the account of his early scientific experiments we feel, indeed, that Freud had to a remarkable degree the gift of intellectual venturesomeness, but we feel, too, that it is precisely this gift of believing too easily on too little evidence, of *plunging* — as it must have seemed to his teachers — too recklessly from one field to another that shocked his innate scientific probity, pulled him to just short of the final prize, and then stopped him, probably more puzzled than anything else that he had not gone through to the end of his "hunch." In this early period, at least, he was, to the extent that he was inwardly the boldest of men, equally uncertain. He was shy about his boldness and ignorant, as yet, of where he would triumph. "I have often," he wrote once, "felt as if I had inherited all the passion of our ancestors when they defended the Temple, as if I could joyfully cast away my life in a great cause. And with all that I was always so powerless and could not express the flowing passions even by a word or a poem. So I have always suppressed myself and I believe that people must notice that in me."

This instinctive self-trust of the gifted man is, paradoxically, a gift that he can mistrust. Freud, then, had good sanction for mistrusting his, since his whole training in the school of Brücke was to avoid the kind of speculation he was prone to make. Indeed, it was just this tendency in himself that probably attracted him to that utterly speculative character, Wilhelm Fliess, who was so busy working out a system of biological time on the basis of the menstrual cycle, and whose attraction to Freud, and Freud's to him, was so obviously founded on their common tendency to intellectual guesswork. But since Freud distrusted this tendency until it could be put on a scientific footing, and Fliess distrusted his own not at all, it is understandable that the relation between them broke down — as was to happen later with the equally speculative Jung. Although Freud was a "son" to Fliess and a "father" to Jung, one can see that, despite the enormous difference between Fliess and Jung, Freud had to assert in both cases not merely the originality but the felt reality of his hypotheses.

In both cases, however, we see that Freud is inherently not the plodder he has been trained to be: he is not a man who will always be abashed by an older and more authoritative type like Fliess. On the contrary, the man who conceived psychoanalysis, who reached into the unconscious, who generalized so confidently from his own dreams and Jewish jokes, was the same man who, in his earlier period, was so excited by the possibilities of cocaine that he tried it on his own fiancée; who caught fire on seeing a particular case of hysteria; who later was to insist that Moses was an Egyptian and that there is a death wish. Obviously this man had the bold reach, the speculative power, the gift of forming radical and breathtakingly fundamental hypotheses to an extraordinary degree. But how typical it was of him, too, to say in a letter, when he was preparing himself to write *Totem and Taboo*: "I am reading thick books without being really interested in them since I already know the results; my instinct tells me that. But they have to slither their way through all the material on the subject. In that process one's insight gets clouded, there are many things that don't fit and yet mustn't be forced." We can see that he was reading these books not for the kind of external proof of his theories, based on someone's research, which in the case of *Totem and Taboo* would have been more formal than real; he was reading in order to make sure that he was not flying in the face of the facts and, I suspect, in order to see whether anyone had thought along this *subject* before. In that case, we can be sure, he would have checked. He was original, not irresponsible.

This is the essential Freud of the portrait — the speculative, the experimenter, the plunger, all of whom add up to the highest scientific rectitude. It is the adventurousness in Freud that explains his break with his old teacher Breuer, with whom he had written the cardinal first book in psychoanalysis, *Studies in Hysteria*. But Breuer was frightened of "sexual studies" and withdrew. On the other hand, with a younger man like Jung, we can see that the break occurs precisely because Freud is wary of what he called in Jung the "mystical" element. Now what is the difference, someone might well demand, between Freud and Jung, since they are both theorists in a highly speculative field and each may be equally right? The difference lies in the extent to which things are real to one. Freud said, my theories are *true*; Jung, my theories are *possible*.

This is not the place for a discussion of Freud and Jung, except as their early association and later quarrel affected the founder of psychoanalysis. But I will say that even someone who is far more sympathetic to the religious imagination than Freud is can hardly help a feeling of revulsion when he compares Jung's *Modern Man in Search of a Soul* with Freud's *The Future of an Illusion*. Freud's book, though limited, sounds as if he is talking about something he believes; while Jung's — "sincere," far more supple and sympathetic to the modern yearning for a faith, for any faith! — has about it the unmistakable suggestion: try it, it may be good for you. One rejects an *illusion*; the other offers us a *search* — for an illusion? The difference between these two books is that Freud thinks like a scientist, and is concerned with what he knows; Jung thinks "psychologically": *i.e.*, he is concerned with what man *needs*; Freud is concerned with what he sees as *truth*.

« 2 »

It is this passion for the sharp edges of truth that makes Freud a hero. It prepares you for whatever surprises in the shape of tigers and jaguars may spring out at you from the underbrush of the human soul. Jones emphasizes this feeling for the truth as the greatest single mark of Freud's mind; and I must confess, as someone who is not a Freudian, that whatever the obscurities and unprovabilities of Freudian doctrine, one gets an overwhelming sense in Freud's own work that he is a man who seeks truth. In Jones's psychoanalytic terms, to seek truth is already to show that one has an instinct for truth; but Freud's sense of reality was surely an individual gift, a mark of unique insight. What a man sees, that is what he is; but he has really to *see* it, as Cézanne saw the apple, and as so many highly theoretical Americans do not see the thing they tell us they are writing about. The more a man really sees, the more absurd and reckless he will seem to those who can see only what the intellectual fashion gets them to see. Freud's sense for the truth is not nullified by the highly speculative character of his mind. Indeed, the two go together: the condition being what I do not find in Jung: the persuasion that these things are unutterably real to the man himself.

Such a mind walks on the thin edge of an abyss. On one side of you is not only all that is unknown, and perhaps unknowable, indescribable, frighteningly obscure and vaguely obscene — but, for a man as religiously trained in science as Freud was, and for whom science was, indeed, a religion, there is the danger of seeming to fly off beyond the sanctioned limits of science. And this danger Freud incurred, as he incurs it still. One leading German psychiatrist stormed at a scientific meeting, when psychoanalysis was brought up, that it was a subject "for the police." At the Academy of Medicine in New York, Freud was denounced as a typical "Viennese libertine." Freud, the most laborious sublimate of men, the man whom his lifelong associate Jones calls "quite peculiarly monogamous," was identified with the Vienna of *La Ronde*. (On the one hand his findings were scoffed at because so many of his first patients were repressed Jewish ladies; on the other hand he was denounced as an example of Viennese immorality.) The German neurologists were so entirely united against him that at one meeting, when Sadger read a study of the influence of his mother in C. F. Meyer's life, a Dr. Braatz cried out that German ideals were at stake and that something drastic should be done to protect them. Freud had hoped that Jung's important place in the early psychoanalytic movement would save it from being thought of as a "Jewish national movement." But Jung withdrew. And similarly, though Jones does not label the point, one can see from his account of Freud's struggle for a hearing that some of the most violent attacks on him came from Jewish doctors. One could wish, however, that the well-known Freudian tactic of showing up every opponent and critic as badly in need of treatment were not so marked even in someone so humanly impressive as Dr. Jones. The opponent Oppenheim has to be labeled a neurotic, and "furthermore, his wife was a bad case of hysteria." Another opponent "was a curious man, a doubtful personality with a shady past." Freud's old teacher Meynert, who had turned unfriendly, is in his turn revealed as a sick man. The heretics in the Freud circle — Adler, Jung, Stekel, Rank, and how many others — are all exposed, more or less regretfully, but with unmistakable certainty. "Nor did it surprise Freud that the so-called arguments brought forward by his opponents were identical with his patients' defenses and could show the same lack of insight and even of logic. All this was therefore in the natural order of things and could neither shake Freud's convictions nor disturb him personally."

So, despite the violent attacks, he persisted (and he never replied; only the disciples do). Why did he persist? Because he believed it. Had psychoanalysis been entirely a subject susceptible to proof, like Newton's or Pasteur's, the early hypothesis might have been confirmed and the discoverer's continuing belief in it would have seemed less remarkable than it does. Nevertheless, all discoveries, all works of art, begin in this gift of conviction, long before experimental confirmation or even realization is possible. And the test of it is always the same: a piece of reality that no one else sees is real to someone, and he makes us see it. In the same way, the original insight is either so real that you can convincingly work it out, or it is no insight at all. The brilliant but marginal thinkers, from Fliess to Rank, end up as episodes in someone else's life. The give-away is always in Jung's suggestion that God may not exist, but that He is good for you.

In Freud's kind of conviction lies the principle of the hero; it is this that gives him his character. Seen from the outside, a life like Freud's, ending as it did not merely in the loss of so many talented disciples, but in his suffering as an old man at the hands of the Nazis, in the loss of his library, in the cancer of the throat that so agonizingly killed him, represents, as we feel, a remarkable ordeal. And the tendency of most Americans who are sympathetic to psychoanalysis is probably to complain, as David Riesman does in *Individualism Reconsidered*, that Freud believed in arduousness, that he could see anything good only as the reward of extreme effort. By contrast with the sloppiness which was a Viennese joke and self-indulgence and boast, Freud's grim laboriousness must have aroused further dislike and hostility. It was *after* seeing patients all day and after writing up his notes and correspondence that he would sit down, after nine in the evening, to his own books. This routine went on day after day, interrupted only by a walk and one evening a week playing cards with his cronies. (Only when he was sixty-five, Jones tells us, did he allow himself a cup of coffee at five o'clock. He rarely drank even wine.) But what both the corrupt society of Vienna, and Americans who think that any extreme kind of moral exertion is somehow unhealthy — what both miss is the extraordinary hold that conviction of the truth has upon such a man as Freud, dominating his life, holding him to his desk late into the night, forcing him at the end, when he was dying of cancer in London, still to see patients. And need it be noted that this was probably not a merciful gesture, that Freud was not so much a healer as a scientist, that his patients were the one laboratory in which this man could confirm and advance his theories? The hero is a hero because he has an heroic destiny, and the very mark of such a destiny is that no one chooses it; it chooses the man it shall be embodied in. The destiny is a cause, an essential idea behind the perplexing surface of things. Just as it chooses the hero, its oracle, its voice to the world, so in this knitting-together of hero and cause lies the essence of a suffering that he cannot reject any more than he could, anticipating the cost ahead, not have chosen it. But truth, choosing him, pledged him to endure what had to be. And it is in this sense of the inescapability of the truth that the characteristic devotion of the hero is found.

[1956]

Psychoanalysis and Literary Culture Today

THERE IS a young Englishman on Broadway who shouts every night that he is angry, very angry. Yet when we open John Osborne's play

Look Back in Anger and try to find out just what he is angry about, we make a curious discovery: he is not angry on specific grounds, as people often are; he is angry at his inability to feel anger, angry that he lacks a cause to be angry about. At one moment, after complaining that "nobody can be bothered. No one can raise themselves out of their delicious sloth," he says, very wistfully indeed for an angry man, "Was I really wrong to believe that there's a — kind of — burning virility of mind and spirit that looks for something as powerful as itself? The heaviest, strongest creatures in this world seem to be the loneliest. Like the old bear, following his own breath in the dark forest. There's no warm pack, no herd to comfort him. That voice that cries out doesn't *have* to be a weakling's, does it?"

This is the truest note in a play which emotionally and artistically seems rather contrived. It is not intensity of feeling but the longing for this intensity that is behind Mr. Osborne's confused and rather forced emotions. And equally, this same pseudo-violence, expressing the dearth rather than the excess of feeling, has struck me in several contemporary literary works that parade an air of militancy and rebelliousness — Norman Mailer's *The Deer Park*, Jack Kerouac's *On the Road*, Tennessee Williams's *Camino Réal* and other plays, the books of essays that Henry Miller has published from California, Allen Ginsberg's *Howl*. What puts all these works together in my mind is the fact that this essential lack of feeling, of direction and point is accompanied by the same extreme yet abstract violence of sexual activity and description. I am reminded of the Marquis de Sade, that famous sexual rebel, that supposed martyr to the cause of sexual freedom — when one actually opens his books, he turns out to be not a rebel at all but a fantasist whose idea of sexual pleasure is always something so extreme, perverse and complicated that only the mind can imagine it — as only the mind can stage it. This is the situation in Norman Mailer's *The Deer Park*, a book that was acclaimed by some left-wing critics as an indictment of Hollywood, and is based in part on the enforced exile from the industry of Communist directors and writers who would not give the names of party members to the investigating committees. One discovers very soon in reading his book that Mailer is not interested in the political significance of his material, though he feels that he *should* be; he is concerned with sex as an ultimate expression of man's aloneness.

The Deer Park takes place mostly in a famous desert resort, and despite the urbanities of luxurious American living, I had the sensation that these people really were in the desert, and with nothing to talk about, nothing to think about, nothing to feel, they were like Eskimos whiling away the eternal boredom of the igloo with unending sexual intercourse.

The sensation of claustrophobia, of something profoundly cheerless and inhuman that I got from Mailer's book was intensified by his article in *Dissent* — "The White Negro: Superficial Reflections on the Hipster." Mailer's theme is that the Negro has been forced by discrimination into an outlaw state in which he has developed the primitive and uninhibited sexuality that white men are not allowed to indulge. As modern capitalist society becomes inwardly more demoralized, certain advanced sectors of white society — the more naturally rebellious, intelligent and unafraid — become white versions of the Negro, seek to become hipsters (spiritual outlaws) rather than "squares" (conventionally conformist men and women). On the model of the Negro, they can find in the sensations of unprecedented orgasm that direct, blazing, ultimate contact with reality of which so many people are deprived by conventional, inhibited middle-class life.

Anyone with experience in Marxist literature will recognize immediately in this essay the adaptation to the hipster of the myth of the proletariat. Mailer's essay is a completely Marxist-revolutionary essay. Although the characters are the same, their names are different; and although the plot is really the same, too, the real difference is that the play is not on the boards, nothing is really taking place except theoretically. There *was* a proletariat once, and a bourgeoisie; people did suffer from starvation, inhuman hours, physical violence. But Mailer's picture of the Negro and of his revolutionary, unprecedented orgasms gives even the interested and sympathetic reader the sense that all this is being relayed to him from far away, for it is all a mental construction. Nothing here is taken from the real life of struggle, from life as actual conflict; it is an attempt to impose a dramatic and even noble significance on events that have not genuinely brought it forth. So desperate is Mailer for something to be revolutionary about, as Osborne is, that after telling us contemptuously that modern psychoanalysis merely softens the patient up by adapting him to modern middle-class society, he says that, by contrast, two strong eighteen-year-old hoodlums beating in the brains of a candy-store keeper do have courage of a sort, "for one murders not only a weak fifty-year-old man but an institution as well, one violates private property, one enters into a new relation with the police and introduces a dangerous element into one's life. The hoodlum is therefore daring the unknown, and so no matter how brutal the act, it is not altogether cowardly."

Jack Kerouac is a far less gifted and intelligent writer than Mailer, but in his recent best-seller, *On the Road*, one finds this same loneliness of emotions without objects to feel them about, this same uprush of verbal violence which, when one looks at it a little closely, seems to be unnaturally removed from the object or occasion. Kerouac, indeed, writes not so much *about* things as about the search for things to write about. When he celebrates the "kick" of ecstasy brought about by drink, drugs and jazz, it is the relief of having so strong a sensation that impresses him, not his communion with some object in ecstatic relatedness. And it is significant that his highest praise is for "the mad ones, the ones who are mad to live, mad to talk, mad to be saved, desirous of everything at the same time, the ones who never yawn or say a commonplace thing, but burn, burn, burn like fabulous yellow roman candles exploding like spiders across the stars and in the middle you can see the blue centerlight pop and everybody goes 'Aww!' "

Though it may seem a far step from the raucous and self-advertising propaganda of Kerouac's Bohemian group to the professional theater world of Tennessee Williams, the very subject of Williams's plays is always this same loneliness. When Williams, minus the stage lights and hocus-pocus of his director, is read for himself, as in his execrable fiction, *The Roman Spring of Mrs. Stone* and the stories collected in *One Arm*, one discovers that his subject is not merely the fantasy world of the utterly lonely, but that in fantasy even the sexual fulfillment of his characters has a brutal and mechanical quality, as if one mental category dully followed another without any stimulus or color from direct experience. In one of the stories in *One Arm*, a Negro masseur not merely violates his white patient, but literally butchers him; this same hellish oppression of sexual fantasy, like a nightmare from which the dreamer may never escape into the unpatterned relief of the real world, dogs us in some of the more violent stories of Carson McCullers, in the most recent novel by Nelson Algren, A *Walk on the Wild Side*, and in the last section of Paul Bowles's *The Sheltering Sky*, where a young American wife, maddened after her husband dies in the desert, is captured by an Arab and added to his harem.

I wish I could describe some of these new novels and plays in greater detail, for what is most striking about so many of them is the fact that despite the surface sexual violence, they seem little concerned with sex itself, with the *physicality* of sex; in many of these books there are simply not enough people about, in actual human relation of any sort, for sexual activity to take place. On the contrary, many of the newer writers use sex exactly as a drunken and confused man uses profanity — as a way of expressing anger, irritation, exasperation, and thus of breaking through the numbing despair of isolation. And indeed, isolation of the most crippling and stupefying sort is the really significant experience behind this literature — the kind of isolation that makes it impossible to break the lockstep of one's thoughts, the isolation that imagines anything because it has contact with nothing, but which, in the imagination of loneliness, cannot give us the color, the tactile feel of anything, only the abstract category to which the experience belongs.

Yet this loneliness does not call itself that; it calls itself revolutionary. In a long and now celebrated American poem simply called *Howl*, the young poet Allen Ginsberg has taken Whitman's long line and has described an hallucinated tour of America that reverses Whitman's celebration and becomes an exultant nightmare of denunciation:

I saw the best minds of my generation destroyed by madness, starving
   hysterical naked,
dragging themselves through the negro streets at dawn looking for an
   angry fix,
angelheaded hipsters burning for the ancient heavenly connection to the
   starry dynamo in the machinery of night,
who poverty and tatters and hollow-eyed and high sat up smoking in the
   supernatural darkness of cold-water flats floating across the
   tops of cities contemplating jazz,

who bared their brains to Heaven under the El and saw Mohammedan
    angels staggering on tenement roofs illuminated . . .
who cowered in unshaven rooms in underwear, burning their money in
    wastebaskets and listening to the Terror through the wall,
who got busted in their pubic beards returning through Laredo with a
    belt of marijuana for New York.

Now this abstractness contrasts very sharply with the lyric and
sensuous imagery with which sexual desire or activity used to be described by writers who were famous for their prophetic, unconven-
tional concern with the subject. I have not the space to spell out in
its required and fascinating detail the kind of imagery which one
finds in Whitman's "Out of the Cradle Endlessly Rocking," in the
love scenes of D. H. Lawrence's *Sons and Lovers*, in the glorious
pages of Colette, who could portray sex as the union not only of
man and woman but of man and the whole physical world of earth
sounds and earth smells, of colors and nuances; in those pages of
Proust where, despite the pain of Swann's jealousy of Odette, one
feels the gasping sharpness of real desire and the excitement of the
great city that is its background and stimulus. Perhaps I have made
it too easy for myself by contrasting so many classically sensuous
writers with American writers who have never had the same tradition
of art as the celebration of the natural world. But as Albert Camus
confessed in his recent Nobel Prize speech, even someone brought
up in the pagan and sunlit world of North Africa finds himself
unable to describe the sensuous joy of life as he once did. As man
increasingly loses his connection with the world, the great world, the
only world, he finds himself playing the moralist and the revolutionary as part of the same imposture — the purpose of which is to
perform *some* action, to see oneself performing any role.

« 2 »

Much of the fiction and poetry I have been describing has been
influenced by the theories of Wilhelm Reich, and in the terms in
which I have been describing them, illustrates the use of psychoanalytical terminology for the sake of an utterly hypothetical rebelliousness, in which a gangster beating out the brains of an old storekeeper is seen as the ritual of a revolutionary terrorist destroying the

old order. Turn to the enormously fashionable and influential literary criticism written under the inspiration of Dr. Jung, and you find in academic and philosophical circles the use of psychoanalysis not as socialism but as religion. In a recent effort to summarize the Jungian conception of literature — the book takes its very title from the loneliest character in American literature, Melville's Ishmael — James Baird explains that what orthodox Christians regard as sacrament is really symbol, and that since art itself deals with symbols, art itself may be viewed as a religious ritual. To anyone who has followed the development of literary criticism since the vogue of neo-orthodoxy began with Eliot, this is old stuff; phrases like symbol, symbolic action, ritual, myth, are the mainstay of fashionable academic criticism. But the themes I have been stressing in this paper — isolation and forced rebelliousness — are paralleled in the pseudo-metaphysics of the following. For just as art is really a religious ritual, so religion is really art; sacrament, says Mr. Baird, is symbol "representing corporateness in which the individual is subsumed, and ultimately these new compensatory symbols transcend the artist in the collective of the archetype."

The abstraction of his created form as sacrament singularly envisions the corporateness of man in a religious act. . . . Each man worships alone on his island. The sacrament which he creates invokes for his comfort and his "salvation" a world of the ideal where what he remembers of lost symbols is mixed with what his heretical allegiance to non-Christian (Oriental) custom supplies. Whether this custom, displayed to him through the aperture of his Oriental journey as experience, was mastered or merely "sampled" cannot very much matter. His symbol suggests the possibility of a new sacramental corporateness. As a maker of sacramentalism he belongs to an unconscious artistic community of his age because, as artist, he is like other workers who find art a better means of affirmation than existential courage. He has cast off convention and traditional theology, and in his act of creating, he descends to the true primitivity of religiousness; he returns to the authority of primitive feeling and the emotive life.

There is not a phrase here which refers to anything real; neither art nor religion, neither the so-called primitive feeling nor the emotive life means anything in this context. But Mr. Baird is not bogus: he is not pretending that he believes in God; he is pretending that

out of something which is not religion, religion may come again, so
that human beings who have lost the traditional objects of their belief, but not the habit of belief, may have something to believe in
again. Just as the Reichians want to believe in Socialism again, because they don't, so the Jungians write as if religion could be had
back for the asking. It is all so easy, so fatally easy — this Socialism
that carefully avoids society; this religion that dares not say that
God exists. It is easy because everything is based on what the self
wants, what the self needs or thinks it needs, and nothing on what
the world is really like. The world — the surrounding and not always friendly reality of nature, history, society — has disappeared for
these writers, and has taken with it everything which has given measure and definition to man's struggles in the world, everything which
has given man a sense of his possibilities and his limits, of his guilt
as well as his desire, of his tragedy as well as his happiness. These
writers are not concerned with winning over nature, with forcing it
to yield up its secrets; they are searching for a world they can believe
in again, and get angry at again. They are tormented not by the
pains of heroism, but by the inability to feel heroic — and often by
the inability to feel anything. The human catastrophes visited upon
our generation by totalitarianism seem too great to understand, to
describe, to cope with. History has become meaningless to them, and
private life a search for sensations — either of unprecedented orgasm
or of God — that may make them feel real to themselves.

« 3 »

This pervasive sense of unreality is authentic, and, as usual, the
writers — those whom Ezra Pound saluted as the "antennae of the
race" — see ahead of everyone else. For the middle-class world which
all of us have depended on so long has itself, as a value system,
ceased to exert any real authority, to arouse real respect. The sense
of unreality that I have been describing arises naturally out of the
bewilderment of people who recognize that history has taken still another turn, and that the solid middle-class virtues on which so many
of us depended, so that we could meaningfully oppose them, are no
longer believed in seriously enough for opposition to mean anything. The real tragedy of our time, as Nietzsche correctly foresaw, is
a nihilism so total, so pervasive, so defeatist even in the midst of the

greatest luxury our world has ever known, that it is no wonder that unimaginative people try to turn back the clock of modern science, to blame Marx and Darwin and Freud for robbing us of the illusion of our omnipotence in the universe. These people are hopeless, yet there is one element of tragic truth in their indictment of the modern spirit: more and more people lack the sense of tradition with which to assimilate the endless shocks and changes of the twentieth century. Just as Marx could not anticipate heirs who would completely lack his culture and tradition, who in the name of his great insights into capitalist society would create a society far more tyrannical and unjust, so Freud, himself so rooted in the Hebraic tradition, the English tradition, the nineteenth-century tradition, the scientific tradition, could not have predicted the destruction of Western civilization at Auschwitz, Maidenek, Belsen. He could not have imagined a psychoanalytically oriented psychiatry divorced from the humanistic and moral tradition, a psychiatry that would be used for market research in consumer motivation and even for the manipulation back to "normal" of political deviants. Psychoanalysis depended enormously on the intellectual and literary tradition out of which it arose, and of which it is an essential part. Now that this tradition of cultivation and intellectual freedom no longer commands allegiance as it used to, one sees an increasing divergence between writers, who are concerned with the tradition itself, and therefore with Freud's classic insights, and those psychoanalysts who, lacking the needed cultural reference, foolishly and self-indulgently suppose that they are living in the same world of bourgeois morality which made Freud grasp the necessary reactions of repression, guilt and shame. In the last few years, the kind of psychoanalytical comment on literary works which used to be so arresting and valuable has come to seem a wholly mechanical jargon. Significantly, it has become the staple of the most pedantic and academic research, unrelated to living literature; for, as with all things academic, this perspective is based on admiration of the static, the enclosed, on the literary tradition that neatly folds itself up and files itself away.

Equally, the use of psychoanalysis as a kind of pampering to merely bourgeois tastes and self-delusions, to the lapdog psychology of Americans whose only problem is to reduce and to save on income tax, is in itself a literary scandal. In this connection I would point to several things. One: the myth of universal "creativity," the assumption that every idle housewife was meant to be a painter and that every sexual deviant is really a poet. From this follows the myth that these unproductive people are "blocked"; whereupon how easy for the hack and the quack to get together! Second: the use of psychoanalytical jargon as a static description of the personality of the artist. There is no doubt that although neurosis can cripple creative artistry or hinder it entirely, talent is always quite separate in function — if not in theme — from the emotional chaos of neurosis, which provides no clue whatever to the reality of creative life. But perhaps the theme I have been stressing in this paper — the contemporary use of psychoanalysis in order to find identity rather than freedom — is seen here, too, since the more unreal people become to us, the more we try to pin them down with a descriptive formula, usually gained these days from psychoanalysis. If we approach literature exclusively by way of the writer's personality, psychoanalytically considered, we not only get even farther away from the real experience of literature than we were before, but we obliterate even the fundamental cultural respect for the health of the creative self in our eagerness to label the writer ill.

A recent example of this is the introduction by Mrs. Diana Trilling to a new selection of the letters of D. H. Lawrence. Mrs. Trilling confesses that Lawrence no longer means as much to her as he did in rebellious youth, and one believes her, since her analysis of Lawrence's work is based not on his real and marvelous creativity, but on an Oedipal conflict which she insists is the root of his ultimate failure as a novelist. More than one great poet, or poetic talent, has known the same kind of failure, which is probably rooted in the gap between the poetic realization of reality, which is always fundamentally "personal," and the kind of novelistic instinct which specializes in *story* — an instinct that Lawrence never really had. But instead of paying the homage to him that his genius deserves — and calls for — homage that would at least see Lawrence as possessing the defects of his genius, Mrs. Trilling regales us with the kind of clinical hindsight which, divorced from literary humility and appreciation, has made this kind of writing a terror to anyone who simply cares for literature.

I think it was this institutionalized conjunction of sex and love that threw Lawrence into the despair of the war years. The conflict raging in the world was an externalized expression of the private sexual struggle which was to absorb so large a part of his emotional energies for the rest of his life.

This is no irrelevant private point I'm making, no psychoanalytical advantage I'm trying to take of Lawrence, need I make that clear? The conflict which was crystallized in Lawrence when he and Frieda finally married seems to me to be the essential conflict, and contradiction, that runs through all his work.

This may not be an irrelevant private point, but it shows an attitude toward literature which has nothing to claim for literature itself. It is odd that the very people who are so quick to see suppressed and wasted creativity in people who are merely emotionally ill should always wish to deny the fundamental creativity of the greatest writers, like Kafka and Lawrence and Dostoevsky — a mistake that, in the case of the latter, Freud pointedly refrained from making. Yet the reason for this relentless psychologizing of art, so often equally irrelevant to both art and psychology, is that it gives the analyst, whoever he may be, the chance to share in the creativity of his subject. There is a sad perversion here of what, in genuine literary criticism, *is* an act of appropriation. Henry James said that the true critic is so much in love with art that he tries to "possess" it — to include it in his personal experience, which means to increase his power of enjoyment and understanding, and thereby of instruction to others. But as Ernst Kris has pointed out, the rise of a wholly "esthetic" attitude toward life — I should call it pseudo-esthetic in effect — is an attempt to appropriate not the work of art, which does exist so that we may possess it, but the artist himself. It exists so as to give us "status" and "prestige" in a world where the old bourgeois claims of money and social position, though they support the life of art, are felt not to be as real in advancing one's prestige as creativity itself. And the myth of creativity, the endless search for it in modern times, is simply a search for identity on the part of people who believe that they can find it in an experience, that of the real creator, utterly foreign to themselves.

I could go on here to speak of many related aspects: of "taste," of corruption, of the demonstrable fact that while psychoanalysis has added nothing to the creation of art, it has added a great deal, perhaps too much, to our modern concern with art. But in conclusion it is more important to note that the most signal fact about our experience today is that it is utterly unprecedented. The protagonist of middle-class literature, from Goethe to Thomas Mann, from Blake to D. H. Lawrence, from Rousseau to Proust, naturally saw life as a struggle against convention. Under the slogan of nature as freedom and truth, man saw himself as a hero reuniting man to the natural destiny of which he had been robbed by the gods. If there had been no profound tradition of repression, no moral code to bind us, Don Juan could never have been a hero or Anna Karenina a heroine; there would have been no guilt to suffer and no rebellion to honor. But the great human symbol of contemporary literature, I suggest, is no longer the rebel, since there is no authoritative moral tradition that he can honestly feel limits and hinders his humanity. It is the stranger — who seeks not to destroy the moral order, but to create one that will give back to him the idea of humanity.

[1958]

The Lesson of the Master

PHILIP RIEFF's book is a brilliant and beautifully reasoned example of what Freud's influence has really been: an increasing intellectual vigilance about human nature. So far as I can tell, Freud has been marvelous for intellectuals and a bit confusing to everyone else. The art of loving (even oneself) seems to be as difficult in the Freudian era as in any other; and the intelligence with which certain writers can get to work on Freud's ideas — sorting them out, pairing them off, relating them to previous ideas and to our sense of crisis — is only further proof that the Eden of our undivided human nature is far behind us, and that, like the Master himself, many an intellectual today has no greater passion than to write a good book.

Freud's own life was quite extraordinarily laborious, ascetic, and intellectual. Despite his concern with civilized man's oppression and

Freud: The Mind of the Moralist, by Philip Rieff. New York: Viking.
Sigmund Freud's Mission, by Erich Fromm. New York: Harper & Brothers.

denial of his instinctual nature, Freud himself believed that this repression is essential to "culture." And in describing human nature as a fundamentally insoluble conflict between two different provinces of human need, Freud was not merely describing human nature but actively interpreting it. Like every true investigator of human nature, he showed that man's difficulties already represent ethical ideas and can lead to new ethical choices. In short, Freud was a moralist, drawing "lessons on the right conduct of life from the misery of living it."

This starting point leads Mr. Rieff really to examine the implications and consequences of Freud's ideas; and the examination is exciting, for Mr. Rieff has not only a sociologist's alertness to the cultural implications of Freud's doctrine but also acute resources — and knowledge — as a student of intellectual history. Fundamentally, his motive in writing the book would seem to be the Freudian motive in so many intellectual enterprises: to lay bare, to disentangle, to establish contradictions and to unveil significances. Just as psychoanalysis has become for many writers what it was for Freud all his life long — an intellectual adventure, a constant sense of discovery related to problems rather than to patients, who merely furnished the problems — so Mr. Rieff's own excitement in the book is to make elegant distinctions, to uncover the mind of this moralist as a descendant and correction of modern thought. Mr. Rieff has a superb last chapter on "Psychological Man" — who has replaced the Political Man of antiquity, the Religious Man of the Middle Ages, the Economic Man handed down by the Enlightenment, and who produces the kind of cultural self-concern that is so characteristic of our period. Once you realize, as Mr. Rieff does, that men live by distinct values and choices, whether they know it or not; that they go from role to role in history as expressions of the philosophy they live by — then you have a sense that our fate depends on the soundness and correctness of the ideas we have now. An intellectual critic like Mr. Rieff can get to work, minutely retracing the implications and correlations of the Freudian world view, as if every step of thought were the only meaningful action for man today.

In a sense this intellectual vigilance duplicates the psychoanalytical session itself, which constantly offers up to the patient the minute significances and implications of his self-interpretation. In analysis, these follow from what Mr. Rieff brilliantly underscores as the Freudian distrust of everything that is not the inner life, private conduct, the self. But what the analyst does for the patient — present the terms for his new choices as a human being — Mr. Rieff does in respect to the cultural significance of Freudianism. His style has the same closeness, the same undertone of hypertense alertness. Again and again he makes brilliant points. Although everyone knows that Freud's ideas are in direct descent from the Romantic poets and philosophers, who valued "that which cannot be described," no one, to my knowledge, has analyzed this relationship as well as Mr. Rieff has. He points out that since Freud "refused to treat mind except as in historical process," no thought or feeling is self-explainable to Freud, and he develops this latter in showing how pitilessly Freud assumed that everything in the psyche is for use, how little he accounted for apathy. This wholly dynamic psychology led Freud to show things in too "emphatic" a setting, to enlarge on purposes and conflicts, equivalences and denials. But "as Freud's sense of the compelling social nature of love grew upon him, he became more aware of sexuality — the secret act of the private individual — as a safeguard to the de-individualizing functions of love as authority."

Mr. Rieff's most moving insight is that "we can measure the speed and distance of the modern retreat from a political doctrine of freedom by this touting of whatever appears refractory in human nature, as if freedom were thereby being proclaimed as inherent in the life-giving act itself." In the particularly brilliant last section of the book, analyzing the increasing privacy with which the individual views his role today, he shows why "the popular drift of psychological science aims at freeing the individual most of all from the burden of opposition" and remarks that "Freud was . . . unable to perceive that our own culture might become highly permissive in the sphere of . . . sexual morals — the better to enforce its public repressions."

The real value of Mr. Rieff's book is that it shows to what extent contemporary thought has assimilated Freud's ideas; the complexities and contradictions he has uncovered in Freud's thought — these are now everyone's, and the only way in which we can conceive getting the better of them is in extending our intellectual vigilance over human nature, in the kind of thoughtfulness which Mr. Rieff's book exemplifies.

« 2 »

By contrast, Dr. Erich Fromm's little book, essentially a hostile analysis of Freud's personal asceticism and authoritarian personality, renders its own points ineffective precisely because of the slightness and discursiveness with which he tries to express in such short space criticisms of Freud's personality and the moral implications of his doctrine. Such criticisms have to be made minutely and thoroughly to have any significance at all.

The trouble with the "revisionists" of Freud, like Dr. Fromm, is not so much in their ideas — many of which, emphasizing the social molding of human nature, are valuable in contrast to the unrelieved solitude of the Freudian arena in which the self struggles for light. It is the utter lack of any system, of intellectual coherence, of decisiveness; the neo-Freudians seem to live intellectually from hand to mouth, and they offer corrections of Freudian doctrine that are not unsound so much as they are inconstant. Dr. Fromm's criticisms of Freud's harsh and puritanical personality would be more significant, surely, if one did not see in his impatient style that he is looking for any stone to fling against this Goliath. Much of what he says about the dismal nineteenth-century bourgeois in Freud is perfectly correct. "The whole mystery of sublimation, which Freud never quite adequately explained, is the mystery of capital formation according to the myth of the nineteenth-century middle class. Just as wealth is the product of saving, culture is the product of instinctual frustration. . . . Freud speaks of . . . love as a man of his time speaks of property or capital." This is an important point, but it is a point in passing; it does not follow from any whole point of view that Fromm offers us in rebuttal to Freud.

Freud's overwhelming influence stems from the fact that he does offer us a new point of view, that with him one goes from idea to idea, from subject to subject. In the same way, the great intellectual systems of the past exerted their appeal by really lighting up the world, by explaining things in extent, by showing the relationship of man to the world and of man to himself. Mr. Rieff, though no disciple, shows the thoroughness and coherence of Freud's system by the closeness with which he is able to analyze every side of it; his book, tight and complete, is the best possible tribute to the comprehensive nature of Freud's genius. Dr. Fromm, who seems to have learned the intellectual caprice of his adopted country, gives away the fundamental eclecticism of his view by trying to evaluate so fundamental a theme as Freud's austerity in this short space. Freud's theory may be more useful to the intelligence than to the passions, but it does answer to certain fundamental requirements of the intelligence.

[1959]

The Conquistador: or Freud in His Letters

EVEN IF the life of Sigmund Freud had been less arduous and heroic, his character less complex, the present selection from his personal letters, edited by his son Ernst, would still have a special claim on our attention. For psychoanalysis was founded not merely by Freud, but in a very real sense *on* him. Freud found the meaning of dreams in his own dreams, and was led to formulate the Oedipus complex by being the favorite of a mother who was twenty years younger than his father. Even at the end of his life, when he had been driven into exile, his enduring conception of himself as a lonely prophet made him cast the Moses of *Moses and Monotheism* in his own image. No one who has read Ernest Jones's marvelously informative biography, or the more purely scientific letters (to Wilhelm Fliess) which have been published as *The Origins of Psychoanalysis*, can miss the dramatic and significant involvement, in the theory of psychoanalysis itself, of Freud's intense puritanism, his anxiety about money, his colossal ambition, his domineering attitude toward women (and in a very real sense his inability to understand women).

Psychoanalysis certainly bears the imprint of Freud's own character. Yet harsh and overstrained as his personality was, it has always puzzled me that "revisionist" critics of Freud like Erich Fromm,

The Letters of Sigmund Freud, selected and edited by Ernst L. Freud. New York: Basic Books.

armed with a wholly social notion of what a "healthy" personality should be, can attribute the excesses and mistakes of orthodox psychoanalysis exclusively to Freud's personal faults. For the cardinal thing about Freud, seen against the history of psychology, is how gifted he was. Without the peculiarly compelling insight that enabled him to grasp what was *typical* in his own experience, Freud would now be as dead as any of the Wundts and Lombrosos who were such great men in their time. There has been very little original insight among Freud's rivals — or, for that matter, among his own followers. Freud stands out not because he was always right, but because he tended, on the whole, to have real insight — to see *some* things as they really are.

Ironically, it is the very indiscrimination with which psychoanalysis has been taken up in this country that makes it so much harder for people to appreciate Freud's real qualities. We now tend to evaluate people as if they were inherently alike, but differ only in their upbringing. We do not share in the intellectual tradition out of which Freud came, and so we cannot recognize what Freud took from it and how he added to it. We overlook the significance of Freud's gift for discovery — that which adds new territories to our awareness. A great intellectual gift is the human element that is most strange to the thinker himself and that makes him strange to us. He *sees* differently. Somehow his life and character get hitched up behind his peculiar intellectual urgency in such a way that he has a more pressing commitment, a sharper impatience with ordinary relationships, than do others.

What interests me in Freud is that side of himself that he called the "conquistador" — the momentum of originality, the driving force in carving out a wholly new field, that makes such a man peculiarly the teacher of others. It is the quality, when all allowances have been made, that unites the great religious teachers, the great poets, the primary scientists. It is clearly his conception of truth as something hidden, repressed, driven underground, but to which he had come closer than others, that made Freud, despite his belligerent positivism, go so far beyond the materialism of his generation in science in saluting the great novelists and poets. Surely it was this sense of truth as a "mystery," to be revealed as the illumination of one's own experience, that made Freud venerate those who like

Joseph could uncover dreams, or like Moses, see God in fire. To have a vision of truth as profound because hidden, hidden by the force of convention, is to see nature as a constant challenge. The "conquistador," the intellectual pioneer, can never rest, for he alone sets his standards and has no one with whom to compromise. To have such a conception of oneself is to embark on a lonely, hard destiny, to be always at war with conventional society and yet not be able to take it seriously. It is to need love more, perhaps, than do other people, and at the same time to believe less in the significance of love.

These are the qualities, as I see it, that lie behind Freud's constant sense of his own arduousness, of his lack of ease and accommodation. At the end of his life he was able to acknowledge these traits in himself with a certain resignation, but even at the end he could not relent. There is this extraordinary passage from a letter of 1929:

All I know is that I had a terribly hard time; the rest followed as a matter of course. It could also have been very much better. I was only aware of the objective, not of myself. My worst qualities, among them a certain indifference to the world, probably had the same share in the final result as the good ones — *i.e.*, a defiant courage about truth. In the depths of my heart I can't help being convinced that my dear fellow men, with a few exceptions, are worthless.

He recognized that he had a peculiar disposition to take life hard; and in fact he did have to wait four and a half years to marry his fiancée, constantly suffered the extreme anti-Semitism of Vienna, and as soon as he had published his first great theories, found himself ostracized. In 1886, when he was studying in Paris under Charcot, he wrote to Martha Bernays, his future wife:

I think it is my great misfortune that nature didn't grant me that certain something that attracts people. When I think back over my life I realize that I would have needed little more than this certain something to assure myself of an easy existence. It took me such ages to win my friends, I had to struggle so long for my precious girl, and each time I am introduced to someone I realize that the new acquaintance is led by some impulse, which defies analysis, to underestimate me. . . . I believe people see something alien in me and the real reason for this is that in my youth I was never young and now that I am entering the age of maturity I cannot mature properly.

Certainly there were "motivations" enough to justify the grimness that Freud always felt about life and himself. No one reading these many letters can doubt why Freud felt constantly that he had to persuade, to cajole, even to beat down, a host of enemies. Once, in a train where all the windows were tightly closed, he had only to open a window to find himself shrieked at, "He's a dirty Jew!" He recounts how the famous Koller, one of the great innovators in eye surgery, found himself, after disagreeing on a scientific point with a colleague, being publicly insulted and having to fight a duel. Freud had to worry about money all through his youth, and no sooner had he begun to feel a little secure than the First World War came in, ruining the Austrian middle class. He lost a beloved daughter when she was still in her twenties. Even after he had become world-famous, he could not get his professorship until a friend virtually bribed a minister. By the Second World War, he had to give up his library, his savings, and barely made it to England. During this period, he suffered atrociously from cancer of the jaw, and underwent a whole series of operations. Four of his five sisters, all too old to escape from Austria, were gassed by the Nazis.

Freud waited for his fiancée, for security, for fame, with the special bitterness of the Middle European Jew who is not at home with himself or the society around him. He suffered from cultural claustrophobia and the lack of fraternity that Kafka and so many others had identified with the Austro-Hungarian Empire. He felt that he was living in a crazy-quilt of nationalities, cut off from the more liberal and humane culture of England and France that he admired. One of the most touching moments in the letters comes when he writes to Martha, during the long exile of his engagement (she was living near Hamburg): "Have you seen the sea yet? Please give it my best regards — we will meet yet."

No wonder that with these many deprivations and postponements, this constant isolation and antagonism, these repeated blows, Freud wanted a marriage that would give him security on at least one flank. During the long engagement, he flew into a rage because his meek, good little Marty refused to stop seeing a certain Fritz Wähle of whom Freud was jealous. (She soon gave way, and

Freud duly congratulated her: "I was patient and finally you did me justice. . . . You will eventually agree with me more fully on this point.") Later, when he had established the psychoanalytic movement, he was almost pathetic in his eagerness for Jung to be his chief lieutenant, and wrote in 1907: ". . . You are more suitable as a propagandist, for I have invariably found that something in my personality, my words and ideas strikes people as alien. . . ." As early as his student days in Paris, Freud had sat at a performance of *Carmen* feeling utterly detached from the pleasure-seeking "masses" around him. The peculiar loneliness of his experience at the opera led him to formulate (in a letter to Martha) a positive value in the repressions. This makes ironic reading for us who have been brought up to distrust repression and to seek satisfaction as our destiny.

> . . . The mob gives vent to its appetites, and we deprive ourselves. We deprive ourselves in order to maintain our integrity . . . we save ourselves for something, not knowing for what . . . we strive more toward avoiding pain than toward seeking pleasure. . . .

Surely it was out of this awareness of what life had cost him that Freud learned to calculate, in every life, the balance that a person must strike between the pleasure-principle that we instinctually seek and the reality-principle to which we must learn to submit. But to an American, living in a culture in which more and more people seek at any price to avoid pain, at all times to be comfortable, cherished, secure, Freud's letters make strange reading. They virtually ask the question: Need his life have been so grim? Would Freud have benefited from a good psychoanalysis? Couldn't the man have arranged things better? Freud, who was certainly aware of not being on the sunny side of life, would not have taken very seriously this proposal to limit and to temper his life. To look too deliberately for happiness — this fear of pain would have reflected to him nothing but the emptiness of our intellectual environment. It is a pleasant irony that, misusing his name, a watered-down psychoanalysis, seeking above all to adjust man to his society, has proved especially pervasive.

Whatever Freud's personal "grimness," to repeat the word that seems central to any discussion of his character, he was concerned not so much with himself as with the "objective." He had a pressing sense of actualities which he could not overlook and which certainly did not overlook him. Freud's despair of his fellow men, his disbelief in their official ideals — all this compared unfavorably in his mind with his own "defiant courage about truth." No wonder that with this stern sense of opposition between his own intellectual virtue and the treacherous, inimical world, he clung, despite his belligerent declaration that he was an "unbeliever," to his Jewishness. He joined the Jewish fraternal organization, the B'nai B'rith, when at the outset of the psychoanalytic movement he found everyone in Vienna against him. In his golden period, the mid-Twenties, when Vienna under a Socialist administration was at last prepared to honor him, he wrote fiercely that "as a Jew I was prepared to be in the opposition and to renounce agreement with the 'compact majority.'" This constant sense of defiance is perhaps more characteristic of the great prophets than of the usual Viennese professor.

Freud saw in the relationship between man and the truth something of the quality which is found in the Biblical confrontation of man and God — a quality at once persistent, tragic, despairing, and exalted. It might have been Moses outraged by the Golden Calf who wrote, as Freud did about the Viennese public: "Truth is unobtainable; humanity does not deserve it." It is true that Freud "had a terribly hard time." But surely the real hardness of his life, the deepest urgency behind it, lay in his commitment to the truth. Men are led by a mysterious destiny that is no less terrible when its moving power, as Freud thought, is our hidden nature, ourselves alone.

[1960]

The Language of Pundits

IT IS curious that Freud, the founder of psychoanalysis, remains the only first-class writer identified with the psychoanalytic movement. It was, of course, Freud's remarkable literary ability that gave currency to his once difficult and even "bestial" ideas; it was the insight he showed into concrete human problems, the discoveries whose force is revealed to us in a language supple, dramatic, and charged with the excitement of Freud's mission as a "conquistador" into realms hitherto closed to scientific inquiry, that excited and persuaded so many readers of his books. Even the reader who does not accept all of Freud's reasoning is aware, as he reads his interpretation of dreams, of the horror associated with incest, of the Egyptian origins of Moses, that this is a writer who is bent on making the most mysterious and unmentionable matters entirely clear to himself, and that this fundamental concern to get at the truth makes dramatis personae out of his symbols and dramatic episodes out of the archetypal human struggles he has described. It is certainly possible to read Freud, even to enjoy his books, without being convinced by him, but anyone sensitive to the nuances and playfulness of literary style, to the shaping power of a great intellectual conception, is not likely to miss in Freud the peculiar urgency of the great writer; for myself, I can never read him without carrying away a deeply engraved, an unforgettable sense of the force of human desire.

By contrast, many of the analysts who turn to writing seem to me not so much writers as people clutching at a few ideas. Whenever I immerse myself, very briefly, in the magisterial clumsiness of Dr. Gregory Zilboorg, or the slovenly looseness of Dr. Theodore Reik, or the tensely inarticulate essays of Dr. Harry Stack Sullivan, or the purringly complacent formulas of Dr. Edmund Bergler, or even the smoothly professional pages of Dr. Erich Fromm, I have a mental picture of a man leaping up from his chair, crying with exultation, "I have it! The reason for frigidity in the middle-aged female is the claustrophobic constitution!," and straightway rushing to his publisher. Where Freud really tried to give an explanation to himself of one specific human difficulty after another, and then in his old-fashioned way tried to show the determination of one new fact by another, it is enough these days for Dr. Bergler to assert why all writers are blocked, or for Dr. Theodore Reik, in his long-winded and inconsequential trek into love and lust, to announce that male and female are so different as to be virtually of different species. The vital difference between a writer and someone who merely is published is that the writer seems always to be saying to himself, as Stendhal actually did, "If I am not clear, the world around me collapses." In a very real sense, the writer writes in order to teach himself, to understand himself, to satisfy himself; the publishing of his ideas, though it brings gratifications, is a curious anticlimax.

Of course, there are psychoanalyst-writers who aim at understanding for themselves, but don't succeed. Even in Freud's immediate circle, several of the original disciples, having obtained their system from the master, devoted themselves to specialties and obsessions that, even if they were more than private *idées fixes*, like Otto Rank's belief in the "birth-trauma," were simply not given the hard and lucid expression necessary to convince the world of their objectivity. Lacking Freud's striking combination of intellectual zeal and common sense, his balanced and often rueful sense of the total image presented by the human person, these disciples wrote as if they could draw upon Freud's system while expanding one or two favorite notions out of keeping with the rest. But so strongly is Freud's general conception the product of his literary ability, so much is it held together only in Freud's own books, by the force of his own mind, that it is extraordinary how, apart from Freud, Freudianism loses its general interest and often becomes merely an excuse for wild-goose chases.

Obviously these private concerns were far more important to certain people in Freud's own circle than was the validity of Freudianism itself. When it came to a conflict between Freudianism and their own causes (Otto Rank) or their desire to be uninhibited in mystical indefiniteness (C. G. Jung), the body of ideas which they had inherited, not earned, no longer existed for them. Quite apart from his personal disposition to remain in control of the movement which he had founded, Freud was objectively right in warning disciples like Ferenczi, Rank, Adler, and Stekel not to break away from his authority. For the analyst's interest in psychoanalysis is likely to have its origin in some personal anxiety, and some particularly unstable people (of whom there were several in Freud's circle), lacking Freud's unusual ability not only to work through his own neuroses but to sublimate everything into the grand creative exultation of founding a movement, committed themselves fruitlessly to the development of their unsystematic ideas, found it impossible to heal themselves by the *ad hoc* doctrines they had advanced for this purpose, and even relapsed into serious mental illness and suicide.

Until fairly recently, it was perfectly possible for anyone with a

Ph.D. (in literature or Zen or philology) to be a "psychotherapist" in New York State. I have known several such therapists among the intellectuals of New York, and I distinguish them very sharply from the many skillful and devoted lay analysts, with a direct training in psychoanalysis, who are likely to have an objective concern with the malady of their patients. The intellectuals with Ph.D.'s who transferred from other professions to the practice of psychoanalysis still seem to me an extreme and sinister example of the tendency of psychoanalysis to throw up the pundit as a type. Like modern intellectuals everywhere, intellectuals as self-made analysts are likely to have one or two ruling ideas which bear obvious relation to their private history, but which, unlike intellectuals generally, they have been able to impose upon people who came to them desperately eager for orientation in their difficulties. In short, the ruling weakness of intellectuals, which is to flit from idea to idea in the hope of finding some instrument of personal or world salvation, has often become a method of indoctrination. All the great figures in psychoanalysis have been egotists of the most extreme sort; all the creative ones, from Freud himself to the late unfortunate Dr. Wilhelm Reich, were openly exasperated with the necessity of having to deal with patients at all. They were interested only in high thinking, though Freud at least tempered his impatience enough to learn from his patients; the objective power, the need to examine symptoms in others, never left him.

By contrast, the intellectual who is looking for an audience or a disciple has often, as a psychotherapist, found one in his patient. And the obvious danger of exploiting the credulous, the submissive, the troubled (as someone said, it is the analyst's love that cures the patient, and certain intellectuals love no one so much as a good listener), which starts from a doctrine held by the analyst in good faith but which may be no less narrow-minded or fanatical for all that, seems to me only an extension of the passion for explaining everything by psychoanalysis which literary intellectuals have indulged in so long. When I think of some of the intellectuals who have offered their services as therapists, I cannot but believe that to them the patient is irrelevant to their own passion for intellectual indoctrination. My proof of this is the way they write. Ever since Freud gave the word to so many people less talented than himself, it has become increasingly clear that, whatever psychoanalysis may have done for many troubled people, it has encouraged nonwriters to become bad writers and mediocre writers to affect the style of pundits. For the root of all bad writing is to be distracted, to be self-conscious, not to have your eye on the ball, not to confront a subject with entire directness, with entire humility, and with concentrated passion. The root of all bad writing is to compose what you have not worked out, *de haut en bas*, for yourself. Unless words come into the writer's mind as fresh coinages for what the writer himself knows that he knows, knows to be true, it is impossible for him to give back in words that direct quality of experience which is the essence of literature.

Now, behind the immense power and authority of psychoanalytical doctrines over contemporary literature — which expresses itself in the motivation of characters, the images of poetry, the symbol hunting of critics, the immense congregation of psychiatric situations and of psychiatrists in contemporary plays and novels — lies the urgent conviction, born with modern literature in the romantic period, the seedbed of Freudian ideas, that literature can give us knowledge. The Romantic poets believed in the supremacy of imagination over logic exactly as we now believe that the unconscious has stories to tell which ordinary consciousness knows nothing of. And just as the analyst looks to free association on the part of the patient to reveal conflicts buried too deep in the psyche to be revealed to the ordinarily conscious mind, so the Romantic poets believed that what has been buried in us, far from the prying disapprovals of culture, stands for "nature," our true human nature. A new world had been revealed to the Romantics, a world accessible through the imagination that creates art. And Freud, who also felt that he had come upon a new world, said that his insights had been anticipated by literary men in particular; he felt that he had confirmed, as scientific doctrine, profound discoveries about our buried, our archetypal, our passionate human nature that philosophers and poets had made as artists.

Had made as artists. Nietzsche, who also anticipated many of Freud's psychological insights, said that Dostoevsky was the only psychologist who had ever taught him anything. No doubt he meant that the characters Dostoevsky had created, the freshness of Dostoevsky's perceptions, the powerful but ironic rationality of Dostoevsky's style had created new facts for him to think of in comparison with the stale medical formulas of psychiatry in his time. Similarly, Freud said of Dostoevsky that "before genius, analysis lays down its arms," indicating that with the shaping power of the artist who can create characters like old Karamazov and Prince Myshkin, with the genius that in its gift of creation actually parallels life instead of merely commenting on it, analysis cannot compete. And in point of fact we do learn more about the human heart from a stupendous creation like the Karamazov family than we ever do from all the formulary "motivations" of human nature. Just as each human being, in his uniqueness, escapes all the dry formulas and explanations about human nature, so a great new creation in imaginative literature, a direct vision of the eternal like William Blake's or an unprecedented and unassimilable human being like old Karamazov, automatically upsets and rearranges our hardened conceptions of human nature.

There is no substitute for life, for the direct impression of life; there is no deep truth about life, such as writers bring home to us, that does not come in the form of more life. To anyone who really knows how rare and precious imaginative creation is — how small, after all, is that procession which includes Dante's Paolo and Francesca, Shakespeare's Othello, and Tolstoy's Natasha — how infinitely real in suggestion is the character that has been created in and through imagination, there is something finally unbearable, the very opposite of what literature is for, in the kind of metallic writing which now so often serves in a novel to "motivate" a character.

Maybe the only tenable literary role which novelists and poets, as well as critics and psychologists, now want to play is that of the expert — the explainer, the commentator, the analyst. Just as so many psychoanalysts want to be writers, so many writers now want to be analysts. And whenever I rise up at intervals from my dutiful immersion in certain specimens of contemporary literature, I find it hard to say who has less to contribute to literature, the psychiatrist who wants to push a few small ideas into a book or the novelist who in the course of a story breaks down into writing like a psychoanalyst.

« 2 »

The deterioration of language in contemporary fiction into the language of pundits is not often noticed by critics — perhaps because the novelists have taken to writing like critics. But it is by no means the highbrow or intellectual novelist — like Mary McCarthy, who in a single story for *Partisan Review* is likely to produce so many deliberate symbols — who is the only offender against art. John O'Hara in *From the Terrace* wrote, of the mother of his hero, that "What had happened to her was that she unconsciously abandoned the public virginity and, again unconsciously, began to function as a woman." Of the Eaton brothers, O'Hara made it clear that "If William slapped Alfred or otherwise punished him, the difference in ages was always mentioned while William himself was being punished; and each time that that occurred the age separation contributed to a strengthening of the separation that was already there because of, among other considerations, the two distinct personalities." This is a novelist? Frankly, I have the impression that many of the younger novelists have learned to write fiction from reading the New Critics, the anthropologists and psychologists. I cannot begin to enumerate all the novels of recent years, from Ralph Ellison's *Invisible Man* to Vance Bourjaily's recent *Confessions of a Spent Youth*, which describe American social customs, from college up, as fulfilling the prescription of tribal rites laid down by the anthropologists. But whereas an angry and powerful novelist, as Ellison is in *Invisible Man*, whatever helpful hints he may get from psychiatrically oriented literary critics, will aim at the strongest possible image of Negro suffering and confusion in a hostile society, Vance Bourjaily, in his recent novel, has his hero preface his description of a business smoker by apologizing that "it would take the calm mind of an anthropologist to describe objectively the rites with which the advertising tribe sent its bachelor to meet his bride."

I don't know what repels me more in such writing, the low spirits behind such prosiness or the attempted irony that is meant to disguise the fact that the writer is simply not facing his subject directly but is looking for something to say about it. No wonder that a passage like this sounds not like fiction but a case history: "I had a good time with Vicky during those two or three months; at the same time, I was learning about the social structure of the town and that of the school which, with certain exceptions for unusual individuals, reflected it; Vicky was more or less middle middle. As a friend of hers, since my own status was ambiguous, it seemed to me that I must acquire hers by association." And Mr. Bourjaily's book *is* a case history, though so meanderingly self-absorbed, for the most part, that it comes splendidly alive when the hero describes a visit to his relatives in the Near East; for a few pages we are onto people whom Mr. Bourjaily has to describe for us, since they are new types, and then we get free of the motivational analysis that is the novelist's desperate response to people who he thinks are too familiar to be conveyed directly. This is a curious idea of a novel — as if it were the subject, rather than the point of view, which made it boring.

The true writer starts from autobiography, but he does not end there; and it is not himself he is interested in, but the use he can make of self as a literary creation. Of course, it is not the autobiographical subject that makes such books as Mr. Bourjaily's flat; it is the relatively shallow level from which the author regards his own experience. The mark of this is that the writer does not even bother to turn his hero into a character; he is just a focus for the usual "ironic" psychological comment. If the writer nowadays sees himself as a pundit, he sees his hero as a patient. What, in fact, one sees in many contemporary American novelists today is the author as analyst confronting his alter ego as analysand. The novel, in short, becomes simply an instrument of self-analysis, which may be privately good for the writer (I doubt it) but is certainly boring to his readers.

« 3 »

The deterioration of language in contemporary "imaginative" literature — this reduction of experience to flat, vaguely orphic loose statements — seems to me most serious whenever, in our psychiatrically centered culture, spontaneity becomes an arbitrary gesture which people can simulate. Among the Beat writers, spontaneity becomes a necessary convention of mental health, a way of simulating vitality, directness, rough informality, when in fact the literary works produced for this pose have no vitality, are not about anything very significant, and are about as rough as men ever are using dirty words when they cut themselves shaving. The critic Harold Rosenberg once referred scathingly to the "herd of independent minds"; when I read the Beat and spontaneous poets en bloc, as I have just done in Donald Allen's anthology of the "new" American poetry, I feel that I am watching a bunch of lonely Pagliaccis making themselves up to look gay. To be spontaneous on purpose, spontaneous all the time, spontaneous on demand is bad enough; you are obeying not yourself but some psychiatric commandment. But to convert this artificial, constant, unreal spontaneity into poetry as a way of avoiding the risks and obligations of an objective literary work is first to make a howling clown out of yourself and then deliberately to cry up your bad literature as the only good literature.

The idea of the Beat poets is to write so quickly that they will not have to stand up for the poem itself; it is enough to be caught in the act of writing. The emphasis is not on the poem but on themselves being glimpsed in the act of creation. In short, they are functioning, they are getting out of the prison house of neurosis, they are positive and free. "Look, Ma, no hands!" More than this, they are shown in the act of writing poems which describe them in the act of living, just about to write poems. "*Morning again, nothing has to be done/ maybe buy a piano or make fudge/ At least clean the room up, for sure like my farther / I've done flick the ashes & buts over the bedside on the floor.*" This is Peter Orlovsky, "Second Poem."

Elsewhere, the hysterical demand for spontaneity as an absolute value means that everything in the normal social world becomes an enemy of your freedom. You want to destroy it so as to find an image of the ecstasy that has become the only image of reality the isolated mind will settle for. It is a wish for the apocalypse that lies behind the continued self-righteous muttering that the world is about to blow up. The world is not about to blow up, but behind the extreme literary pose that everything exists to stifle and suppress and exterminate us perhaps lies the belief, as Henry Miller plainly put it in *Tropic of Cancer*, that "For a hundred years or more the world, *our* world, has been dying. . . . The world is rotting away, dying piecemeal. But it needs the *coup de grâce*, it needs to be blown to smithereens. . . . We are going to put it down — the evolution of this world which has died but which has not been buried. We are swimming on the face of time and all else has drowned, is drowning, or will drown."

The setting of this apocalyptic wish is the stated enmity between the self and the world, between the literary imagination and mere reality — a tension which was set up by Romanticism and which Freudianism has sharpened and intensified to the point where the extreme Romantic, the Beat writer, confesses that the world must be destroyed in order that the freedom of his imagination proceed to its infinite goal. Romanticism put so much emphasis on the personal consciousness that eventually the single person came to consider himself prior to the world and, in a sense, replacing it; under Romanticism, the self abandoned its natural ties to society and nature and emphasized the will. The more the single conscious mind saw the world as an object for it to study, the more consciousness was thrown back on itself in fearful isolation; the individual, alone now with his consciousness, preoccupied in regarding himself and studying himself, had to exercise by more and more urgent exertions of will that relationship to the world which made consciousness the emperor of all it could survey — the world was merely raw material to the inquiring mind.

Freud, himself a highly conservative and skeptical thinker with a deeply classical bias in favor of limitation, restraint, and control, could not have anticipated that his critique of repression, of the admired self-control of the bourgeoisie, would in time, with the bankruptcy of bourgeois values, become a philosophy for many of his followers. Freudianism is a critique of Victorian culture; it is not a prescription for living in the twentieth century, in a world where the individual finds himself increasingly alienated from the society to which he is physically tied. Freud once wrote in a letter to Romain Rolland: "Psychoanalysis also has its scale of values, but its sole aim is the enhanced harmony of the ego, which is expected successfully to mediate between the claims of the instinctual life [the id] and those of the external world; thus between inner and outer reality.

"We seem to diverge rather far in the role we assign to intuition. Your mystics rely on it to teach them how to solve the riddle of the universe; we believe that it cannot reveal to us anything but primitive, instinctual impulses and attitudes . . . worthless for orientation in the alien, external world."

It was the Romantics who handed down to modern writers the necessity to think of the world as "alien and external." By now so many writers mechanically think of it this way that it is no wonder that they look for a philosophy of life to the "primitive, instinctual impulses and attitudes," though, as Freud knew, they are "worthless for orientation in the alien, external world." Man cannot cheat his own mind; he cannot bypass the centrality of his own intelligence. Yet is not sole reliance on the "primitive, instinctual impulses" exactly the *raison d'être* of so many Beat poems and novels; of neurotic plays dealing with people whose only weakness, *they* think, is that they are repressed; of literary studies whose whole thesis is that the American novel has always been afraid of sex? What is wrong with such works is not that the single points they make are incorrect, but that they rely upon a single point for a positive philosophy of life. It is impossible to write well and deeply in this spirit of Sisyphus, pushing a single stone up the mountain. It is impossible to write well if you start from an arbitrary point of view, and in the face of everything that is human, complex, and various, push home your *idée fixe*. It is impossible for the haunted, the isolated, the increasingly self-absorbed and self-referring self to transcend itself sufficiently to create works of literature.

Literature grows out of a sense of abundant relationships with the world, out of a sense that what is ugly to everyone else is really beautiful to you, that what is invisible to many men is pressingly alive and present to your writer's eye. We can no longer, by taking thought, transcend the life that consists in taking thought. The English novelist and philosopher Iris Murdoch has recently helped clear the air of desperate self-pity by saying that "We need to return from the self-centered concept to the other-centered concept of truth. We are not isolated free choosers, monarchs of all we survey, but benighted creatures sunk in a reality whose nature we are constantly and overwhelmingly tempted to deform by fantasy. Our current picture of freedom encourages a dream-like facility; whereas what we require is a renewed sense of the difficulty and complexity of the moral life and the opacity of persons."

By now the self-centered mind fashioned by romanticism, constantly keeping itself open only to adjurations of absolute freedom and spontaneity, has traveled about as far along the road of self-concern as it can; it has nothing to discover further of itself but fresh despair. The immediate proof of this is in the quality of so much of the literature that has been shaped by Freudianism — only because all other creeds have failed it. It is not possible to write well with one's own wishes as the only material. It is not possible any longer to think anything out without a greater reality than one-self constantly pressing one's words into dramatic shape and unexpected meaning. All our words now are for our own emotions, none for the world that sustains the writer. And this situation is impossible, for it was never the self that literature was about, but what transcended the self, what comes home to us through experience.

[1961]

VIII
History

Edmund Wilson on the Thirties

ONE OF THE many things that I miss in American writing today is the frankly "literary" reportage of national events that used to be done by writers like Theodore Dreiser, H. L. Mencken, John Dos Passos, Edmund Wilson. One reason for the decline of this kind of journalism is the assumption by writers that there is nothing to investigate, that ours is the dead calm that comes after or between wars, that the literary man on a news story belongs only to a blazing time of troubles. The younger writers complain that they are too far from the peaks of power to be able to say what is really happening. Some of the writers who came out of the 1930s have reacted so sharply against their youthful radicalism that they now have a vested interest in contentment. The only Victorians left in the world today are the exhausted, guilt-ridden, tediously accommodating ex-radicals who want peace at any price. Some years ago an English magazine edited by such intellectuals announced in its very first issue that the mood of the present period could be summed up as "After the Apocalypse." This was on the eve of the H-bomb, the revolts in Eastern Germany, Poland, Hungary, and the intercontinental ballistic missile; but veterans of the 1930s, as we know from the example of Whittaker Chambers and how many other ex-revolutionaries, project their sense of depletion into the world itself.

Still, it cannot be denied that writers turn to reportage in times that are warlike — times when issues are wholly on the surface, when society is visibly in flux, when there are disturbing social tensions which everyone feels in his own life. The 1930s, an era of incessant social violence, depression, revolution, war, lent themselves to reporting because writers felt themselves carried along by history. So much happened in the 1930s, from the depression to another world war, from Roosevelt to Hitler, from the Japanese attack on Manchuria to the Spanish Civil War, that it can be said of a great many writers that nothing has happened to them since. If the

The American Earthquake, by Edmund Wilson. New York: Doubleday and Company.

nineteenth century did not end until 1914, the twentieth did not fully begin until the 1930s, for it was then that we began to see even in our innocent and long-protected country the onset of the all-powerful state, the security police, the governmental manipulation of mass opinion, the establishment of the "common man" as an absolute good — all of which have become so much part of our lives, especially since 1945, that we no longer recognize how much we have changed. But in the 1930s all these things emerged out of the unexpressed admission that the crisis was permanent and uncontrollable; in America, virtually the last symbol of pure capitalism, one could see the old order of ideas actually disintegrating, while millions of people sought salvation from the welfare state, Communism, Father Coughlin, Dr. Townsend, Huey Long. And if this continuing ferment made so many writers turn to reportage, so there arose, under the whiplash of now unbelievable despair, that dependence on the state which by now has made the state the only loyalty that people profess.

But we are all wise after the event. The 1930s were not only a fearful beginning to our characteristic mid-century world but an immediate shock; while a great many people understandably lost their heads, no one now can admit it — one is supposed to have looked at fifteen millions unemployed, the country desperate, Hitlerism and Fascism overriding Europe, without feeling anything. The tragedy of so many radicals of the 1930s is precisely that they believed in justice, in freedom, in co-operation. They were not prepared for politics as tragedy; Americans so rarely are. It is easier to rewrite history now, to portray Franklin Roosevelt as more calculating than he really was. So the New Deal appears, in the works of John T. Flynn, Whittaker Chambers, James Burnham, as planned, theoretical, coherent; and the picture becomes really grotesque in the last works of Charles A. Beard, who saw Roosevelt tricking the Japanese into attacking at Pearl Harbor, so that the United States would have an excuse for coming to the aid of the British Empire.

Such interpretations of the New Deal show a remarkable forgetfulness both of the mass suffering which no government during the 1930's could entirely have overlooked and of the confusion, amazement, and powerlessness of those in office. If the 1930s mark the beginning of the contemporary history — the century of mass society — it is because in the 1930s anyone could apply to society Henry Adams's saying that modern man has mounted science and is run away with. With the 1930s, one could see in force the unavailingness of intelligence and good will in a world where political order is continually flying apart under the pressure from ideological new states. Men like Roosevelt, who fundamentally lacked ideas, were able to give the impression that they were planning or plotting a new society, when actually their greatest gift was one of charismatic leadership, the ability to hold up images of stability and national tradition during the storm.

« 2 »

It is this quality of flux, of storm, of violent change, that Edmund Wilson has summoned back so vividly in *The American Earthquake*, a literary expansion of his articles from the *New Republic* about the 1920s and his book reportage of the depression.

It may be that the impression of chaos and intellectual helplessness that Wilson ascribes to the New Deal appeals more to the literary imagination than it does to political historians. Arthur Schlesinger, Jr.'s, recent book on the background of the New Deal (*The Age of Roosevelt: The Crisis of the Old Order; 1919-1933*) presents a picture of intellectual foresight which Wilson, drawing on his actual writings in the 1930s, obviously does not share. And perhaps the gift for seizing and holding personal impressions, the capacity for swift observations and revealing contrasts, gives Wilson an oversensitized capacity for descriptions of social change. Writers like Wilson, with their instant feeling for the literary image that will convey the feeling of social crisis, for the scene that will instantly evoke a historical moment, are so strong on history as literature, on swift and brilliant passagework, that they tend to impress upon us, as Carlyle does, a picture of history as a series of picturesque accidents. The stream of time bursts into iridescent foam for a paragraph or two, then retires into brutal inconsequence again.

But on the other hand, Wilson's chronicle is so unflinchingly personal, it presents so dramatically the confrontation of the period by a mind obviously unused to social ugliness, that it catches perfectly the revolutionary and unsettling impact of the 1930s on those who were least suited to it. The shock of the times comes through in the reactions of someone like Wilson, whose instincts are always for culture and tradition, and who never ceases to think of himself as an unattached man even when he comes closest to Marxism. It is the radicals who committed themselves intellectually who now have to revise history, for it is themselves that they have to disengage from the past. Similarly, it was never the "proletarian" novelists who caught the drama of the 1930s — they lost themselves in the general hysteria. Much of the Communist writing done in the 1930s, by people who were honest enough but who gave away such brains as they had, now looks like the fever chart of a patient *in extremis*. Such writers are now wrecks of the 1930s, writers who fell to pieces under the last disillusioning blow of the Soviet pact with Hitler, precisely because they had no culture to abdicate from, no wit to surrender. The pseudo science of Marxism gave them all the ideas they ever had, worked on them like strong drink; and their personal confusion was stepped up by incessant political manipulation and propaganda. It was precisely these Communist writers, who saw the 1930s as a time when everything was breaking up and who deliriously joined in the *Götterdämmerung* of "bourgeois" values, who became the real victims of the period. It was not a lack of integrity that doomed so many of these writers. It was a lack of background and perspective, an inability to see that their movement, too, would have its natural and inevitable end.

Wilson's cultural imagination saved him from this loss of perspective. If anything, he had too much of it, and his extraordinary gift for turning every assignment into a superb literary article is a symbol of his inability to lose himself, as many writers did, in a purely human situation. The reins are always tight, and the horses always go the same way. On the other hand, Wilson's detachment certainly never made him incurious. The secret of his durability as a writer is his patient, arduous effort to assimilate, to clarify for himself and for others, subjects from which he feels excluded by temperament. The same hard-won intellectual triumph that as an agnostic he gets out of the Dead Sea Scrolls Wilson used to get, also as a bystander, out of descriptions of the Ziegfeld Follies, police beating up Communist marchers at New York City Hall, the Scottsboro case, the career of Henry Ford, the miseries of depression Chicago. Amid the laziest minds in the world, he is the most Puritanical of intellectual students, the most exacting in the correctness of his language and his learning.

Unsympathetic critics like to portray Wilson as a popular writer who sacrifices the ambiguity and complexity of his subjects. In truth, all his strength comes from the fact that he seeks to understand, to know; and it is his habit of willed attention, of strained concentration, that explains the exciting luminousness and tension of his prose.

Wilson is not a reporter but a literary artist driven by historical imagination — like Henry Adams and Carlyle. Such writers are lightning-quick to see the many metamorphoses of modern man. In Europe, where the succession and contrast of different epochs can be seen on every hand, writers who appeal to the historical imagination can be read for their merit as artists. But in this country, where we are likely to overvalue single traditions as such but to overlook the beauty of history itself, the creative side of such writers is unappreciated. Wilson's sense of historical contrast is documented entirely from his own life and that of his family in relation to America. The points of the compass for him are "the old stone house" of his ancestors in upstate New York that he describes so movingly in this book; New York, the great symbol of the cosmopolitan 1920s, a city that he always describes with distrust; and the ancient greatness embodied in Lincoln.

Only someone who has read much of this old material before can recognize how fine a work of art Wilson has made out of his records of the 1920s and 1930s — based always on the overriding fact of American instability. To see this as coldly as Wilson does, without for a moment allowing oneself to become cold to America, is to have the gift of perspective. When Wilson writes about a buccaneer of the 1920s, "Sunshine Charlie" Mitchell of the National City Bank, he notes that "the boom produced its own human type, with its own peculiar characteristics." When he writes about "the old stone house" in Talcottville, New York, he writes with appreciation of the old farmers that "they were very impressive people, the survivors of a sovereign race who had owned their own pastures and fields and governed their own community."

The section on the solitaries in his family significantly ends with a tribute to Herndon's unsentimental biography of Lincoln, and when Wilson writes about Lincoln, his prose rises to an uncontrollable emotion and we understand why, in the face of so much misery, so much helplessness, thinking of Lincoln inspires him "with a kind of awe — I can hardly bear the thought of Lincoln."

If the historical imagination lives on metamorphosis, it expresses itself as personal impressions. Wilson writes cultural reminiscences as novelists and dramatists write scenes and dialogue. His strong suit is never ideas as such (any more than ideas as such were the strength of Carlyle or, despite his pretensions to philosophy, of Henry Adams); the end of the book, with its halfhearted approval of Beard's thesis on the war, simply emphasizes Wilson's stubborn and romantic isolationism. What makes Wilson's reporting good is the impression of actual experience brought to white heat on the page; it is the re-creation of a scene that relates Wilson to history, not the significance of history in itself. Wilson's writing depends entirely on the strength and flexibility of his style, and its unusual quality lies in the coupling of his intellectual tense style with the lower depths, the city junk heaps and bread lines, the strikes and demonstrations, the agony of mass fear.

The subtler achievement of the book is in the rapid succession of these sketches, which are run together to create a sense of history in motion. In Wilson, reportage becomes a series of impressions united only by the writer's temperament. Like all writing that is fundamentally personal, it depends almost too much on the writer's spirits, his wit, his virtuosity of style. Once the tone flags, the whole threatens to become commonplace. This is what above all things it dare not become, since it is so close to life that only the personality of the writer keeps it from relapsing into meaninglessness. Nothing in such a book dare appear in its objective crudity; everything must be assimilated by imagination. Nothing is held too long, for when the attention is fixed so sharply on cultural detail, it may easily tire, and in any event, the essential point has usually been made swiftly. But the assembling of details, the movement of ideas — these give us the orbit, the "spread" of life in a particular time, the picture of history behaving organically, through a hundred filaments and cells of the social body, lighting up together.

[1958]

The Historian at the Center

SOME YEARS ago, during the Truman era, when Arthur Schlesinger, Jr., began thinking of *The Age of Roosevelt,* he understandably felt that it was a bad time to be writing about Roosevelt. Whatever Truman's endearing personal qualities, his administration certainly did not add to the reputation of the New Deal; and Truman's weaknesses as the heir of the Roosevelt administration so quickly made him the sacrificial goat when the Republicans in the McCarthy period came up with their retrospectively long knives that Schlesinger must have felt that he was writing dead against the spirit of the times. Moreover, Eisenhower, at least in those now far-off first months when he seemed to be coherent and occasionally even sage, offered up so powerful a glamour in opposition to F.D.R.'s that it intensified the disenchantment with Roosevelt that had set in with Stalin's obvious exploitation of Allied victory.

But a work of history takes so long to produce that it sometimes sees changes — either in the public taste or in the historian himself — that make for an ironic reversal of expectations. The Truman era may have been a bad time to begin *The Age of Roosevelt,* but .the last years of Eisenhower's have certainly made it a good time for publishing it. By 1957, when Schlesinger published his first volume, *The Crisis of the Old Order,* it was impossible not to see parallels on every hand between the obstinacy of Hoover and the obtuseness of Eisenhower.

No wonder Schlesinger's account of how the first New Deal emerged has proved so unexpectedly rousing. Not only was the depression the most significant social experience of the generation now increasingly in the ascendancy; it so colored its experience of the war that anyone who came of age in the 1930s recognized not only that war is politics carried on by other means but that the war was in some sense an extension of the depression. Everything since 1933 has taken place outside the domain of the "normal," the tradi-

The Age of Roosevelt, Vol. II; The Coming of the New Deal, by Arthur Schlesinger, Jr. Boston: Houghton Mifflin Company.

tionally hopeful American experience. The increasing weakness of middle-class standards and traditions, of the faith in progress and of the habitual insistence on freedom; the increasing frivolity of popular culture; the political nihilism and cynicism of which McCarthy was the largest postwar symbol — all this had its beginnings in the bitterness of the depression and the intellectual bankruptcy of business leadership. It is the great merit of Schlesinger's history that he describes the breakdown of public order, then the first excitement of the New Deal and the hoped-for revival of the national faith, with complete emotional authenticity.

This is because Schlesinger really believes in the New Deal as a tradition, a political idea, a historical legacy. He believes that it was one of the great expressions in our time of historical intelligence and moderation, that it symbolizes the vitality still possible at the center. Schlesinger believes in the New Deal even more than do most of the New Dealers, for whom it represented a whole series of inconclusive compromises. He is sure that as a philosophy the New Deal has coherence and that as a national tradition it has distinct shape. This, while historically debatable, is so deeply felt a conviction that he includes among the dramatis personae of the New Deal the ancestral figures of many American social philosophers with whom Roosevelt had no intellectual connection.

Schlesinger has conviction, and what among so many historians is merely a liberal prejudice is for Schlesinger a way of separating all sheep from all goats. Very few American historians have a real point of view. The amorphous liberalism of so many intellectuals works with particularly numbing force on historians who are so full of American history (i.e., *modern* history) that they are too much a part of what they are writing about to describe it with required force and edge and interest. American historians are deficient in ideas. Whether their lack of perspective is due to their lack of general historical interests or whether it is the other way around, they need a gimmick, a tool, a formula. (No wonder that the conservative and Catholic de Tocqueville is always invoked by American historians; he knew what he thought.) But the gospels are all contradictory — de Tocqueville, Turner, Beard, Marx, Freud — and now Riesman. Schlesinger, whose ease embodies some of the characteristic glibnesses of the present historical guild, certainly has a point of view. It was this, in a period when few historians will try a "big" book, in the grand style, that led him to attempt the whole age of Roosevelt. One reason for this is his evident wish to re-create, as an intellectual tradition, the New Deal for the Democratic party. But even more, Schlesinger's book represents an interest in history as seen from the top, from the inside, among the policy makers — and it is this, actually, that gives the book its old-fashioned *literary* interest, for the great nineteenth-century historians also wrote as if they were operating from the center of things.

« 2 »

Schlesinger's notable sense of literary organization and drama, his ability to describe the Washington scene and the New Dealers as episodes in a historical drama — these have distinct literary overtones (there is even a reminiscence of John Dos Passos's style in the early portrait of Hoover's childhood) and literary value. Because Schlesinger writes as a partisan, with enormous confidence in his cause, he lacks the literary freedom of a Van Wyck Brooks or Edmund Wilson; but he is also free from the mawkish and desperate psychologizing of the academic historian who feels that he writes from the outside, far from the centers of power. Schlesinger's history embodies the admiration of an American intellectual, who feels himself part of a new elite outside the business ethos, for the one great recent American leader who was also outside it. Radicals are usually interested in ideology, not politics; liberals tend to see themselves as sympathizers, not leaders. Schlesinger has reversed this pattern among American historians, just as he believes that F.D.R. reversed it in government.

It was Roosevelt the "country squire," who was patrician in tradition and in fact undistinguished at both law and business, who became the idol of all those people in this country — minorities, labor, Southern peons and Southern aristocrats, intellectuals — who also felt themselves outside the business community as an activity and a tradition. In particular, Roosevelt gave new sanction to those academic intellectuals and theorists who, until the New Deal came along, had always been baffled by their inability to make use of, even to test, their explicit analysis of modern society. The more the businessmen hated Roosevelt because, as they correctly thought, he despised business as a way of life, the more the intellectuals and

academicians clung to him. They had all been thrown together by
their common exclusion from "normal," commercial, American experience. The Roosevelt haters were wrong when they charged
that Roosevelt hated business because he had failed in it. Schlesinger quotes a remarkable letter Roosevelt once sent to a Harvard
dean: he really thought business "absurd." It was this freedom from
the most powerful tendency in American life that gave Roosevelt
his inner freedom; it is this, surely, that gave him his sense of the
dramatic, of the "forward" movement in American life at a time
when the old order, in Schlesinger's phrase, was not merely in crisis
but had actually collapsed.

Schlesinger's first volume, *The Crisis of the Old Order,* though
highly partisan and sometimes downright unfair in its black-and-
white scheme of values, was exciting because it represented the actual drama in the passing of the old order. *The Coming of the New
Deal* is far more technical in its detail and minutely carries the history of the administration up to the 1934 elections. It is not merely
his sense of historical responsibility, it is his New Deal mystique, as
it were, that has made Schlesinger in this volume stick so closely to
the inner history of the new reform agencies — the AAA, the NRA,
the PWA, and all the rest. Yet the image of Roosevelt is always in
the reader's mind, obviously because it is in the author's. The book
concludes with a character study of Roosevelt in office that is an extension of the biography of Roosevelt with which the first volume
ended; I suspect that future volumes in *The Age of Roosevelt* are
likely to close on this same magnetic human image.

« 3 »

The administrative point of view, I have suggested, is a brilliant
literary and dramatic device that gives the reader the old-fashioned
sense of commanding history as a drama and a spectacle. The conflict of administrators, the sensitivities of Henry Wallace, the prick-
liness of Harold Ickes — all these become problems of policy, as
they must have been to Roosevelt; and, like Roosevelt, we feel ourselves to be patient, sage, endlessly resourceful. The trouble with
this is that while it gives us a sense of being at the center and almost
in command of things, it tempts Schlesinger into sacrificing the
truth that cannot be fitted in, the jagged edges that would detract

from the straight frame and the smooth design. From the center of the administrative web, all things appear in relation to itself. The historian in this position, like the President, gets a sense of the whole that is exciting, but some things look flatter to him than they need to; he must cover too much in a hurry; he cannot help being a little condescending and mechanical. Just as Roosevelt said "my old friend" too easily, so Schlesinger is a little offhand in describing a New Deal politician as "irresistible and penetrating."

More serious is the intellectual unctuousness that comes from thinking inside the position of power. It is true, as Schlesinger says in his moving portarit of Roosevelt, that "the American system remained essentially a presidential system; in the end, all things came to the man in the White House." But the White House is more likely to hear of things than it is to initiate or even to understand them, and here Roosevelt's famous "pragmatism," his lack of ideas, has turned out to be far more sterile and even dangerous than Schlesinger's account of Roosevelt in his favorite image of himself — the "quarterback," the shifting center of operation — suggests. Roosevelt's freedom from the business ethos was more an accident of birth and a quality of personality than a matter of personal philosophy. When one recognizes the intellectual poverty and spiritual thinness with which he defended democracy during the war — has there ever been so notable an American leader whose public papers are so insignificant as political literature? — and remembers how Wilson, by contrast, always had historical reasons for what he did and recognized the historical tragedy of what he was forced to do, one sees the tragedy of a diminishing democratic leadership that Schlesinger, who sees F.D.R. always in winning human terms, does not bother with. Wilson, demonstrably a failure in his own terms, a "foolish" and obstinate idealist, nevertheless left behind him concepts that the Democratic party could think about. The use of a political philosophy, after all, is that it be carried on. Roosevelt's pragmatism, which his enemies thought opportunism and which in Schlesinger's book becomes an exciting democratic vitalism and pluralism, was in fact conducted so far beyond the limits of "normal" politics that it signified neither the bankruptcy that his enemies saw nor the inspired common sense that Schlesinger sees. It represented the extreme of administrative maneuvering, Roose-

velt's only knowledge, in a world in which — as with Stalin at
Yalta — gestures and smiles and personal charm deceived the actor
far more than they did his audience. It had been Roosevelt's great
good luck that he was socially an anachronism, but by the end of
the war he was really one politically: only his growing inaccessibility
inside the web permitted him not to realize that stratagems had replaced principles.

The New Deal did not destroy the old order. Like all modern
revolutions, it came in after the old order had collapsed. It operated, as all governments must operate nowadays, under the shadow
of extremes, in a world of improvised solutions. But Roosevelt
could not know how much he had gone beyond the traditional
morality, the clear sense of good and evil, that at least left Woodrow Wilson historically lucid.

It is this failure to show the growing uncontrol within and behind the New Deal, the hidden dimension of moral extremism,
that I object to in Schlesinger's new book. He writes as if, by recounting on so minute a scale the first year of the New Deal, he
were reporting from some irrefutable center the established truth.
Actually, it has become increasingly clear that the New Deal represented, against the will and sometimes without the knowledge of
many people who participated in it, a series of adventures in a void
that was created by the decay of tradition.

When Roosevelt was asked once for his philosophy, he replied
testily: "I am a Christian and a Democrat." This was the legacy
passed on to him, and was purely personal; it was not one he could
hand on to his successors. And in fact, he has no disciples, only admirers. Since, in Schlesinger's total argument, the New Deal represents a philosophy of moderation, a middle way between *laissez
faire* and the Communist specter, I think that one clear intention of
his book — to create a canon, to show the New Deal as a viable
tradition — is an illusion. What makes his volumes so notable is really their literary sense, their dramatic organization, their feeling
for the personalities of administrators who were swept up by the
times as by a tidal wave. It is in such pages that Schlesinger shows
his awareness of the plight of democracy, of the increasing pressure
of mass society on the eighteenth-century machinery of American
government. Schlesinger's book, which becomes thin in its compla-

cent New Deal references, is actually exciting and moving whenever, in seeking to render the facts, it hints of the permanent crisis that is the truth of our times.

[1959]

The President and Other Intellectuals

SOME YEARS AGO, when Sherman Adams was still grand vizier of the Eisenhower administration, a famous American poet and long-time friend of Adams's, while sitting in his office in the White House, expressed a desire to meet the President. Adams went in and came out again and tactfully explained that the President was not curious to meet the famous poet.

That same poet, however, was prominently displayed at the inauguration of John F. Kennedy. And although many of us who admire Robert Frost's poetry and enjoy Robert Frost's conversation and have not shared his political views may well be surprised to hear that he has *returned* to the Democratic fold, Frost's enthusiasm says a good deal about Kennedy's charm for some of the most interesting minds in the United States. During the campaign and afterwards, Kennedy certainly never hid his allegiance to the fundamental principles of the New Deal — which Robert Frost has always detested. Yet no sooner did the New Frontier get itself named (somewhat mechanically) than Robert Frost heralded "an Augustan age of poetry and power, with the emphasis on power."

For Robert Frost even to think of himself as Virgil to Kennedy's Augustus in this new age of American power shows how deeply Kennedy not only affected some writers but encouraged them to feel a new confidence about America's role in the world. During the campaign, the very literary and "socialist" columnist of the *New York Post*, Murray Kempton, confessed that although he was pledged to vote for Norman Thomas, his heart belonged to Kennedy, while Walter Lippmann must have carried many votes for Kennedy by certifying his faith in Kennedy as a thinking politician who promised to be a statesman.

It was particularly on the more intellectual and liberal correspondents with him that Kennedy seemed to make the greatest
immediate impression. At Los Angeles, watching his first press conference before the nomination, Norman Mailer thought that Kennedy did not seem too popular with the general run of reporters; he
was "too much a contemporary, and yet difficult to understand."
But Richard Rovere in the *New Yorker* not merely testified with increasing warmth and affection to Kennedy's abilities, but that July
was able to say "with a fair amount of certainty that the essence of
his political attractiveness is his extraordinary political intelligence.
. . . The easy way in which he disposes of the question of Church
and State . . . suggests that the organization of society is the one
thing that really engages his interest." In his recent book on the
campaign, *The Making of the President, 1960*, Theodore H.
White describes Kennedy on tour as one "who enjoys words and
reading, is a Pulitzer Prize winner himself and a one-time reporter;
he has an enormous respect for those who work with words and
those who write clean prose. He likes newspapermen and their company. Kennedy would, even in the course of the campaign, read
the press dispatches, and if he particularly liked a passage, would tell
the reporter or columnist that he had — and then quote from its
phrases, in an amazing effort of memory and attention."

Norman Mailer at Los Angeles, preparing the article that *Esquire*
was to insist on calling "Superman Comes to the Supermart," was
staggered on interviewing Kennedy when the candidate said he
had read *"The Deer Park* . . . and the others." The conventional
remark on meeting Mailer is, of course, that one has read *"The
Naked and the Dead* . . . and the others." But Kennedy, happily,
was not conventional. The man who was very possibly the next
President of the United States had read the scandalous hip novel
about Hollywood doings in Palm Springs that had enraged and disgusted so many publishers and critics. Mailer's brilliant if over-
written article expressed the same hope for Kennedy that in their
different ways Lippmann and Rovere and Kempton and even Robert
Frost had openly felt. Given the "vacancy" in American life, as
Lippmann had put it during the last days of the Eisenhower administration, the increasing divorce between private thought and
the public realm, could it be that here at last was one of the

"creative innovators" in politics, one man with brains and vision enough to pull our people to world reality, away from business as usual? Could it be, dared one hope, that with this rich, handsome, literate and courageous young man the sickening cycle of underground life and public inanity had at last been cut? *Esquire*, more hip than Mailer himself, advertised his article as "The Outlaw's Mind Appraises the Heroes' Dilemmas." But what Mailer said, with moving hope as well as concern, was that perhaps, with Kennedy, there might at last be some positive awareness of the ever-growing disrespect of intellectuals for politics. Too long, as he said, had politics quarantined us from history, and too long had we left politics to those who "are in the game not to make history but to be diverted from the history which is being made." Although the convention at Los Angeles was actually dull, full of seedy machine politicians, "The man it nominated was unlike any politician who had ever run for President in the history of the land, and if elected he would come to power in a year when America was in danger of drifting into a profound decline."

Mailer was stirred enough to romanticize Kennedy with faintly derisory analogies to Marlon Brando. Yet whatever Mailer's personal symbol of an American hero, what he said was no more than what so many intellectuals felt. "It was a hero America needed, a hero central to his time, a man whose personality might suggest contradictions and miseries which could reach into the alienated circuits of the underground, because only a hero can capture the secret imagination of a people, and so be good for the vitality of his nation. . . ."

And just recently there has come to hand the most moving expression of the wretchedness and the positive sense of unreality that political alienation can suggest to a sensitive mind. It is the brilliant excerpt, recently published in *Esquire*, from Saul Bellow's new novel, *Herzog*. The hero is a university teacher and writer, racked by the collapse of his marriage and by his spiritual loneliness, who wildly scribbles in his notebook letters to public leaders as well as to private individuals. At the end of this excerpt, he suddenly writes a letter to President Eisenhower, and this defines not only the ground of his private unhappiness but his feeling that it has a public source: ". . . it seems a long time since chief executives and private citizens had any contact. The President is briefed by experts or informed by committees on the problems of the nation. That is too bad. Sometimes obscure citizens are wildly intelligent, without the disabilities of special training. But we have to recognize that intelligent people without influence have a certain contempt for themselves. This partly reflects the contempt the powerful have for them, but mainly it comes from the contrast between strength of mind or imagination and social weakness or political impotence. . . . It seems to them that society lets them think everything, do nothing. The private resentment and nihilism that result are due to a private sense of failure which possibly comes from the intellectual's faulty definition of himself and his prospects. What should his thought do? What power ought he to have from it?"

The Russians speak of many disaffected and silent people in their country as "internal *émigrés*"; increasingly it has become natural for many American writers and scholars and intellectuals to think of themselves as "internal *émigrés*." In the very Thirties that now seem to some young people an unrecapturable time of *engagement* and public responsibility, Nathanael West said that we have no outer life, only an inner one, "and that by necessity." By the 1960 Presidential campaign, it was perfectly possible for writers like Robert Frost and Norman Mailer (who, whatever the outer life, are not so hilariously divergent as they seem) to herald, with varying tones of enthusiasm and private distrust, what Frost called "a new Augustan age" and Mailer an end to the "alienated circuits of the underground." I grant that writers welcome an audience in high places, that "the new Augustan age" is pure rhetoric — much more so (whatever the phrase) than Mailer's felt and even obsessive feeling that now there are "alienated circuits of the underground." But if the writer is good, even his egotistical affections are intelligent. And of course one reason for this pro-Kennedy feeling was the contrast he made with the General and the General's Westerns and the General's sentences — to say nothing of the General's party, which a year after the campaign announced a major new campaign to enlist "the specialized knowledge and experience of the nation's intellectuals," which has now drawn plans in every state "to facilitate the utilization of friendly academicians in party affairs at all levels."

Truman, even more than Eisenhower, showed himself to be intemperate in denouncing "advanced" American pictures that had been selected by museum officials for exhibition abroad, while F.D.R., whatever his spontaneous shrewdness in answering to immediate situations, had the landed gentleman's repugnance to excessive intellectual labor. No wonder that so many writers and scholars have felt that they can at least *talk* to Kennedy. He reads, he reads endlessly, his reading is constantly an amazement in a country where the strongest minds often on principle declare a positive contempt for the reading of serious books. Addressing a newspaper publishers' convention, the President of the United States recalled that Karl Marx had been correspondent for the *New York Tribune*. Before leaving for his talks with De Gaulle and Khrushchev, the President at his birthday dinner in Boston quoted William Lloyd Garrison's famous thunder-cry from the opening number of the *Liberator*. When he was welcomed to Paris by De Gaulle, the President graciously replied by invoking Jefferson's love for France and Franklin's popularity in the *salons*. When Hemingway died, the President quickly issued a tribute in which he made reference to Paris in the 1920s, the lost generation and the fact that Hemingway had helped to end the old provincialism of American letters. The President, as James Reston has said, takes printer's ink for breakfast, and by now his bookishness and intellectual sophistication are so well known that one is no longer surprised to hear that C. P. Snow has been invited to the White House and that E. E. Cummings has been in to tea, or that at a certain juncture Kennedy alone, of all his intellectual entourage, knew the title of Churchill's first book. It did not seem at all pretentious to me that the First Lady, interviewed on her plans for redecorating the White House, should have spoken of her interest in antique furniture as natural to the wife of a "historian." Not only has "history" been the President's strongest intellectual interest, but so far as he has been trained to any profession, it has been to the study and the writing of "history." The son of the American Ambassador to Great Britain in 1940 had positive reasons to remember that during the Civil War the son of the American Ambassador to Great Britain was Henry Adams, and there learned a great deal that was to be important to the life of politics and the writing of history. President

Kennedy, who before the war thought of becoming a newspaperman, reminds me, in the range of his sophistication, of a great many "intellectual" newsmen and editors. The author of *Why England Slept* and *Profiles in Courage*, the President whose favorite book has been given out as Lord David Cecil's *Melbourne* and favorite novel as Stendhal's *The Red and the Black* is in his personal interests alone far more of a "historian" than many who teach history rather than learn it.

Now it is also true that President Kennedy's anecdotes from American history tend to be trotted out rather irrelevantly to formal occasions, and that the punch line quoted in Paris from Samuel Adams is unaccountably accredited in Vienna to someone else. And if he cited a little-known detail from Karl Marx's biography to an audience of publishers, it was to joke that Marx had vainly asked the *New York Tribune* for a raise — look, said the President, what you fellows may get us all into by not giving a correspondent a raise! William Lloyd Garrison's "I will not equivocate and I will be heard!" is in excess of what a birthday dinner among Massachusetts politicians, even on the eve of his going to Europe to meet Khrushchev, seems to call for. And *Profiles in Courage*, perhaps because it was indubitably *written* by the author himself (as he replied to reviewers who doubted it), is certainly far more interesting for its personal emphasis on "courage," courage by *anybody* in the United States, whether Taft or Norris, than for any significant political ideas of his own. *Profiles in Courage* always reminds me of those little anecdotes from the lives of great men that are found in the *Reader's Digest*, Sunday supplements, and the journal of the American Legion. It is the kind of book that reads like a series of excerpts even when you read it through; and indeed it seems composed of excerpts — excerpts of reading, excerpts of anecdote. Nor, quite apart from his conventional public statements, am I impressed with the tales of a voracious reading that seems to be concerned largely with getting the "facts," the highly separable material and statistical facts that can be shoveled into the executive mind. And with everything that has been said about Kennedy's being a Catholic, almost nothing, so far as I can tell, has emerged about the personal and intellectual side of his Catholicism. Unlike Senator Eugene McCarthy and other American politicians whose thoughtfulness and sense of philosophical principles owe so much to the traditional teachings of their church, John F. Kennedy seems to have been more aware of Catholics as a source of political support than of the Church as a source of intellectual inspiration. And although Kennedy's narrow victory, which owes so much to Catholics, has caused many Catholic writers and intellectuals to rally almost defensively around him, some of them, before Kennedy was nominated, were positively bitter about his political exploitation of Catholic support.

Yet with all these limitations and conventionalities and sales tricks, it is interesting to see how much of an "intellectual" Kennedy wants to be and how eagerly his bookishness, his flair and sophistication, his very relish for the company of intellectual specialists, have been advertised to the public without any fear that it might dismay a people so notoriously suspicious of these qualities in others. Obviously in Kennedy's case an "intellectual" taste does not suggest a fastidious withdrawal from anything — not even normal passion. Adlai Stevenson in his two campaigns seemed to be running not only against the bluff, smiling General, but against the General's philistine supporters. It is interesting to learn from the autobiography of T. S. Matthews that when Matthews warned Stevenson against "Ohio" (meaning the Yahoos), Stevenson's advisers just stared at him, while Stevenson smiled and went back to work. The extraordinary identification that so many American intellectuals make with Stevenson has often struck me as loyalty not to a lost cause but to lostness as a cause. I have never been sure just how much of an "intellectual" Adlai Stevenson is, but he has certainly been cherished among intellectuals more for his obvious sensitivity than for the strength of his ideas. In 1956 even more than in 1952, and at Los Angeles in 1960 even more than in 1956, he seemed the peerless leader of intellectuals who boasted that they had never had a candidate before — and who warned that if he were counted out for positively the last time, they could never be that much concerned again: they would have suffered just too much. And since Stevenson's public style seemed to combine self-demeaning wit and vulnerability to such a degree that some of his closest friends condoled with him on having to face the public at all, perhaps it is no wonder that the candidate who publicly yearned that the cup might pass from him was defeated by the General who listens with particular respect to the head of any large American corporation.

By contrast, of course, Kennedy has not only surrounded himself with many of the liberal historians, economists and political scientists who were reputedly such a liability to Stevenson, but despite certain necessary political favors to be paid back he has made a point of appointing as Ambassador to Japan a professor of Japanese history, as Ambassador to India a John Kenneth Galbraith, as Secretary of the National Security Council the former dean of the Faculty of Arts and Sciences at Harvard, as one of his immediate advisers the author of a scholarly study of Presidential power, as another adviser a young man in his twenties who was first in his law class at Harvard. Although the Secretary of State obviously was chosen to be one of a team, it is interesting that his last previous job should have been as president of the Rockefeller Foundation; although the Secretary of Defense was president of the Ford Motor Company, he came to Ford and rose at Ford because he was a brilliant statistician; although the Secretary of the Interior necessarily comes from the West, the present one really is crazy about Robert Frost. Even the Postmaster General in this administration has written a novel; even the new Military Adviser to the President has written a superb book on American defenses. No wonder that Arthur Miller and John Steinbeck and W. H. Auden were asked to the inauguration as publicly declared assets of the Republic; that even the Kennedys' French chef is felt to be a compliment to their good taste rather than to their wealth — to say nothing of the *fête champêtre* thrown for the Pakistan President at Mount Vernon, which (it is safe to guess) irritated some congressmen not because of its reputed cost, but because, with its announced links to classic entertainments in the past, it represented a bit of intellectual swagger that not all Americans are likely to admire.

In short, the President has gladly let it be known that he is in fact a highbrow, an intellectual, an omnivorous reader. There was once a Tammany mayor of New York who, in private, talking with a favorite magazine reporter, confided that he indeed knew and enjoyed Joyce's *Ulysses*. But this was a secret, not a boast. President Kennedy's acquaintance with some minor details in the life of Karl Marx is rather more a boast than a secret, like his open espousal of

Robert Frost, his invocation of William Lloyd Garrison in Boston and of Jefferson in Paris; all these and more are attempts to form his public style. As has often been said, Kennedy is the most "intellectual" President since Woodrow Wilson — some even say since Theodore Roosevelt. Hoover may have been a brilliant mining engineer on three continents and with his wife he did translate a medieval Latin treatise on mining; but in public he gave the appearance of suffering fools miserably, and stimulated no one. Wilson had been a political scientist and had written books; but he, too, tended rather to patronize and to moralize, and at Versailles in 1918 was hopelessly outclassed in wit and learning, to say nothing of his not knowing a single blessed word of French. (President Kennedy's French is primitive, but even on a state visit to Canada he was able to make a virtue of his limitations by likening it to Prime Minister Diefenbaker's.) Like Theodore Roosevelt (also trained to no profession but that of "historian"), Kennedy has cultivated as his public style the bookman-in-office. Although Kennedy has not yet publicly found jobs for poets (as T.R. did for Edwin Arlington Robinson), he, like Roosevelt, has praised the strenuous life as if he were promoting a historical revival and, like T.R. again, he lets his literary opinions be known. He has helped to establish taste. And it is just this cultivation of the highbrow world as an executive taste and Presidential style, his turning the poor old suffering American egghead into something better than a martyr to popular culture, that I find most suggestive about Kennedy-as-intellectual. If during the campaign he grew on many thoughtful observers who distrusted his family background and despised his failure to say a single word about McCarthy, so in his first weeks, at least, he was able to persuade many cool observers that his was the necessary style of administration in these times — like Churchill, like De Gaulle. Before Cuba, one English joke was that Kennedy talked like Churchill but acted like Chamberlain; even after Cuba, it was said that there had been an *unaccountable* lapse of his dominant executive style. But Cuba apart for the moment, it is obvious that Kennedy's reputation as an "intellectual" has been an asset to him at a time when government operates on a scale of such complexity, requires so deft an ability at least to show a nodding acquaintance with many subjects. It has often been said that Kennedy turned the tide in his first television debate with Nixon by the precise answers he was able to supply to questions raised from so many different fields. Before his nomination, says Theodore H. White in *The Making of the President, 1960,* Kennedy astonished his own staff by analyzing without notes his chances in every single state of the union, and, in the "honeymoon" weeks of the administration, Vice President Johnson let it be known that he was positively awestruck by the President's ready handling of so many different subjects.

This smooth and easy assimilation of fact, this air of over-all sophistication, is what Americans have learned more and more to admire in journalism, in business, in conversation and on television quiz shows — whether the man in the dock is Charles Van Doren or the President of the United States being questioned mercilessly (and pointlessly) about everything from Laos to Tammany. The quiz show did not die out with the exposure that the contestants had been briefed; the candidates in the 1960 campaign were also briefed, as is the President of the United States today, and the show goes on. If the reporters sometimes act as if they wanted to trip the President up, the President knows that he can impress the country by way of the reporters. This over-all style, so much like the division of even the arts and sciences into departments of *Time* magazine, became a "research" style among the military during the war, and it has now invaded the big universities and "scientific research and development." It is our national style, *intellect-wise.* We now admire it — when it comes unaccompanied by personal stress. A recent article in a liberal weekly on "The Mind of John F. Kennedy" turns out to be an entirely admiring study of Kennedy's range as an administrator. This vocational or psychological use of the word "mind" is so typical of our time and place that it probably never even occurred to the author to extend the word to cover "beliefs." Instead we are told that Kennedy's "marshaling of related considerations" defines Kennedy's mind "as political in the most all-encompassing sense. The whole of politics, in other words, is to such a mind a seamless fabric, in which a handshaking session with a delegation of women is an exercise directly related to hearing a report from a task force on Laos." And this ability to assimilate on the jump necessary quantities of fact, to get statements of a problem that carry "action consequences" — this is what we have come to value as the quality of intellectual all-roundedness or savvy. It is a style that depends always on research done by other people, on a swift and agile reaction to the statement of the problem *set* by other people, on the professional politician's total recall for names and faces, the professional communicator's ability to wham the effective phrase right down the mass media to the great audience. The more complex and insoluble the problems become, the more intellectuals are needed to pile up research on them; the incoming trays are piled higher, ever higher, with Freedom Riders, Latin American poverty, education bills, recalcitrant congressmen, the Congo, obstinate Englishmen and offended Nigerian diplomats who were refused a cup of tea in a Maryland restaurant. The professors who coasted along on two courses and one committee now work from eight-to-eight before they go out to the big dinner every night: "I don't have time to put my shoes on in the morning." Since the boss is the man who takes his problems home with him, the boss proves that he is the boss by a certain air of tense vigilance and unsleeping physical resiliency and readiness. Never in any administration have we been told so constantly how little sleep the President gets.

The boss nowadays does not have to be an expert himself; in the normal course of nature he cannot be one and boss too. But he has to know who the experts are. So much is this executive style — with its dependency on batteries of advisers, experts, "researchers" — the admired "intellectual" style because it works with intellectuals, that the President of this nation of boastful pragmatists, in a public tribute to Robert Frost, told the story of a mother's writing the principal of a school, "Don't teach my boy poetry; he's going to run for Congress" — and affirmed: "I've never taken the view that the world of politics and the world of poetry are so far apart." No wonder that some who suffered with Stevenson in 1956 for being too good for the American public felt with Kennedy in 1960 that intellect was at last in touch with power. He had read the essential books; and the essential names, the principal formulae, the intellectual shorthand, were at his disposal. No wonder that, conversing with certain Kennedy advisers in March, one felt about them the glow of those who have not merely conceived a great work but are in a position to finish it. The boss *understood*; he was just as savvy as anyone else, but less "sensitive" (meaning destructible). It took half the time to explain highly technical problems to Kennedy that it had to Stevenson, and it turned out, too, that Stevenson actually wasn't much of a reader. During the Eisenhower administration, I heard a famous scientist say with some satisfaction that the President was "actually very intelligent." And Robert Frost, when he finally did get to an Eisenhower stag dinner at the White House, made a point of saying afterwards that President Eisenhower was extremely intelligent. I understood. When a really good mind, suffering from the natural loneliness of really good minds, gets the ear of a man smart enough to make his way to the very top, even to make the topmost pinnacle an attribute of himself, there is a natural sense of satisfaction. For when all is said and done, action *is* the natural sphere of a mind sane and hopeful, eager to revive the classic center of man's public activity. To real intellectuals, power means not Caesarism but right influence; and it must be said that the type of Henry Adams, who wants to be near power so that he can deride it but feels that he is too intelligent to influence it, is really the prisoner of his own despairing rationality. Adams did not want his private obsessions interrupted by any new dimension of experience. And while the *quality* of mind is not necessarily better among those who are more "healthy-minded," it is a fact that the capacity of certain intellectuals to wield influence, the belief that they not only can but that they should, is interpreted maliciously by those who are so alienated from the body politic (to say nothing of politics) that they must explain everything as self-seeking.

« 2 »

I would suggest that what drew certain historians, political scientists, economists and lawyers to Kennedy was the fact that he, too, was outside the business community, had grown up independent of the main influence, and that Kennedy's very adroitness and eagerness of mind, his sense that there were deeper sources which he could employ, pleased them as the style of a politician no more limited by the business ethos than they are. In many ways the current intellectual style brings together people who have nothing

in common but their indifference to the conventional values. It is
the style of labor lawyers from immigrant families; of university
administrators with a family tradition of diplomacy and liberal
Republicanism in the tradition of Stimson, not the shabby rhetoric of "free enterprise" set up by professional demagogues; of professors themselves brought up in professors' families; of economists
who remember with bitterness what young men with brains had to
fight in the way of prejudice and snobbery when they first made
their way up the university ladder. Such figures, whether their background was too patrician or too scholarly or too radical or too
foreign for the majority view, represent the accelerating war of the
"specialists" (or the "engineers," as Veblen called them) with the
"price system." They have grown up on ideas, they have made their
way up on ideas, they live on ideas. And in some way that must be
both exciting to them and yet frustrating, Kennedy is also not limited
to business and by business. He shares with his advisers a certain
intellectual freedom from the dominant prejudices and shibboleths.
But what for them is often a positive article of belief may, for him,
be only freedom from vulgar prejudice — and it is exactly here that
Kennedy's use of his advisers has already proved so much more
significant than their influence on him.

About Kennedy one *has* to make psychological guesses, for unlike
his advisers, one does not know what he thinks by reading him —
nor even by talking to him. His most essential quality, I would think,
is that of the man who is always making and remaking himself. He
is the final product of a fanatical job of self-remodeling. He grew up
rich and favored enough not to make obvious mistakes or to fall for
the obvious — he has been saved from the provincial and self-pitying
judgments that so many talented Americans break their teeth on. He
has been saved, not merely from the conventional, but from wasting
his time on it. Even now there is an absence in him of the petty
conceit of the second-rate, and a freshness of curiosity behind which
one feels not merely his quickness to utilize all his advantages, but
also his ability to turn this curiosity on himself. He turns things over
very quickly in his own mind; he gets the angle. Yet all the while he
stands outside, like a sculptor surveying his work. He is what a certain time has made, has raised highest, and he can see himself in
perspective in a way that perhaps only Americans can — since only

they have *made* so much of themselves. The father made a killing in liquor and even as ambassador managed to sound like a district boss; the son has as many European "connections" as royalty. The father worked it so that each of his children would have at least a million dollars; the son, starting out high above the economic motive, asked advice of fatherly gentlemen in New England as if he had all the world to choose from. The grandfathers in Boston still had to look at *No Irish Need Apply*; their grandson, as the Attorney General of the United States said with grim pride when he urged Negroes to fight more for their *political* rights, is now President of the United States. He is President of the United States, he is a millionaire, he has the sex appeal of a movie hero, the naturalness of a newspaper-man and as much savvy as a Harvard professor — and whereas you and I would be scared even to imagine ourselves taking on such responsibilities as face him every moment of the day and night, the highest office is what he wanted, this is what he went straight for, this is what he has. He has learned so continuously, so brilliantly, even so greedily, that one observer, noting that the author of *Profiles in Courage* didn't show his profile on the McCarthy issue, dryly wonders "if the book didn't, on some very private level, instruct him in what to avoid." The determination to succeed, the guardedness against vulnerability of any sort, the constant vigilance not to show himself wanting (his health has been the only admitted "weakness") — this is so sharp that another writer has brilliantly compared Kennedy to the type of Whig who in the eighteenth century entered the rising House of Commons: "of large and comparatively recent fortune, intelligent, elegant, tremendously determined to make a place for himself, desiring above all to be effective and to succeed, contemptuous of the aristocratic condescensions and concerned not to be condescended to."

But unlike those Whigs, it is to be doubted that Kennedy represents a definite social interest. What has given him his influence, even over the "brain power," as he describes this resource passingly in *The Strategy of Peace*, is his sophisticated freedom from conventional prejudice. When one adviser, submitting a memorandum on Latin American problems, noted that certain recommendations could be highly irritating to American business, Kennedy waved the hypothetical objection aside. This elasticity makes him exciting to work for, and to pass from so detached a mind to the endless analysis of itself that Washington goes in for might well make an intellectual in Washington feel that "brain power" is at the center of things again, that the few have again the chance to do well by the many.

« 3 »

Yet as this is being written, nothing stands out so clearly about the Kennedy administration as its frustrations. The occasion is piled higher with difficulty than ever before, and "the most intellectual and idea-seeking President since Woodrow Wilson" must find it as hard to remember some of the ideas he came in with as it is to promote some he has acquired since. Only in the White House, it may be, will Kennedy know the "contradictions and miseries" that other men have always lived with. And perhaps it is only in the White House, too, that the intellectual advisers who have gone smoothly from academic success to academic success may for the first time experience rebuff, defeat, obloquy. The "decisions" get more and more "educated," to use the President's interesting word, but they do not grow more decisive. And when I think of the increasing ugliness of American "conservatives," the political stalemate that Kennedy is faced with by Russia, the impossible difficulty of getting Americans to limit their smallest economic privileges enough to create a new social sense in this country, the conflicting views of so many different groups of advisers who were meant to counteract each other but who can produce administrative chaos, I anticipate that so restless and so ambitious a man as Kennedy will want to cut through the ever-deepening morass.

The most striking side of the Cuban disaster, to me, was the virtually official apologia that since Kennedy inherited the invasion scheme from Eisenhower and found that the C.I.A. had been arming and training an invasion army that could no longer be "contained," the technical approval by the Joint Chiefs of Staff and the approval of a majority of his advisers were enough to make him approve not merely an immoral but an impractical scheme to invade Cuba. Even a literary man reading up on Castro and his revolution could guess that Castro was much too popular to be overthrown from a small landing at the Bay of Pigs. Yet, faced by so many conflicting and in a sense mutually canceling bodies of advice, Kennedy allowed the gun to go off. And nothing has been said by him since, or by his advisers, that indicates it was anything but the *failure* of the Cuban invasion that they regret. It has given a "bad mark" to the administration that wants so much to succeed. What is immoral and downright stupid about the invasion, what represents not merely faithlessness to our traditions but an executive temperament restless, tricky, irritable — this has not been understood by the administration and its advisers. And seeking out Hoover and MacArthur at the Waldorf in an effort to make a show of national unity at the first sign of national dismay! The only defense that I have heard against the frightening impatience displayed in the Cuban adventure has been that so-and-so wasn't in on the decision, and that intellectuals on the outside never recognize how many important decisions are improvised and uncalculated. Where, then, is the meaningful relation of intellectuals to power? Is it only to write memoranda, to "educate" the decisions that others make? History will not absolve them that cheaply. What troubled me about the Cuban adventure was that although its failure was attributed to "erroneous" advice, the essential philosophy behind it was perhaps uttered by the adviser who, when asked for a show of hands, said "Let 'er rip," and by another who said pompously that it was time to come to a power confrontation with Communism in this hemisphere. (Stewart Alsop reporting.) In short, actions may be excused as "improvised," but is the essential philosophy a longing to come to a power "confrontation" in this hemisphere? Is it possible that the very freedom from conventionality that I interpret as the essential mark of Kennedy's intellectuals and of his receptivity to them — that this may yet create an abstract and virtually ideological conception of American power?

The famous State Department "White Paper" on Castro, published before the invasion attempt, listed many distinguished Cuban liberals, democrats, intellectuals, who had fled from Castro after being part of the 26 July revolutionary movement against Batista. Various pro-Castro "progressives" in this country noted that the White Paper quite conveniently omitted mention of any of the privileges lost by American business in Cuba. But although it is not for me to prove this, I suspect that in the mind of the author of the White Paper was not so much the desire to overlook the resentment of American business against Castro as the intellectual bitterness of an American liberal democrat against a political adventurer (Castro), who began as a "reformer" and has since shown himself a cynical and dangerous ally of totalitarianism. Perhaps business just did not come into it for the principal author of the White Paper. Hard as it is for pro-Castro intellectuals in this country to take this, I believe that economic determinism seems to explain as little of our bellicosity as it does Russian bellicosity. Anyone who has studied Castro's political development can see that his gravitation toward totalitarianism has had nothing whatever to do with American economic policies in Cuba. Khrushchev's stated belief to Walter Lippmann that Kennedy takes orders from "Rockefeller" is as mechanical a piece of Communist rhetoric as Stalin's stated belief that Hitler's policies were dictated by German capitalists. Indeed, the Russian Revolution itself, launched entirely by intellectuals whose historic dissociation from the great mass of the Russian people explains the very structure of the Communists as a party of intellectual managers, offers the most devastating proof that, especially in our times of centralization, history is made not for material interest but out of intellectual fanaticism often divorced from the most elementary social interest.

After the invasion attempt against Cuba, Kennedy replied to Khrushchev's professed indignation by cautioning him not to support Castro militarily. He ended his message with this emphatic burst: "I believe, Mr. Chairman, that you should recognize that free people in all parts of the world do not accept the claim of historical inevitability for the Communist revolution. What your government believes is its own business; what it does in the world is the world's business. The great revoluton in the history of man, past, present and future, is the revolution of those determined to be free." This is stirring language quite different from the usual muddle of Eisenhower's public statements. But I find it hard to believe that for Kennedy the Soviet government's philosophy is "its own business"; I find it also hard to believe Khrushchev when he says (on alternate Tuesdays) that he himself does not plan to attack the socially backward nations and explains that the well-known law of Marxist development will take care of that. Of course Kennedy is not driven by a fanatical creed of political messianism that is taken as the only universal law of history; nor is he as driven as Russians have been by a profound resentment of the creeds and relative good fortune of the West. But to the extent that Kennedy has been liberated by his own good fortune from the intellectual torpidity of American business, he may have been thrown back on the intellectual's natural outlet in causes. And the most significant side of Kennedy-as-intellectual seems to lie, not in his public cultivation of the "intellectual" style that is now admired in the highest echelons, but in the fact that, as a would-be intellectual who happens to be President of the United States, his natural tendency may be to identify the United States with a crusade, a cause, with "liberty." It was exactly this accessibility to causes that now constitutes, retrospectively, the disagreeable and even false side of Theodore Roosevelt. Similarly, what one fears about Kennedy is the other side of what one admired and was prepared to admire more in him — that he has been left free by his immense power to adopt a cause forged out of his energy and the depths of his restless ambition. Hard as it is for most of us to imagine ourselves arguing the fate of humanity with Khrushchev, it does not seem to bother Kennedy. And when I ask myself, as I increasingly must, what it is in Kennedy's ambition to be an "intellectual" statesman that steels him for his awesome responsibility, what in his *convictions* can carry him over the sea of troubles awaiting all of us, I have to answer that I do not know. At this juncture, Kennedy's shrewd awareness of what intellectuals can do, even his undoubted inner respect for certain writers, scholars and thinkers, is irrelevant to the tragic issues and contributes nothing to their solution. To be an "intellectual" is the latest style in American success, the mark of our manipulatable society.

[1961]

Uprooted Writers

SIGMUND FREUD. Thomas Mann. James Joyce. Samuel Beckett. Bertolt Brecht. Vladimir Nabokov. Erich Auerbach. Ernst Cassirer. Claude Lévi-

Strauss. Maurice Maeterlinck. Jules Romains. Georges Bernanos. Jacques Maritain. Erwin Panofsky. Karl Wolfskehl. Elsie Lasker-Schuler. Paul Tillich. Américo Castro. Hermann Broch. Andre Breton. Erik Erikson. Franz Werfel. Elias Canetti. Sigrid Undset. Robert Musil. Oskar Maria Graf. André Maurois. St.-John Perse. Arthur Koestler. Renato Poggioli. Erich Maria Remarque. Wilhelm Reich. Hannah Arendt. Erich Heller. Herbert Marcuse. Nelly Sachs. Michael Polanyi.

These at least made their way to safety. But Ernst Toller, dead by his own hand in New York; Kurt Tucholsky in Sweden; Stefan Zweig in Brazil; Walter Benjamin after being turned back on the French-Spanish frontier; Egon Friedell in Vienna; Paul Celan in Paris; Theodore Lessing, murdered in Prague as he sat at his desk; Erich Muhsam, tortured to death in Oranienburg; Anne Frank, fifteen when she died in Belsen; Simon Dubnow, author of the greatest history in Russian of the Jews, eighty-four years old when he was shot to death in the Riga ghetto. Max Jacob died in Drancy, Simone Weill in London of malnutrition induced by her solidarity with the occupied French. We do not know just how many writers in Yiddish, Hebrew, Russian, Lithuanian, Latvian, Polish died in the gas chambers. We do not know the fate of those gifted young children who were actually smuggled out of the Vilna ghetto so that they at least would continue the story of their people.

We will never know the full score of the Hitler horror. What began in 1933 did not end in 1945. To discuss the particular talents that made it to America, to ours and the world's good fortune — Mann, Brecht, Werfel, Nabokov, Arendt, Auerbach, Maritain — is to recall not only the many who did not but the unequal contest between the individual talent and murderous totalitarianism. To have been of age during the Hitler period is to be stamped forever with the image of an unlimited destructiveness that now seems no less grotesque for being so suicidal. In what many consider the greatest German poem of the Holocaust, *Todesfuge*, Paul Celan wrote of the death inflicted on so many helpless people

wir trinken und trinken

Black milk of dawn we drink it at dusk
    we drink it at noon and at daybreak we drink it at night
    we drink and we drink
    we are digging a grave in the air there's room for us all

Goethe said that the "shudder of awe" was man's highest tribute to the power of the universe. That shudder we still feel at the proscription, exile, hardships, and death of so many gifted people.

Yet just now I prefer to think of a German philosopher someone told me of. He guarded his family in an Amsterdam attic near where the Otto Frank family was betrayed. With a rifle on his knees day after day he wrote a philosophical treatise — and lived to publish it. I think of Thomas Mann, in Princeton and in Pacific Palisades, completing the great Joseph tetralogy and going on to write *Dr. Faustus*; of Erich Auerbach, for me the greatest of modern literary scholars, writing his magisterial study of representation, *Mimesis*. Auerbach was grateful that the Turkish libraries were so poor, he was not distracted by secondary literature. Simone Weil, first on Riverside Drive in New York, then in London, was working out that extraordinary personal theology, *Waiting for God, Supernatural Knowledge*, that was to have such a marked effect on T.S. Eliot and so many English, French, and American intellectuals. Sigmund Freud was in London, stoically enduring the pain of cancer in his jaw, for which he would not take even aspirin lest it diminish the lucidity with which, at eighty-three, he was still seeing patients and rewriting *Moses and Monotheism*. Describing himself as "an island of pain in a sea of indifference," he was to die just as Hitler unleashed his war.

The most gifted of Russian writers in exile, Vladimir Nabokov, had while still in Paris begun to write his first novel in English, *The Real Life of Sebastian Knight*. He wrote it in the bathroom of a tiny flat so as not to disturb his infant son Dmitri. When the Nazis overran France in 1940, Nabokov had to save his Jewish wife; he was able to get on one of the last ships to America thanks to a Jewish rescue service that gratefully remembered the support given to persecuted Jews under Czarism by Nabokov's father, an aristocratic liberal whose real legacy to his gifted son was the Russian democratic tradition. Nabokov in America was bitterly to complain to his good friend and sponsor Edmund Wilson that American intellectuals seemed to know nothing of this tradition, thoughtlessly disseminated the Leninist lie that Russian exiles were all "white guards." No other writer in exile was to make such brilliant use of the English language and the American scene.

After passing through France and Denmark, Bertolt Brecht was in Hollywood. He was to pass through America, too. In a litany addressed to those who come after us, *An Die Nachgeborenen*, Brecht cried, "Truly, I live in dark times" — *Wirklich, ich lebe in finsteren Zeiten* — " ... Whoever laughs/Has simply not yet received/The dreadful news. .... /Accidentally I have been spared./The roads led into the swamps in my time/Language betrayed me to the butcher. .... /After all, we passed — changing countries more often than shoes — .... /Yet we know well enough:/Hatred of baseness, too,/Distorts one's features."

Hannah Arendt, who had taken her doctorate at Heidelberg under Karl Jaspers with a famous thesis on St. Augustine's concept of love, was on West 95th Street in New York, struggling with her adopted English to write *The Origins of Totalitarianism*. She was an editor at Schocken Books, where her passion for Kafka, for her the greatest modern writer in German, had much to do with his influence on American writers. As soon as the war ended, she devoted herself to Jewish cultural reconstruction, striving to locate and to find safe homes for the libraries and religious articles stolen *en masse* by the Nazis. With her philosopher husband Heinrich Bluecher, a German Protestant who bravely went back to Germany time and again to save people and to bring out their possessions, she was now devoting herself to political philosophy. Totalitarianism was the central fact of our era that she was determined to trace to its roots in the alienation of modern society and thought from tradition. For her this went deeper than the Marxist description of the worker's estrangement from his daily task.

Herbert Marcuse of the Frankfurt Institute of Social Research, headed by Max Horkheimer and T. W. Adorno, was soon to mix Freud and Marx into a cumbersome potion that would be swallowed easily, especially in California, by young American Ishmaels looking for a Captain Ahab to direct their life voyage. Wilhelm Reich, a left-winger amid conservative Freudians, a determined radical visionary who extended Freud's dictum of sexual repression from a bourgeois nineteenth-century problem into *the* twentieth-century malady that explained the proliferation of all disease, even Fascism, was to find a small fanatical audience here for his apocalyptic vision. The orgone energy at large in the universe was *not* being sufficiently absorbed by traumatized slaves of a sexual inhibition programmed by capitalism's work ethic. Claude Lévi-Strauss was at the New School for Social Research, sometimes moonlighting as a French cultural attaché, spending his limited funds on the vast literature of Indian ethnology. Erwin Panofsky at The Institute for Advanced Study was helping to make art history a significant American enterprise. The French poet and diplomat St.-John Perse (Alexis Léger) was in Washington writing *Exil*,

Vents, Amers, Franz Werfel was in California, publishing *The Forty Days Of Musa Dagh* and writing *The Song of Bernadette.* Nelly Sachs was in Stockholm, recovering from the shock of her transplantation and the revelations of Treblinka and Auschwitz to write, with a piercing new simplicity based on the Psalms and mystical imagery of Hasidic origin. The Holocaust almost literally drove her out of her mind, but she recovered by writing those poems, *In den Wohnungen des Todes,* of which she said, "If I could not have written, I could not have survived. ... Death was my teacher... my metaphors are my sounds."

Freud said that the intellect is soft but persistent. These writers were weak and vulnerable, struggling with new countries, new customs, often enough a difficult new language to write in, but they were persistent. A common theme in the face of Nazi destructiveness was History as the human memory, our common past, the human labyrinth. Think of Freud's insistence that our past is always within us, of Thomas Mann's concern in the Joseph novels with what he called the deep well of the past, of the Greek *polis* as the background of Hannah Arendt's political philosophy, of the way in which tradition and the break with tradition haunted Nabokov and Lévi-Strauss no less than the Germans. An irony of the Fascist age was its war against people who above all else believed in continuity — and so were never as death-fascinated as their tormenters were.

Continuity means not just the past but the past *behind* the past we think we know. The real drama of European exiled writers in America — I limit myself to Mann and Arendt — is the contrast between their instinctive European sense of history and the optimistic American belief — should I call it the *old* American optimism? — that the future is as real as the present. Only a great European poet, Rilke, could have defined poetry as "the past that breaks out in our hearts." Huck Finn, on learning that the Bible story he was forced to learn dealt with characters dead a powerful long time ago, said that he took no stock in dead people. Americans, especially of recent immigrant vintage, thought of the past as a mistake. The America that began to rearm in 1940, miraculously recovered from the depression, had a bounce, a new faith in progress as its destiny, that contrasted with the exhaustion and fearfulness of many exiles.

In any event, severe German intellectuals like Thomas Mann and Hannah Arendt had to acquire a taste for America. Mann, somehow protected from many disorderly things in the New World by his outward propriety, gave the impression in Princeton and Pacific Palisades, 1938-1953, of being as rigid as Gustav von Aschenbach on his arrival in Venice. This may just have been his favorite disguise; Mann liked to think of himself as antibourgeois, a literary subversive, a mischievous satirist who just happened to look like a German field marshal with a taste for reading. He certainly made the best possible use of his contradictions. A novelist where there had so few German novelists before him, a natural conservative who had astonishingly begun his career, at twenty-five, with *Buddenbrooks*, whose theme is the decline and fall of his tradition, Mann knew how to make exemplary fiction by playing on a reality that, as German philosophy and poetry have demonstrated, may not be taken literally, that literally may not even exist.

The great work of Mann's life, *Joseph and His Brothers*, was appropriately begun the year Hitler came to power, 1933, and was completed in 1942. The novel owes more than we will ever know to an exile like the biblical Joseph's, and to Joseph's wayward, mischievous family loyalty rather than religious loyalty to the monotheism which his father Jacob represents as the last of the patriarchs and the wrestler with God to whom God gave the name Israel. At the end of *Joseph the Provider*, when after more than a thousand pages Joseph is reunited with the father who never ceased to mourn his favorite son, "the son of the promise," Jacob nevertheless reminds Joseph that the latter's success has been worldly; it is not a part of the spiritual epic begun by Abraham.

So one can say of Mann's achievement, incomparable in its modern rendering of the biblical story, that it triumphs as story *because* it is detached. Although there is something symbolic in Mann's spending so many of the Hitler years writing his book, Mann did not consciously write it as an act of participation and sympathy. He stands outside the Bible's claim to revelation and the religious destiny of mankind; he is preoccupied, literally and almost dreamingly, with the biblical world as a storybook, a mythical coat of many colors. Did all that actually exist? If any of it did, how can we reach it? History may be the greatest fiction; and thus an invitation to write fiction that weaves speculation, legend, and the prototypes within our own minds.

What his God was to Jacob — the mysterious, unspeaking but audible force of destiny, the mystery of mysteries because He is One yet his works are forever contradictory — the most ancient world is to Mann the storyteller who works here as a sorter out of myths, creating his story by examining and eluding one myth after another. There is a pattern here, but *what* is it? The "ironic German," as the critic Erich Heller has called Mann, is not likely to believe that his characters are as God-appointed as *they* say they are. Jacob, Esau, Laban, Leah, Rachel, Joseph, Benjamin, Reuben become more real to us than ourselves, as is required of a great novel. But to wonder *what* they are, with all their exaltations, jealousies, sufferings, and wanderings up and down that hot desert — this is to make us wanderers ourselves. Early in the first volume, *Tales of Jacob,* Mann likens himself to Jacob the wanderer, who preferred to dwell in tents. "As for me," he writes at the close of his wonderful opening meditation on the pastness of the past, "I will not conceal my native and comprehensive understanding of the old man's restless unease and dislike of any fixed habitation. For do I not know the feeling? To me too has not unrest been ordained, have not I too been endowed with a heart which knoweth not repose...? For the storyteller makes many a station, ... pauses only tent-wise, awaiting further directions, and soon feels heart beating high, ... a sign that he must take the road, toward fresh adventures which are to be painstakingly lived through, down to their remotest details, according to the restless spirit's will."

Mann surely owed this to his inner homelessness in America. Nabokov came here in 1940 prepared to write in English, to teach in America, to learn all he could from America; he certainly got the native scene down cold in *Lolita, Pnin, Pale Fire.* But of course Nabokov was unknown and had to make his way; Mann, sixty-three when he arrived, was not without a German sense of his own importance. His publisher Alfred Knopf may have called him Tommy, but I am sure no one else would have thought of it. Mann was an American citizen when he returned to Switzerland in 1953 by way of East Germany; he disappointed many of his greatest admirers by responding more pessimistically to American disorder during the McCarthy madness than to older traditions of liberty that he never really absorbed.

Yet *Joseph and His Brothers,* and of course *Doctor Faustus,* came out of Mann's intellectual alienation from America as well as his unrealizable hopes for Germany. It is not necessary for a great artist to be at home in exile, perhaps just the contrary. Adroit and even devilish in his quick use and parody of the American scene, Nabokov had already been twice exiled — from Russia and Germany — before he came here from France. Nabokov's fiction, especially in English, is relativistic, duplicitous in technique, devoted to protagonists driven by *idées fixes.* It was easier for

Nabokov than for Mann to get absorbed in America; his sense of the comic and the perverse, plus his need to show off all he learned from a language and culture not his own, fed on America. And he too ended up in Switzerland!

Mann's unweaving the Bible into a modern novel somehow depended on his ability to live in Princeton and Hollywood without quite taking in the sounds around him. Kissinger's brother, asked why *he* spoke without an accent, is reported to have said — "I played with the boys on the block." This may not be the way to ultimate success.

In *Joseph and His Brothers* it is not only Joseph who is in exile, and by extension, his lonely God-intoxicated father. The Hebrew God Himself, we learn in two extraordinary passages, is notoriously jealous because He is alone, having promised Himself to this one family. Only Mann, with his knowing humor at the expense of self-importance, has developed — perhaps from some old Jewish legend — a long-buried fact in the story of Potiphar's wife, who is mad for Joseph; Potiphar is a court eunuch. When Mann's Joseph learns this, he reflects that Potiphar must be lonely, as lonely as God. "Yes, God too, the Lord, was lonely in His greatness; and Joseph's blood and his memory spoke in the realization that the isolation of a wifeless and childless God had much to do with the jealousy of the bond He had made with man." Later Joseph astonishingly says to Potiphar, "Our God has dedicated Himself to us, and is our blood-bridegroom in all jealousy, for He is solitary and on fire for our loyalty. And we for our part are the bride of His loyalty, consecrate and set apart."

No Jewish writer coming out of the terrible years, whether as victim or survivor, could have described the Hebrew God with such mischief. The destruction, to use a term more fitting than the outworn and unprovoking term Holocaust, sent many baptized Jews, like Arnold Schoenberg, back to their Old Testament God. In the immense loneliness of Jewish history, there has often been no one else to turn to. Like most modern Jewish thinkers, but more especially German Jewish thinkers, Hannah Arendt was more influenced by Christianity than by Jewish tradition. Her first work had been on St. Augustine; she and Hans Jonas, who was to become the great authority on the Gnostics, were the only Jews in Bultmann's famous New Testament seminar at Marburg. Arendt was also profoundly indebted to the classical tradition. Her first book in English, *The Origin of Totalitarianism* (1951), was based on unfashionable perspectives. In the face of all the usual left and ex-left-wing illusions about Communism, she believed that totalitarianism was the same everywhere if it meant absolute one-party rule; this was still too shocking for students of Nazism in the early fifties. In Franco Spain, there remained power centers not entirely creatures of the state; there was not the *total* kind of domination that she found in the Nazi and Leninist police systems. In the last and best chapters of *The Origins of Totalitariansim,* she demonstrated their fatal resemblance.

The *Origins* began with the so-called Jewish problem and its relation to the German catastrophe. Unlike so many exiled writers, Arendt faced this "problem" directly. She had never been a radical even during the Weimar period, and was not under the illusion, familiar in Marxist literature from Marx to Isaac Deutscher, that the so-called Jewish problem is merely a reflection of social and economic tensions. On the other hand, Arendt did not comprehend from within the extent to which the Jewish masses of Eastern Europe, faithful to their religion, had no Jewish problem; just enemies. Kafka, Arendt's favorite twentieth-century writer in German, a writer whose superiority to Thomas Mann was with her an article of faith, was willing to suffer his Jewishness but not to accept it. Arendt was religious in a very private sense. Her emerging political philosophy, drawn from a host of classical authorities, Montesquieu, Tocqueville, John Adams and other conservatives, came down to a vision of the Greek *polis* as the great political condition and of the rootlessness of the individual, the incessant struggle of politics, as symbols of some underlying modern disorder.

She was indeed very theoretical. Even her acquired taste for republican liberty rather than social meliorism reflected her basic conditioning in the profound sense of the self at the heart of German Protestantism and German philosophy. Her constant maxim was "we must think what we are doing." Emerson, who as his admirer Nietzsche laughed, had only one fault, he had been too much influenced by German philosophy, characteristically said: To think is to be free. That was Hannah Arendt's profession of faith, her life, her example to the many American writers who learned from her that there was indeed another Germany.

Hannah Arendt became a remarkably vivid figure at Berkeley, Chicago, Columbia, as the first woman professor at Princeton, at the New School for Social Research. She seemed not another scholar-in-exile but became such a personality as only America can make out of a European inheritance and a mind not just gifted but fearless. What America did for her was to give her still another intellectual loyalty and an audience literary even more than it was scholarly. Writers responded to her, and she to writers, in a way that professional scholars never could. She would not have been altogether pleased to register the fact that she was actually more of a writer than a philosopher and historian. She set great store by her philosophical training, her long relationship with Karl Jaspers, ambitious treatises like *The Human Condition* (1958), and her last, unfinished two-volume work, *The Life of the Mind* (1978). Only a writer would have been sent by *The New Yorker* to cover the Eichmann trial, and only a writer could have tossed off the fatal phrase "the banality of evil."

Hannah Arendt was a great moralist. She held very firm views on what the condemned Jews should have done in the face of the Hitler terror. One reason *Eichmann in Jerusalem* (1963) disturbed many people was its unrecognized German *egoismus*, from the sidelines of philosophy, at the expense of people who were not in a condition to "*think*" freely. Although she disparaged the historic tendency of German intellectuals to live above the battle, and professed admiration for the opposite trait in American intellectual life, in the end she could not avoid the noble German trap: to think is to think yourself free. To think and to think well was not the prerogative of the Nazi murderers any more than it was of their victims. The theoreticalness of her approach to the destruction of European Jewry was in contrast to the passion with which she described the terrible events themselves.

When I first read *Eichmann in Jerusalem* I was overwhelmed by the power with which she reported the court testimony and the mountain of records which the Nazis themselves left of their crimes. I remember in particular her account of one Private Schmidt, who alone on the Eastern front seems to have asserted his conscience as a Christian and refused to kill; he was beheaded. I did not understand the "banality of evil" thesis, and in view of the facts, wondered whether *she* altogether understood what such a phrase implies. Her gift as a writer was indeed superior to her philosophizing on what Churchill called the worst episode in human history. Her lifelong refrain, "we must think what we are doing," applied to Eichmann and his murder squads, simply meant: they were too ignorant, coarse, bureaucratic, in a word unthinking. Therefore the extermination of even a million children could seem "banal," like a computer error.

So we are led back to that fatal discrepancy between German intellectuals and political beastliness. I do not know how much her gratitude for America included the recognition that her admired John Adams was in politics all his life, or that the noble Jefferson, *our* Goethe, was not ashamed to play the political game. His only regret, and ours, is that inferior men played it more successfully.

Can we always think what we are doing? No. But can we *do* what we have been thinking? William James said we should. So did Emerson, Thoreau, John Quincy Adams, and Lincoln before him. By now pragmatism has an ugly sound, and in the hands of many an American totally absorbed by the commercial culture, it should. It may be that by now Americans are too far removed from the Enlightenment even to vote for the Bill of Rights. The idea of a republic, of republican liberty, thrilled Hannah Arendt and made her passionate about her citizenship. She quoted the great German historian of antiquity Theodor Mommsen — "My great dream was to live in a free German republic; lacking that, I wrote the history of Rome." Perhaps in the end she was too impatient with her old German political frustration, but too devoted to German intellectual *virtù*, to accept the mediocrity that so many of us now do accept in the face of a commercial rapacity that invades every side of American life.

She did not accept mediocrity; she did not really understand it. When the great Jewish scholar Gerson Scholem, an old friend, reproached her for not sufficiently loving the Jewish people, she tartly responded that the expression was nonsense. One could love God, not a people. The austerity of this is breathtaking. It is positively unthinkable among American intellectuals just now. Even to recall a perception like this is to remember how different European writers in exile could be.

[1980]

New York from Melville to Mailer

My impression is that in New York anything might happen at any moment. In England nothing could happen, ever.

John Sparrow, Warden Of All Souls

Have you ever seen an inch worm crawl up a leaf or twig, and there clinging to the very end, revolve in the air, feeling for something to reach something?

*That's like me. I am trying to find something out there beyond the place on
which I have a footing.*

> Albert Pinkham Ryder
> (visionary painter 1847-1917)

"It is because so much happens. Too much happens."

> Mrs. Hines, in Faulkner, Light In August

*In New York who needs an atom bomb? If you walked away from a place
they tore it down.*

> Bernard Malamud, The Tenants

NO NEW YORK streets are named after Herman Melville, Henry James,
Walt Whitman, Edith Wharton. New York does not remember its own; it
barely remembers Poe in Fordham, Mark Twain on lower Fifth Avenue,
William Dean Howells on West 57th Street, Stephen Crane in Chelsea,
Dreiser and O'Neill in Washington Square, Willa Cather on Bank Street,
Thomas Wolfe and Marianne Moore in far-off Brooklyn, Hart Crane on
Columbia Heights, Allen Tate in the Village, Cummings on Patchin
Place, Auden on St. Mark's Place, Lorca at Columbia. It will not remem-
ber Ellison and Bellow on Riverside Drive, Mailer in Columbia Heights,
Capote in the U.N. Plaza, Singer on West 86th any more than it remem-
bers having given shelter to European exiles from Tom Paine to John But-
ler Yeats, Gorky to Nabokov. It — and you — will be astonished to hear
that the following effusion —

My City, my beloved, my white! Ah, slender,
Listen! Listen to me, and I will breathe into thee a soul,
Delicately upon a reed, attend me —

was written by — Ezra Pound.

New York the city has been one of the great subjects of American writing; more than New England, the South, the West, it has been a great
home to American writers as well as the chief marketplace. But New York
is so intent on whatever it is that is more important than writing that its
writers usually feel as ignorable, evanescent, and despisable as those poor
storekeepers on newly smart renovated Columbus Avenue now being re-

moved because they cannot pay four thousand a month for a grocery that last month rented for nine hundred. "In New York who needs an atom bomb?" someone says in Bernard Malamud's *The Tenants*. "If you walked away from a place they tore it down."

The ever accelerating pace of New York, its historic fury, its extremes of culture and deprivation, ostentation and misery, leave whole segments of the population historically mute, not even aware of a greater life that goes on far away from them at the Manhattan center of the storm. Anonymous particles of dust trudging invisibly within places that could be Yazoo City for all their connection with New York. My parents lived out their lives in total insignificance, not even knowing that a child of theirs might some day speak for them.

But a writer can himself be the wound that remembers. Herman Melville, born to those Edith Wharton called "qualified by birth to figure in the best society," was always to feel that New York was his nemesis and that living in it again the last twenty-five years of his life, he had to be as indifferent as it was to him. New York uprooted him as a little boy after his father's sudden bankruptcy and death. New York (or the savage ups and downs of economic life that seem New York incarnate) broke up his family, forced him to become a sailor, deserter, adventurer — and thus an author howling against this most hazardous of trades. When he finally confessed his worldly failure as an author and returned to New York in 1866 to eke out a living as a customs inspector, the New York in which he was totally forgotten as an author was somehow bearable *because* it ignored him. He now confined himself to poetry, privately published and paid for by relatives, though his anxious wife was afraid to have the family know that he was writing poetry at all, his reputation for instability was already so dark. At the very end, conserving in retirement the energy left him, he wrote the now famous short novel *Billy Budd* that he may not have intended to have published at all — long after his death the entangled and barely legible drafts were recovered from a tin box by a graduate student, Raymond Weaver, the first to resurrect obliterated Herman Melville.

Yet without all this disorder and early sorrow, without New York "the terrible town" as Henry James called it, Melville might very well have lived the sterile upper-class life that Edith Wharton fled to live in Europe. The protagonist of James's marvelous story "The Jolly Corner" returns to New York from many years abroad to seek what *he* would have been if he had lived the life of his class. He finds it in the ghost of himself, in the old house off Fifth Avenue he grew up in — a figure beautifully elegant in appearance but brutalized and frightening.

Melville was swept out of this life into an oceanic space that for sheer extent and metaphysical terror resembles the outer space into which our astronauts go — those heavenly spaces into which, as Melville well knew, man carries forever the image of himself and tries to transcend it — "The immense concentration of self in the midst of such a heartless immensity, my God! who can tell it!" Melville confronted his self not as Narcissus but as Ahab: strike through the mask! New York was the threshold, the jumping-off place. *Moby-Dick* opens at the Battery on "a dreamy Sabbath afternoon, ... thousands of mortal men fixed right here in ocean reveries.... Nothing will content them but the extremist limit of the land; loitering under the shady lee of yonder warehouses will not suffice. No. They must get just as nigh the water as they possibly can without falling in."

This longing for the sailor's life, pointedly compared to Cato throwing himself upon his sword, was all too soon to be crushingly realized by the young boy bound for Liverpool, the sailor on the whaler *Acushnet*. The sea turned out to be the open universe. Beyond the happy valley of the Typees, the Galápagos where he had a premonition of what Darwin was to publish in *The Origin of Species*, and all that mystery buried in "my dear Pacific," lay the enigma of man's relationship to what is forever unchangeable by man. This presses hardest on Americans, the people who thought they could change anything.... By contrast New York was the closed world: fashionable Grace Church on lower Broadway from which Melville describes himself in "The Two Temples" being ejected by the sexton; Wall Street in "Bartleby the Scrivener," where a man had to starve himself to death to demonstrate his freedom; *Pierre*, where Melville describes the throes of finishing *Moby-Dick*; finally "The House-Top," the extraordinary Coriolanus poem in Melville's *Battle-Pieces* that describes Melville on the rooftop of his house on East 26th Street scorning the immigrant mob that in the heat of July 1863 violently attacked the city in its protest against the draft.

The life of an author in the New York summer! To Hawthorne he wrote in 1851, "In a week or so, I go to New York, to bury myself in a third-story room, and work & slave on my 'Whale' while it is driving thro' the press. That is the only way I can work now — I am so pulled hither and thither by circumstances." Later in the same month: "The Whale is only half through the press; for, wearied with the long delays of the printers, and disgusted with the heat & dust of the Babylonish brick-kiln of New York, I came back to the country to feel the grass, and end the book by reclining on it, if I may." In *Pierre* we read:

> The chamber was meager even to meanness. No carpet on the floor, no picture on the wall; nothing but a low, long, and very curious-looking single bedstead, that might possibly serve for an indigent bachelor's pallet ... a wide board of the toughest live-oak, about six feet long, laid upon two upright empty flour-barrels, and loaded with a large bottle of ink, an unfastened bundle of quills, a pen-knife, a folder, and a still unbound ream of foolscap paper, significantly stamped, "Ruled, Blue." ...
>
> Now look around at that most miserable room, and at that most miserable of all the pusuits of a man, and say if here be the place, and this be the trade, that God intended him for. A rickety chair, two hollow barrels, a plank, paper, pens, and infernally black ink, four leprously dingy white walls, no carpet, a cup of water, and a dry biscuit or two ... Civilization, Philosophy, Ideal Virtue! behold your victim!

Melville's distrust of authorship extended to his distrust of literature as a vehicle for his agonized search for a constant in the duplicitous universe. Failure on failure: *Moby-Dick*, 1851; *Pierre or The Ambiguities*, 1852; the intended hack novel *Israel Potter*, 1855; *The Piazza Tales*, 1856, first sold to New York magazines like *Putnam's* for less than $20 a story; *The Confidence Man*, 1857, the last work of prose fiction he was to publish in his lifetime, the veritable end to Melville's career as a professional author as well as the most tangled secret assault on shallow American Christianity as the support of an American optimism that lasts only so long as the money holds out. From 1866 to his death in 1891 Melville is captive in the city he associates with failure, indigence, anonymity. In the aftermath of the Civil War, when so many were seeking a new start, Melville becomes an out-of-doors inspector of customs at a salary of $4 a day (it was later reduced to $3.60 a day). At a time when bright prophetic Britishers, like Robert Buchanan, for whom the author of *Moby-Dick* was "a Titan," came looking for him, astonishing important literary mediocrities of the day like E.C. Stedman, who could only report that Melville was "dwelling somewhere in New York," Melville did not even have assurance of tenure in his job. His brother-in-law John Hoadley wrote to the Secretary of the Treasury

to ask you, if you can, to do or say something in the proper quarter to secure him permanently, or at present, the undisturbed enjoyment of his modest, hard-earned salary, as deputy inspector of the Customs in the City of New York — Herman Melville. Proud, shy, sensitively honorable — he had much to overcome, and has much to endure; but he strives earnestly so as to perform his duties as to make the slightest censure, reprimand, or even reminder, — impossible from any superior. Surrounded by low venality, he puts it all quietly aside, quietly declining offers of money for special services — quietly returning money which has been thrust into his pockets behind his back, avoiding offence alike to the corrupting merchants and their clerks and runners, who think that all men can be bought, and to the corrupt swarms who shamelessly seek their price; quietly, steadfastly doing his duty, and happy in retaining his own self-respect.

During the Gilded Age, the Brownstone Decades, the Iron Age that made New York (until our day) the supreme capital — of money, money-making, of the power panorama in architecture, art, publishing, the cosmopolitan intellectualism fused by mass immigration — Melville in his evenings, "nerve-shredded with fatigue" as his wife said, worked at poetry that she was afraid to tell the family he was writing ("you know how such news gets around") but which a relative paid to have published. *Battle-Pieces,* his poems on the Civil War impelled, he said, by the fall of Richmond, had already been above the battle, just as in "The House-Top", the most personal poem in the collection, he was on his rooftop scorning the New York mob whose insurrection against the Draft Act he heard as

          a mixed surf
Of muffled sound, the Atheist roar of riot.
Yonder, where parching Sirius set in drought,
Balefully glares red Arson — there — and there.
The Town is taken by its rats — ship-rats
And rats of the wharves. All civil charms
And priestly spells which late held hearts in awe —
Fear-bound, subjected to a better sway
Than sway of self; these like a dream dissolve,
And man rebounds whole aeons back in nature.

Now, in *Clarel*, he was in the Holy Land; in *Timoleon*, in the Villa Albani — removed from New York just a century ago that Edith Wharton remembered with a shudder as row on row of brownstones put up by venal landlords in the 1860s. "Out of doors, in the mean, monotonous streets, without architecture, without great churches or palaces, or any visible memorials of an historic past ... cursed with its universal chocolate-covered coating of the most hideous stone ever quarried, this cramped horizontal gridiron of a town without towers, porticoes, fountains or perspectives, hide-bound in its deadly uniformity of mean ugliness...."

Melville, who was to spend many Sundays with his granddaughter Eleanor in the newly opened Central Park, had nothing to say about the urban scene in this first great public park in the New World, nothing about the thousands pouring every year into New York harbor. Henry Adams in the *Education* at least did the huddled masses seeking to breathe free the courtesy of attacking them. Melville writing in his poetry of the Pyramids, of tormented Confederate veterans in Jerusalem, of the Age of the Antonines, of conflict with his own androgyny, had nothing to say of the rapacity of finance capitalism in the age of Jay Gould and Jim Fiske — nothing of the crime and squalor of the lower New York streets so conveniently adjacent to Police Headquarters. Jacob Riis, taking his extraordinary photographs of destitution for *How the Other Half Lives*, used to obtain his flash in the dark rooms by firing a pistol; this often set off a fire, but a cop laughed that dust was so thick on the walls that it smothered the fire.

If there is nothing in Melville "dwelling somewhere in New York" of the world that Stephen Crane was soon to describe in *Maggie* and in his sketches of the Bowery and the Tenderloin district, material that enraged the police forever shaking down prostitutes and practically excluded Crane from New York, neither is there anything of Whitman's feeling for the people, the streets, the sheer life-giving vitality that made Whitman describe *Leaves of Grass* and his city as counterparts. "I can hardly tell why, but feel very positively that if anything can justify my revolutionary attempts & utterances, it is such *ensemble* — like a great city to modern civilization & a whole combined clustering paradoxical unity, a man, a woman."

The port, the greatest harbor, as it used to be thought of, was to stupefy and alarm Henry Adams at the end of the old century and Henry James at the beginning of the next. But Melville the "isolato" (his word), reminds us in his New York secretiveness of so many poets, artists, and visionaries who

in New York found perfect solitude even if they were afraid of dying in it —
a creative race that tolerated New York, even loved it from the distance of
Washington Heights, Brooklyn, Queens. Like Ishmael clinging for life to
the coffin that Queequeg had lovingly cut into designs showing the gods
and the whole cycle of life — they had more freedom than they ever could
in a small town. Freedom to write, to love as you please, freedom to write
of your own Spoon River, Winesburg, Asheville, without your neighbors
looking into your pots.

But is Melville the first of these New York hermits — before Albert
Pinkham Ryder, Edward Arlington Robinson, O. Henry, Louise Bogan,
Joseph Cornell? Can a writer or painter now get away from the radio and
television next door, the tenants' association, the investigator, the drug
pushers, the muggers? Immigrant New York, ethnic New York, making a
living from the streets, living in the streets, making it, living the dream of
making it, faster, faster! forced its children out into the open, made them
seek every public arena in the city — turned the city itself into their chief
image of love and frustration, the city as *the* great preoccupation of American thought. From the same period of Melville's retreat into New York,
the late 1860s, we get the conjunction of New York with creativity about
the future: as in the Roeblings' Brooklyn Bridge, the incomparable center
promenade overlooking New York harbor (the last of its kind) as well as the
curveship that Hart Crane from Ohio described as lending a myth to God:

O harp and altar, of the fury fused
(How could mere toil align thy choiring strings!)
Terrific threshold of the prophet's pledge,
Prayer of pariah, and the lover's cry, —

The best things written about the American city as a stupendous new
fact were usually by Midwesterners who caught the new sense of scale involved just in moving to a city — Dreiser, Anderson, Cather, Lindsay,
Sandburg, Fitzgerald, Lewis, Dos Passos, Hemingway, Bellow. Much of
modern American writing was conceived in the outsider's dream of the big
city, by those relatively new to it — and much of America was still new to
it up to 1945. Only those amazed by the commonplace, like Dreiser, could
uncover the clash of interests, the vital struggles below the surface, the
shock and clamor of the unexpected, the savagery that is so rooted in
temptation and so precious to temptation.

This is where American writing came of age, if you like; or ceased to find the New World new. What vanished openly, with New York as the theater and great arena of modern corporate life and mass life, had subtly vanished long before — the totally independent sense of divinity that Emerson, Thoreau, Whitman knew as essential to their own modern quest for personality — that bitter Melville never ceased to look for — that Dickinson in far-off Amherst handled as traditional allegory rather than as an article of belief. The problem of the nineteenth century *was* the death of God, precisely because, as Marx said, man cannot confront his pressing conviction of immortality so long as he is brutalized by the struggle for existence. The modern world is not so much political as ideological; the new wars of religion, left wing and right wing, reveal their character by proving interminable.

But this is getting ahead of our story; the onset was physical in every sense, starting with the freedom of the body. Eros, as Auden wrote in New York, is the builder of cities. Dreiser's Carrie, Crane's Maggie, even James's New York heroine Milly Theale in *The Wings of the Dove*, along with the ladies in his other two spacious and astonishing novels from London in the earliest 1900s, *The Ambassadors* and *The Golden Bowl*, turn on a long-buried sexuality that only Whitman the commoner had had the wit to celebrate in himself because it was so wickedly and beautifully alive in New York. The connection between sex and the physicality of New York was equally clear to Gertrude Stein after her first affair with a woman — the very look of New York conveyed to her a message about purity; it corresponded to her new, cleansed state of mind. "I simply rejoiced in the New York streets, in the long spindling legs of the elevated, in the straight high undecorated houses, in the empty upper air and in the white surface of the snow. It was such a joy to realize that the whole thing was without mystery and without complexity, that it was clean and straight and meager and hard and white and high."

Yehudi Menuhin said in 1943 that one of the great war aims was to get to New York. This became a great rush just before and after what Dos Passos called "Mr. Wilson's War," when many native sons stopping in New York on their way to Paris came to love New York. To this day Francis Scott Key Fitzgerald of St. Paul remains the dramatic poet of New York's luxurious upper-class landmarks, like the Plaza Hotel. New York was a dreamland to Fitzgerald, as it was to his acolyte John O'Hara from Pottsville, Pennsylvania. But O'Hara's mind was too ordinary, a mirror of his own brutal characters, to duplicate Fitzgerald's delicate and tragic triumph. O'Hara loved and aped the privilege that lies in large amounts of cash, the chance to sit with the racing set and to name their horses. To Fitzgerald upper-class New York represented the imagination of whatever is charming, touched by the glamor of money, romantically tender and gay.

No writer born to New York's constant pressure can ever associate so much beauty with it — can ever think of New York as the Plaza Hotel. Fitzgerald felt about New York that it was a woman too exciting to be trusted. New York was the pleasure capital — and thus, to the active American conscience, unreal, a mirage, surely treacherous. At the end of *The Great Gatsby*, when the tale of Gatsby's foolish hopes has all been told, Fitzgerald suddenly, piercingly, begins a great litany over the Middle West as the source of American innocence and hope. Nick Carraway the narrator is gripped by the realization that New York — the East incarnate — has spoiled and ruined all his Midwestern friends. "That's my Middle West — not the wheat or the prairies or the lost Swede towns, but the thrilling returning trains of my youth, and the street lamps and sleigh bells in the frosty dark and the shadows of holly wreaths thrown by lighted windows on the snow."

Of course Fitzgerald never wrote about St. Paul as much, or as brilliantly, as he did about New York. He had the feeling for the textures and lights of the great metropolitan glitter that the enraptured guest gets — or used to get? — at the great New York feast. He wrote of "the enchanted metropolitan twilight," of "forms leaning together in taxis," of New York on summer afternoons as "overripe, as if all sorts of funny fruits were going to fall into your hands," of Negroes in cream-colored limousines being driven by white chauffeurs across Queensboro Bridge. For Fitzgerald all paradoxes then were spectacles. The name of the American dream was still New York.

Fitzgerald's dream was not shared by the writer who admired him so much that he was killed at thirty-seven rushing to Fitzgerald's funeral — Nathan Wallenstein Weinstein — who became Nathanael West. Those immigrants of a century or so ago might see America as promises, but certainly not as beauty. When their descendants became the authors of *Miss Lonelyhearts, Jews Without Money, Call It Sleep, Awake and Sing, Franny and Zooey, Barbary Shore, An American Dream, The Victim, Seize the Day, The Assistant, The Little Disturbances of Man*, books with which one must associate such testaments of hard American experience by the descendants of slaves as *Native Son, Notes of a Native Son, Invisible*

Man, no one could miss a grimness behind certain lives projected on the imperial city. This gave release to a few, all too few, new imaginations. Despite the masses of Jews, Italians, blacks, and Hispanics who have found opportunity in the big cities if nothing else — and often not even that — it is chilling to remember how few *lasting* works have come out of their lives, have done justice to the mass experience in the big city.

Fitzgerald wrote proudly of "the stamp that goes into my books so that people can read it blind, like Braille." It is possible, in the current reign of conceptualism and ideological rage, that literature itself is out of date. In the best universities criticism has been replaced by literary theory, which is convenient when you consider how little students read for pleasure. In lesser places it has been replaced by sawdust for the intellect like Black Studies, Women's Studies, and that chain of fraudulent liberations that clanks its way through every convention of the Modern Language Association: the novel of androgyny in New South Wales. It is hard for the children of oppression to think of art as engaging faculties subtler than anger. Black writing often seems drowned in the urgency of struggle, and since there is little interest outside the once liberal community, which now seems to be evaporating, it is not surprising that most black authors have never published a second book.

It is hard to be a Jew, said Sholom Aleichem; it is peculiarly hard to be a Jewish writer. The enemies of the Jewish writer predominate in his own household, demanding to know why Isaac Bashevis Singer writes about sex, Norman Mailer about violence, Saul Bellow about himself. It was not until the end of the nineteenth century that Jews from Eastern Europe, which used to mean orthodoxy, felt free to flout the commandment against engraving images. Though there seem to be legions of Jewish novelists today, the so-called Jewish novel, the novel of emancipation from the commandments, the bourgeoisification of the immigrants' children, is visibly over. The real subject that haunts the Jew cannot be treated in literature, for a civilization capable of accepting the murder of a million Jewish children is still the only civilization we know.

The creative element ungraspable by criticism, the element that makes for independent beauty, for the touch of life in itself, the psychic moment, the particular scene that brings the wonder of our existence home to us — that is not easy to find in the literature of an always beleaguered people, precarious, isolated, and unloved. What the Israeli novelist Amos Oz complains of is true for more than Jews — "I'm not terribly happy with the Jewish-American novelists. ... too wise, their characters always exchange punchlines instead of talking to each other, their books are just clever sociology. They don't have the echo of the universe, you don't see the stars in their writing."

One reason for this weakness among black writers is the exaggeration of powerlessness, the discursiveness that as in the case of so talented but floundering a writer as James Baldwin shows itself in the projection of sexual tangles onto a political cause — the latest cause year after year. Baldwin doesn't seem to have recovered from the onslaught against him by black nationalists. Political anger is hardly his natural turf, and of course he has never had an audience in the black community anyway. But novel by novel Baldwin, who is actually an expatriate and a very elegant writer, writes books out of an unforgettable family situation that afford him no catharsis, that seem to get bigger and windier with each reiteration of the fraternal tangle.

His old sidekick and rival Norman Mailer *is* a political imagination. Whatever may be said of Mailer's career as a whole — I admire him because he really gives and destroys himself with each hallucinating subject — it is a fact that while fascinated with outlaws, murderers, criminals, people broken on the wheel of American disorder, he knows that his characters are *not* powerless and spiritually indigent. They are alive and fighting. It revolts me to sit in a New York subway car mucked up from floor through seats to ceiling with graffiti so thick on the windows already crusted with dirt that you cannot see where to get out. But only Mailer had the solidarity with the unknown vandals working through the night in the subway barns to imagine what they felt, what they wanted, what in their secret writing *they* are dreaming.

What Mailer recognizes, especially in the context of destructive and ferocious New York, is that Americans are drunk on a sense of power, induced by good money and the wars that bring in the good money and the cars they drive without listening to the drivel on the radio. The good life is their idea of freedom. Mailer, secretly obsessed with the ancestral idea of God as the only lasting power, has made this duplicitous American freedom the obsessive theme of his work. It is the labyrinth of his own guilt as a moralist in this profane world. Pent-up maddened New York is the symbol. He has not been afraid to look ridiculous, reeling like a possessed man from one dispossession to another, from subject to subject, book to book. The excessiveness, the unreality, the violence and the *dreck* that weigh on my battered sensibility in the big city — Mailer has made these his preoccupation, has turned himself into an urban laboratory. I admire and envy his recklessness. These days it may indeed be necessary to plunge into a book as into a jungle, not knowing what you will meet — or whether you will come out at all.

[1981]

The Self as History

Every man has reminiscences which he would not tell to everyone, but only to his friends. He has other matters in his mind which he would not reveal even to his friends, but only to himself, and that is secret. But there are other things which a man is afraid to tell even to himself, and every decent man has a number of such things stored away in his mind. The more decent he is, the greater the number of such things in his mind. . . . A true autobiography is almost an impossibility . . . man is bound to lie about himself.

Dostoevsky: Notes from Underground

Whoever undertakes to write a biography binds himself to lying, to concealment, to flummery, and even to hiding his own lack of understanding, since biographical material is not to be had, and if it were it could not be used. Truth is not accessible; mankind does not deserve it, and wasn't Prince Hamlet right when he asked who would escape a whipping if he had his deserts?

Sigmund Freud

We are all special cases.

Albert Camus

I do not know what "autobiography" is; the genre changes with each new example. What I have tried to write in A *Walker in the City, Starting Out in the Thirties, New York Jew,* is personal history, a form of my own influenced by the personal writings of Emerson, Thoreau, Whitman. Its passion and beat come from my life in history, recorded since I was a boy in notebooks that I value not for their facts but for the surprise I attain by writing to myself and for myself. "I write for myself and strangers," said Gertrude Stein. The strangers, dear reader, are an afterthought.

In my experience, Americans sooner or later bring any discussion around to themselves. The American writers with whom, more than any others, I have lived my spiritual life, tend to project the world as a picture of themselves even when they are not writing directly about themselves. No doubt this has much to do with the emphasis on the self in America's ancestral Protestantism. Theology in America tends to be Protestant. The self remains the focal point of American literary thinking. From Jonathan Edwards to Hemingway we are confronted by the primitive and un-mediated self arriving alone on the American strand, then battling opposing selves who share with us only the experience of being an American.

The deepest side of being an American is the sense of being like nothing before us in history — often enough like no one else around us who is not immediately recognized as one of our tradition, faith, culture, profession. "What do you do, bud?" is the poignant beginning of American conversation. "Who are you? What am I to expect from you?" put into history's language, means that I am alone in a world that was new to begin with and that still feels new to me because the experience of being so much a "self" — constantly explaining oneself and telling one's own story — is as traditional in the greatest American writing as it is in a barroom.

What is being talked about is inevitably oneself as a creature of our time and place, the common era that is the subject of history. Every American story revolving around the self, even Henry Miller as a derelict in Paris, is a story of making it against a background symbolically American. Miller made it to Paris after years of being an indistinguishable big-city nobody. In Paris this American nobody wrote himself up as somebody, a symbol of the free life. The point of the story — as it was for Ben Franklin arriving in Philadelphia, Emerson crossing "a bare common" in ecstasies at his newly recognized spiritual powers, Whitman nursing the helpless wounded soldiers in the Civil War hospitals, Henry Adams in awe of the dynamo at the 1900 Paris exposition, E.E. Cummings observing his fellow prisoners in The Enormous Room, Hemingway in Parisian cafés writing about his boyhood in Upper Michigan — is that he is making a book out of it, a great book, an exemplary tale of some initiating and original accomplishment that could have been imagined only in an American book. The background seems to say that although the creative spirit is peculiarly alone in America, it is alone with America. Here the self, the active, partisan, acquisitive self, born of society, is forever remaking itself, but not in the direction that Keats called "a vale of soul-making."

We tend to emphasize the self as a creature of history and history as a human creation. Even Emerson, the last truly religious, God-oriented writer we have had, the last to believe that the world exists entirely *for* the individual and that "Nature is meant to serve," even Emerson wobbles on the ultimate existence of the individual soul, feels easier with a universal cloud cover called the "Oversoul" than he does with the traditional religious soul in God's keeping, i.e., the soul as the human index and analogue of a spiritual world. What Emerson is talking about in *Nature, The American Scholar, The Divinity School Address,* is the "active soul" of the writer as a teacher to humanity. Emerson, whose doctrine gave full faith and comfort to rugged individualism, is a great modern writer not yet altogether secularized. He despises fiction, calls poet and prophet interchangeable terms, *preaches* the necessity to leave the church behind and find God in one's "immeasurable mind." Yet Emerson was so typically double-sighted that he also wrote the first great American book on the old country — *English Traits.* How strange that the same man in his journals, as well as in his famous lectures on everything at large, nevertheless plays the preacher. What he habitually says is that he has taken himself out of the church, out of formal Christianity, in order to prove that one man, by himself, can be a bridge to divine truth.

And that man is you, my fellow American. You can become as great an artist in words as Ralph Waldo Emerson: all you have to do is become a church to yourself and preach from your own immortal genius. July 15, 1838, a Sunday evening before the senior class at Divinity College, Harvard:

And now, my brothers, you will ask, What is these desponding days can be done by us? ...

Wherever a man comes, there comes revolution. The old is for slaves. When a man comes, all books are legible, all things transparent, all religions are forms. ... Yourself a newborn bard of the Holy Ghost, cast behind you all conformity and acquaint man at first hand with Deity. ... Live with the pleasure of the immeasurable mind.

America itself seemed immeasurable in opportunity: "Nature," which meant everything outside of man, existed to serve man on this continent. An American armed with the primacy of the self can do anything. Especially in words. Like Emerson, he can invent a religion just for free spirits and call it literature. Like Thoreau, he can turn a totally lonely life, the death of his beloved brother John, his penny-pinching, lung-destroying, graphite-owning family, into the most beautiful prose fable we have of man perfectly at home with nature. Like Whitman, who took self-revelation as his basic strategy, he can propose a whole new self — which for millions he has become. Whitman, who wrote a great book in the form of a personal epic, compelled and still compels many readers to believe him not only the desperado poet he was but one of the supreme teachers of a troubled humanity. And then in prose, this worldly failure used the Civil War as an abundant backdrop to his picture of himself as tending the wounded soldiers, an American St. Francis who reincarnated himself as a poet, thanks to war and the assassination on Good Friday of his beloved Lincoln. Henry Adams in the *Education* reverses his loneliness as a widower, his isolation as a historical imagination, into the exquisite historical myth of a Hamlet kept from his rightful kingship — a Hamlet too good for Denmark — a Hamlet who nevertheless knew everybody in the world worth knowing — a Hamlet who finally turned the tables on science, the only knowledge worth having. Adams's last superlative myth is a world that in the twelfth century stood still to worship the Virgin but in the twentieth is racing madly, whirling into outer space in its lust to satisfy Emerson's "immeasurable mind" — intellectual power.

Henry James in his autobiographical prefaces to his collected works and in that staggering personal reverie over what the New World has become, *The American Scene*, showed what mastership over the visible world the literary American self could attain. William James in the personal testimony that is among the most valuable sections of that Emersonian manual in spiritual self-help, *The Varieties of Religious Experience*, showed — in the classic pattern of Protestant autobiography from *Pilgrim's Progress* to John Woolman's *Journal* — that a basic function of such writing is to cure oneself of guilt and self-division.

William James was not the first psychiatrist in America, though he was the student and colleague of those at Harvard who helped to inaugurate this still indefinable therapy. But Dr. James was a genius — it was his best gift — at putting himself together again, in words. To heal thyself is a classic reason for a worried man's becoming a physician, especially a psychiatrist. But no psychologist to my knowledge confessed his divided self so eloquently as did William James; no other has so clearly erected a whole system of *belief* to deal with it. James is Emerson's true successor at the end of the century. Emerson never confessed to doubts and was, as Henry James,

Sr., said bitterly, a man impossible to get hold of, "without a handle."
William James more than anyone in his time understood the American
idea that religion helps us shed our sickness, especially in books.

Hemingway was to say that the only psychiatrist *he* needed was a Smith-
Corona. But Hemingway, like Saul Bellow in our day, used his own experience obsessively in the form of fiction. So Hemingway kept up the pose
to the end that he was invulnerable, famous for "grace under pressure,"
until the gun in his mouth made it too late for him to admit that his public
pose was one great fiction. For the nonfiction writer, as I can testify, personal history is directly an effort to find salvation, to make one's own experience come out right. This is as true of Edmund Wilson in his many
autobiographical essays and notebooks as it is of James Baldwin, Malcolm
X, Claude Brown. It is even true of straight autobiography by fiction
writers. Hemingway's account of his apprenticeship to letters in Paris, *A
Moveable Feast*, is an effort to save himself by recovering an idyllic past.
Fiction is never simply autobiography — not when it is written by a genuine novelist. The autobiographical impulse in fiction takes the form of
satire, burlesque, grandiose mythology, as in *Moby Dick*. It often mocks
the hero and the novel form itself; it generally becomes something altogether different from autobiography by introducing so many other leading characters.

Even the most lasting autobiographies — St. Augustine, Rousseau,
Henry Adams — tend to be more case histories limited to the self, as its
own history to begin with, than the self as the history of a particular
moment and crisis in human history. Saul Bellow has written only one
novel, *The Victim*, in which he has not sat for a leading character. Samm-
ler and Charles Citrine, Herzog, and even Henderson, represent Bellow
in various stages of his life, different moods, different wives. But there are
so many other people and points of interest in his novels, like the frolic-
some portrait of the poet Delmore Schwartz in *Humboldt's Gift*, that it is
clear that what makes the human comedy balance out right is the creative
process for this self-renewing novelist, not Bellow's own history.

Still, wholly personal documents like Whitman's *Specimen Days*,
Adams's *Education*, Conrad Aiken's *Ushant*, Malcolm X's *Autobiography*
can be more lasting than many a novel. What preserves such books is the
news they bring us of history in a new form. In every notable case of this
form, from Franklin's *Autobiography* to Richard Wright's *Black Boy* and
Frederick Exley's *A Fan's Notes*, we have the epic of personal struggle, a

situation rather than a plot. The writer turns himself into a representative sinner or Christian or black or Jew — in Exley's case a comically incurable drunk.

This person, we say to ourselves as we encounter Franklin arriving in Philadelphia, has *lived* history. These are people recounting their fame. Here is Edward Gibbon, "It was at Rome, on the 15th of October 1764, as I sat musing amid the ruins of the Capitol, while the barefooted friars were singing vespers in the temple of Jupiter, that the idea of writing the decline and fall of the city first started to my mind." But Gibbon's book is all about how important he was; he is incapable of making fun of himself. It is not from his innocently pompous memoirs that we learn that the great historian as a member of Parliament from a rotten borough fell asleep during the debates on the American Revolution. One can *live* history in a quite different way, as witness Franklin's comic account of himself walking up Market Street, carrying two rolls, eating a third, and seeing his future wife "when she standing at the door saw me, and thought I made, as I certainly did, a most awkward appearance."

To "live" history is not of course to command it, or even one's fate in life. To live history is to express most memorably a relationship to the past, to a particular setting, to a moment, sometimes even to a particular set of buildings, as Henry James does so vibrantly in that travel book of sheer genius, *The American Scene*, where buildings begin talking to one another because James's mind is so busily interrogating them.

My favorite example of history-to-the-life is Henry Adams's account of being taken as a boy to Washington. He has already told us in many indirect and delightful ways that he is the grandson and great-grandson of presidents. He is staying with his grandmother, the widow of John Quincy Adams:

> Coming down in the early morning from his bedroom in his grandmother's house — still called the Adams building — in F Street and venturing outside into air reeking with the thick odor of the catalpa trees, he found himself on the earthroad, or village street, with wheel tracks meandering from the colonnade of the Treasury hard by, to the white marble columns and fronts of the Post Office and Patent Office which faced each other in the distance, like white Greek temples in the abandoned gravel-pits of a deserted Syrian city.

This is a passage of historical music. The key words are sacred names, as Proust said of Combray, as Gibbon rang the litany of historical names in the great passage enumerating Rome, the ruins of the Capitol, barefooted friars singing vespers in the temple of Jupiter. Adams is also rendering the art of history by locating himself as a boy of twelve wandering from the house of "Madame President" through the ancient, sleepy, undistinguished, unfinished Washington of 1850. Unlike Gibbon's Rome, all in ruins, Adams's Washington is seen by *us* as the powerful America of the future, but strangely ignorant of its future as we see the earth-road, the village streets, wheeltracks. But note that the Treasury has a Greek colonnade and, a most rewarding detail, the white marble columns and fronts of the Post Office and Patent Office in the distance face each other like white Greek temples in the abandoned gravel-pits of a deserted Syrian city. The innocently pompous all-marble Washington of the future, where Adams wrote this passage in 1905 sitting in his great house just across Lafayette Square from the White House, must contend in our minds with the beautifully supple historical imagination of Adams the great historian picturing Syria forgotten in the ruins of the Roman Empire.

When Adams wrote this passage America had just acquired, out of the goodness of its heart, the Philippines, Puerto Rico, Cuba. Adams's sometime friend Theodore Roosevelt, whom he amusedly tolerated as a gentleman from his own set (he thought the President insane), was enjoying the presidency with unholy zest. The moment had already come at the great Paris exposition of 1900 when Adams discovered that his "historical back" was broken by the sight of the dynamo:

The planet itself seemed less impressive, its old-fashioned, deliberate, annual or daily revolution, than this huge wheel, revolving within arm's length at some vertiginous speed, and barely murmuring — scarcely humming an audible warning to stand a hair's breadth further for respect of power — while it would not wake the baby lying close against its frame. Before the end, one began to pray to it; inherited instinct taught the natural expression of man before silent and infinite force. . . .

This is the self living history as its own fate. The barely murmuring dynamo will turn soon into the rocket, Adams into Norman Mailer at Cape Kennedy awed by the towering hangar built to house the moon rocket. The mountebank in the White House, Theodore Roosevelt, will become the succession of presidents after Vietnam unable to halt their own powerlessness. History as our own fate is what the grandiose theoretical last chapters of the *Education* have to teach us. And that is the deepest meaning of "autobiography," historically considered. Adams in Washington,

1850, yields to Adams in Washington, 1900, to ourselves in Washington and New York in 2000. The infinite universe mocks the American belief that our power is constant and growing, surrounded by empires without our ancient belief in the goodness of all people brought up under constitutional democracy.

Walt Whitman is another great example of the self living history — first as a mere spectator; then as our common fate, history as the ultimate explanation of our individual fortunes in life. In *Song of Myself* Whitman wrote of the historical visions he painted of America at mid-century — *"I am the man, I suffer'd, I was there."* In his great diary of the Civil War, *Specimen Days*, Whitman describes himself going down to Washington to look for his brother George, wounded in the second battle of Bull Run. What Whitman does not say is that he was at his lowest ebb as poet and man. *Leaves of Grass* had failed, he really had nothing to occupy himself with at the moment, and he must have had an instinct that the war would be one of those historical tragedies in which the rejected of history find their souls again, in which the epics of the race are reborn.

Early in *Specimen Days* Whitman describes the beaten Federal soldiers in retreat lying along the streets of Washington. Only Whitman would have caught the peculiar poignance of the contrast between the marble Capitol and the helpless, often neglected suffering in what was now a very confused capital. The most splendid instance of Whitman's eye picking out such historical ironies is the description of the wounded soldiers lying in the Patent Office:

A few weeks ago the vast area of the second story of that noblest of Washington buildings was crowded close with rows of sick, badly wounded and dying soldiers. They were placed in three very large apartments. I went there many times. It was strange, solemn, and with all its features of suffering and death, a sort of fascinating sight. ... Two of the immense apartments are filled with high and ponderous glass cases, crowded with models in miniature of every kind of utensil, machine, or invention it ever entered into the mind of man to conceive; and with curiosities and foreign presents. ... It was indeed a curious scene, especially at night when lit up. The glass cases, the beds, the forms lying there, the gallery above, and the marble pavement underfoot. ...

Whitman does not neglect to tell us at the end of this description of the Patent Office that the wounded soldiers have now been all removed. There *was* an historical moment; he was there. Just in time to record fully the typical American contrast between our technical genius and what war does. Whitman was not a soldier, not even a real nurse. History may well wonder if he gave as much to the soldiers as they gave him. They made possible his great poems and prose of the war. But there is present in *Specimen Days* and in the cycle of war poems, *Drum-Taps*, a kind of historical light or atmosphere that is extraordinary. It is a quality one finds only in the greatest books — from the *Iliad* to *War and Peace* — that show history itself as a character. A certain light plays on all the characters, the light of what we call history. And what is history in this ancient sense but the commemoration of our common experience, the unconscious solidarity of a people celebrated in the moments of greatest stress, as the Bible celebrates over and again history as the common experience of the race, from creation to redemption?

But something new has entered into twentieth-century experience. We no longer identify ourselves *with* history. Joyce's Stephen Dedalus said, "History is the nightmare from which I am trying to awaken." History since 1914 has become for the "educated classes" of the West not so much a memory as a threat. This may be one reason for the marked failure of "history" to awaken enthusiasm or even much intellectual curiosity among the young. To have a sense of history one must consider *oneself* a piece of history. Although our age will be remembered most of all for the endless multiplication of technological innovation and scientific information, the "feel" of the present — at least to the white middle class that still writes its history as the history of the world — is that history is out of control, beyond all the prophecies and calculations made for it in the nineteenth century, when the organization of industrial society was plainly the pattern of the future. Hence the unconscious despair of people whose first legend is the city of peace built on a hill, a new world to be born, a new man to be made.

But to the others, who are just arising in history and for whom history is their effort alone, the self knows history only as nemesis and liberation from oppression. Hence, in our immediate culture we get more and more a view of literature as political rhetoric. Imaginative literature even in our privileged society is now so much under the pressure of journalism, documentary, the media, the daily outrage and atrocity, and above all unconscious mass fright, that autobiography of one kind or another, often the meanest travel report through contemporary life, has become all too fashionable, omnipresent.

On every hand I seem to see people saying *I am the man, I got the story first, I was there*. Even that miserable schemer who tape-recorded himself out of the presidency had no higher aim than to write a best-seller called *Nixon as History*. The public gets more and more submissive to instant history. Looking at the endless news reports on television, we resemble savages cowering from the storm in their caves, waiting on the gods to decide our fate. Society, as we draw to the end of our century, resembles the primitive idea of nature as reward or punishment. The man on the spot may only be a ventiloquist's dummy, like most news commentators, reading what he has been given to read. But literature essentially does nothing different when it appeals, as our most gifted writers do, only to the public experience of politics, the moon voyage, the political assassination, the seeming irreconcilability of the sexes.

The real problem for "personal history" now is how to render this excess of outer experience as personal but not private experience. This is the feminine tradition, and women writers know better than men how to turn the glib age of incessant reportage back into personal literature. But there is at the same time so clamorous a cry of personal weakness, so much confessional poetry and fiction, that I ask myself, as a "personal historian," what the spell is on all of us — not least our readers. For of course Plath, Lowell, Berryman, Rich, Olsen, Duncan, Ginsberg, Sexton, Wakoski would not have written such texts, would not be the stars of the classroom nowadays if there were not so many readers who seem to read no poetry and prose that is not confessional, who demand that literature be about the confessional self — an invitation to become confessional themselves.

Does this mean that the theme I began with, the autobiographer as a triumph over his own life, has changed into the self-proclaimed disaster? Of course not. Confession is possible, even popular. We live in a society whose standards of personal conduct have been mocked by all our recent presidents, to say nothing of our leading corporation executives. The open lust for political advantage over human rights and belief in our American superpowers have made breakdown and confession, Vietnam, Watergate and investigation, a pattern of our time.

Erik Erikson says that all confession is an effort to throw off a curse. Guilt seems more endemic than it ever did. It is certainly more popular. Why? No doubt it makes possible a confessional literature that is self-dramatizing in the absence of moral authority. At the same time the dramatization of the self in American literature goes back to a very old theme. How well have *I* made out? What am I to think of *my* life, all things considered? Could it have been any different? Let us not deceive ourselves: Each person, especially in this historically still most hopeful of countries, is constantly making up the progress report of his life, and knows that in this respect everyone we know, love, and hate, everyone to whom we have ever been tied, shares our interests exactly — this life, my life, this time. . . .

So the anxious but somehow thrivingly preoccupied self, in a culture where personal fortune and happiness are more real than God has become even to many believers, cannot help connecting himself with people like himself in this period, with a history that betrays the most intimate passions. Once gods of the earth, presidents now seem all too much like ourselves. More and more the sexes are compelled to admit that men and women — alas! — are more alike than we had dreamed, egotists before anything else. Everywhere we turn we seem to be within the same bedroom walls, under pressure from the same authorities. Hence, not equality but *identity* becomes the condition of life as we get mashed into shape by the same corporations, shopping plazas, ranch houses, mass universities, television programs, instant replay of the same public atrocities.

In all this the self becomes freely articulate about itself, recognizing a *psychological* bond with other selves that is negative. Every confession becomes a progress report of the most intense interest to others. And if the confession is an attempt to ward off a curse, writing it out is also a boast: to be able to write one's life, to make one's way successfully through so many ghosts, between so many tombs, is indeed a boast.

All I have to boast about is that I have at least tried to express my life. I have been saved by language. My sixty years have been lived directly *and* symbolically in the storm centers of the twentieth century. Nothing seems more remote than the illusion of security and tranquility as the century accelerates the violence and nihilism that have marked all our lives since 1914-1918. The concentrated power of modern weapons can be even more suicidal than private despair.

Yet I believe that history exists, that it is still meaningful, and that we can read our fate in the book of history. That gives me the courage to write. To write is in some way to cut the seemingly automatic pattern of violence, destructiveness, and death wish. To write is to put the seeming insignificance of human existence into a different perspective. It is the need, the wish, and, please God, the ability, to reorder our physical fate by mental means, a leap of the imagination, an act of faith. Wallace Stevens once wondered in an essay whether it is not "the violence within that protects us from the violence without." The "violence within" is the effort to make a mental construct that shall hang together — that shall be within the inner landscape a seamless and uninterruptible web — that can prove, as Henry James said, that "the whole truth about anything is never told; we can only take what groups together."

Violence is distinguished by gaps, discontinuities, inconsistency, confusion condensed into power — but no less blind and chaotic for that. The life of mere experience, and especially of history as the supposedly total experience we ridiculously claim to know, can seem an inexplicable series of unrelated moments. But language, even when it is most a mimicry of disorder, is distinguished from violence, atrocity, deceit by relating word to word, sentence to sentence, thought to thought — man to this final construct on a page — always something different from mere living.

So that is why I write, to reorder an existence that man in the mass will never reorder for me. Even autobiography is a necessary stratagem to gain something more important than itself. By the time experience is distilled enough through our minds to set some particular thing down on paper, so much unconscious reordering has gone on that even the naïve wish to be wholly "truthful" fades before the intoxication of line, pattern, form.

Stephen Crane said that art is a child of pain. Existence is itself an anxious matter for many Americans in the twentieth century precisely because the material power is greatest in this country; we have had the greatest illusion of control. And so the disappointment and anger are greater still. In the writing of our time and place, one sees a greater questioning, philosophical and moral rootlessness, a despair that is often just the other side of the most romantic and reckless hope. So the self becomes the accuser, as it so often seems only the target — the self adrift in a private universe. This, to Americans caught off base, as we all are now, can seem as frightening as the silence of those infinite spaces seemed to Pascal:

When I consider the short duration of my life, swallowed up in the eternity before and after, the little space which I fill, and even can see, engulfed in the infinite immensity of spaces of which I am ignorant, and which know me not, I am frightened, and am astonished at being here rather than there; for there is no reason why *here* rather than *there*, why *now* rather than *then*. Who has put me here? By whose order and direction have this place and time been allotted to me?

So one writes to make a home for oneself, on paper, despite Milton's *blind Fury with the abhorrèd shears, who slits the thin-spun life.* In our time history, too, can be "the blind Fury." But to write is to live it again, and in this personal myth and resurrection of our experience, to give honor to our lives.

[1978]

Index

Alfred Kazin lectures and teaches in the United States and abroad. He is Distinguished Professor of English at the Graduate Center of the City University of New York and Hunter College. He established his critical reputation in his mid-twenties with his classic study of American literature, *On Native Grounds*. The list of books he has written and edited appears at the beginning of this volume.